MALEVOLENT SPIRITS:

MONONOGATARI

1

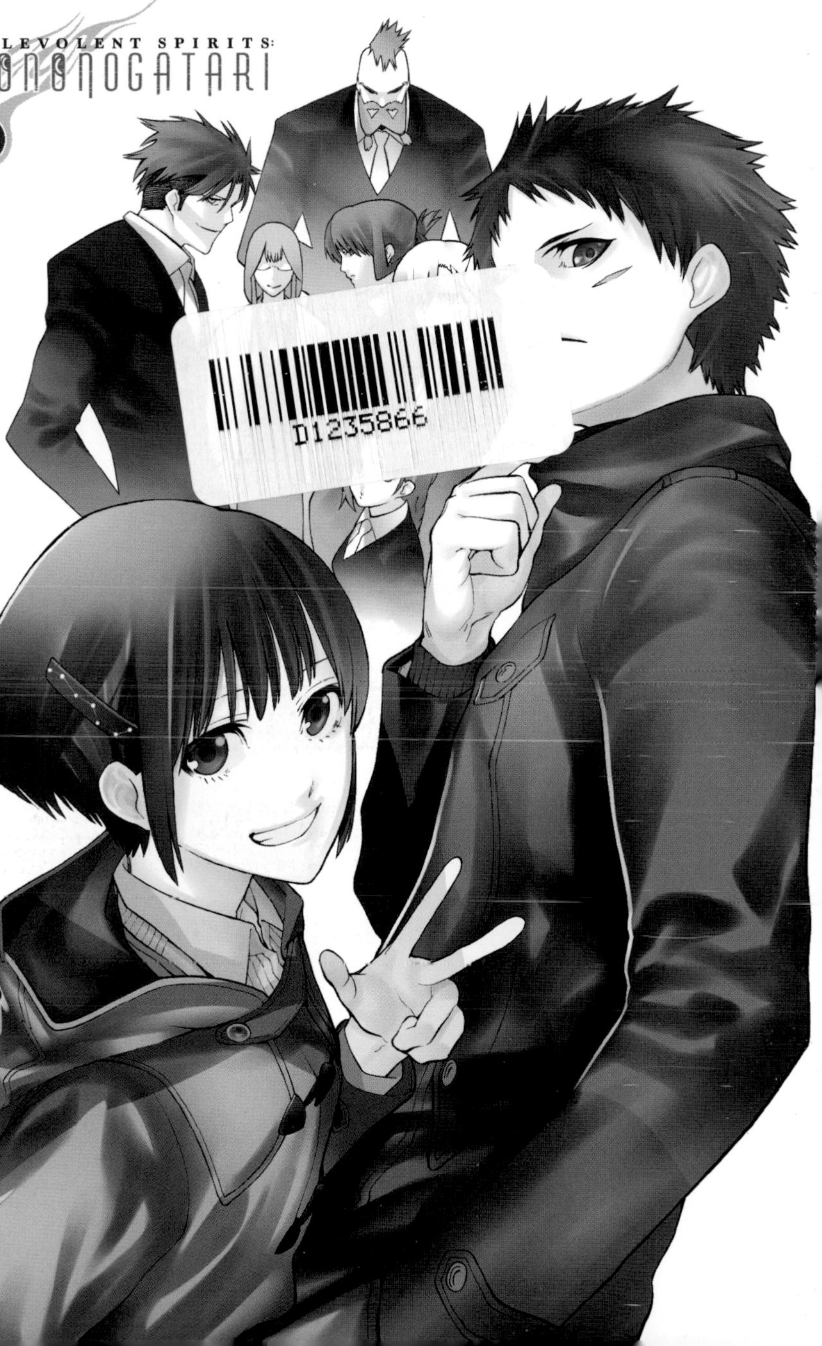

MONONOGATARI

CONTENTS 1

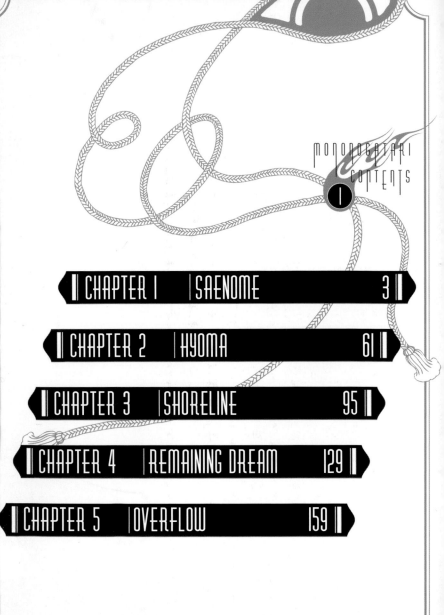

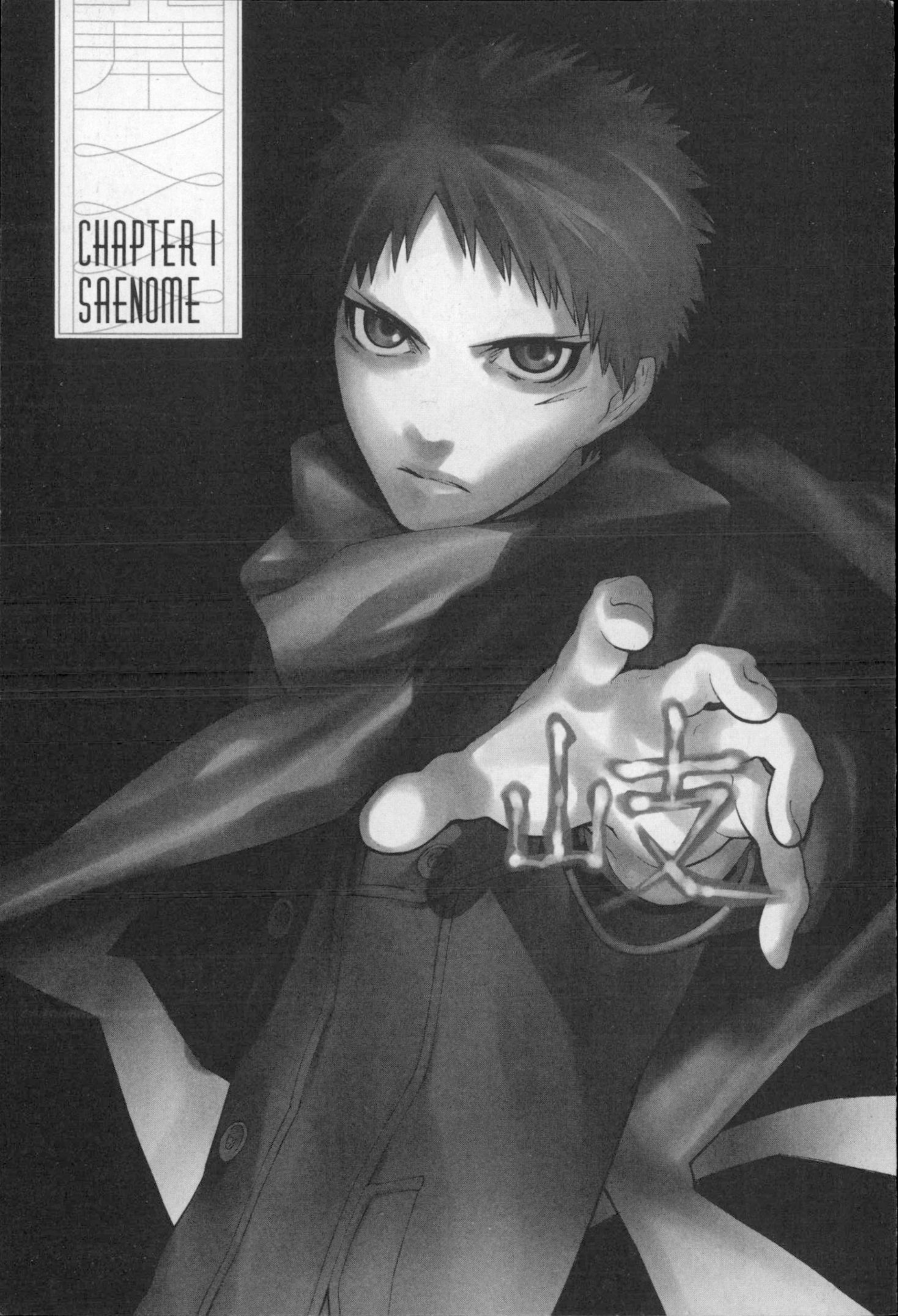
CHAPTER 1
SAENOME

MONONOGATARI

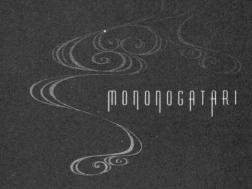

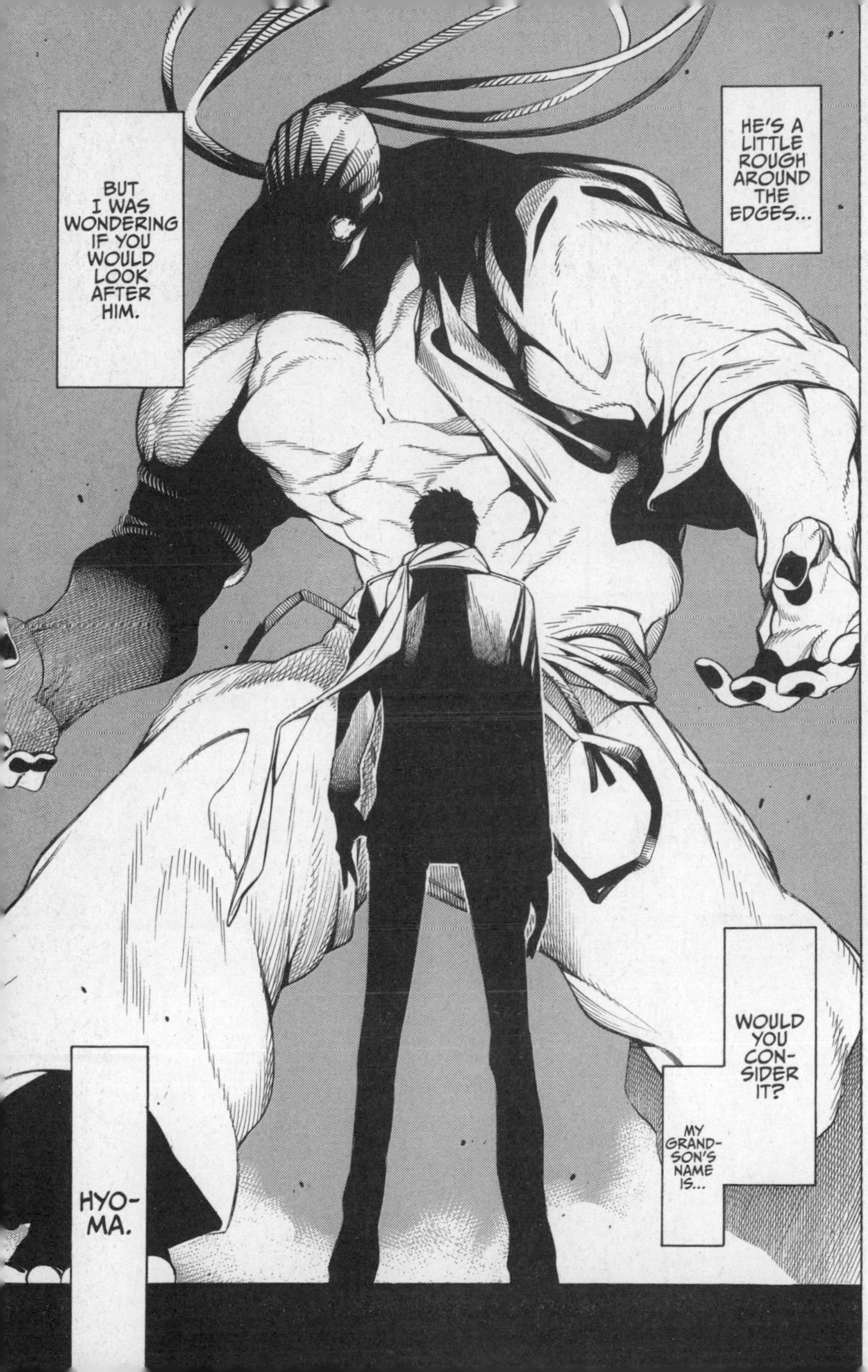
HE'S A LITTLE ROUGH AROUND THE EDGES...
BUT I WAS WONDERING IF YOU WOULD LOOK AFTER HIM.
WOULD YOU CON-SIDER IT?
MY GRAND-SON'S NAME IS...
HYO-MA.

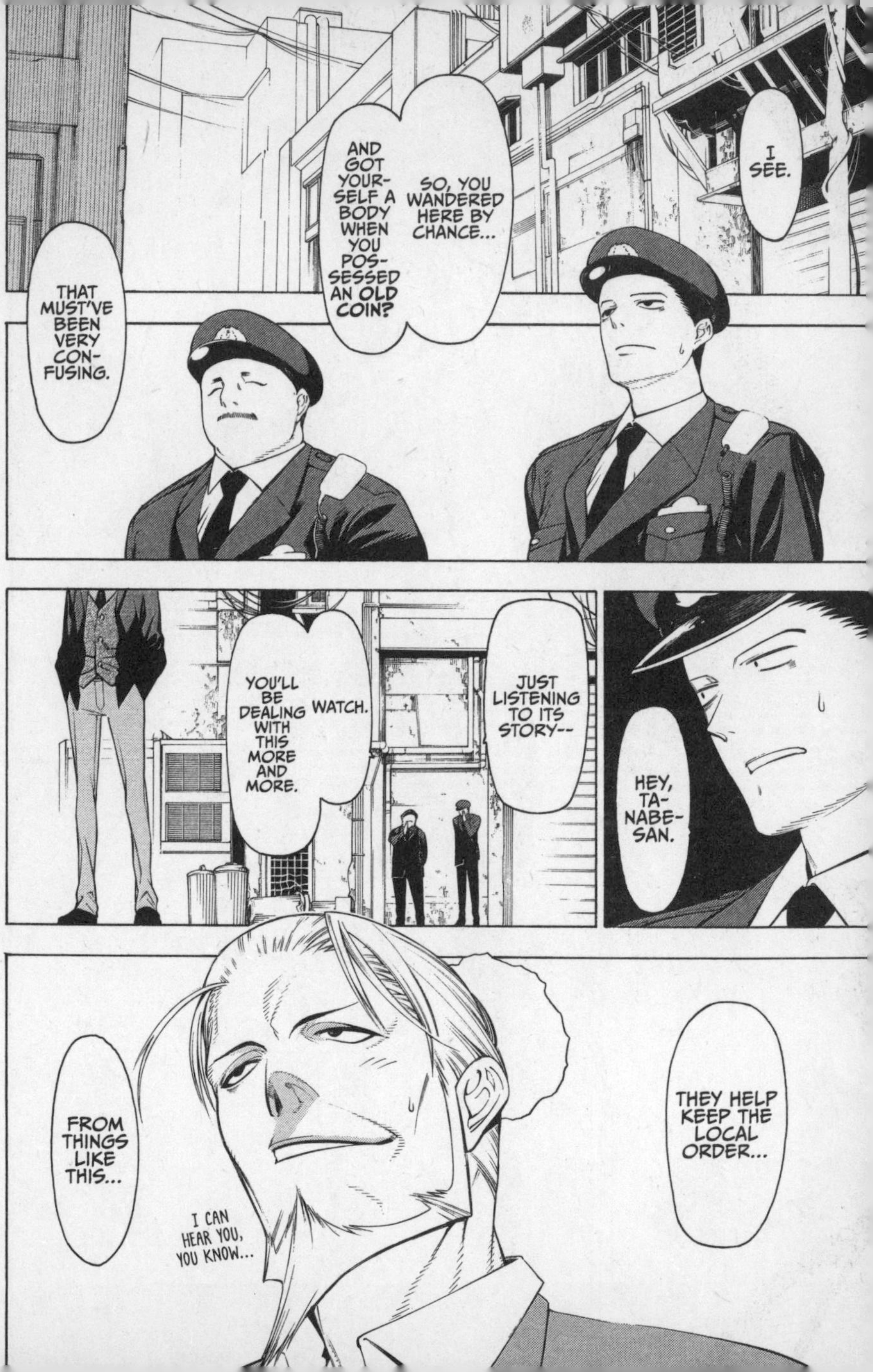
I SEE.
SO, YOU WANDERED HERE BY CHANCE...
AND GOT YOURSELF A BODY WHEN YOU POSSESSED AN OLD COIN?
THAT MUST'VE BEEN VERY CONFUSING.
HEY, TANABE-SAN.
JUST LISTENING TO ITS STORY--
WATCH. YOU'LL BE DEALING WITH THIS MORE AND MORE.
THEY HELP KEEP THE LOCAL ORDER...
FROM THINGS LIKE THIS...
I CAN HEAR YOU, YOU KNOW...

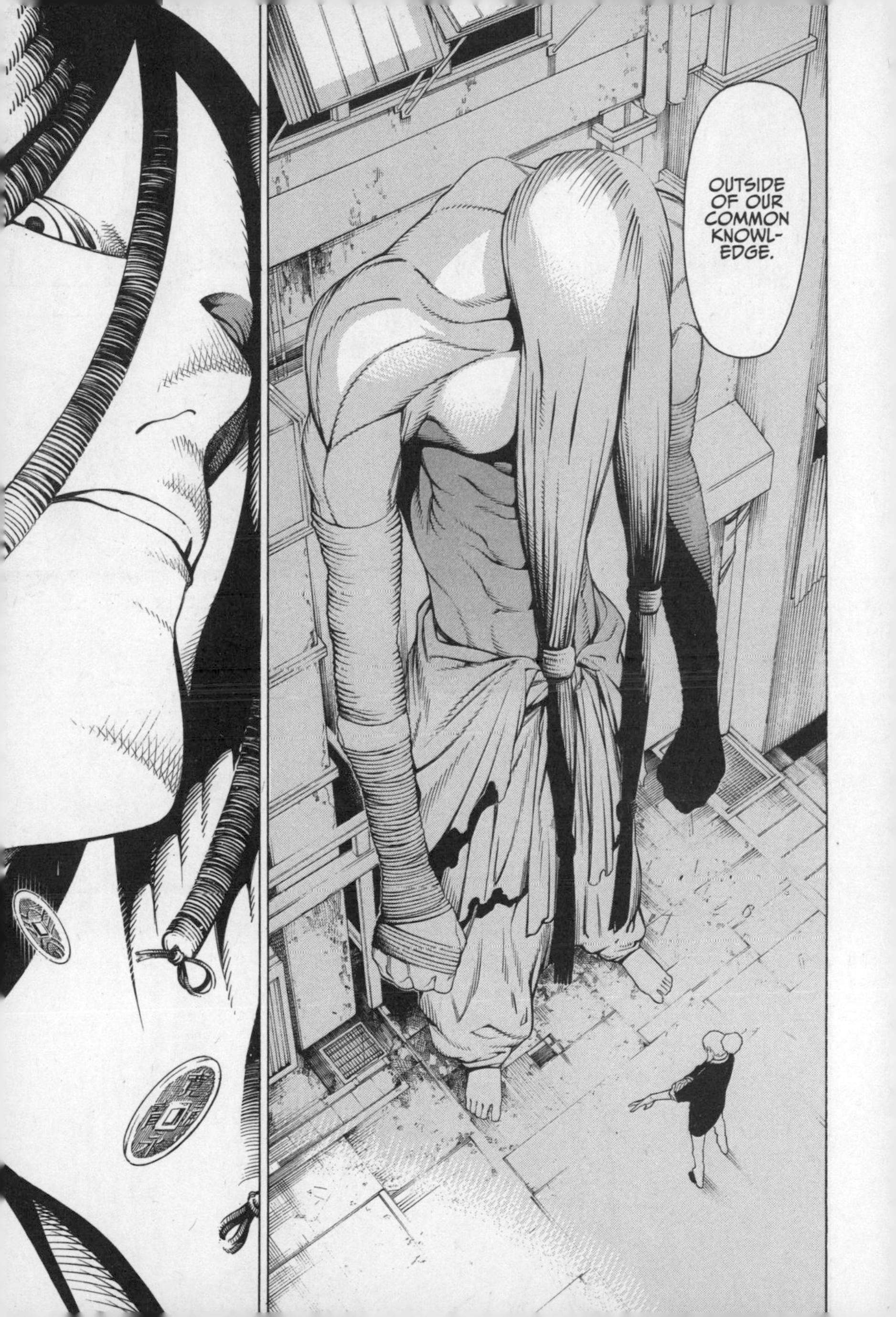
OUTSIDE OF OUR COMMON KNOWL-EDGE.

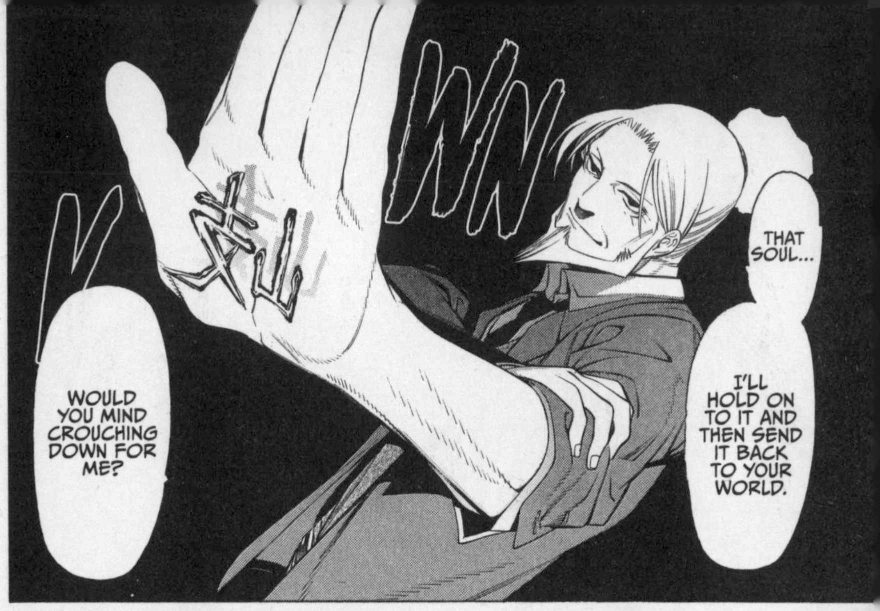
THAT SOUL...
I'LL HOLD ON TO IT AND THEN SEND IT BACK TO YOUR WORLD.
VWN
WOULD YOU MIND CROUCHING DOWN FOR ME?

Hand: Kunato

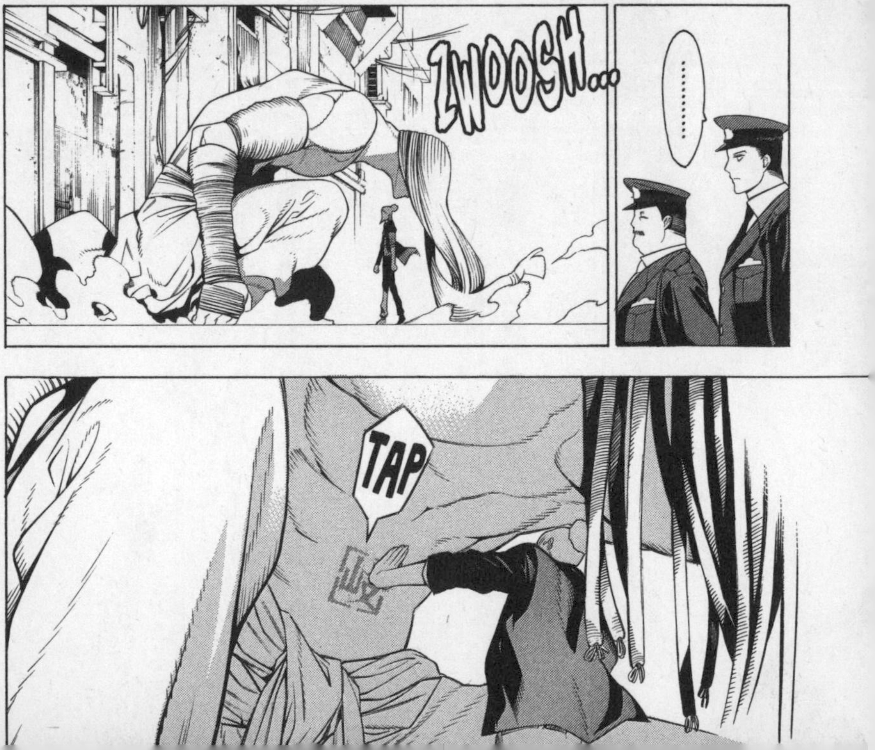
......
ZWOOSH...
TAP

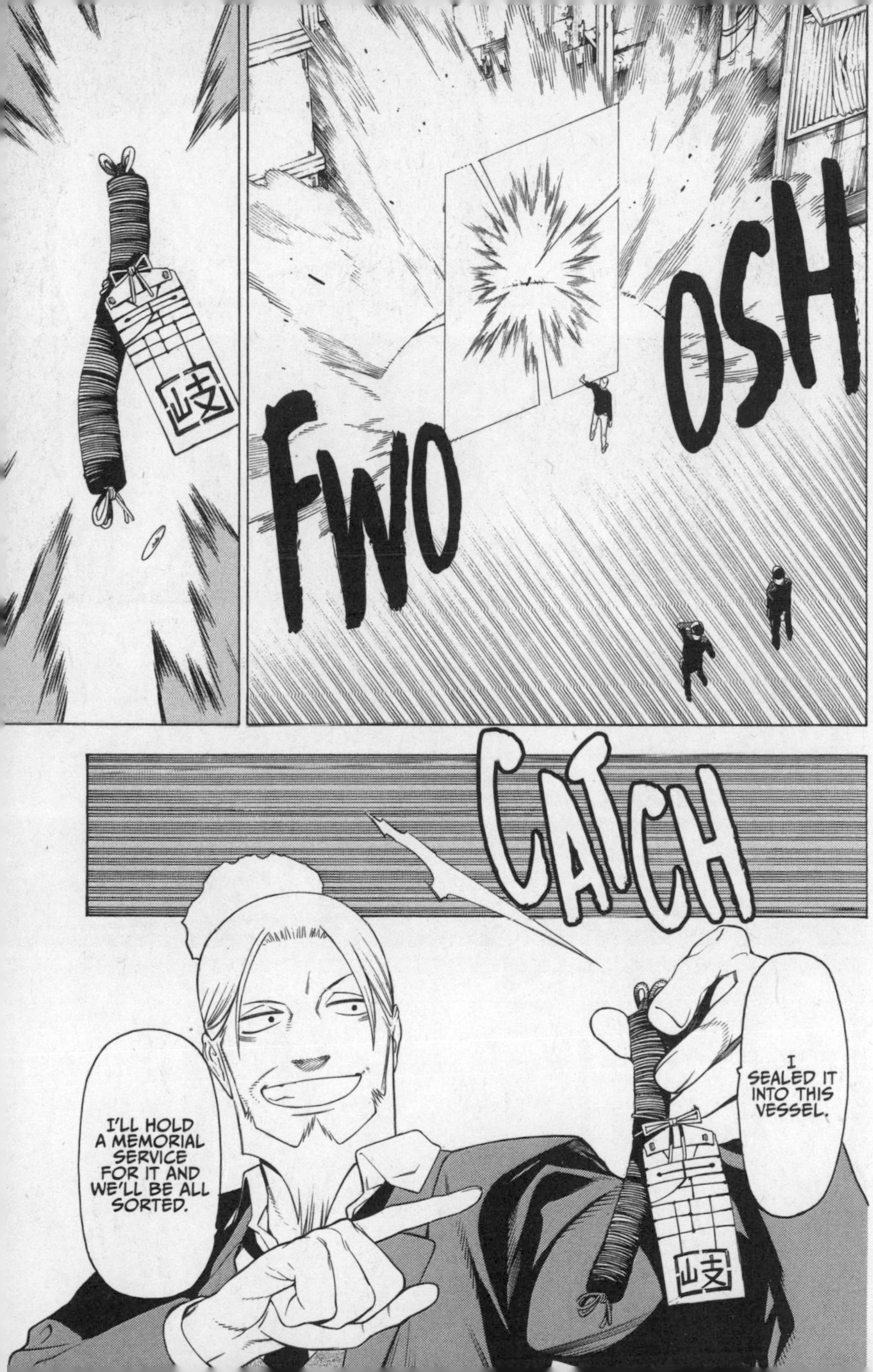
FWOOSH
CATCH
I SEALED IT INTO THIS VESSEL.
I'LL HOLD A MEMORIAL SERVICE FOR IT AND WE'LL BE ALL SORTED.

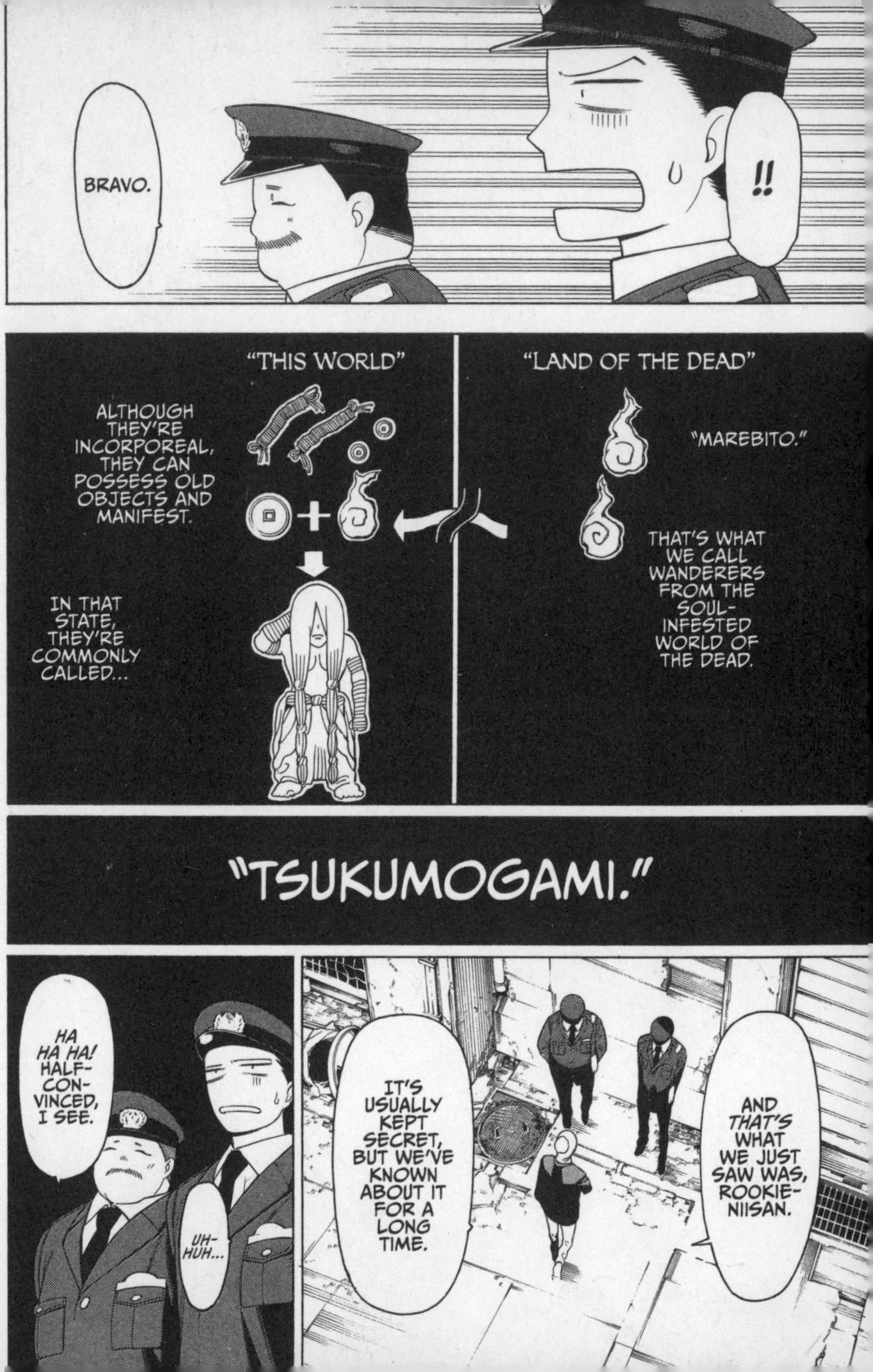
!!
BRAVO.
"LAND OF THE DEAD"
"MAREBITO."
THAT'S WHAT WE CALL WANDERERS FROM THE SOUL-INFESTED WORLD OF THE DEAD.
"THIS WORLD"
ALTHOUGH THEY'RE INCORPOREAL, THEY CAN POSSESS OLD OBJECTS AND MANIFEST.
IN THAT STATE, THEY'RE COMMONLY CALLED...
"TSUKUMOGAMI."
AND *THAT'S* WHAT WE JUST SAW WAS, ROOKIE-NIISAN.
IT'S USUALLY KEPT SECRET, BUT WE'VE KNOWN ABOUT IT FOR A LONG TIME.
HA HA HA! HALF-CONVINCED, I SEE.
UH-HUH...

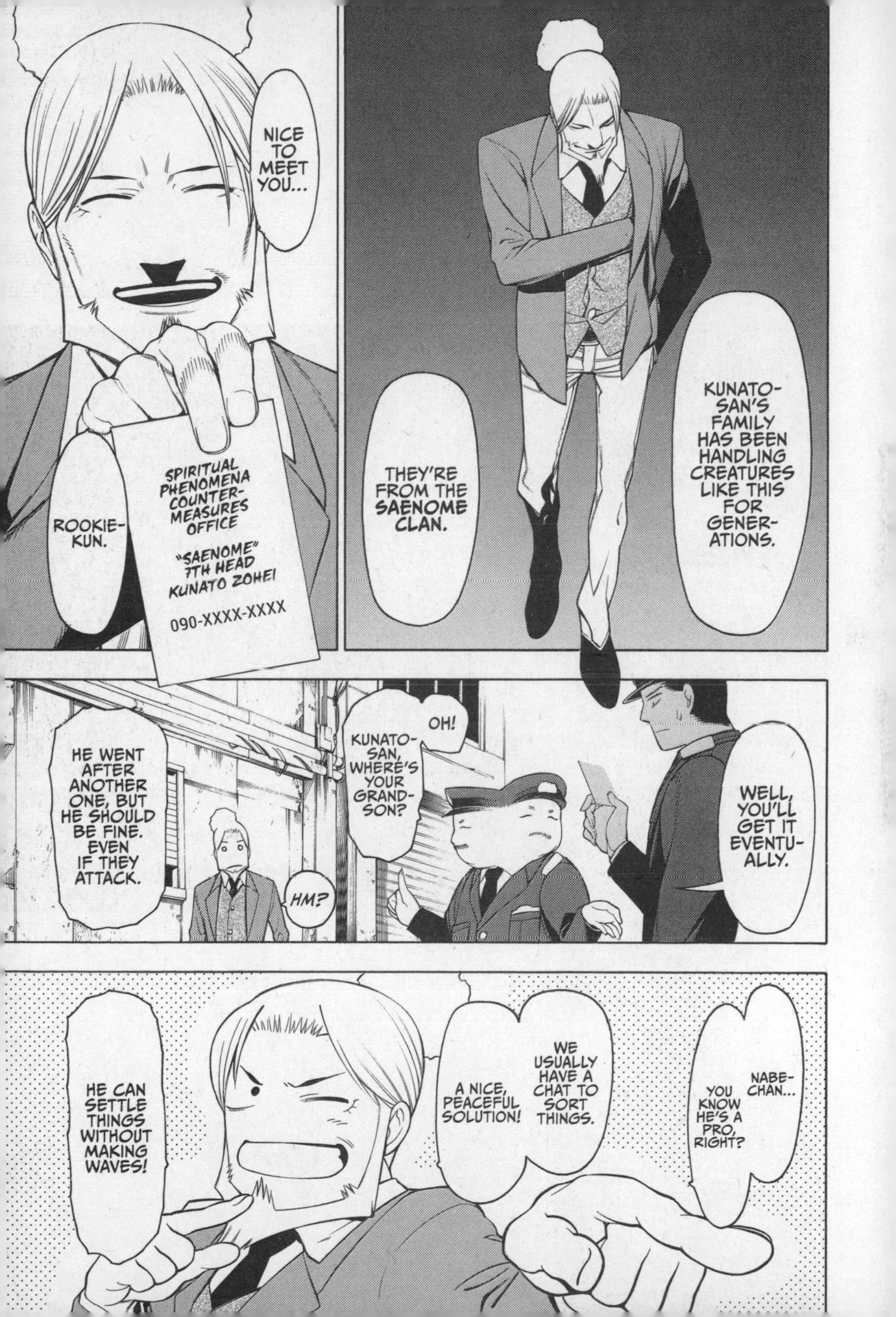
KUNATO-SAN'S FAMILY HAS BEEN HANDLING CREATURES LIKE THIS FOR GENERATIONS.
THEY'RE FROM THE SAENOME CLAN.
NICE TO MEET YOU...
SPIRITUAL PHENOMENA COUNTER-MEASURES OFFICE
"SAENOME" 7TH HEAD
KUNATO ZOHEI
090-XXXX-XXXX
ROOKIE-KUN.
WELL, YOU'LL GET IT EVENTU-ALLY.
OH!
KUNATO-SAN, WHERE'S YOUR GRAND-SON?
HM?
HE WENT AFTER ANOTHER ONE, BUT HE SHOULD BE FINE. EVEN IF THEY ATTACK.
NABE-CHAN...
YOU KNOW HE'S A PRO, RIGHT?
WE USUALLY HAVE A CHAT TO SORT THINGS.
A NICE, PEACEFUL SOLUTION!
HE CAN SETTLE THINGS WITHOUT MAKING WAVES!

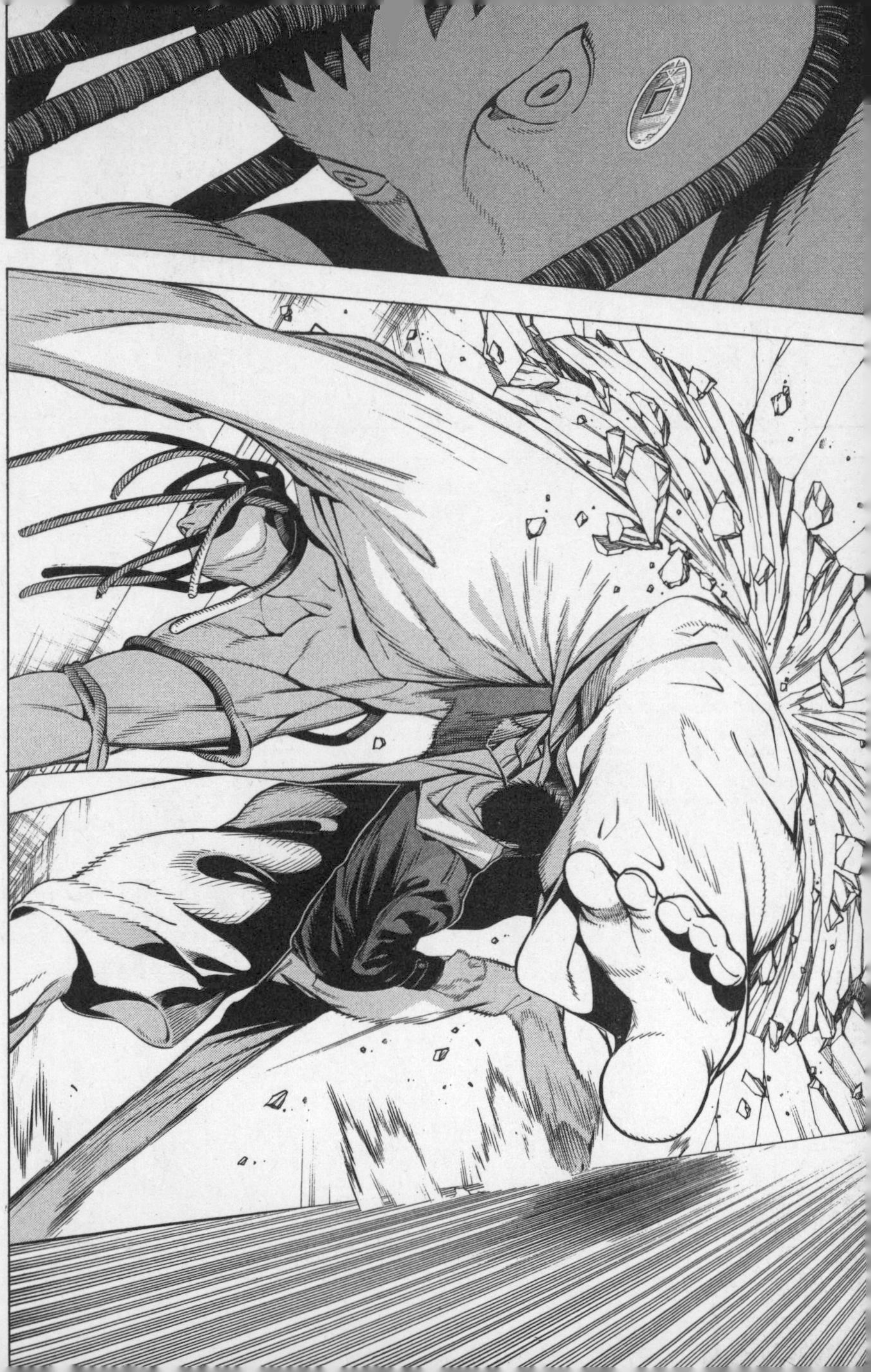

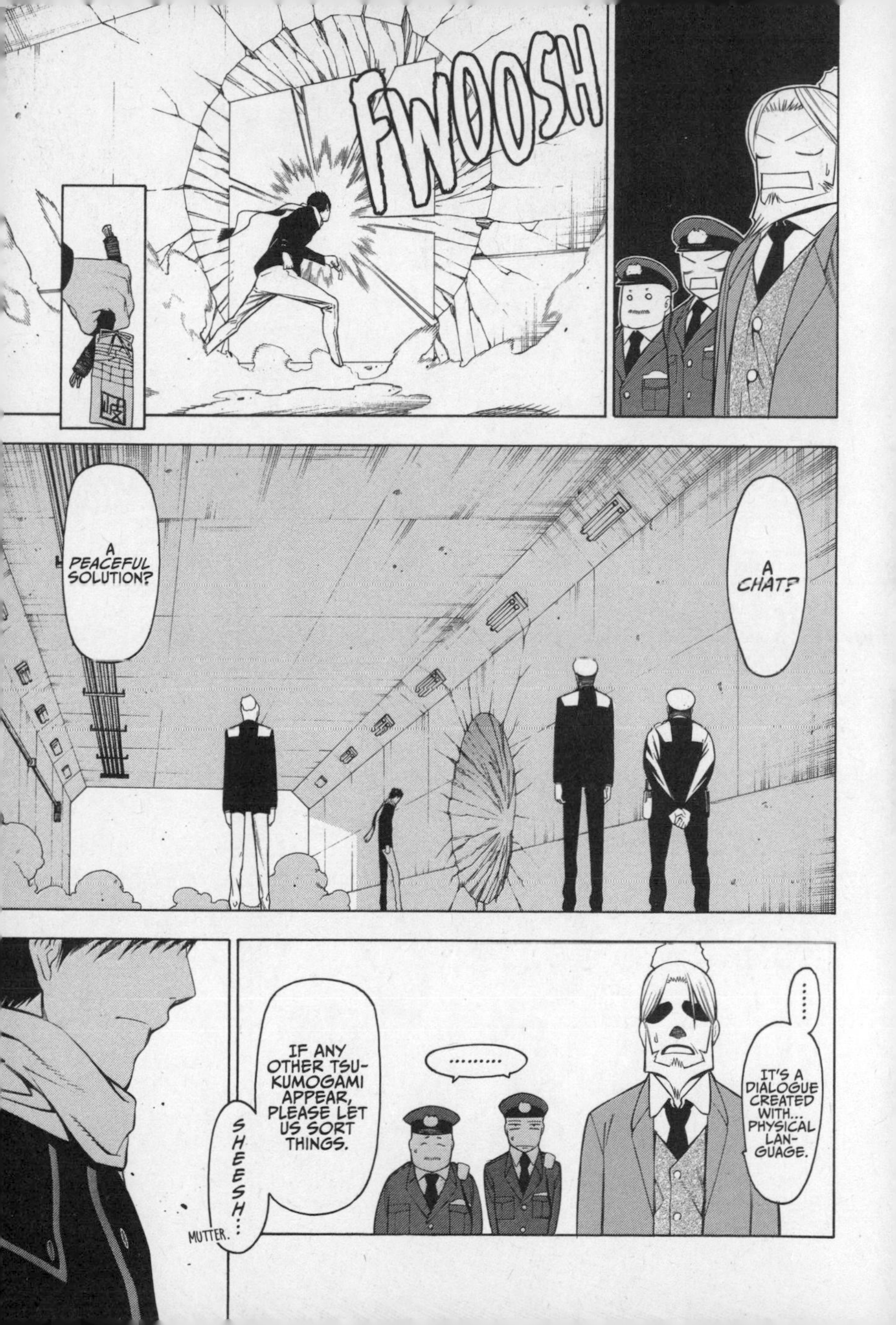
FWOOSH
A CHAT?
A PEACEFUL SOLUTION?
……
IT'S A DIALOGUE CREATED WITH… PHYSICAL LANGUAGE.
………
IF ANY OTHER TSU-KUMOGAMI APPEAR, PLEASE LET US SORT THINGS.
SHEESH…
MUTTER.

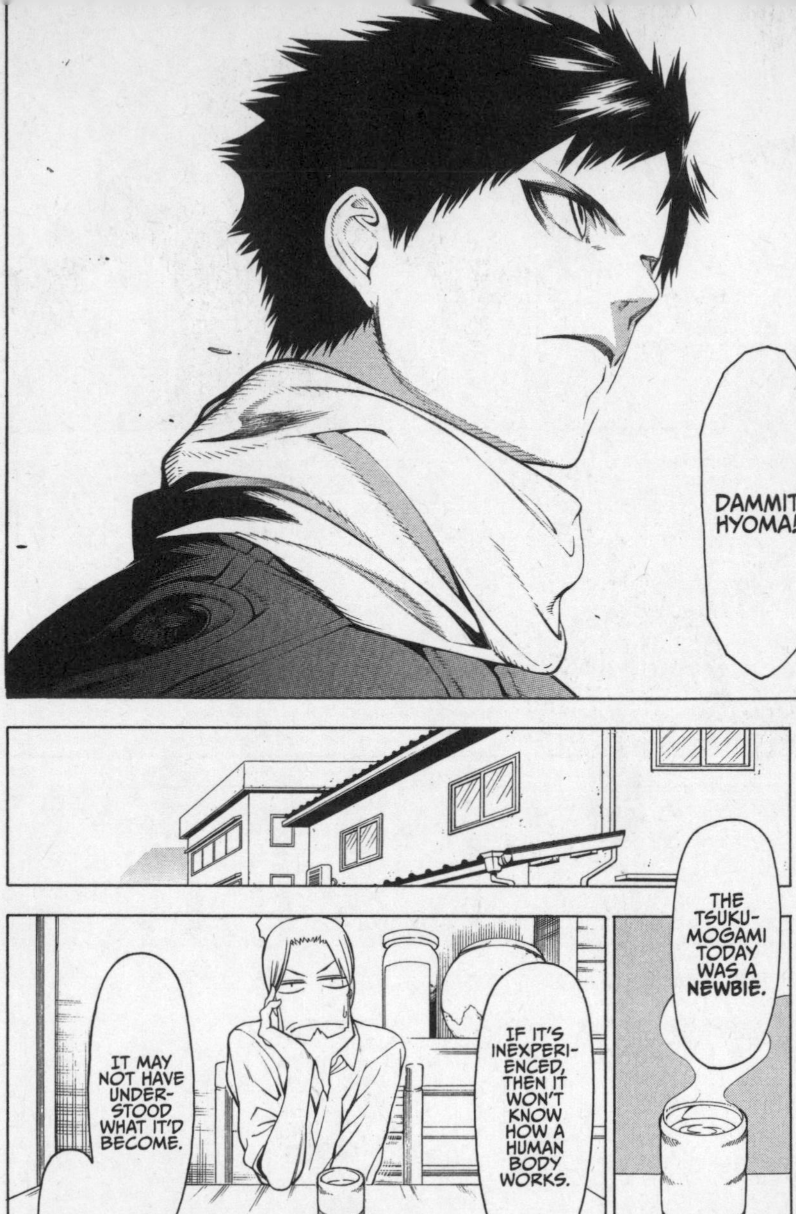
DAMMIT, HYOMA!!
THE TSUKU-MOGAMI TODAY WAS A NEWBIE.
IF IT'S INEXPERI-ENCED, THEN IT WON'T KNOW HOW A HUMAN BODY WORKS.
IT MAY NOT HAVE UNDER-STOOD WHAT IT'D BECOME.
SO...

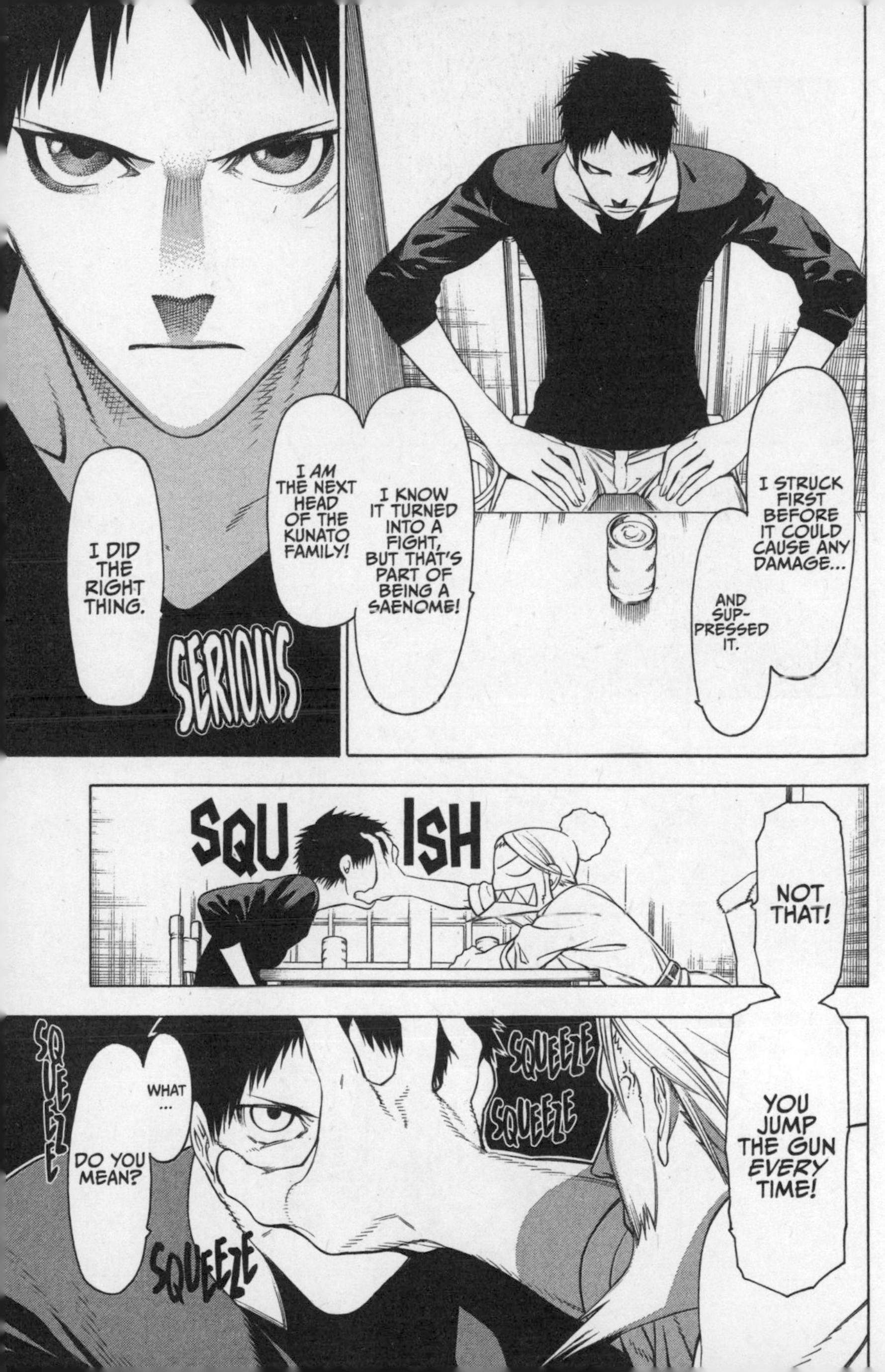
I STRUCK FIRST BEFORE IT COULD CAUSE ANY DAMAGE...
AND SUP-PRESSED IT.
I KNOW IT TURNED INTO A FIGHT, BUT THAT'S PART OF BEING A SAENOME!
I *AM* THE NEXT HEAD OF THE KUNATO FAMILY!
I DID THE RIGHT THING.
SERIOUS
NOT THAT!
SQU ISH
YOU JUMP THE GUN *EVERY* TIME!
SQUEEZE
SQUEEZE
WHAT...
DO YOU MEAN?
SQUEEZE
SQUEEZE

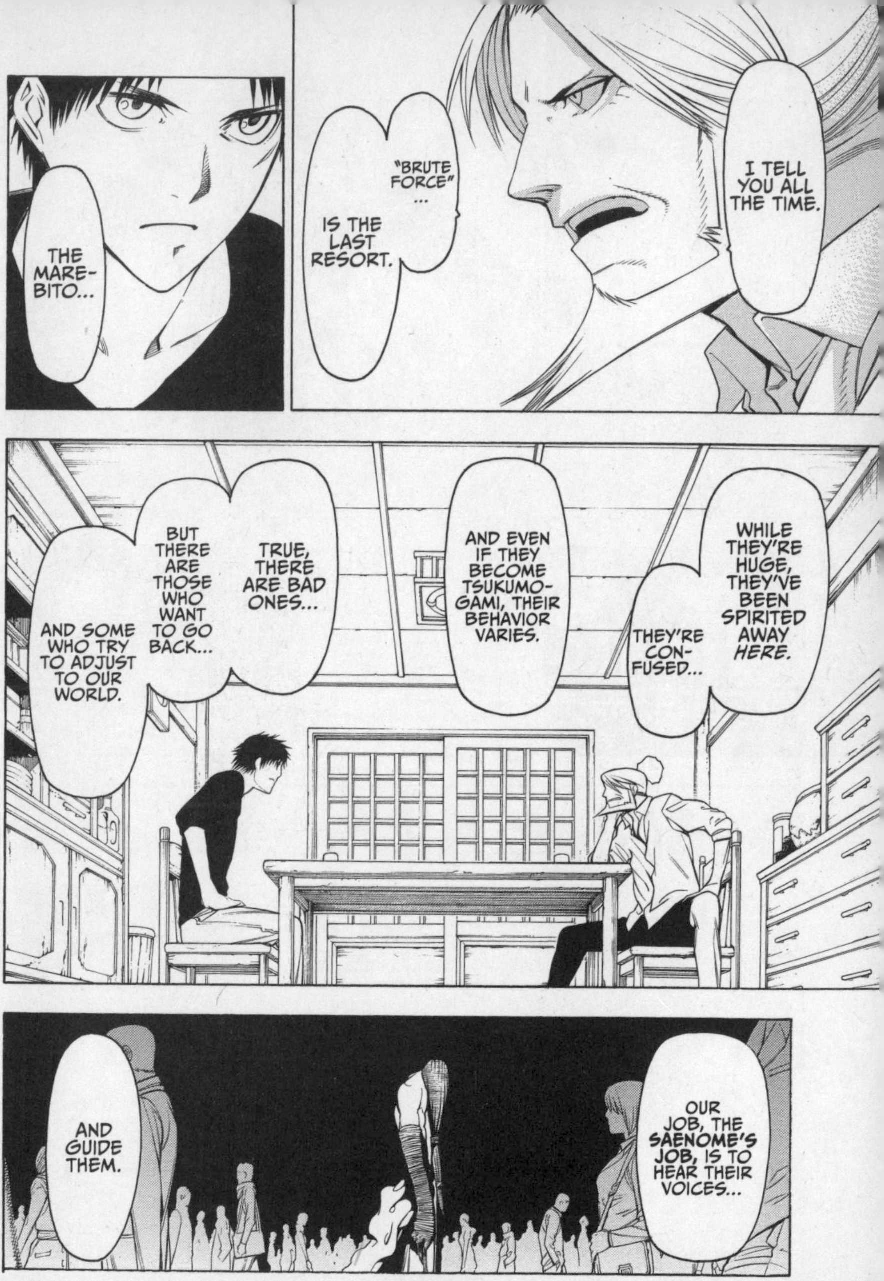
I TELL YOU ALL THE TIME.
"BRUTE FORCE"...
IS THE LAST RESORT.
THE MARE-BITO...
WHILE THEY'RE HUGE, THEY'VE BEEN SPIRITED AWAY *HERE.*
THEY'RE CON-FUSED...
AND EVEN IF THEY BECOME TSUKUMO-GAMI, THEIR BEHAVIOR VARIES.
TRUE, THERE ARE BAD ONES...
BUT THERE ARE THOSE WHO WANT TO GO BACK...
AND SOME WHO TRY TO ADJUST TO OUR WORLD.
OUR JOB, THE SAENOME'S JOB, IS TO HEAR THEIR VOICES...
AND GUIDE THEM.

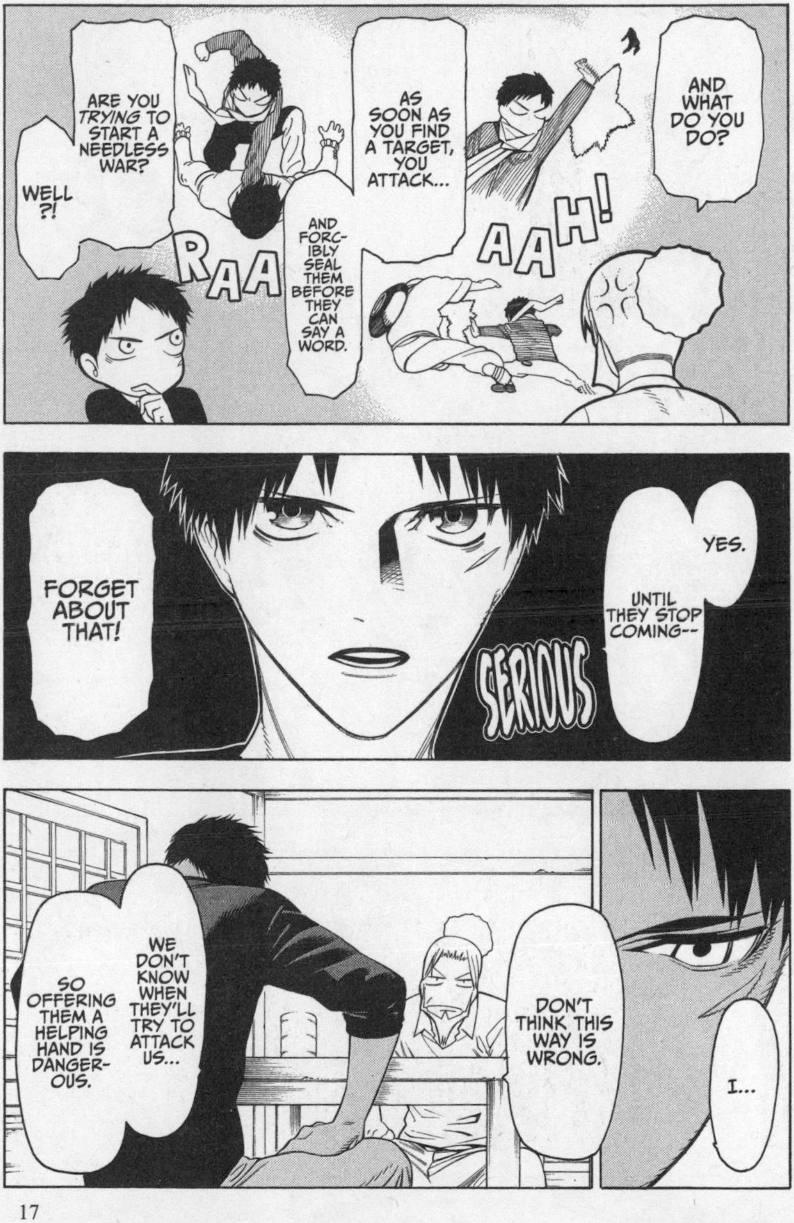
AND WHAT DO YOU DO?
AS SOON AS YOU FIND A TARGET, YOU ATTACK...
AND FORCIBLY SEAL THEM BEFORE THEY CAN SAY A WORD.
RAAAAH!
ARE YOU *TRYING* TO START A NEEDLESS WAR?
WELL ?!
YES.
UNTIL THEY STOP COMING--
SERIOUS
FORGET ABOUT THAT!
I...
DON'T THINK THIS WAY IS WRONG.
WE DON'T KNOW WHEN THEY'LL TRY TO ATTACK US...
SO OFFERING THEM A HELPING HAND IS DANGER-OUS.

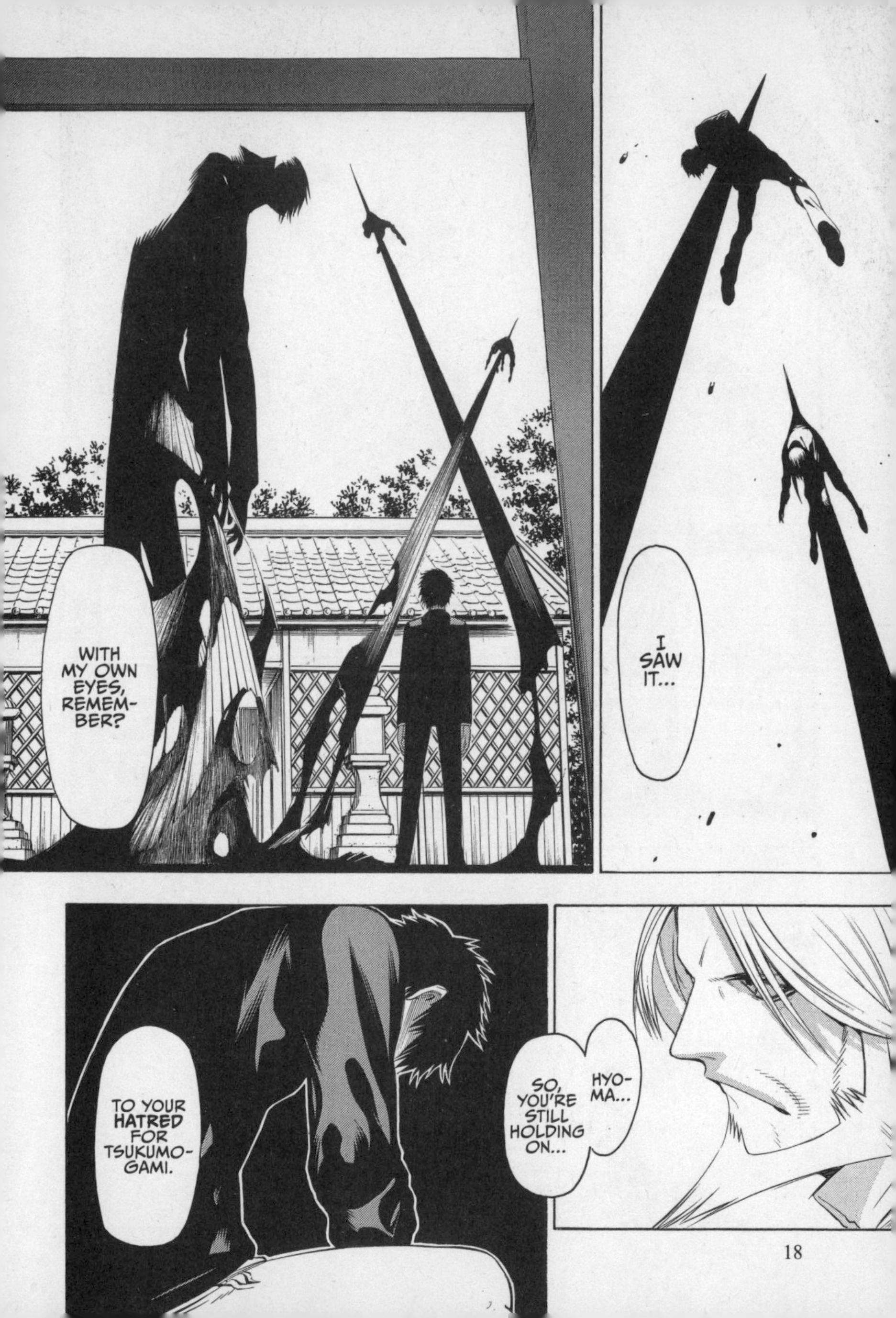
I SAW IT...
WITH MY OWN EYES, REMEMBER?
HYOMA...
SO, YOU'RE STILL HOLDING ON...
TO YOUR HATRED FOR TSUKUMOGAMI.

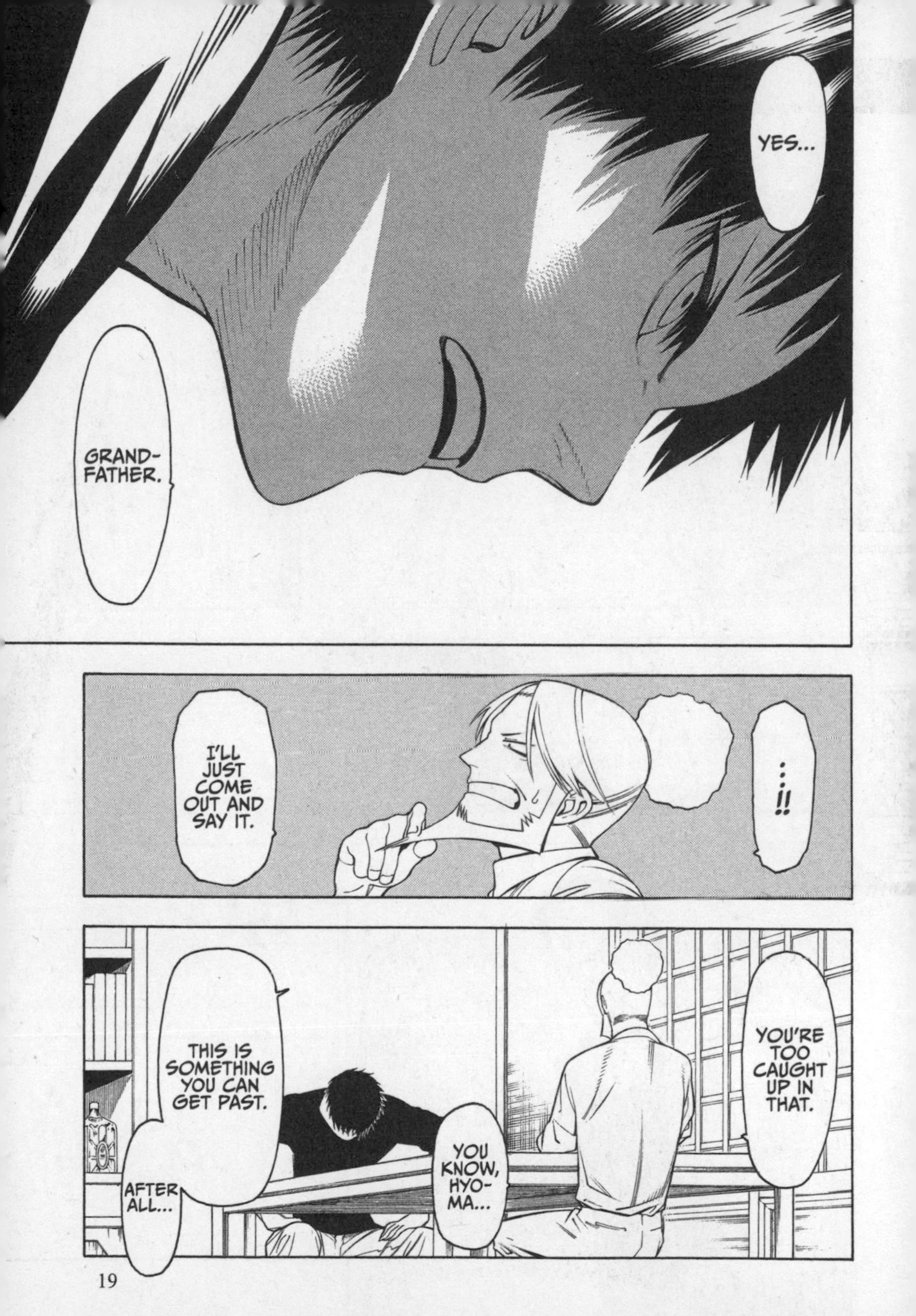
YES...
GRAND-FATHER.
...!!
I'LL JUST COME OUT AND SAY IT.
YOU'RE TOO CAUGHT UP IN THAT.
YOU KNOW, HYO-MA...
THIS IS SOMETHING YOU CAN GET PAST.
AFTER ALL...

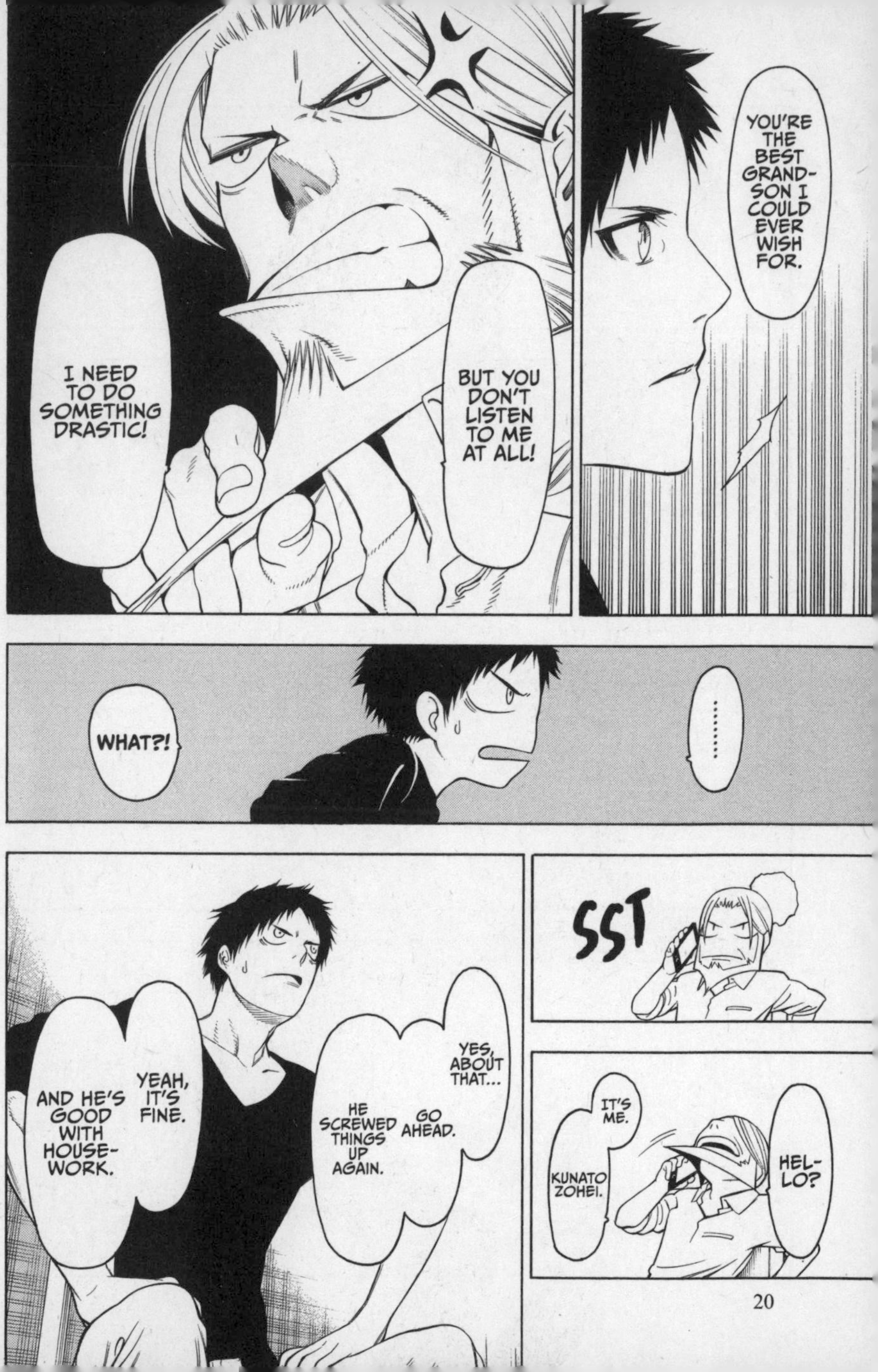
YOU'RE THE BEST GRAND-SON I COULD EVER WISH FOR.
BUT YOU DON'T LISTEN TO ME AT ALL!
I NEED TO DO SOMETHING DRASTIC!
......
WHAT?!
SST
HEL-LO?
IT'S ME.
KUNATO ZOHEI.
YES, ABOUT THAT...
GO AHEAD.
HE SCREWED THINGS UP AGAIN.
YEAH, IT'S FINE.
AND HE'S GOOD WITH HOUSE-WORK.

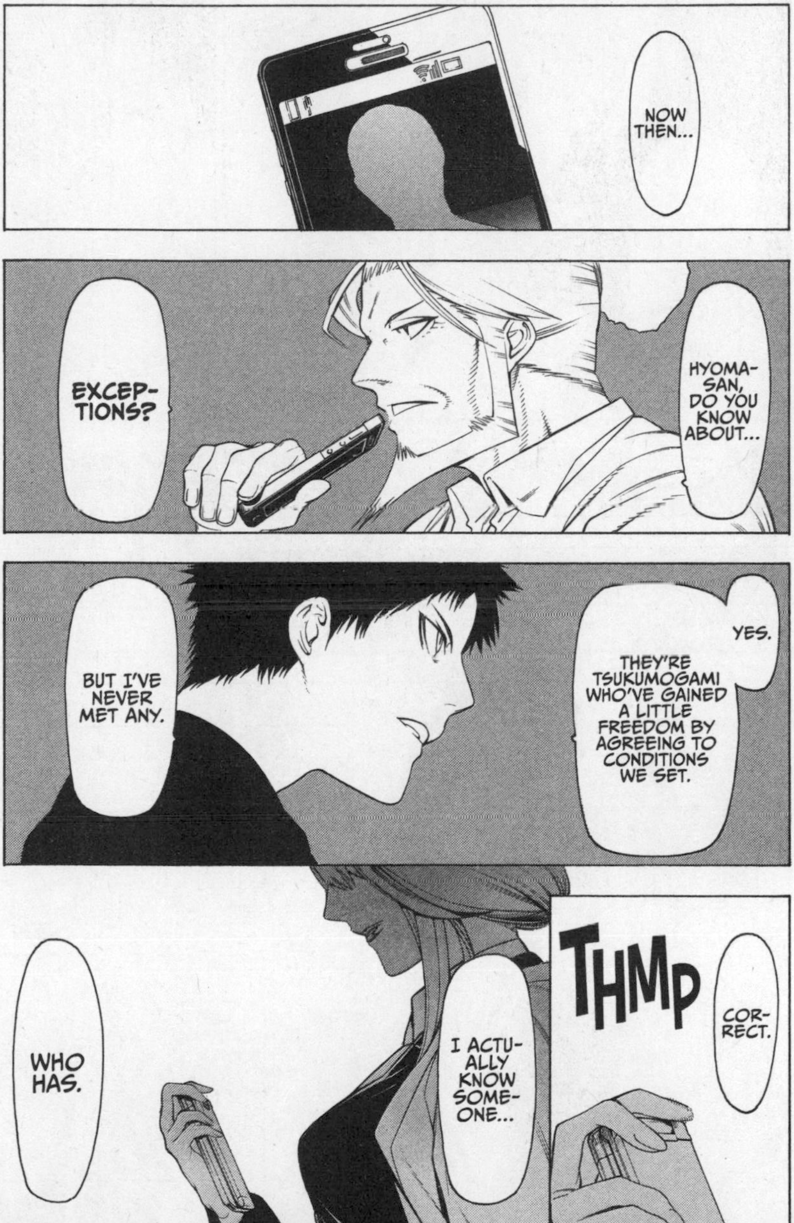
NOW THEN...
HYOMA-SAN, DO YOU KNOW ABOUT...
EXCEPTIONS?
YES.
THEY'RE TSUKUMOGAMI WHO'VE GAINED A LITTLE FREEDOM BY AGREEING TO CONDITIONS WE SET.
BUT I'VE NEVER MET ANY.
CORRECT.
THMP
I ACTUALLY KNOW SOMEONE...
WHO HAS.

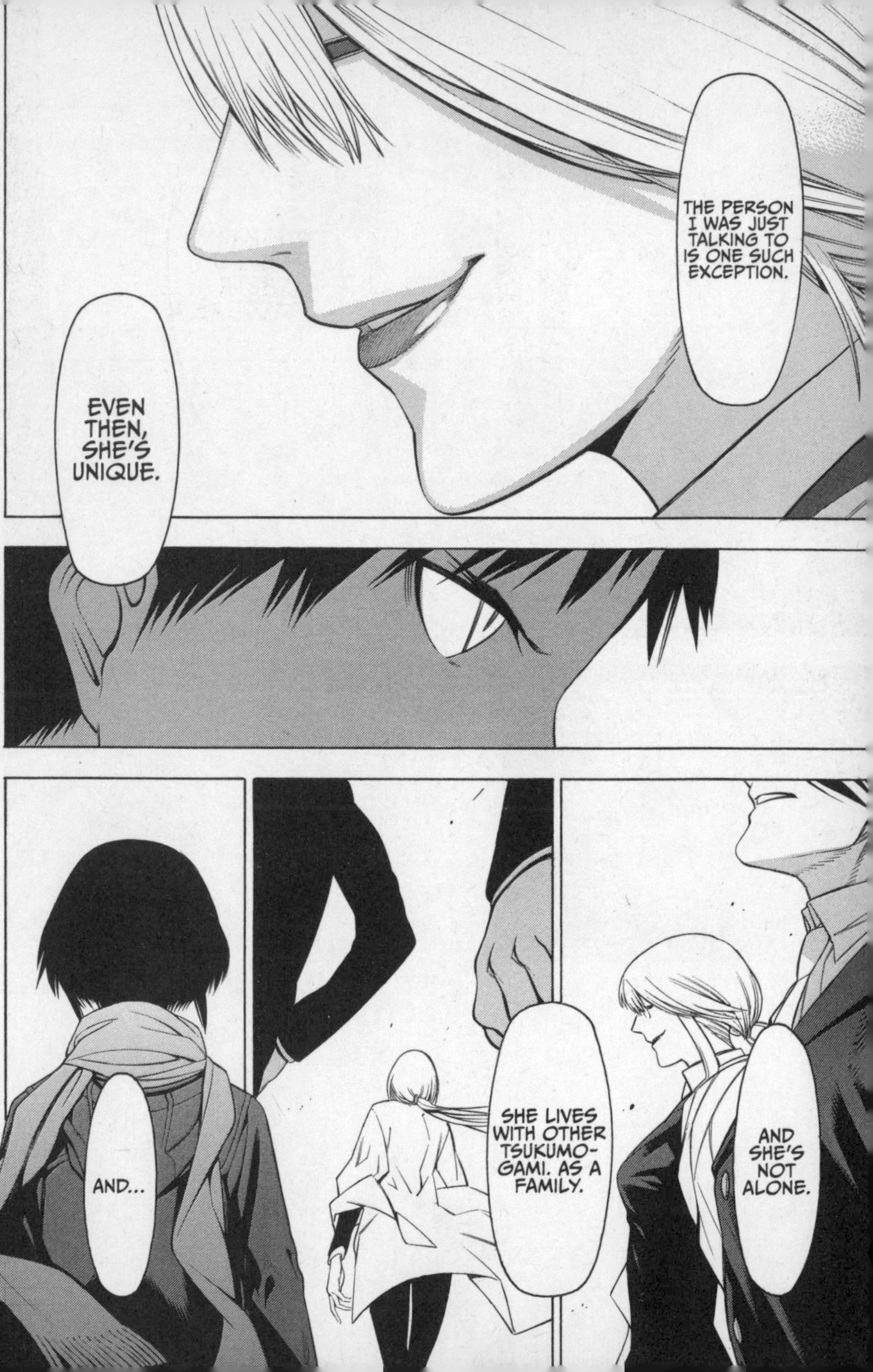
THE PERSON I WAS JUST TALKING TO IS ONE SUCH EXCEPTION.
EVEN THEN, SHE'S UNIQUE.
AND SHE'S NOT ALONE.
SHE LIVES WITH OTHER TSUKUMO-GAMI. AS A FAMILY.
AND...

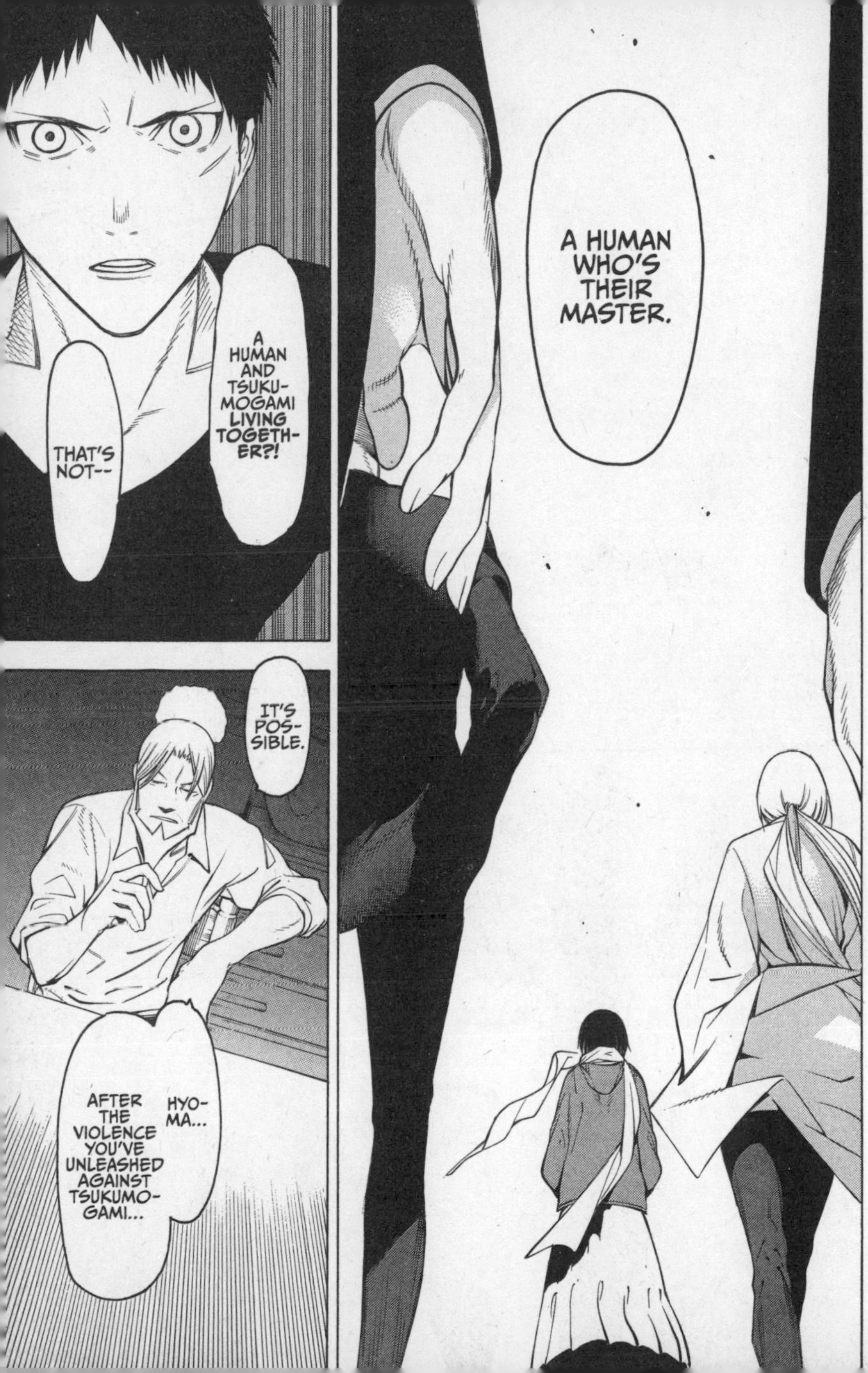
A HUMAN WHO'S THEIR MASTER.
A HUMAN AND TSUKUMOGAMI LIVING TOGETHER?!
THAT'S NOT--
IT'S POSSIBLE.
HYOMA...
AFTER THE VIOLENCE YOU'VE UNLEASHED AGAINST TSUKUMOGAMI...

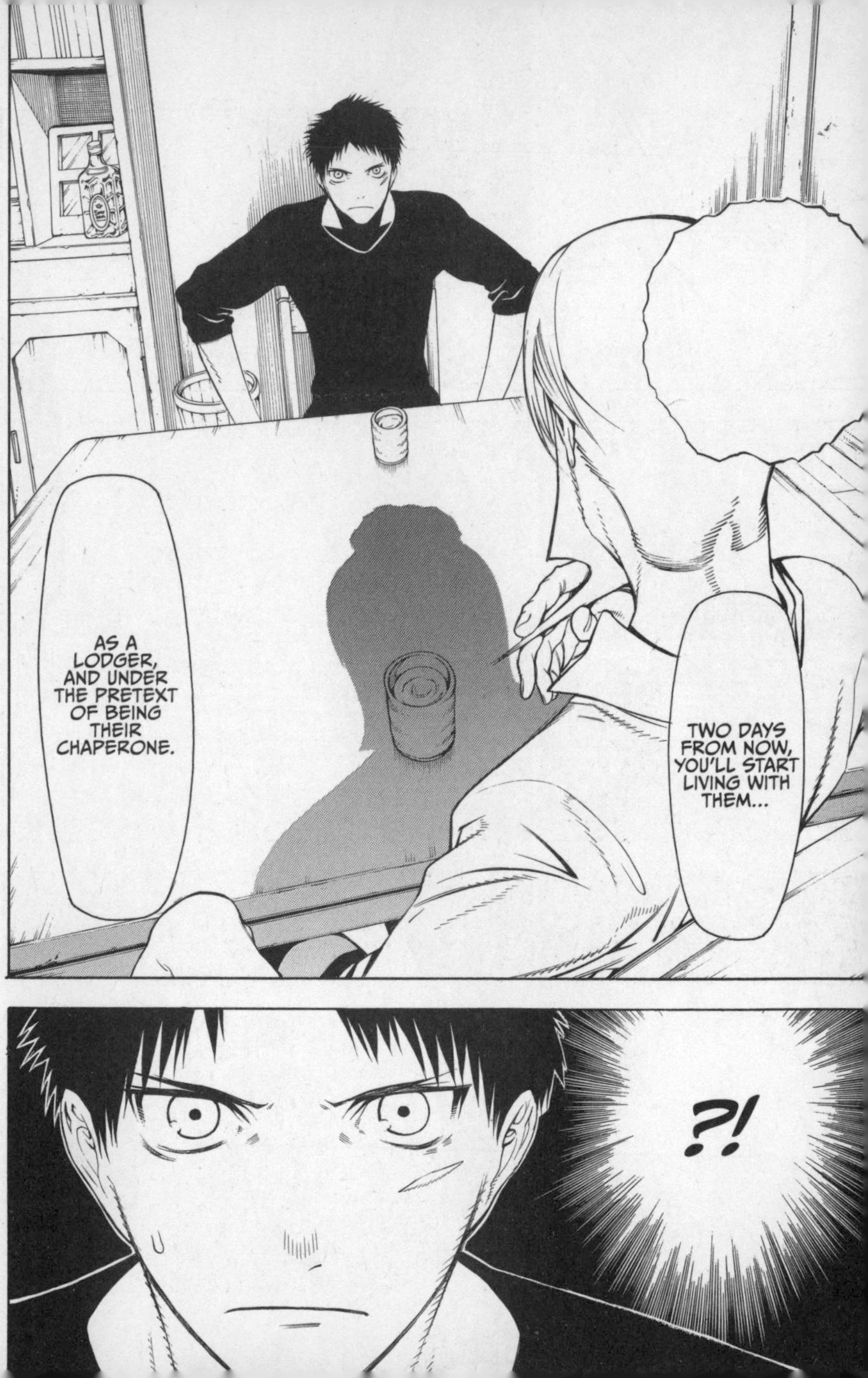
TWO DAYS FROM NOW, YOU'LL START LIVING WITH THEM...
AS A LODGER, AND UNDER THE PRETEXT OF BEING THEIR CHAPERONE.
?!

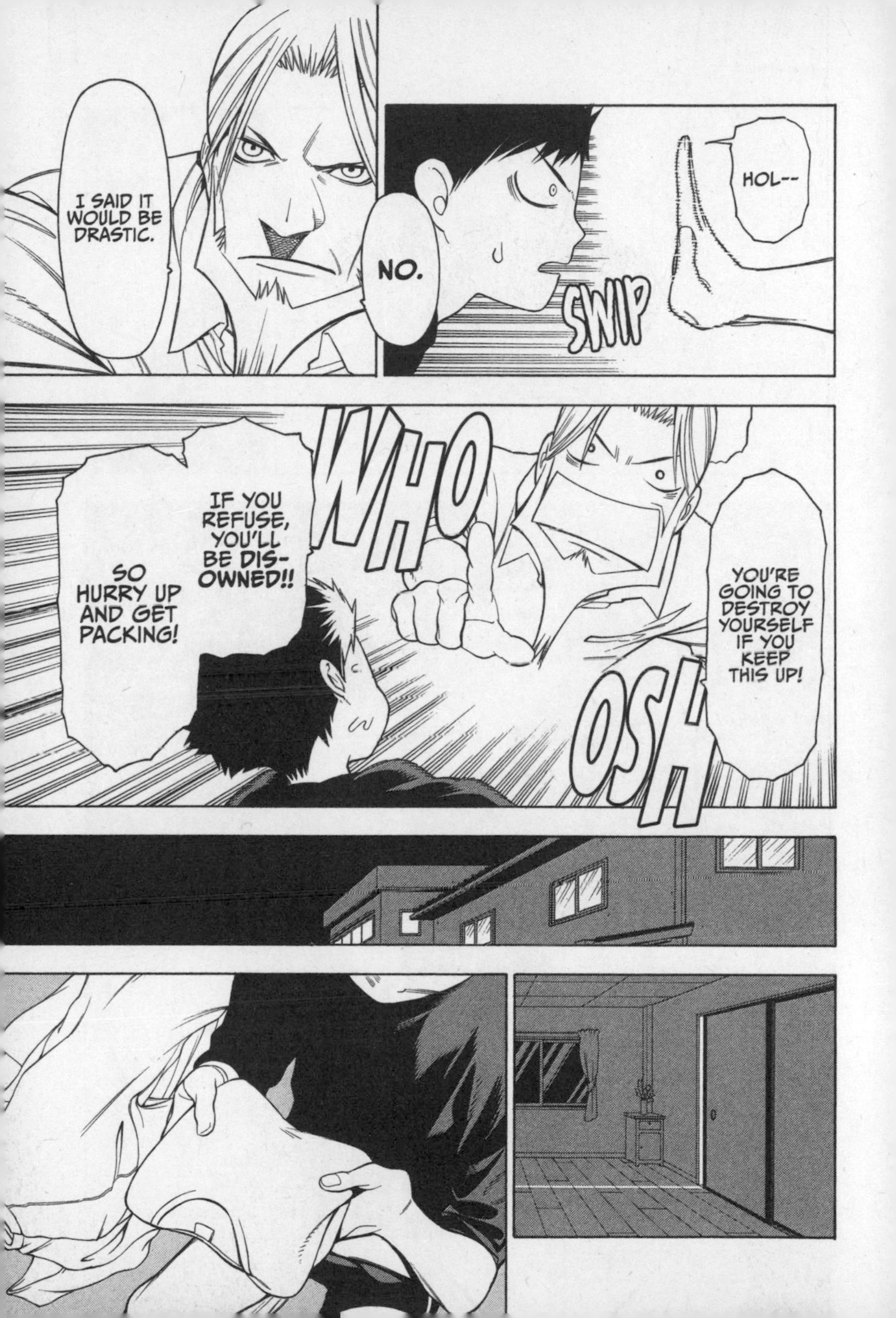
HOL--
NO.
SWIP
I SAID IT WOULD BE DRASTIC.
YOU'RE GOING TO DESTROY YOURSELF IF YOU KEEP THIS UP!
WHOOSH
IF YOU REFUSE, YOU'LL BE DIS-OWNED!!
SO HURRY UP AND GET PACKING!

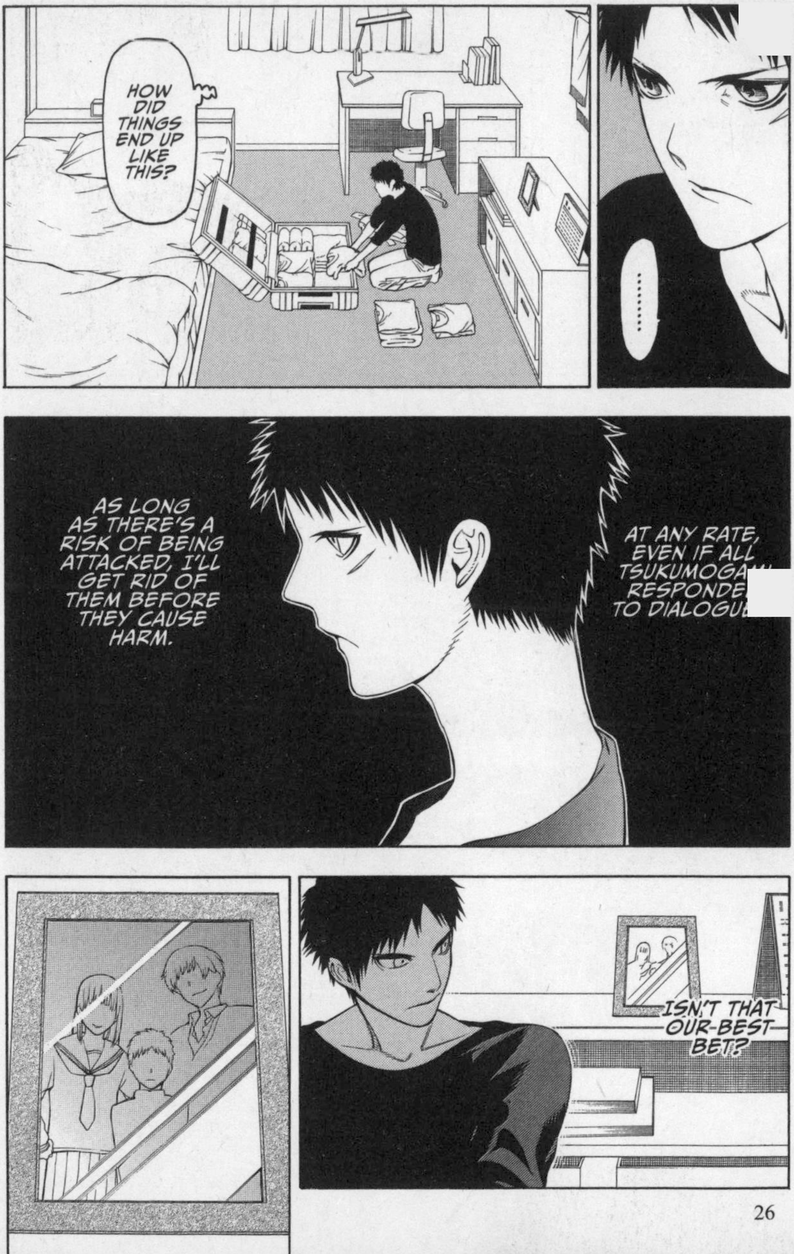
......
HOW DID THINGS END UP LIKE THIS?
AT ANY RATE, EVEN IF ALL TSUKUMOGAMI RESPONDED TO DIALOGUE
AS LONG AS THERE'S A RISK OF BEING ATTACKED, I'LL GET RID OF THEM BEFORE THEY CAUSE HARM.
ISN'T THAT OUR BEST BET?

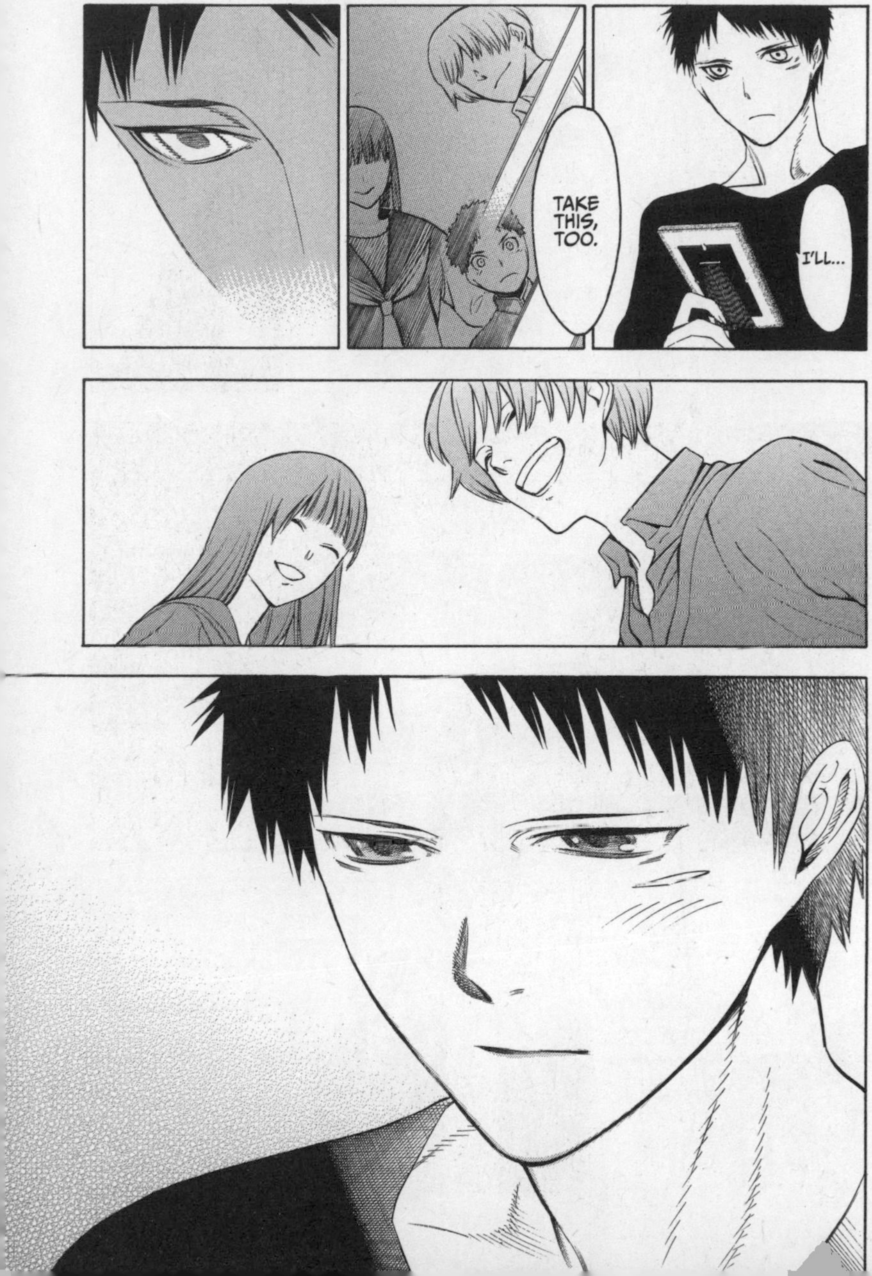
I'LL...
TAKE THIS, TOO.

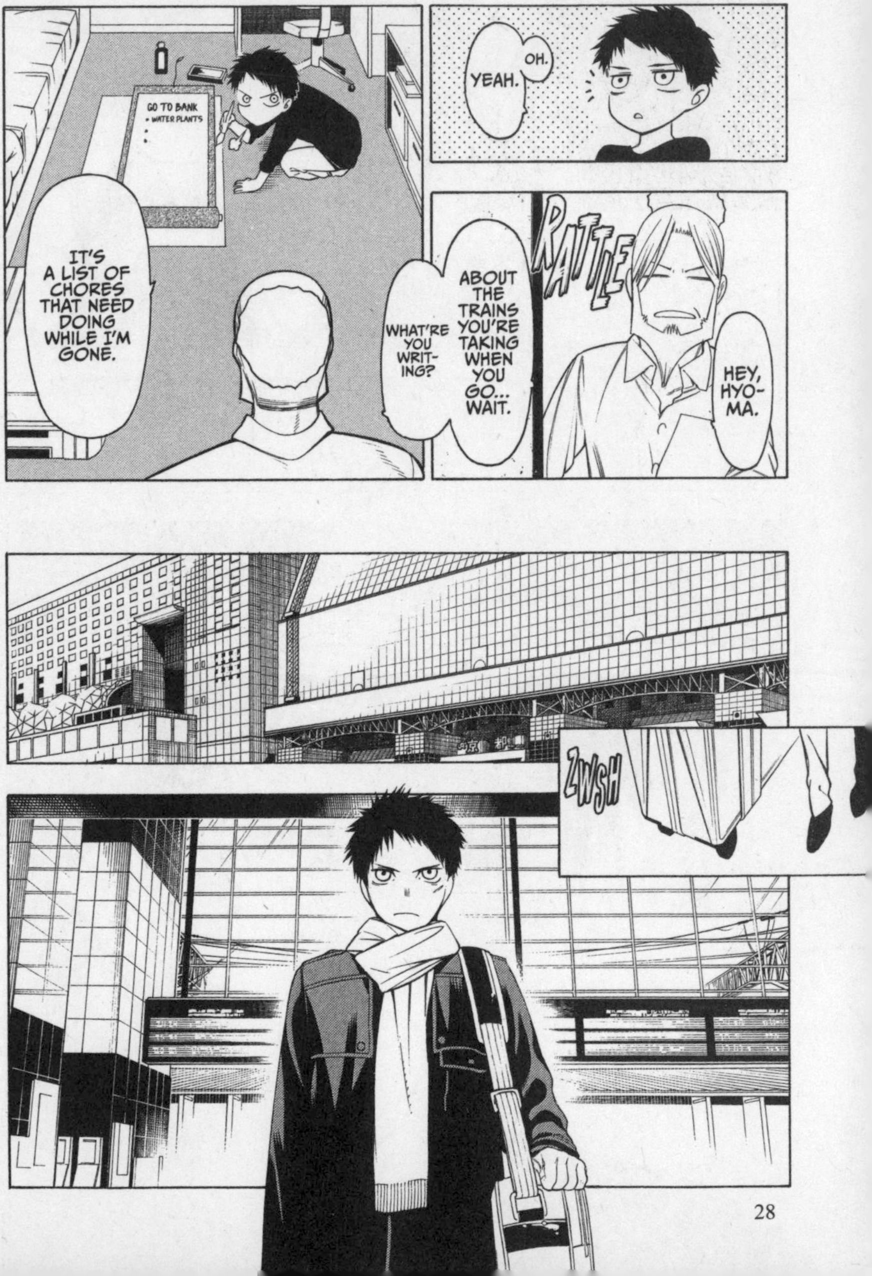
OH.
YEAH.
RATTLE
HEY, HYO-MA.
ABOUT THE TRAINS YOU'RE TAKING WHEN YOU GO... WAIT.
WHAT'RE YOU WRIT-ING?
GO TO BANK
• WATER PLANTS
IT'S A LIST OF CHORES THAT NEED DOING WHILE I'M GONE.
ZWSH

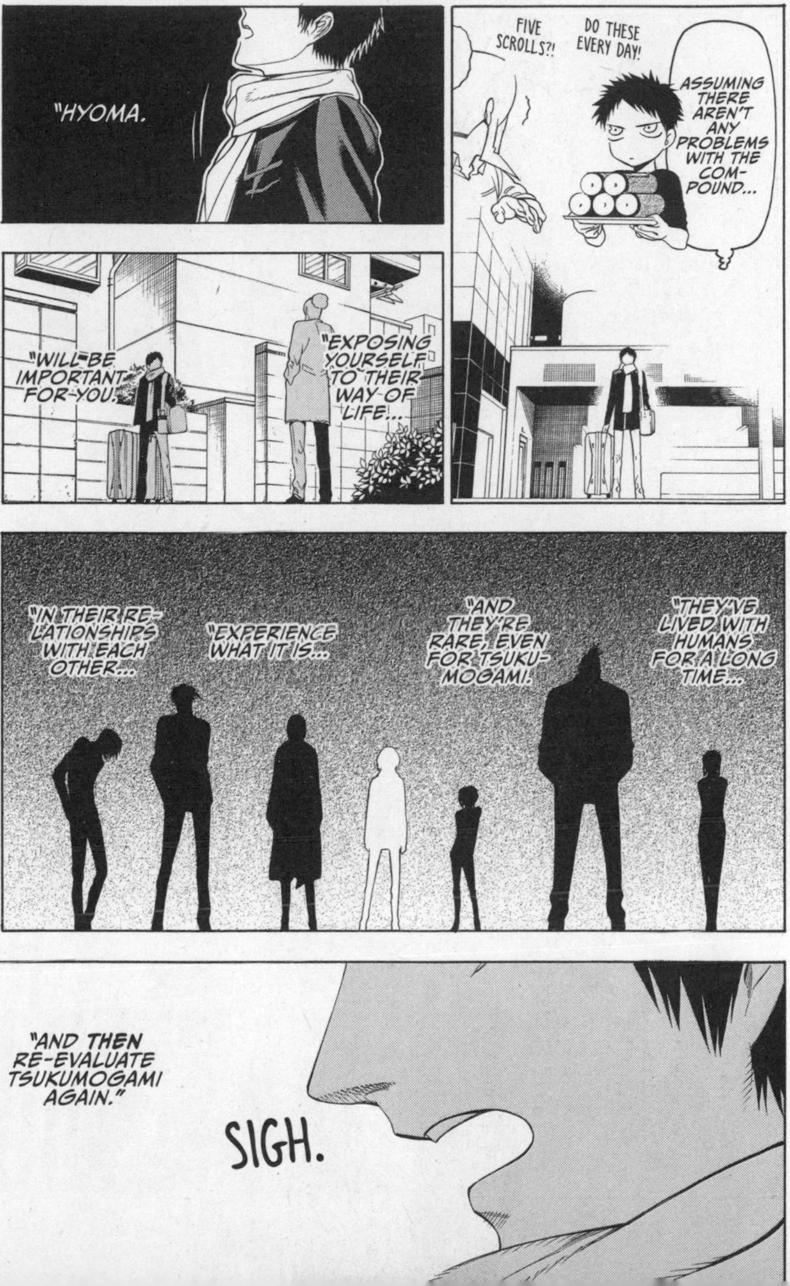
ASSUMING THERE AREN'T ANY PROBLEMS WITH THE COM-POUND...
DO THESE EVERY DAY!
FIVE SCROLLS?!
"HYOMA.
"EXPOSING YOURSELF TO THEIR WAY OF LIFE...
"WILL BE IMPORTANT FOR YOU.
"THEY'VE LIVED WITH HUMANS FOR A LONG TIME...
"AND THEY'RE RARE, EVEN FOR TSUKU-MOGAMI.
"EXPERIENCE WHAT IT IS...
"IN THEIR RE-LATIONSHIPS WITH EACH OTHER...
"AND THEN RE-EVALUATE TSUKUMOGAMI AGAIN."
SIGH.

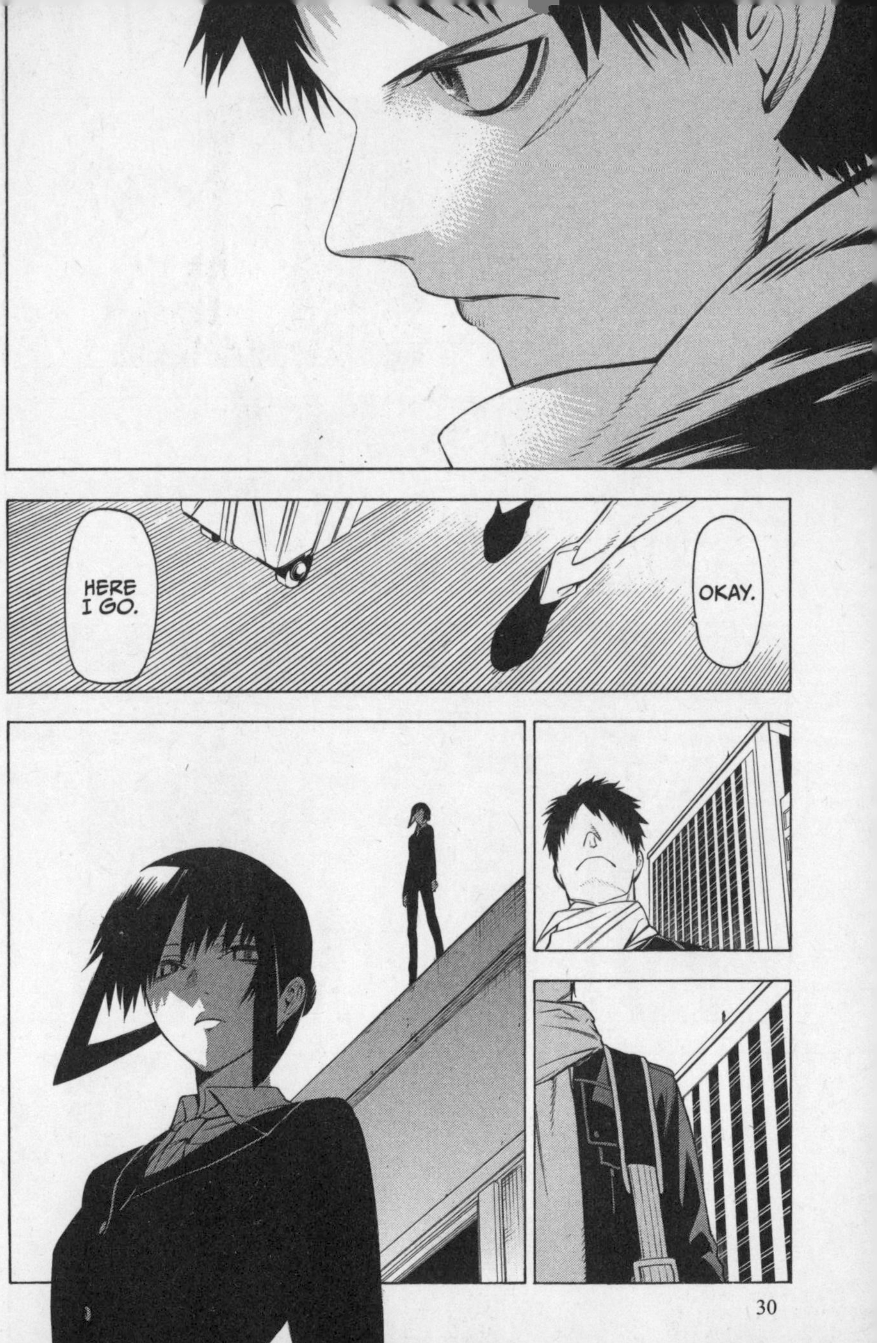
OKAY.
HERE I GO.

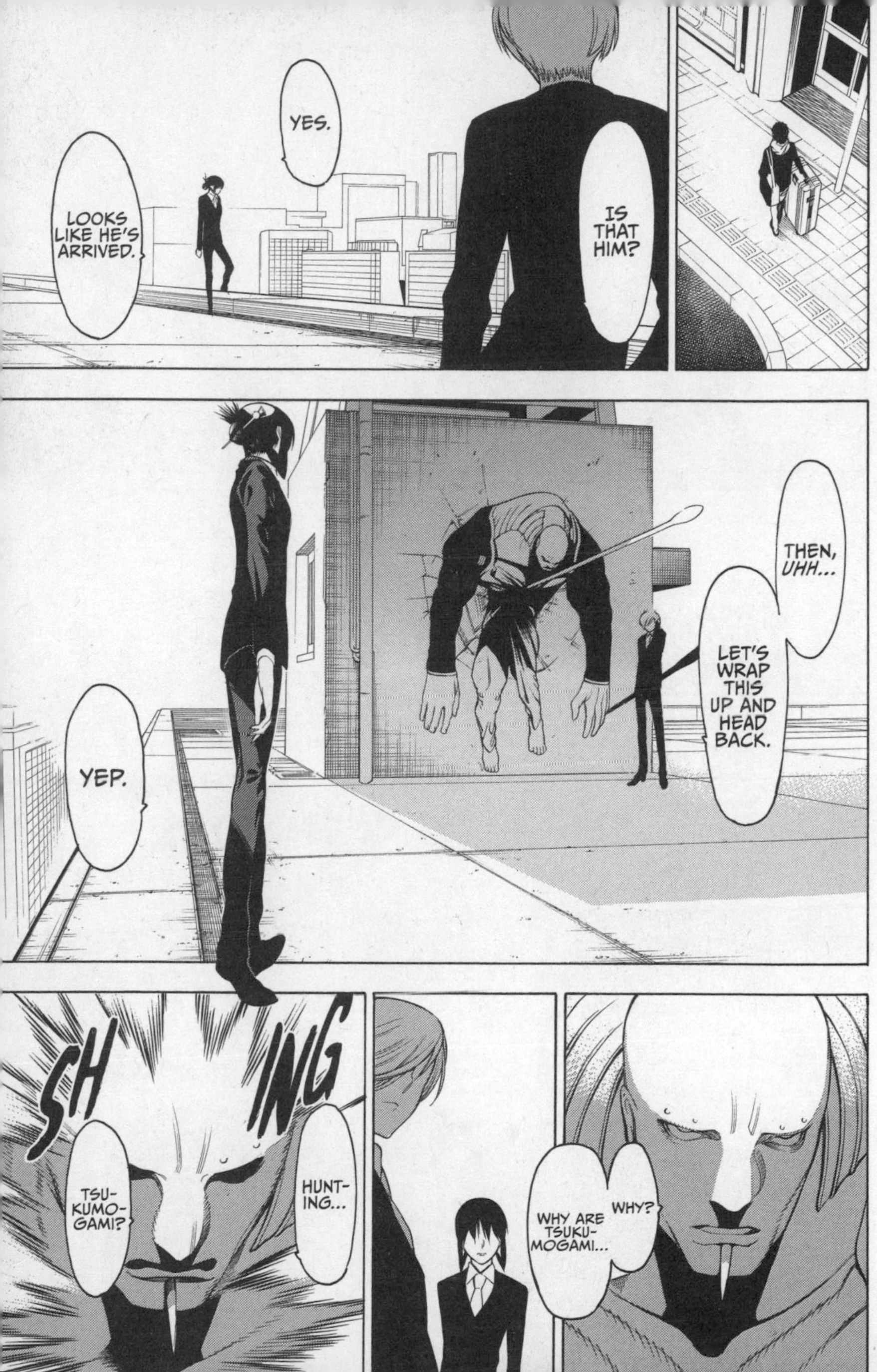
IS THAT HIM?
YES.
LOOKS LIKE HE'S ARRIVED.
THEN, UHH...
LET'S WRAP THIS UP AND HEAD BACK.
YEP.
WHY?
WHY ARE TSUKU-MOGAMI...
HUNT-ING...
SHING
TSU-KUMO-GAMI?

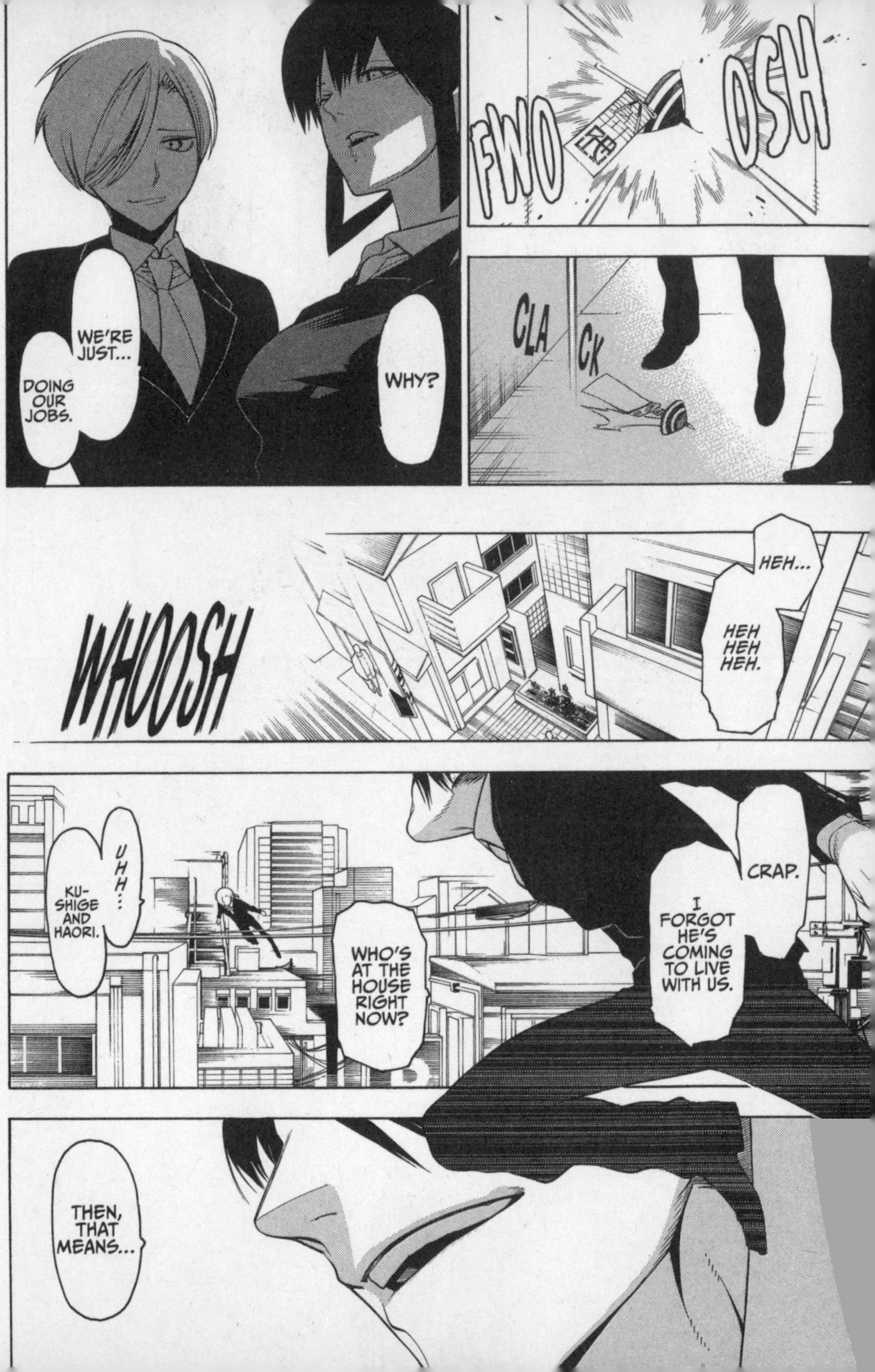
FWO OSH
CLA CK
WHY?
WE'RE JUST...
DOING OUR JOBS.
HEH...
HEH HEH HEH.
WHOOSH
CRAP.
I FORGOT HE'S COMING TO LIVE WITH US.
WHO'S AT THE HOUSE RIGHT NOW?
UHH...
KU-SHIGE AND HAORI.
THEN, THAT MEANS...

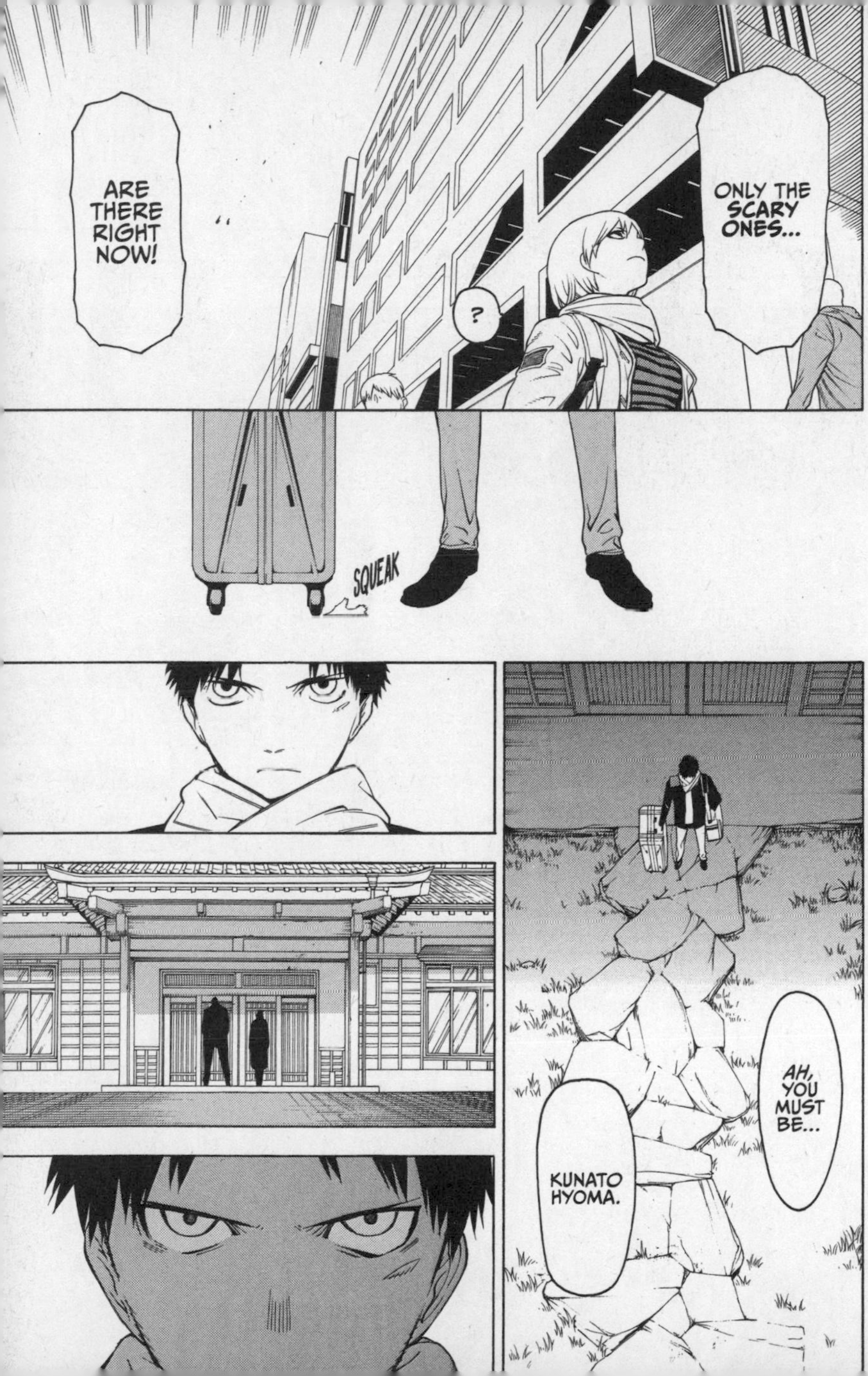
ONLY THE SCARY ONES...
ARE THERE RIGHT NOW!
?
SQUEAK
AH, YOU MUST BE...
KUNATO HYOMA.

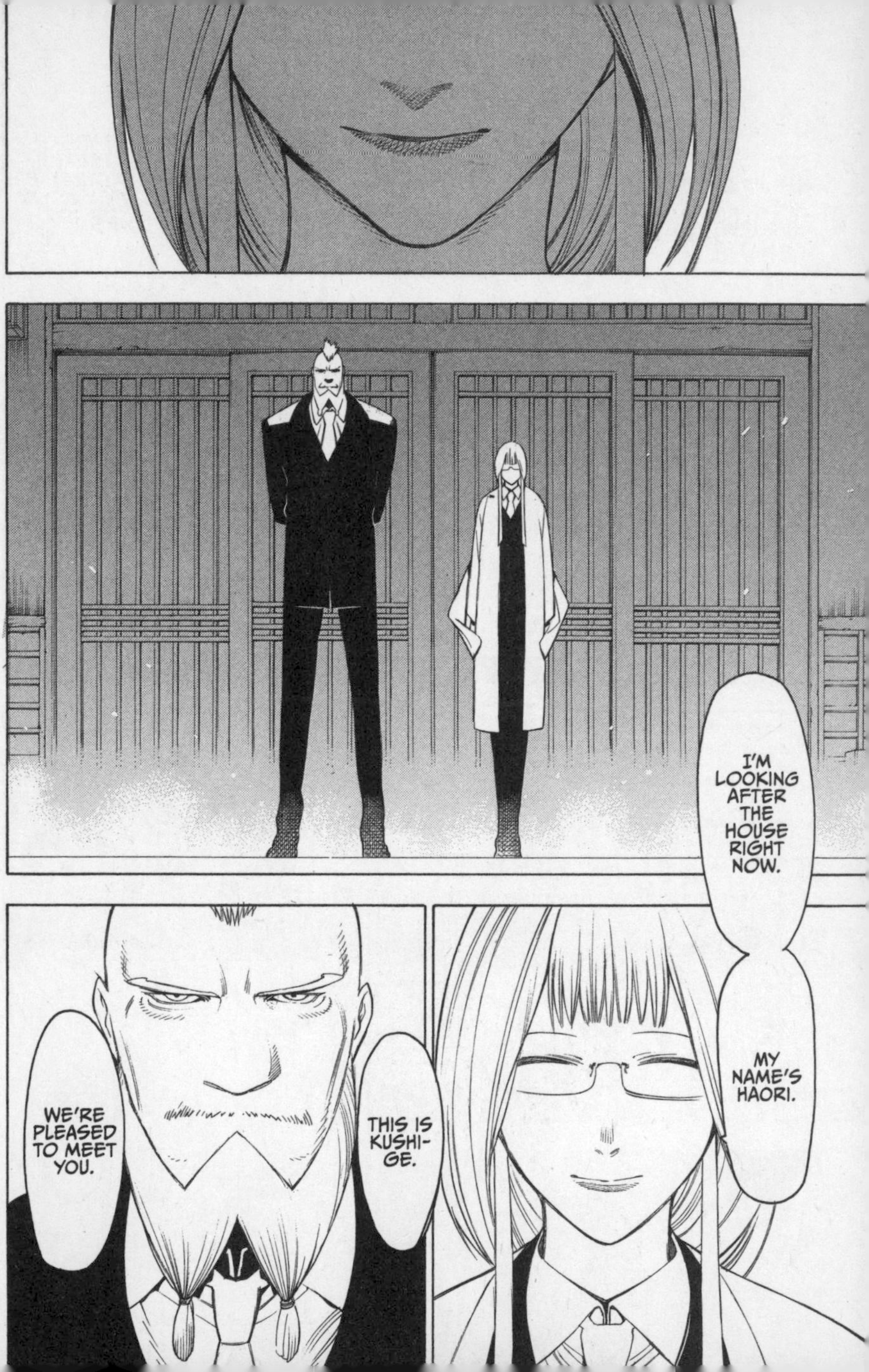
I'M LOOKING AFTER THE HOUSE RIGHT NOW.
MY NAME'S HAORI.
THIS IS KUSHI-GE.
WE'RE PLEASED TO MEET YOU.

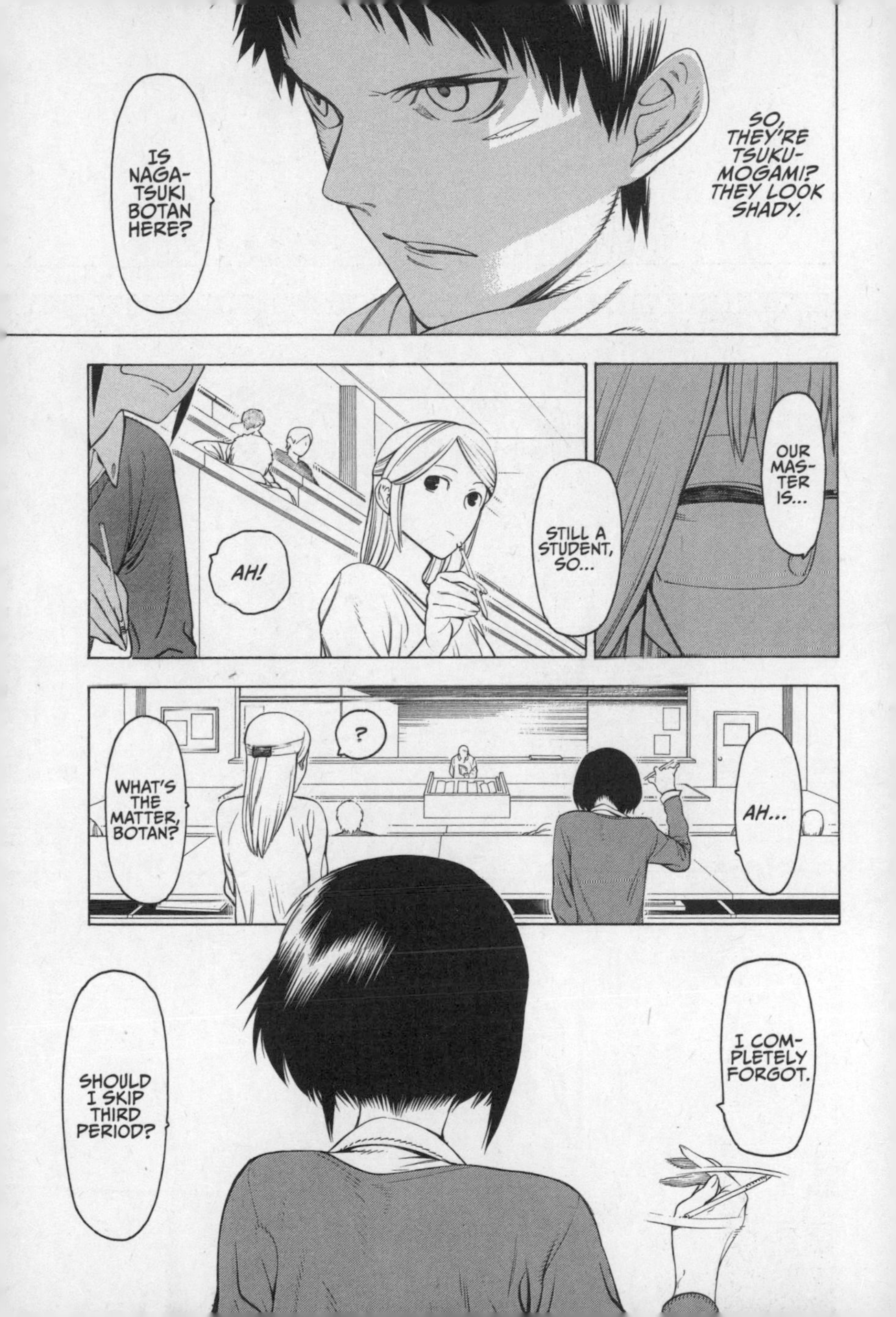
SO, THEY'RE TSUKU-MOGAMI? THEY LOOK SHADY.
IS NAGA-TSUKI BOTAN HERE?
OUR MAS-TER IS...
STILL A STUDENT, SO...
AH!
AH...
?
WHAT'S THE MATTER, BOTAN?
I COM-PLETELY FORGOT.
SHOULD I SKIP THIRD PERIOD?

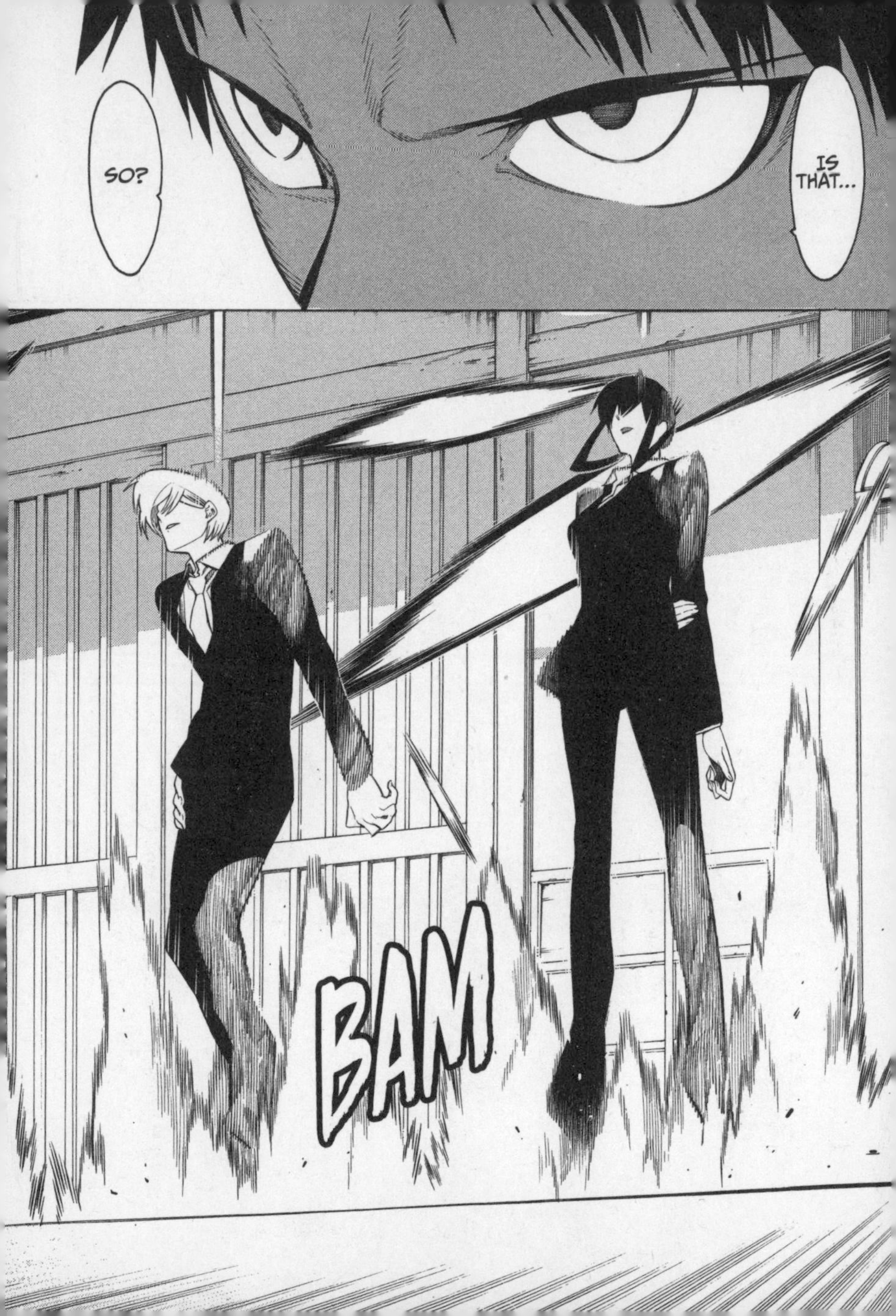
IS THAT...
SO?
BAM

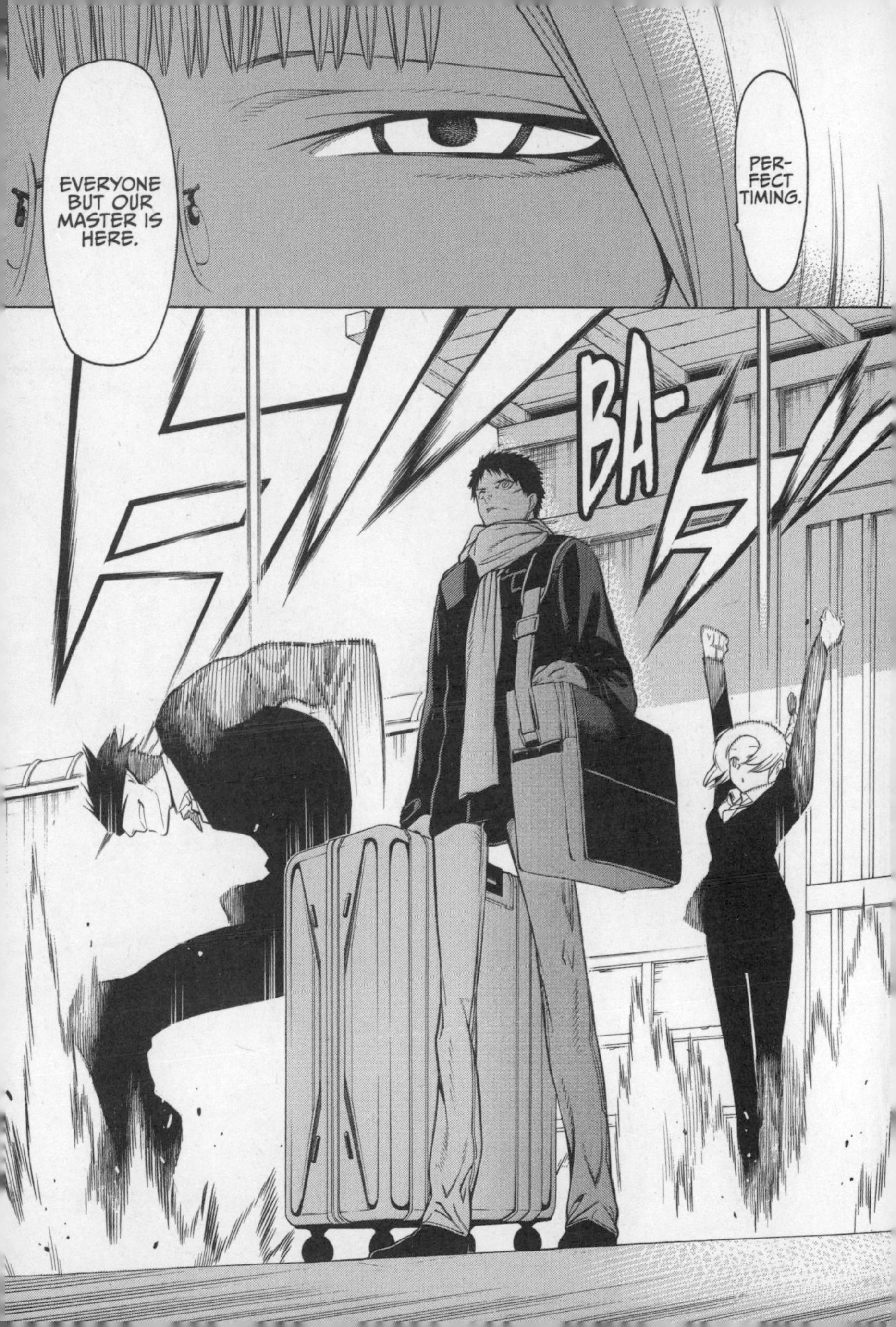
PER-FECT TIMING.
EVERYONE BUT OUR MASTER IS HERE.
BA-

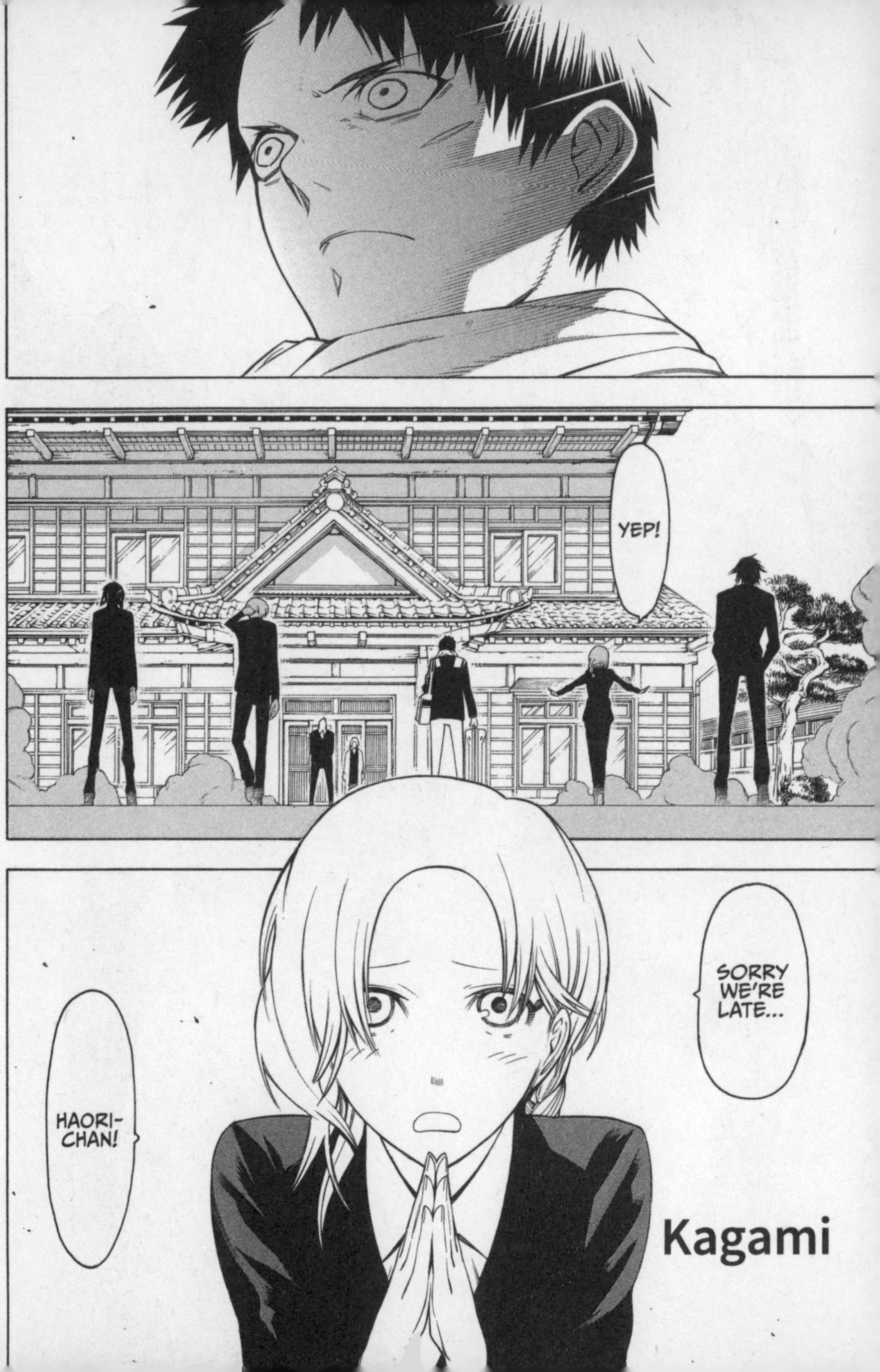
YEP!
SORRY WE'RE LATE...
HAORI-CHAN!
Kagami

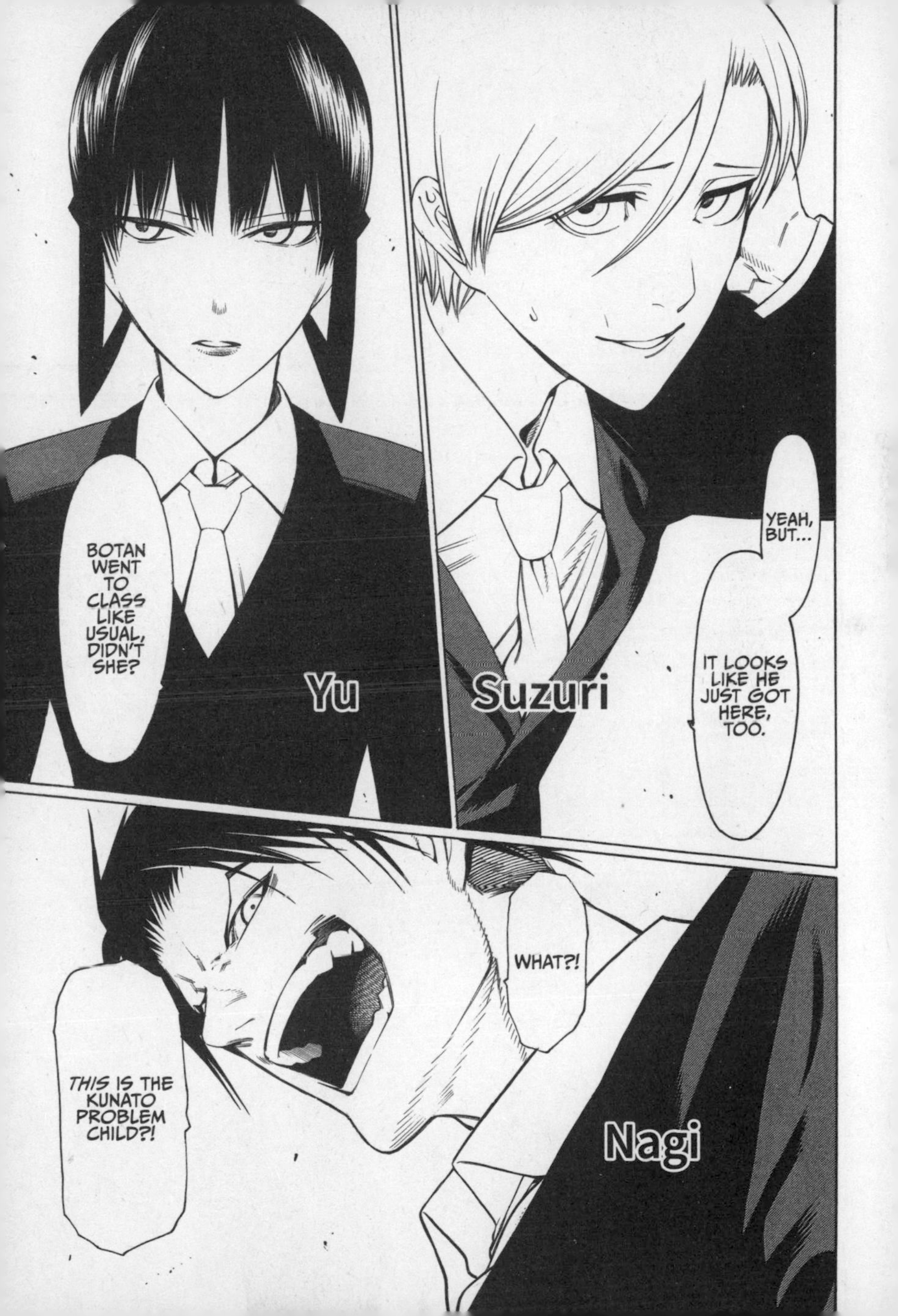
YEAH, BUT...
IT LOOKS LIKE HE JUST GOT HERE, TOO.
Suzuri
BOTAN WENT TO CLASS LIKE USUAL, DIDN'T SHE?
Yu
WHAT?!
THIS IS THE KUNATO PROBLEM CHILD?!
Nagi

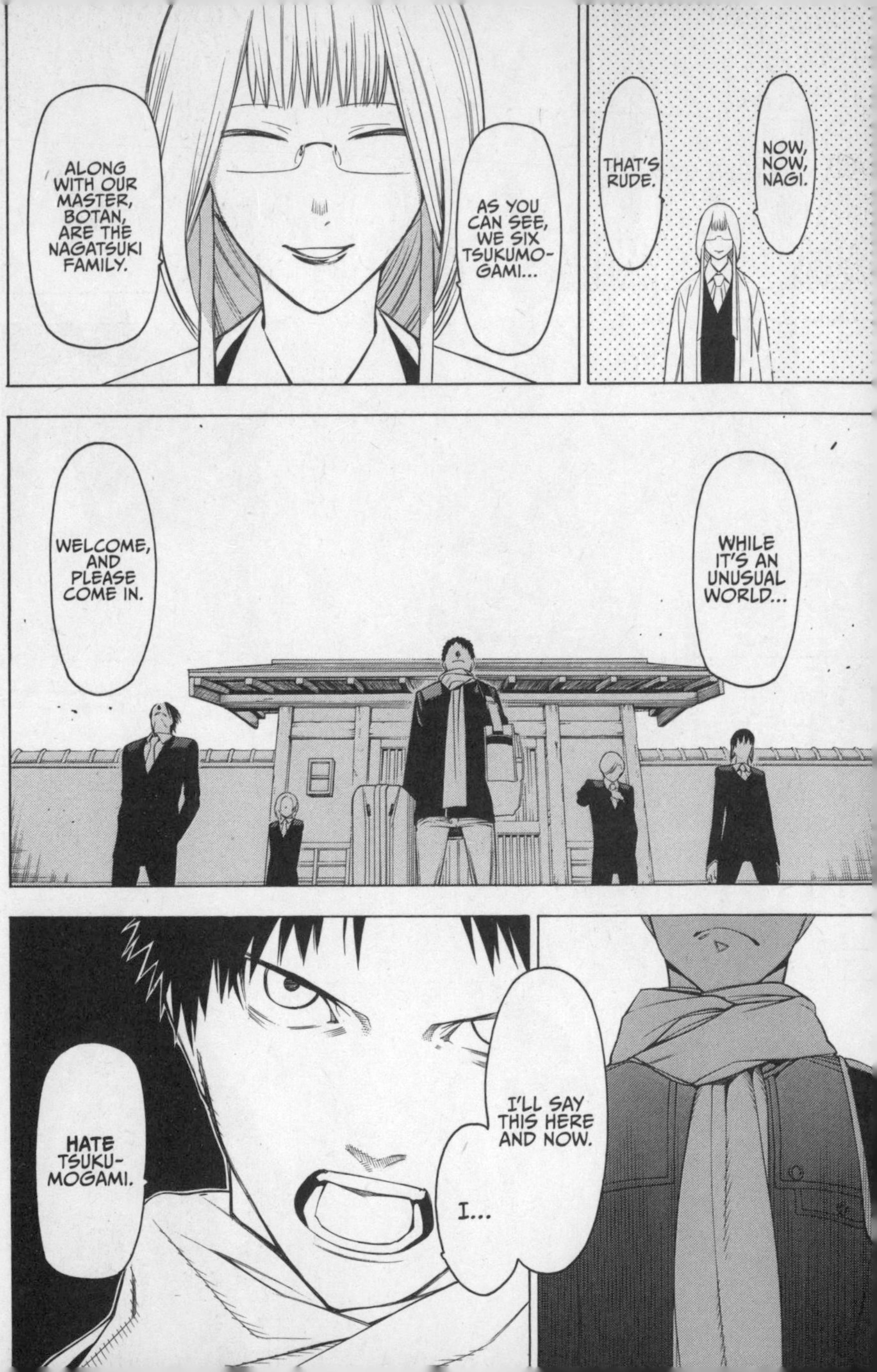
NOW, NOW, NAGI.
THAT'S RUDE.
AS YOU CAN SEE, WE SIX TSUKUMO-GAMI...
ALONG WITH OUR MASTER, BOTAN, ARE THE NAGATSUKI FAMILY.
WHILE IT'S AN UNUSUAL WORLD...
WELCOME, AND PLEASE COME IN.
I'LL SAY THIS HERE AND NOW.
I...
HATE TSUKU-MOGAMI.

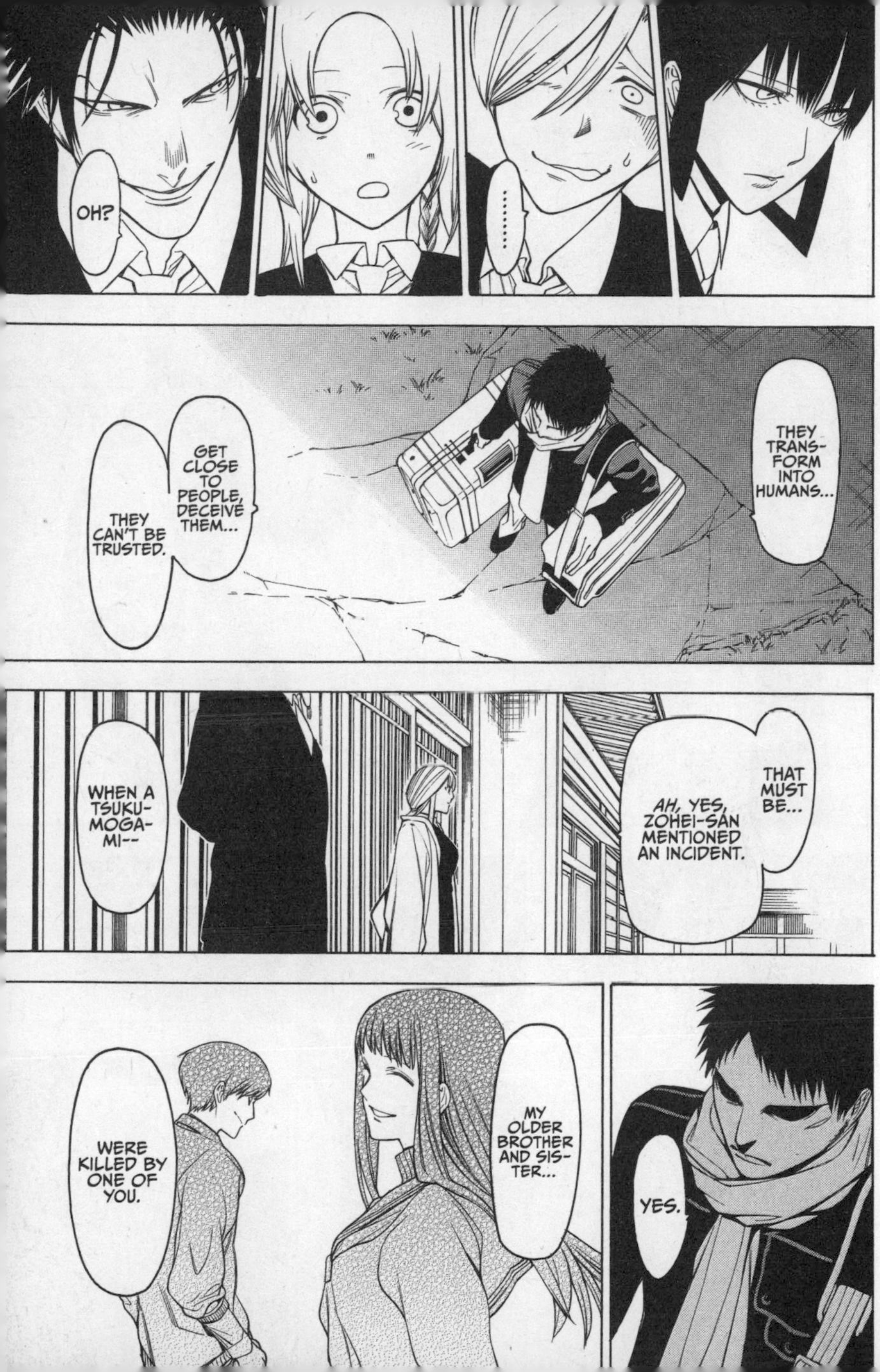
......
OH?
THEY TRANSFORM INTO HUMANS...
GET CLOSE TO PEOPLE, DECEIVE THEM...
THEY CAN'T BE TRUSTED.
THAT MUST BE...
AH, YES, ZOHEI-SAN MENTIONED AN INCIDENT.
WHEN A TSUKUMOGAMI--
YES.
MY OLDER BROTHER AND SISTER...
WERE KILLED BY ONE OF YOU.

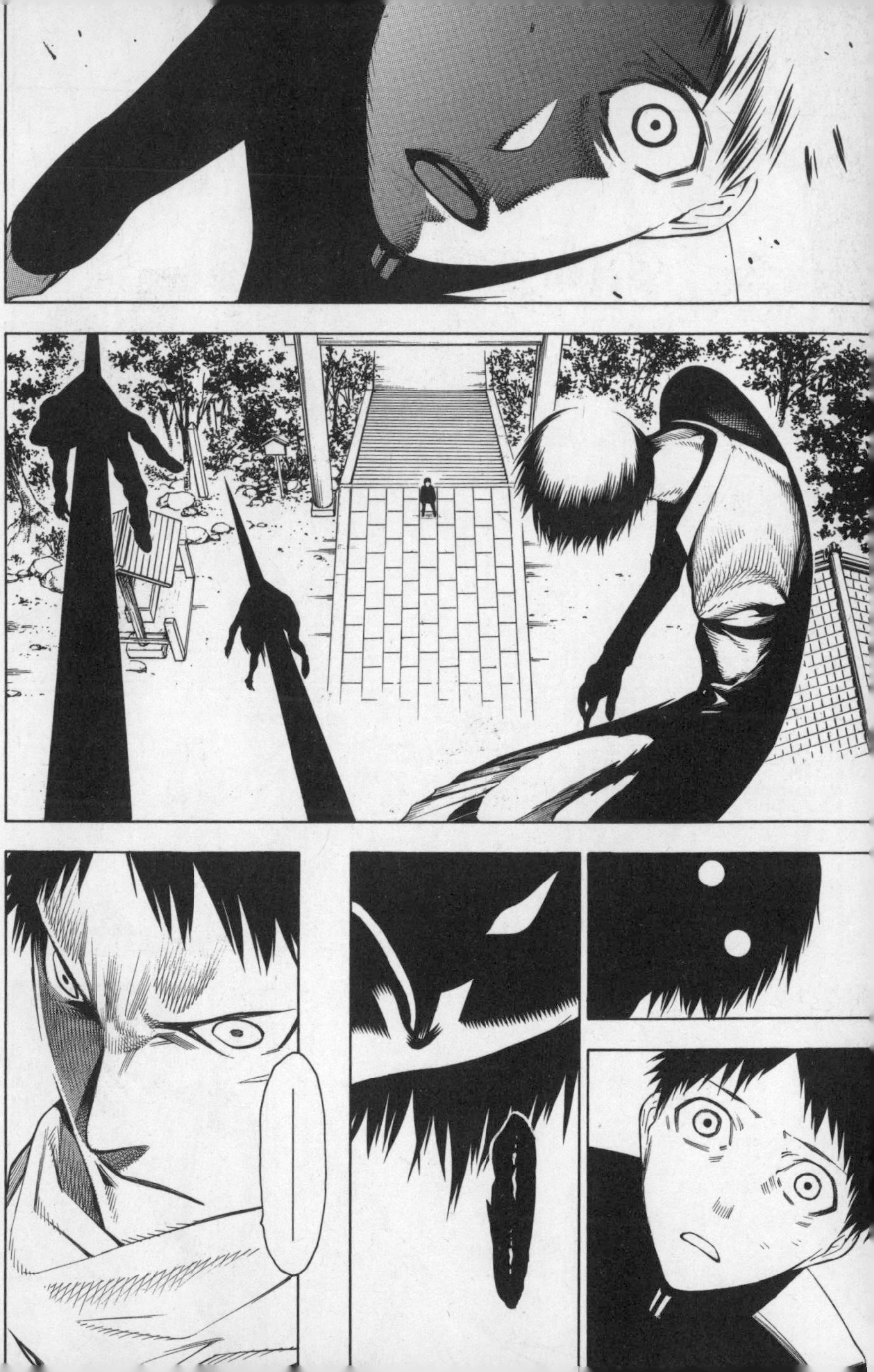
—

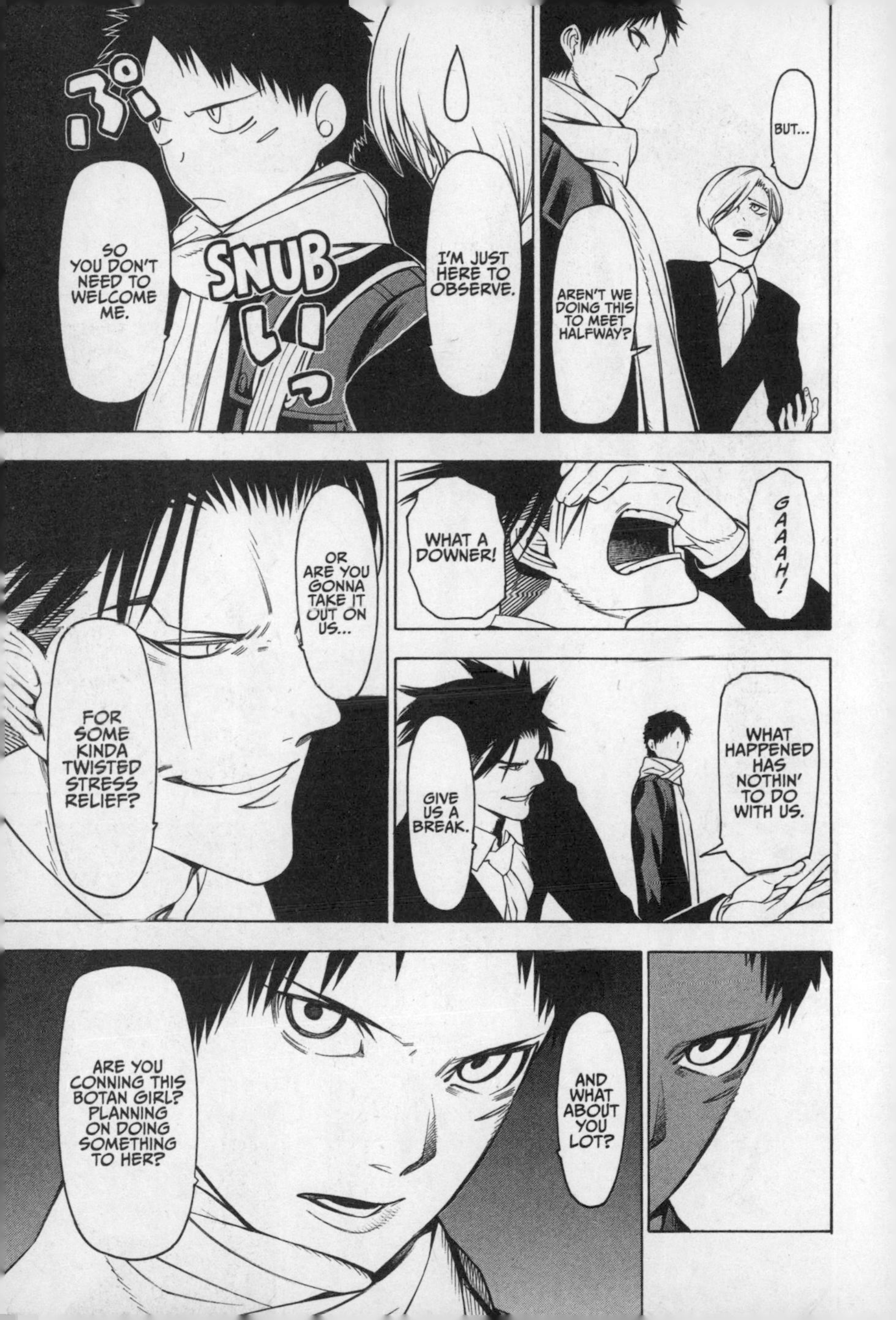
BUT...
AREN'T WE DOING THIS TO MEET HALFWAY?
I'M JUST HERE TO OBSERVE.
SO YOU DON'T NEED TO WELCOME ME.
SNUB
GAAAH!
WHAT A DOWNER!
WHAT HAPPENED HAS NOTHIN' TO DO WITH US.
GIVE US A BREAK.
OR ARE YOU GONNA TAKE IT OUT ON US...
FOR SOME KINDA TWISTED STRESS RELIEF?
AND WHAT ABOUT YOU LOT?
ARE YOU CONNING THIS BOTAN GIRL? PLANNING ON DOING SOMETHING TO HER?

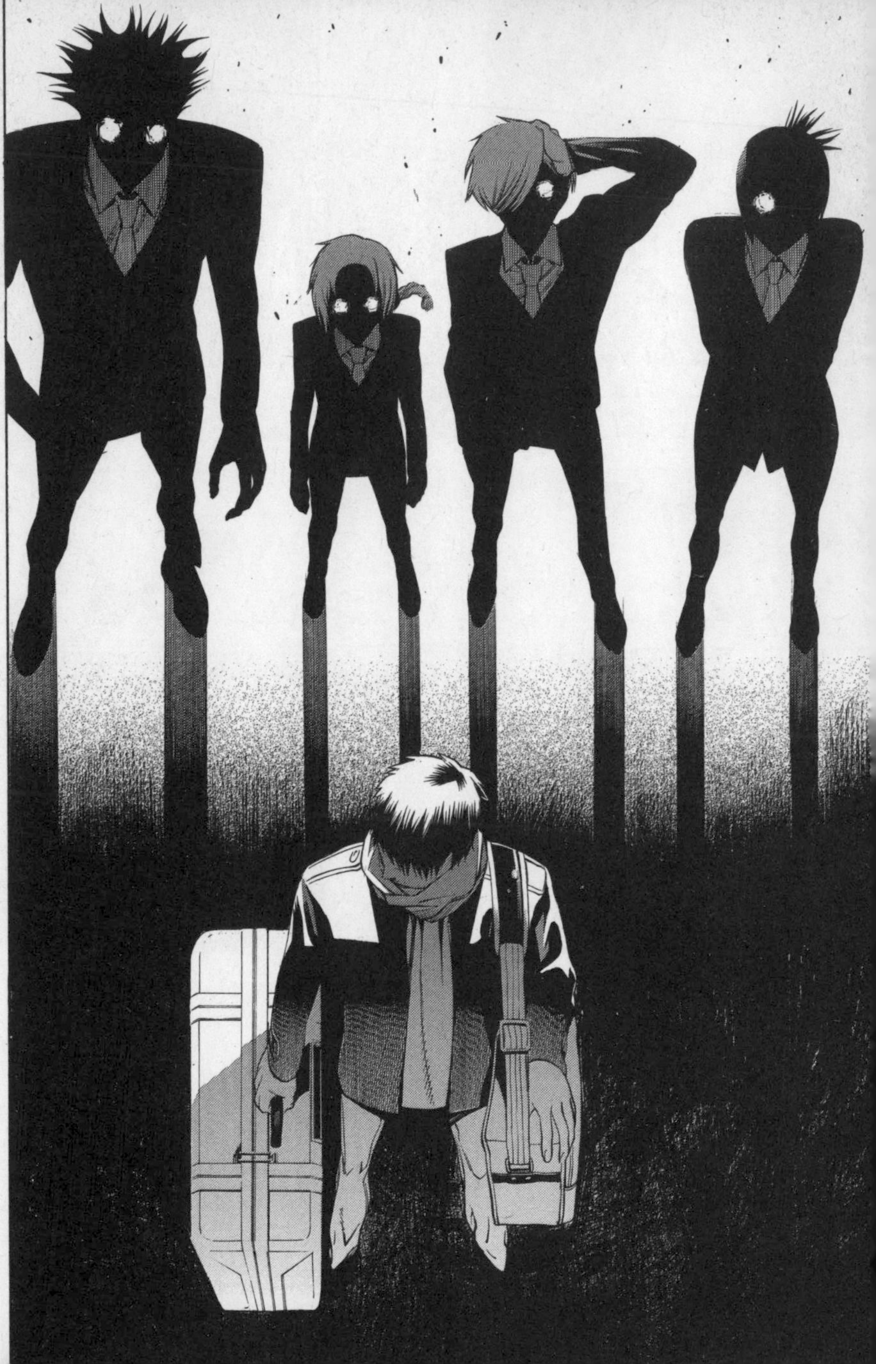

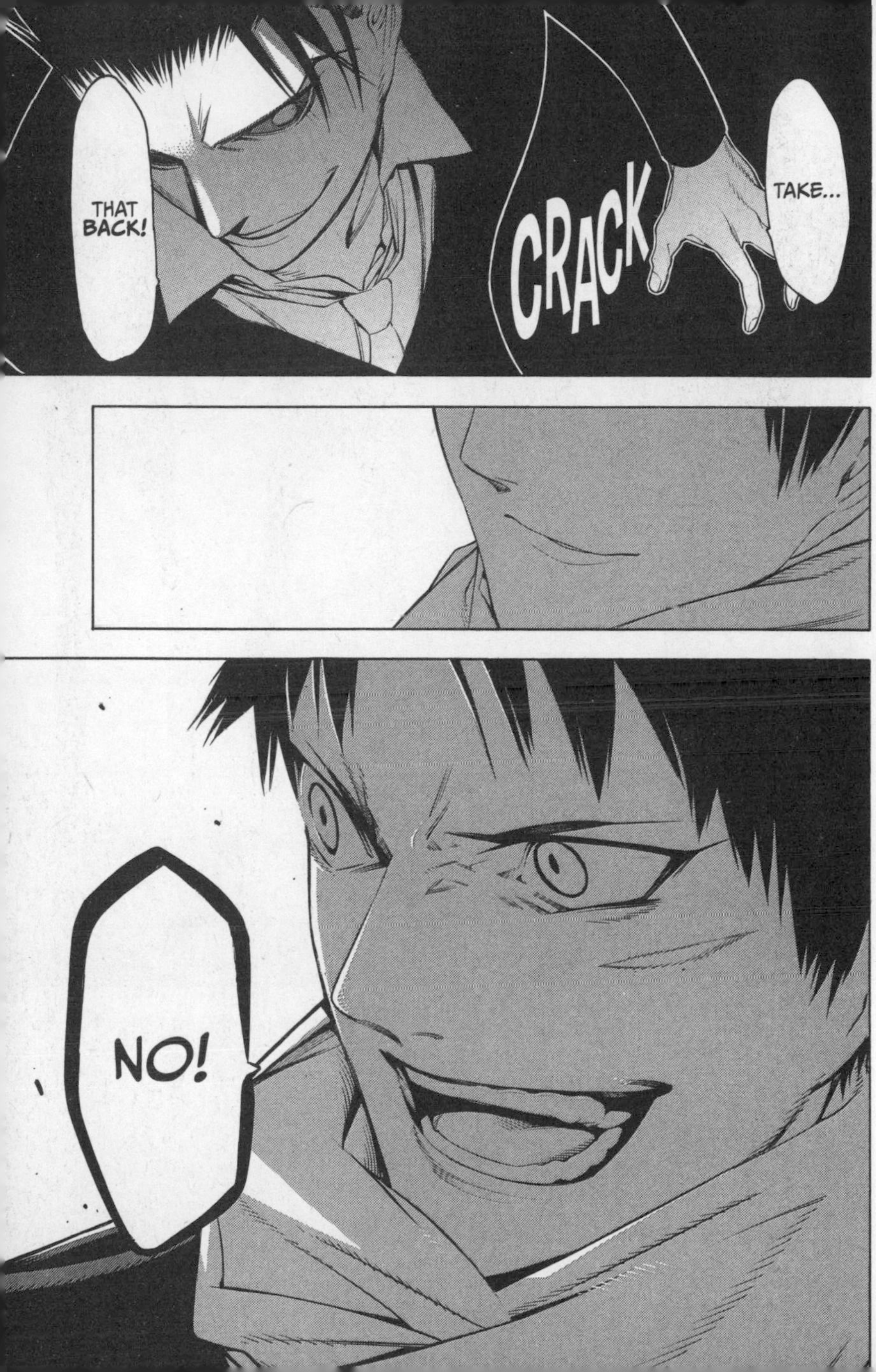
TAKE...
CRACK
THAT BACK!
NO!

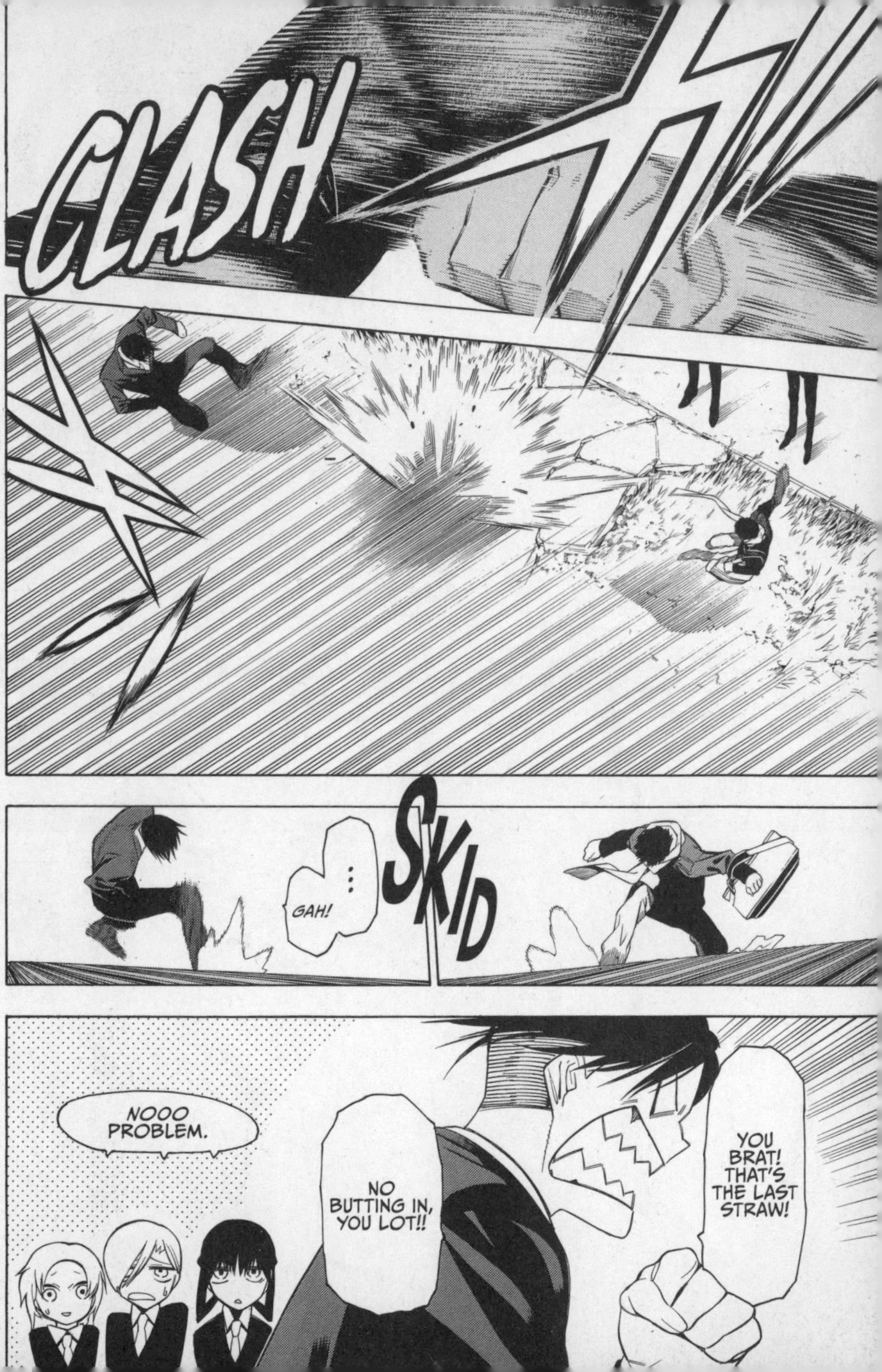
CLASH
SKID
... GAH!
YOU BRAT! THAT'S THE LAST STRAW!
NO BUTTING IN, YOU LOT!!
NOOO PROBLEM.

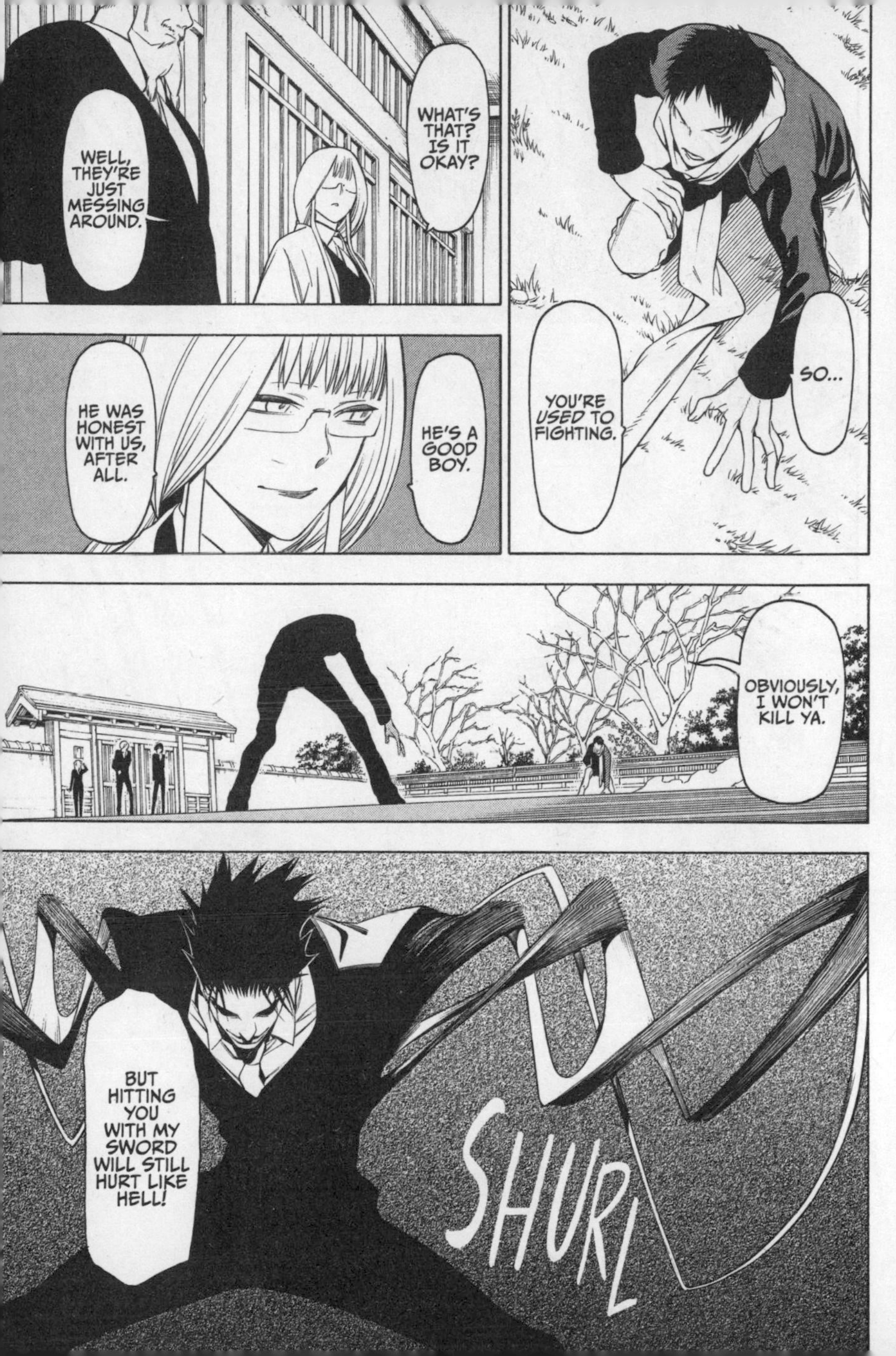
SO...
YOU'RE *USED* TO FIGHTING.
WHAT'S THAT? IS IT OKAY?
WELL, THEY'RE JUST MESSING AROUND.
HE'S A GOOD BOY.
HE WAS HONEST WITH US, AFTER ALL.
OBVIOUSLY, I WON'T KILL YA.
BUT HITTING YOU WITH MY SWORD WILL STILL HURT LIKE HELL!
SHURL

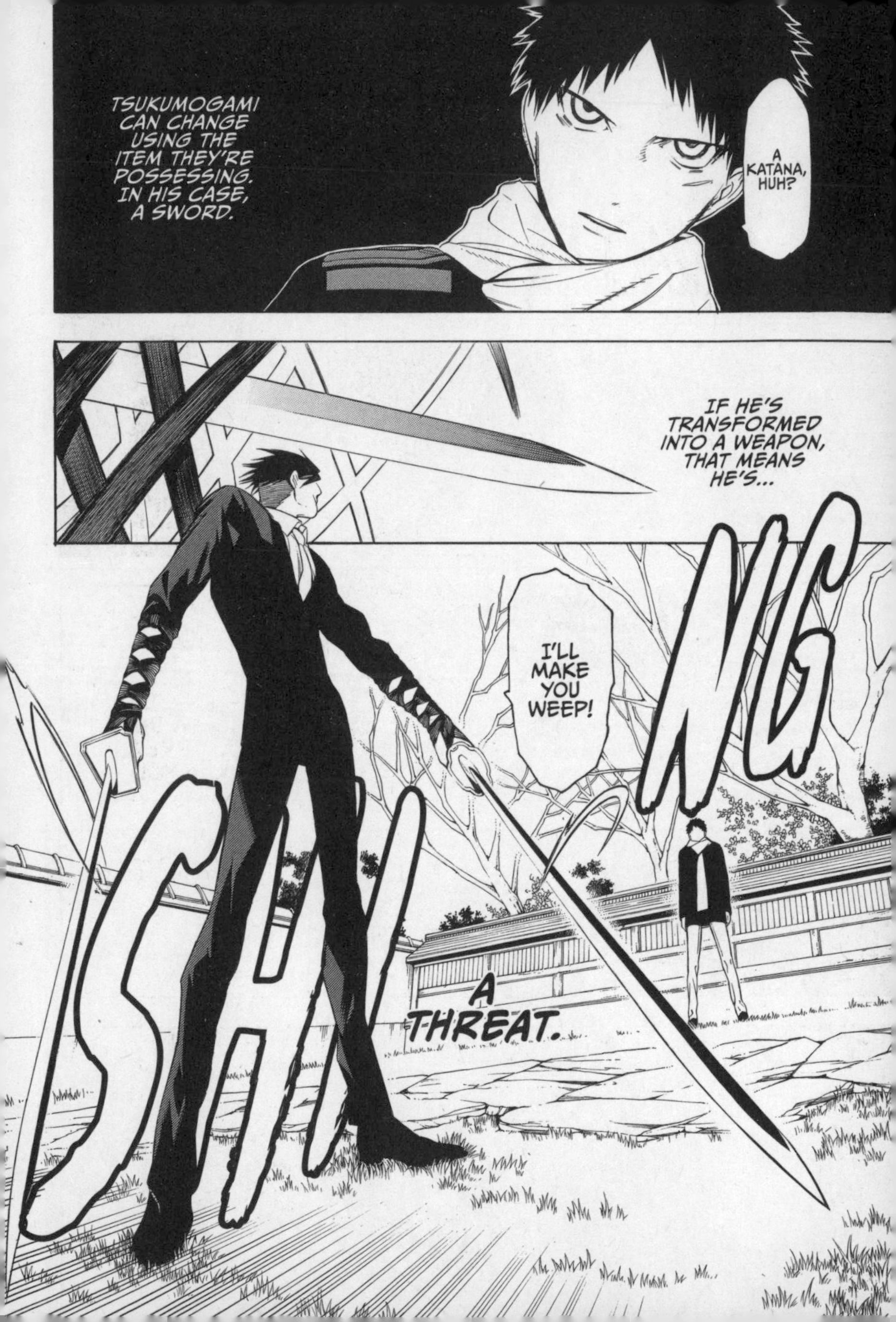
A KATANA, HUH?
TSUKUMOGAMI CAN CHANGE USING THE ITEM THEY'RE POSSESSING. IN HIS CASE, A SWORD.
IF HE'S TRANSFORMED INTO A WEAPON, THAT MEANS HE'S...
NG
I'LL MAKE YOU WEEP!
A THREAT.

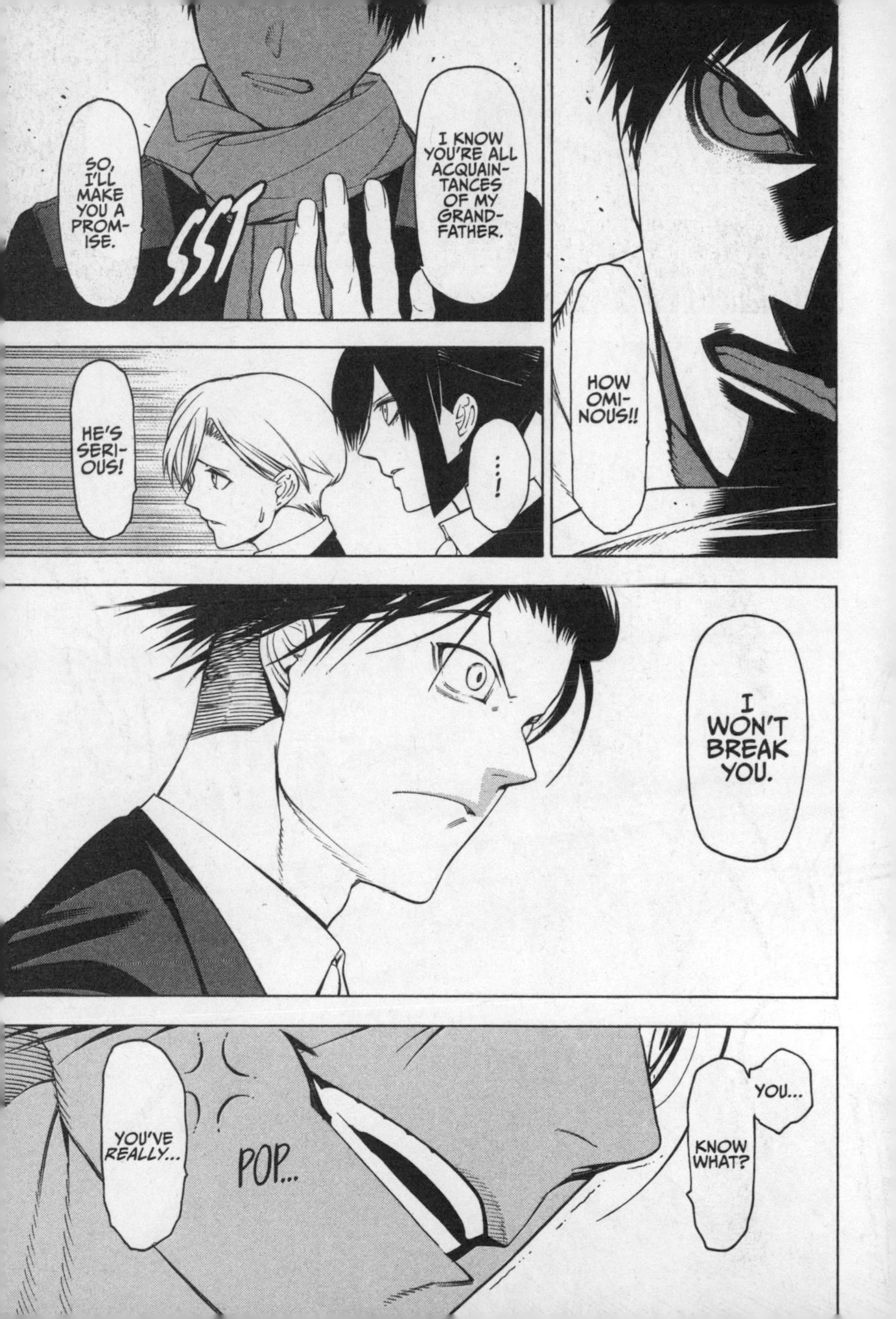
HOW OMINOUS!!
I KNOW YOU'RE ALL ACQUAINTANCES OF MY GRANDFATHER.
SST
SO, I'LL MAKE YOU A PROMISE.
...!
HE'S SERIOUS!
I WON'T BREAK YOU.
YOU...
KNOW WHAT?
POP...
YOU'VE REALLY...

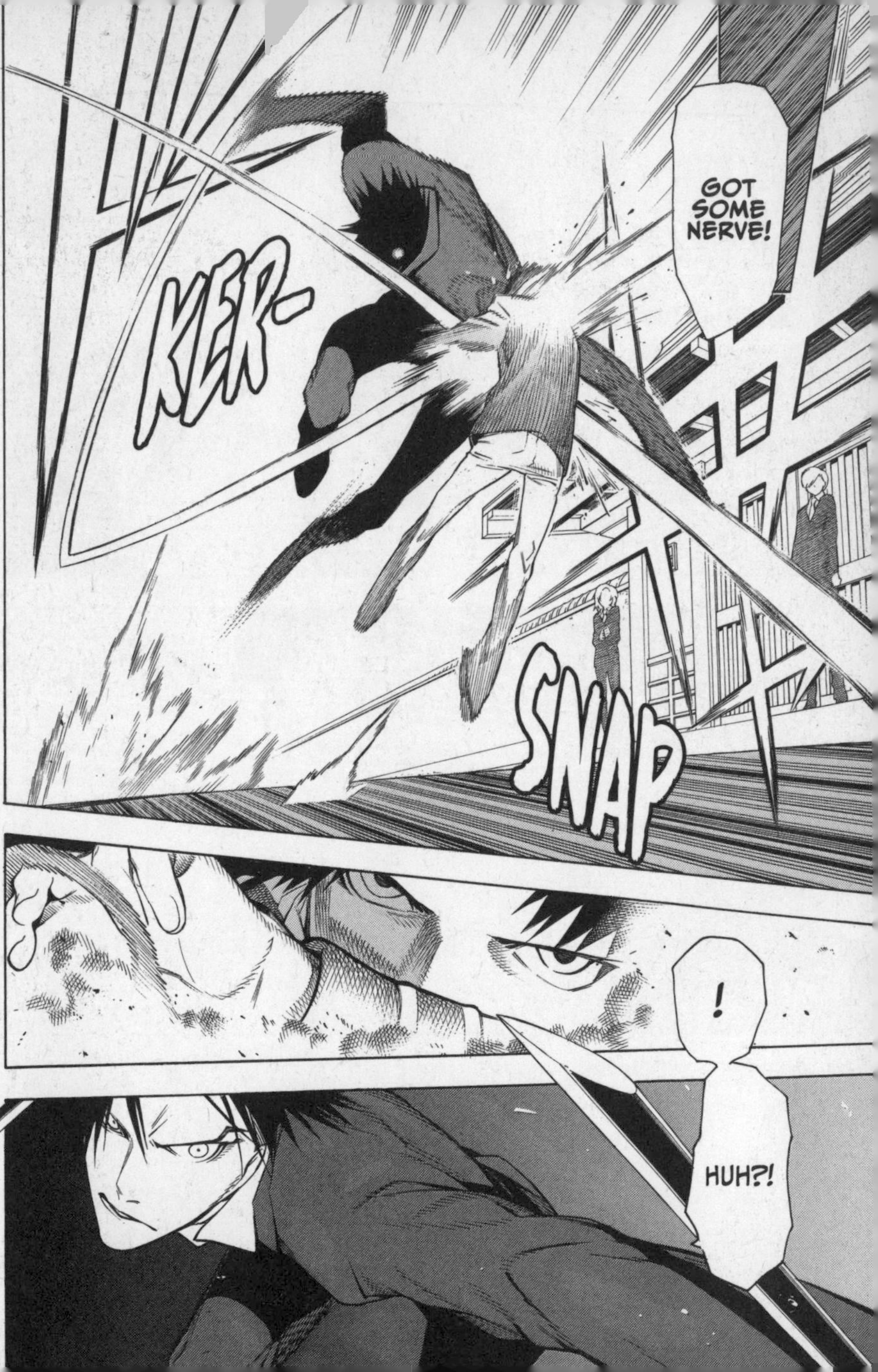
GOT SOME NERVE!
KER-
SNAP
!
HUH?!

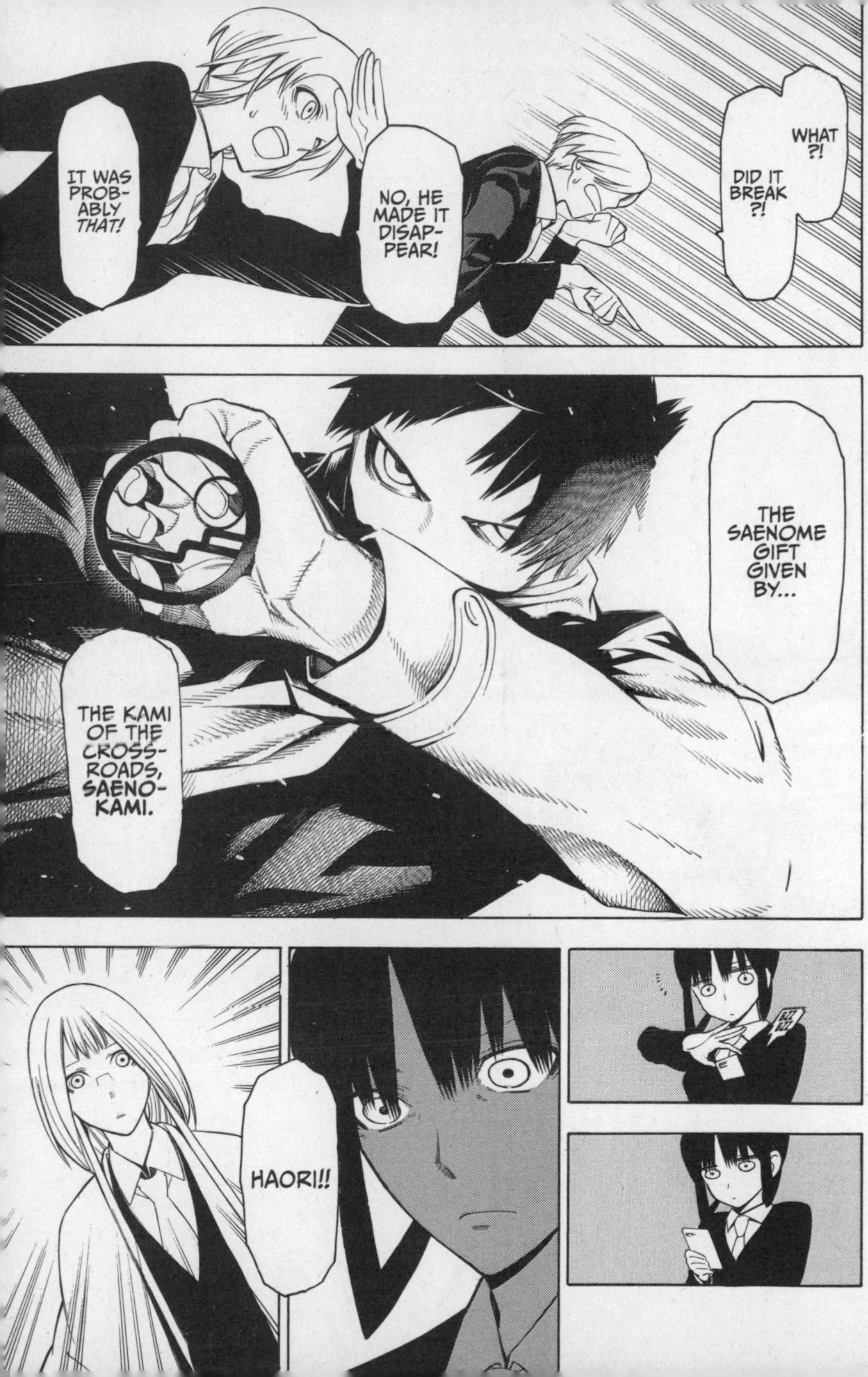
WHAT?! DID IT BREAK?!
NO, HE MADE IT DISAP-PEAR!
IT WAS PROB-ABLY THAT!
THE SAENOME GIFT GIVEN BY...
THE KAMI OF THE CROSS-ROADS, SAENO-KAMI.
HAORI!!

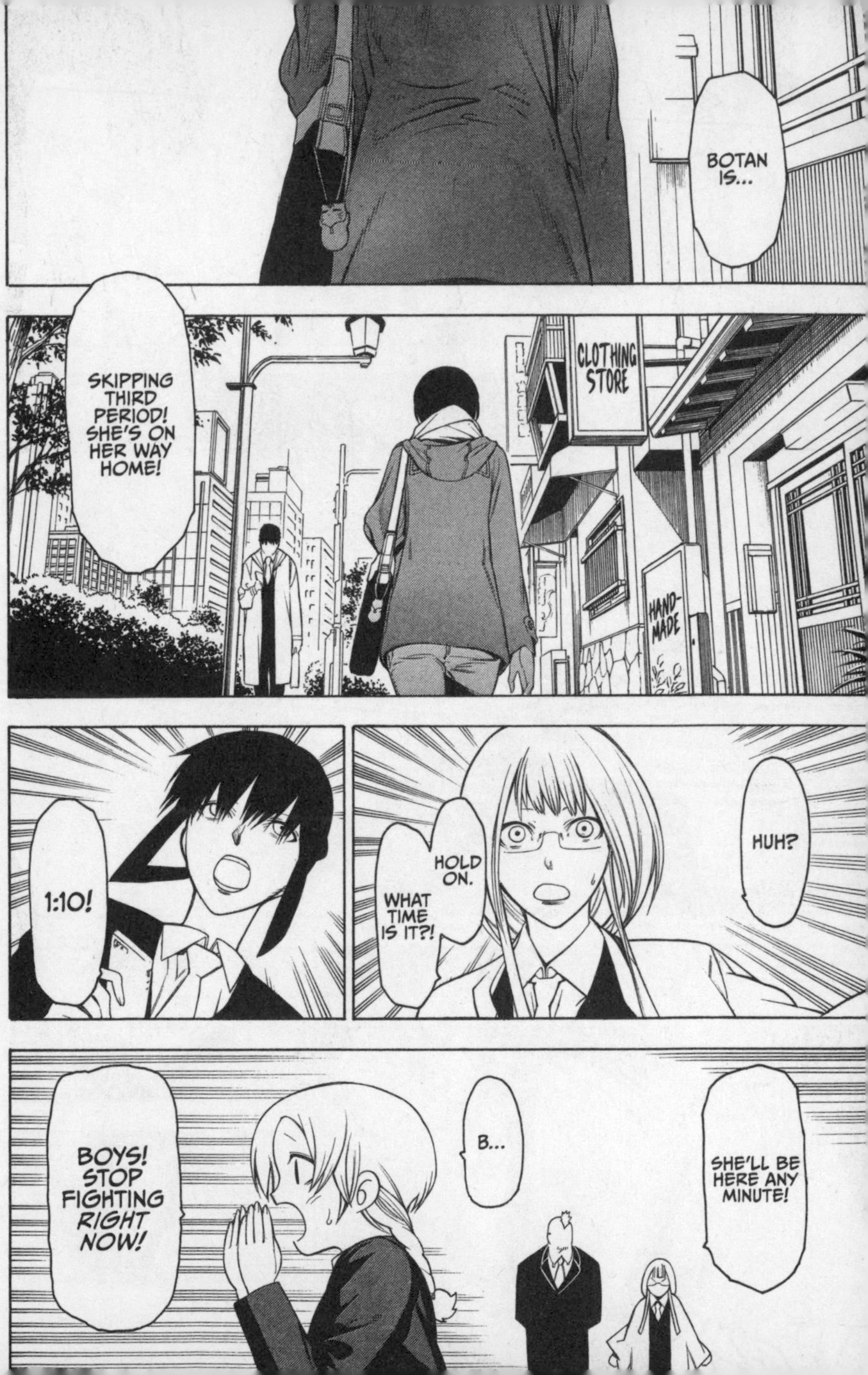
BOTAN IS...
SKIPPING THIRD PERIOD! SHE'S ON HER WAY HOME!
CLOTHING STORE
HAND-MADE
HUH?
HOLD ON.
WHAT TIME IS IT?!
1:10!
SHE'LL BE HERE ANY MINUTE!
B...
BOYS! STOP FIGHTING *RIGHT* NOW!

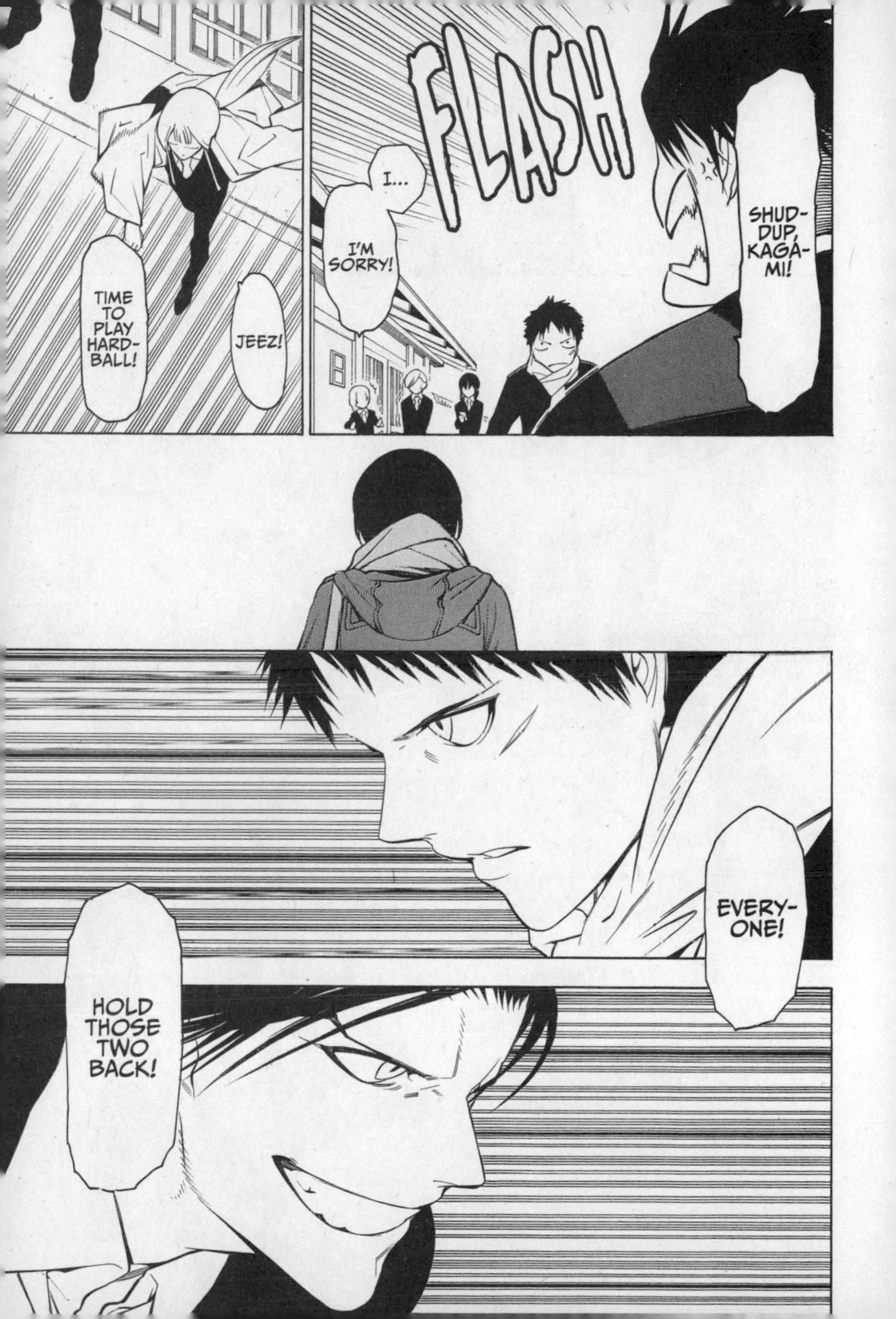
SHUDDUP, KAGAMI!
FLASH
I...
I'M SORRY!
JEEZ!
TIME TO PLAY HARDBALL!
EVERYONE!
HOLD THOSE TWO BACK!

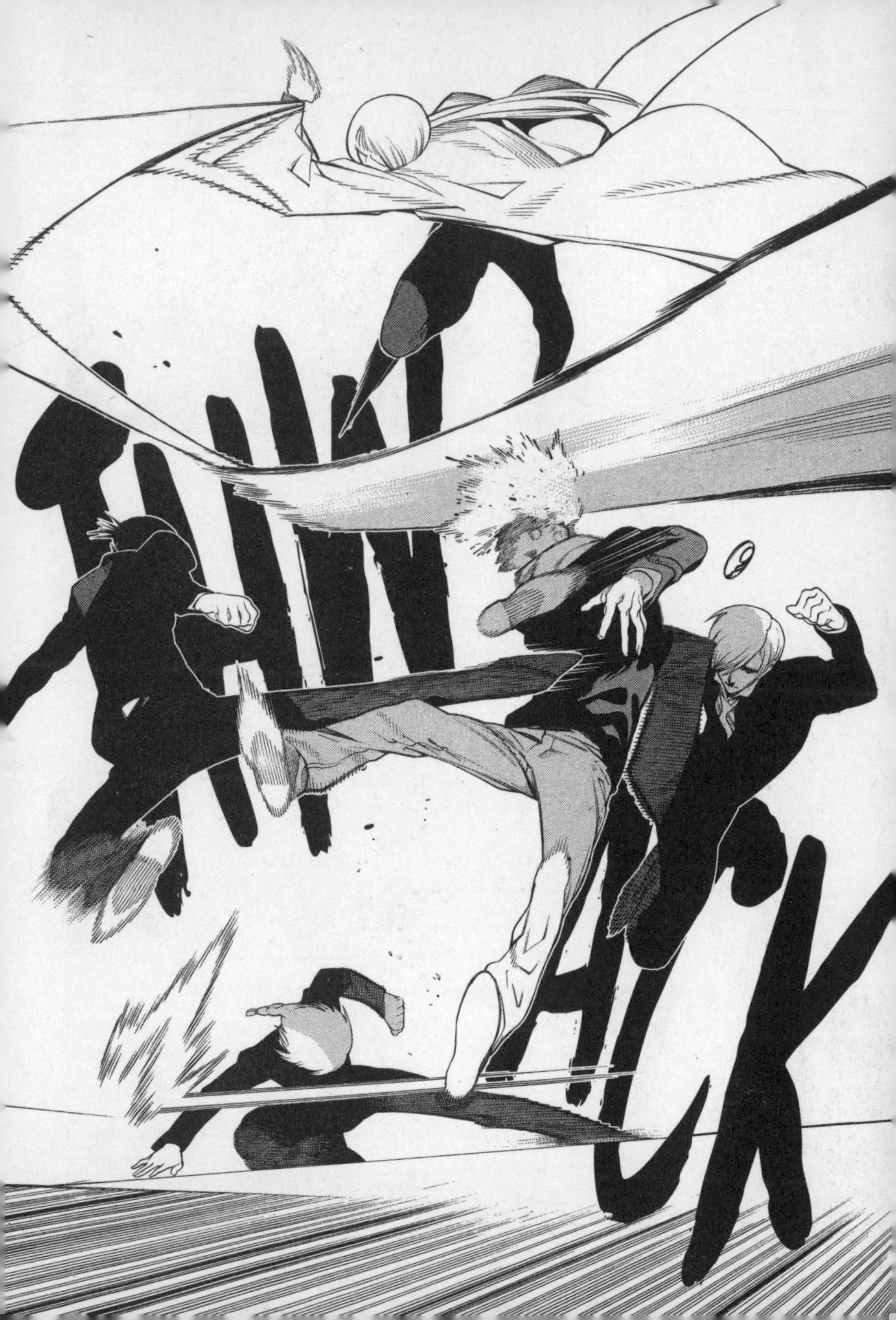
THWACK

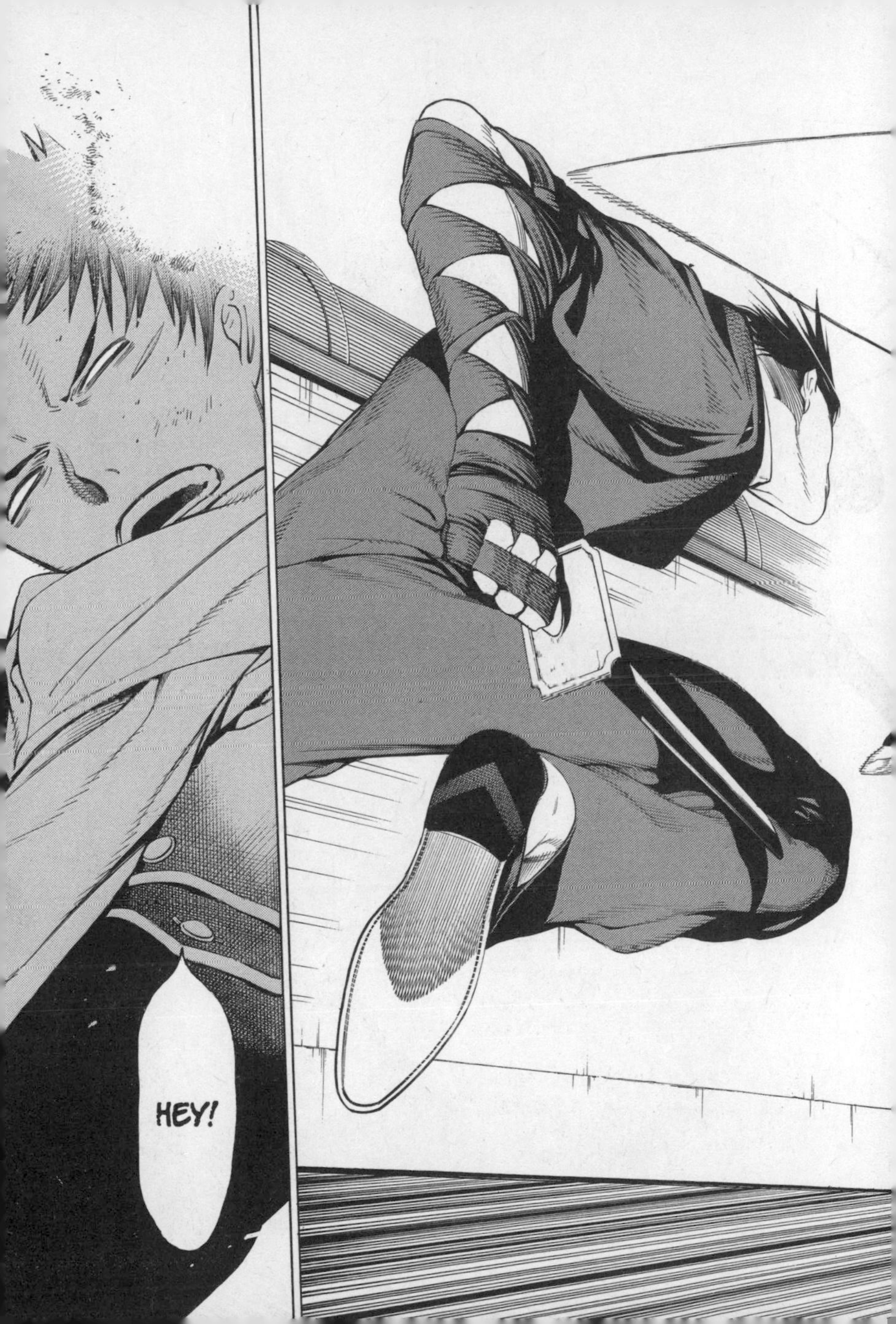
HEY!

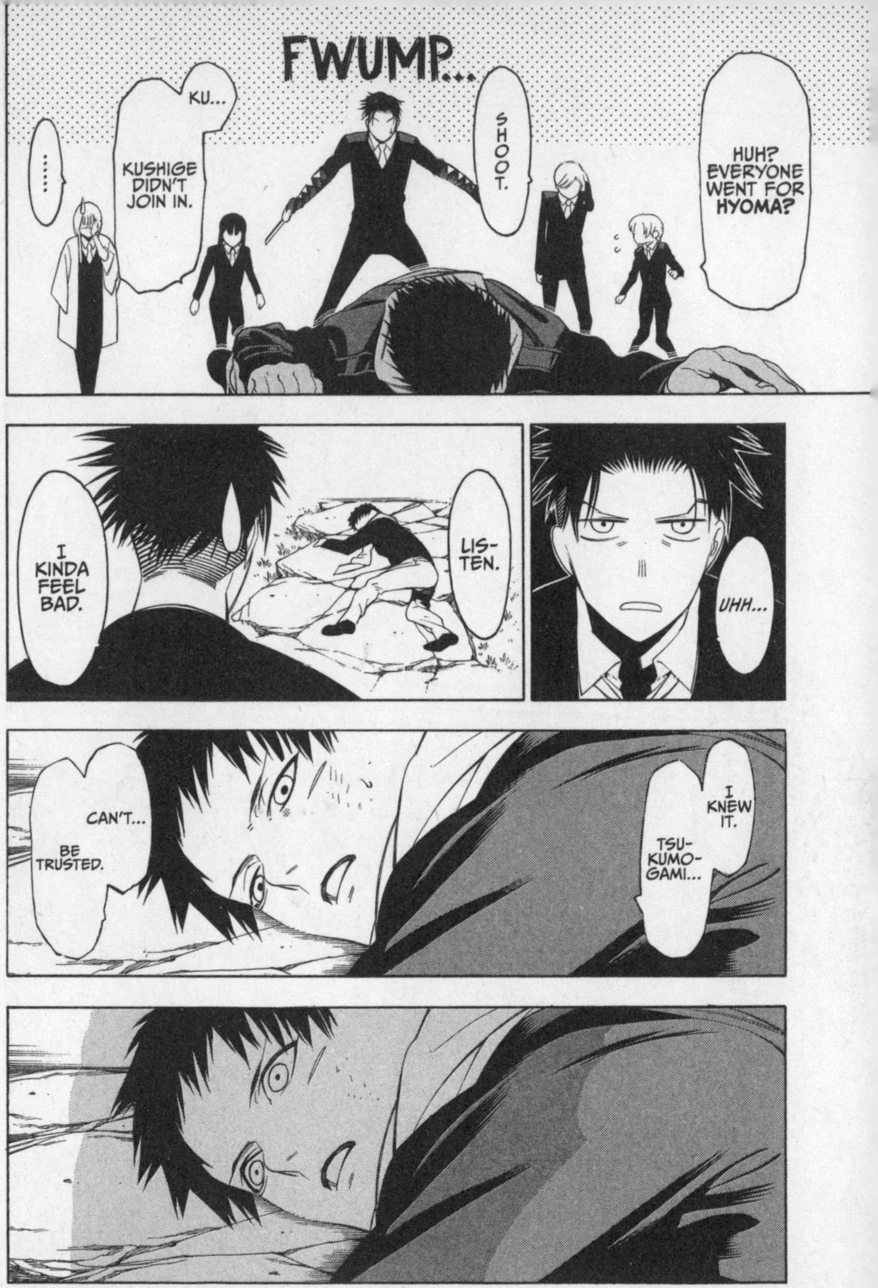
HUH? EVERYONE WENT FOR HYOMA?
SHOOT.
FWUMP...
KU... KUSHIGE DIDN'T JOIN IN.
......
UHH...
LIS-TEN.
I KINDA FEEL BAD.
I KNEW IT. TSU-KUMO-GAMI...
CAN'T... BE TRUSTED.

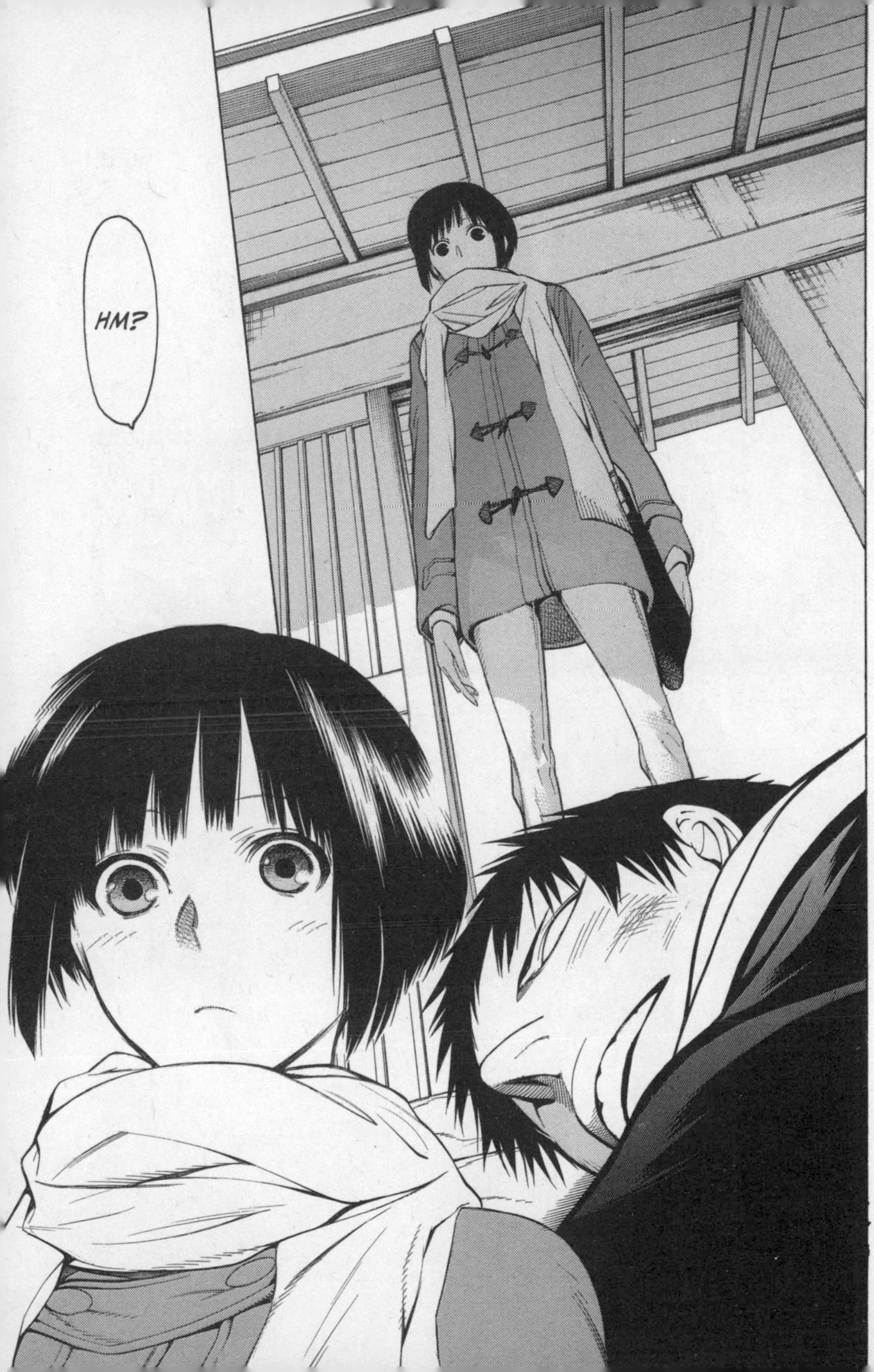
HM?

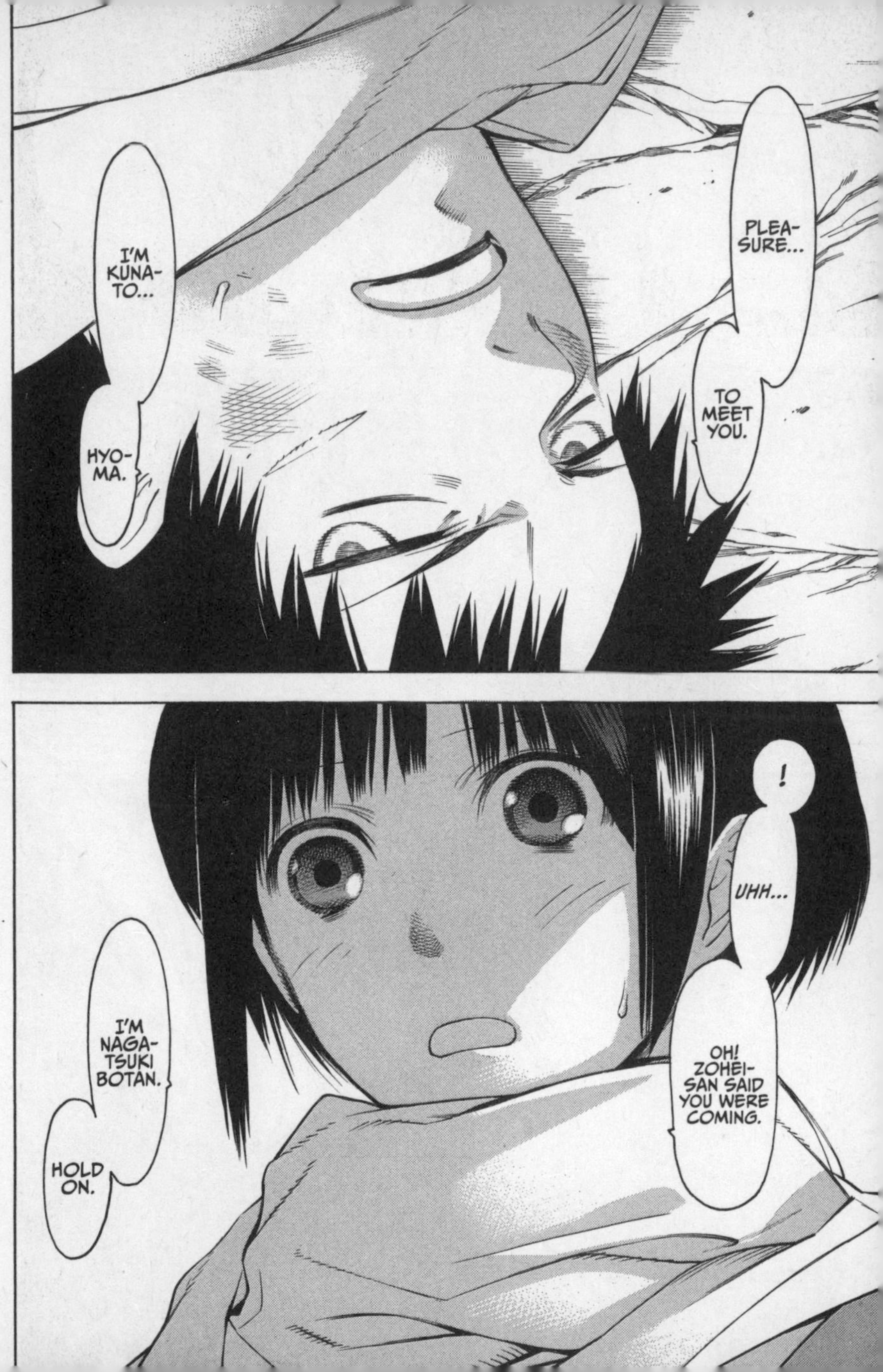
PLEA-SURE...
TO MEET YOU.
I'M KUNA-TO...
HYO-MA.
!
UHH...
OH! ZOHEI-SAN SAID YOU WERE COMING.
I'M NAGA-TSUKI BOTAN.
HOLD ON.

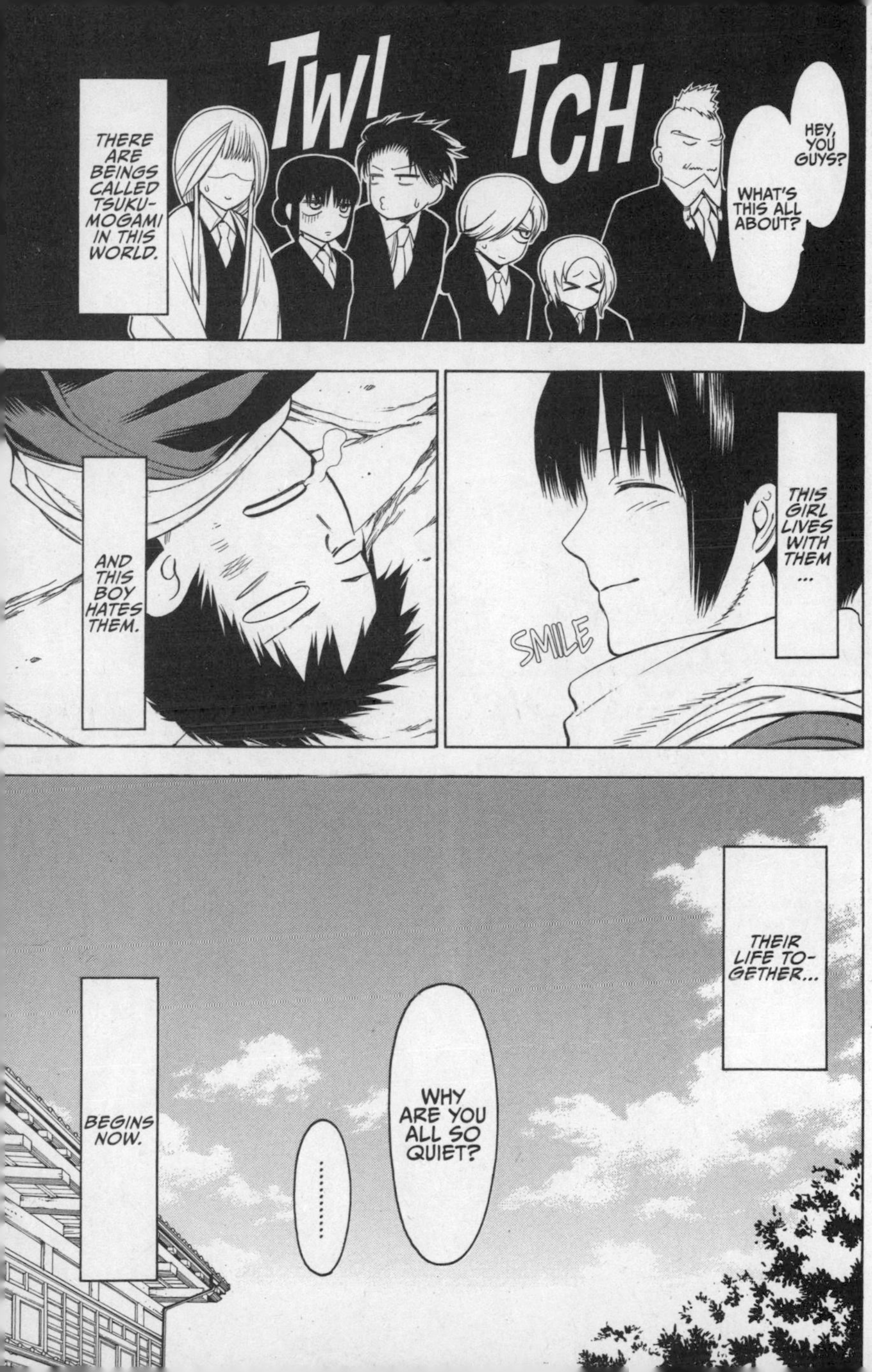
HEY, YOU GUYS? WHAT'S THIS ALL ABOUT?
TWI TCH
THERE ARE BEINGS CALLED TSUKU-MOGAMI IN THIS WORLD.
THIS GIRL LIVES WITH THEM ...
SMILE
AND THIS BOY HATES THEM.
THEIR LIFE TO-GETHER...
WHY ARE YOU ALL SO QUIET?
....
BEGINS NOW.

MONONOGATARI

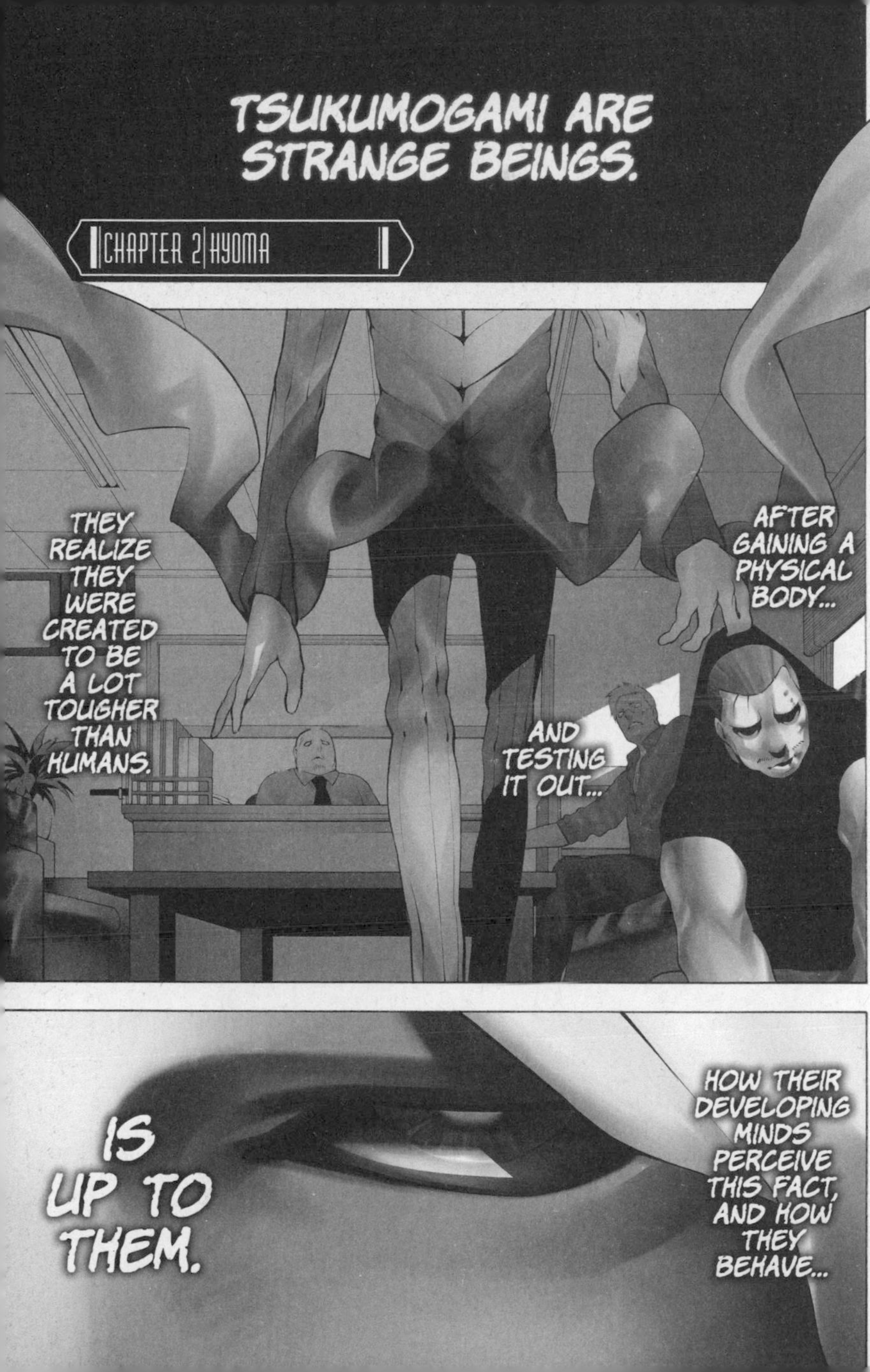
TSUKUMOGAMI ARE STRANGE BEINGS.
CHAPTER 2 | HYOMA
AFTER GAINING A PHYSICAL BODY...
AND TESTING IT OUT...
THEY REALIZE THEY WERE CREATED TO BE A LOT TOUGHER THAN HUMANS.
HOW THEIR DEVELOPING MINDS PERCEIVE THIS FACT, AND HOW THEY BEHAVE...
IS UP TO THEM.

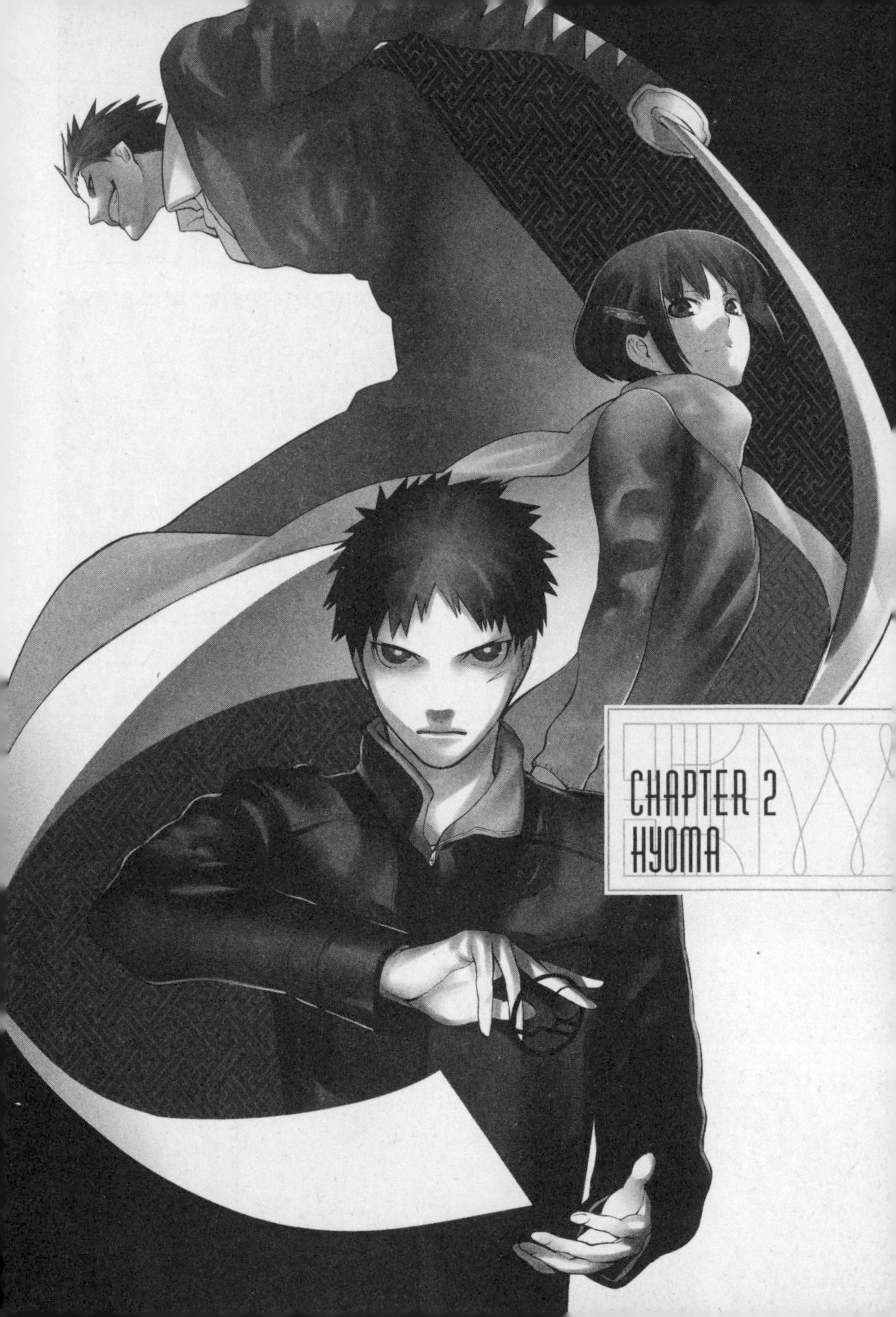
CHAPTER 2
KYOMA

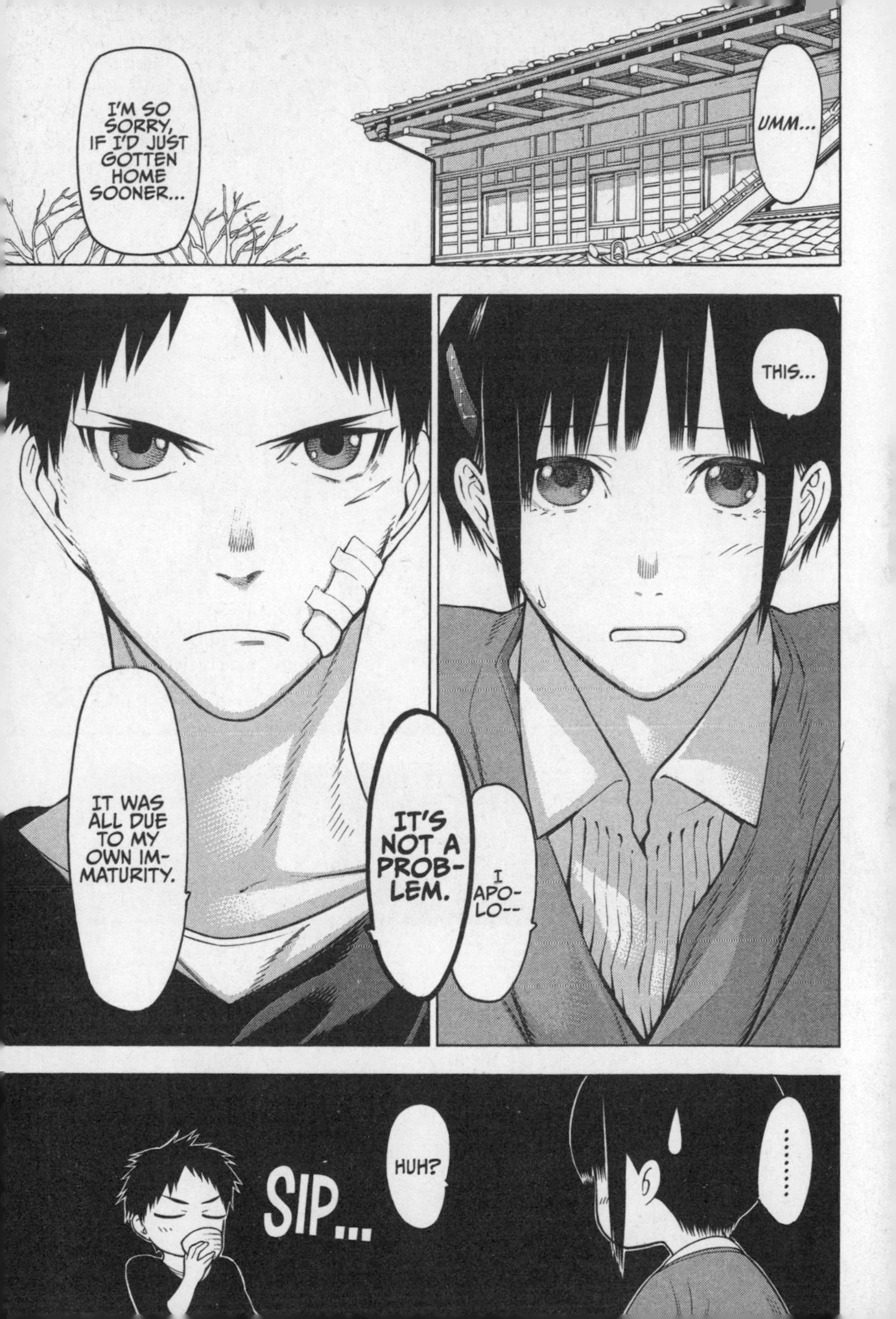
UMM...
I'M SO SORRY, IF I'D JUST GOTTEN HOME SOONER...
THIS...
I APOLO--
IT'S NOT A PROB-LEM.
IT WAS ALL DUE TO MY OWN IM-MATURITY.
......
HUH?
SIP...

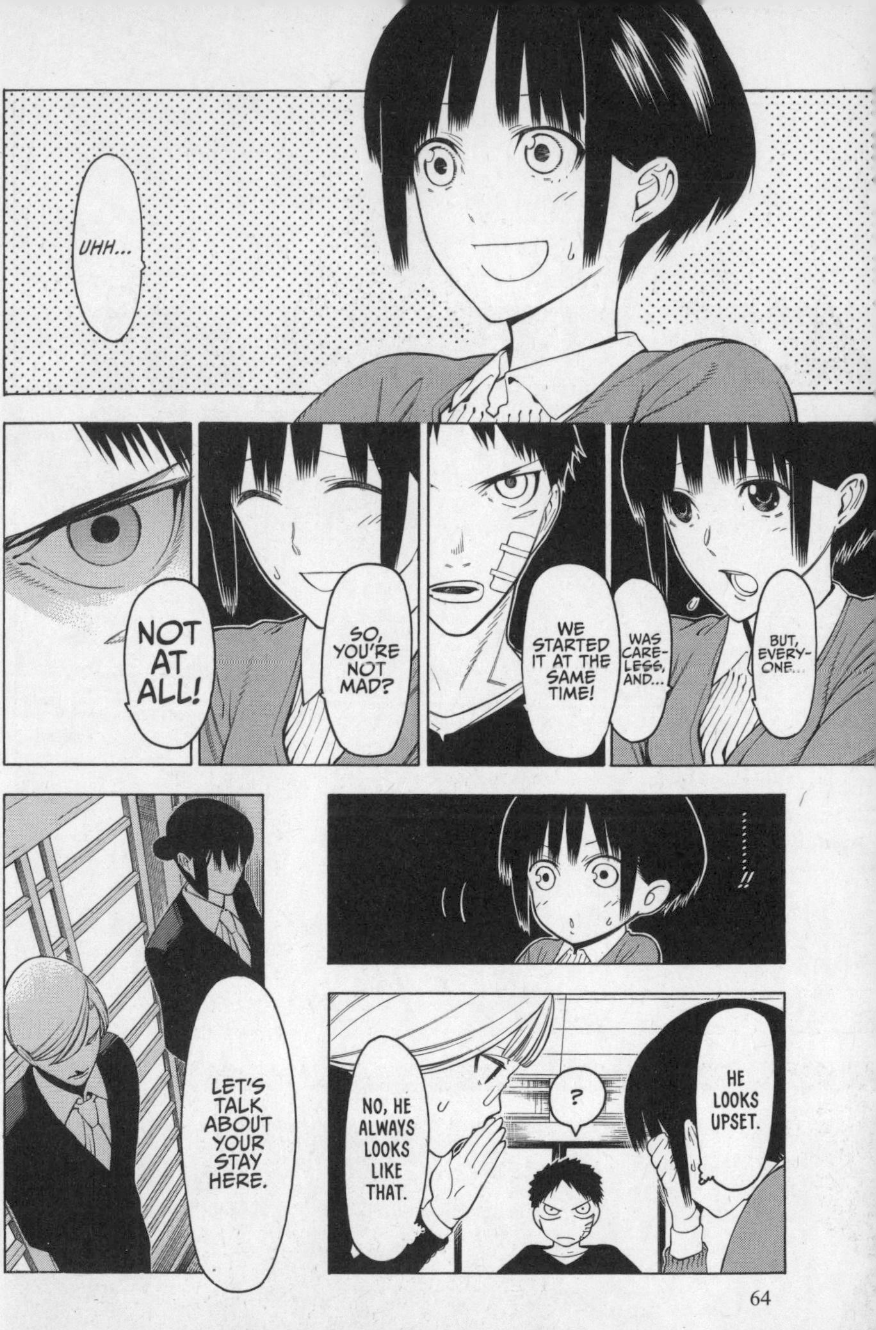
UHH...
BUT, EVERYONE...
WAS CARELESS, AND...
WE STARTED IT AT THE SAME TIME!
SO, YOU'RE NOT MAD?
NOT AT ALL!
......!!
HE LOOKS UPSET.
?
NO, HE ALWAYS LOOKS LIKE THAT.
LET'S TALK ABOUT YOUR STAY HERE.

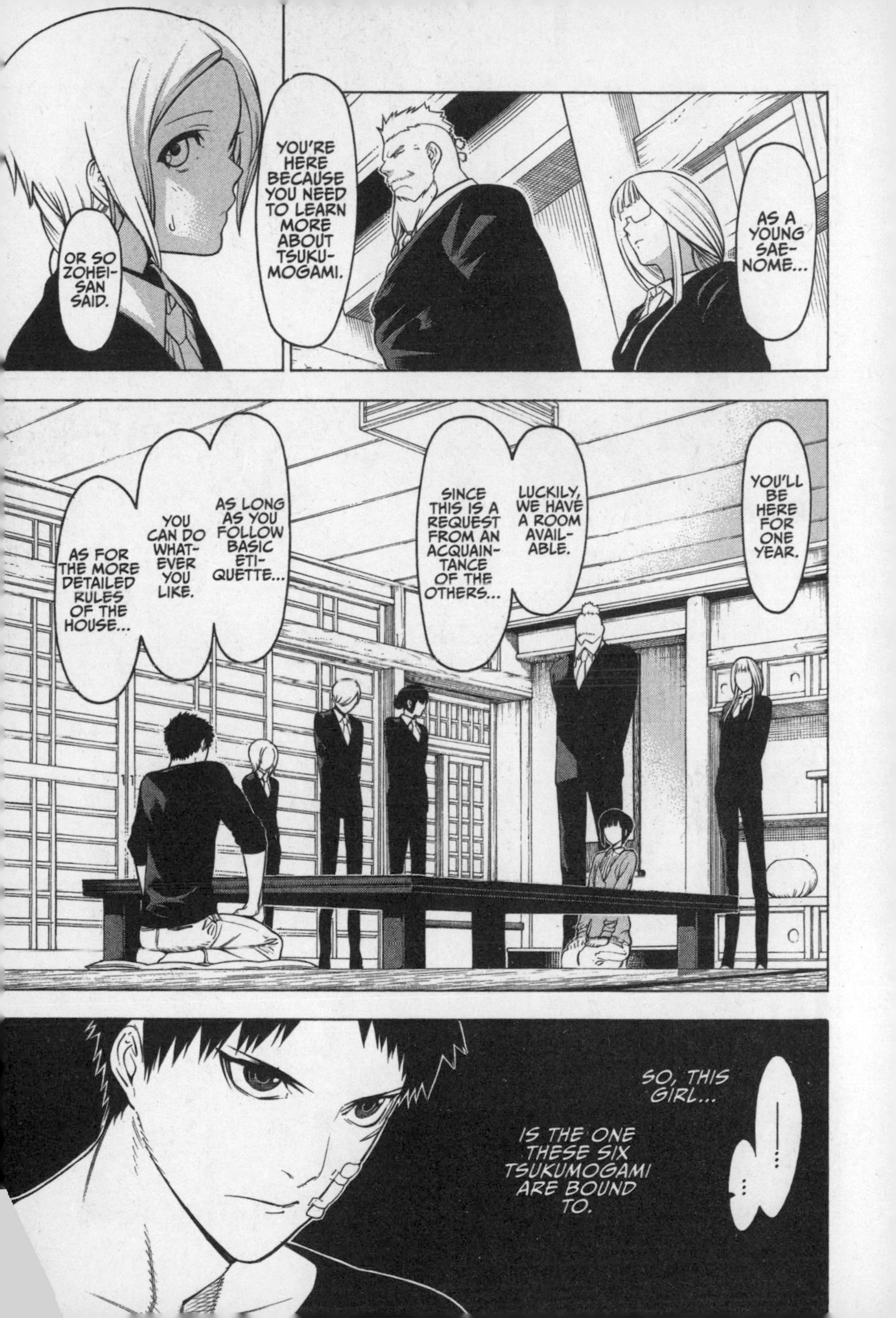
AS A YOUNG SAE-NOME...
YOU'RE HERE BECAUSE YOU NEED TO LEARN MORE ABOUT TSUKU-MOGAMI.
OR SO ZOHEI-SAN SAID.
YOU'LL BE HERE FOR ONE YEAR.
LUCKILY, WE HAVE A ROOM AVAIL-ABLE.
SINCE THIS IS A REQUEST FROM AN ACQUAIN-TANCE OF THE OTHERS...
AS LONG AS YOU FOLLOW BASIC ETI-QUETTE...
YOU CAN DO WHAT-EVER YOU LIKE.
AS FOR THE MORE DETAILED RULES OF THE HOUSE...
......
SO, THIS GIRL...
IS THE ONE THESE SIX TSUKUMOGAMI ARE BOUND TO.

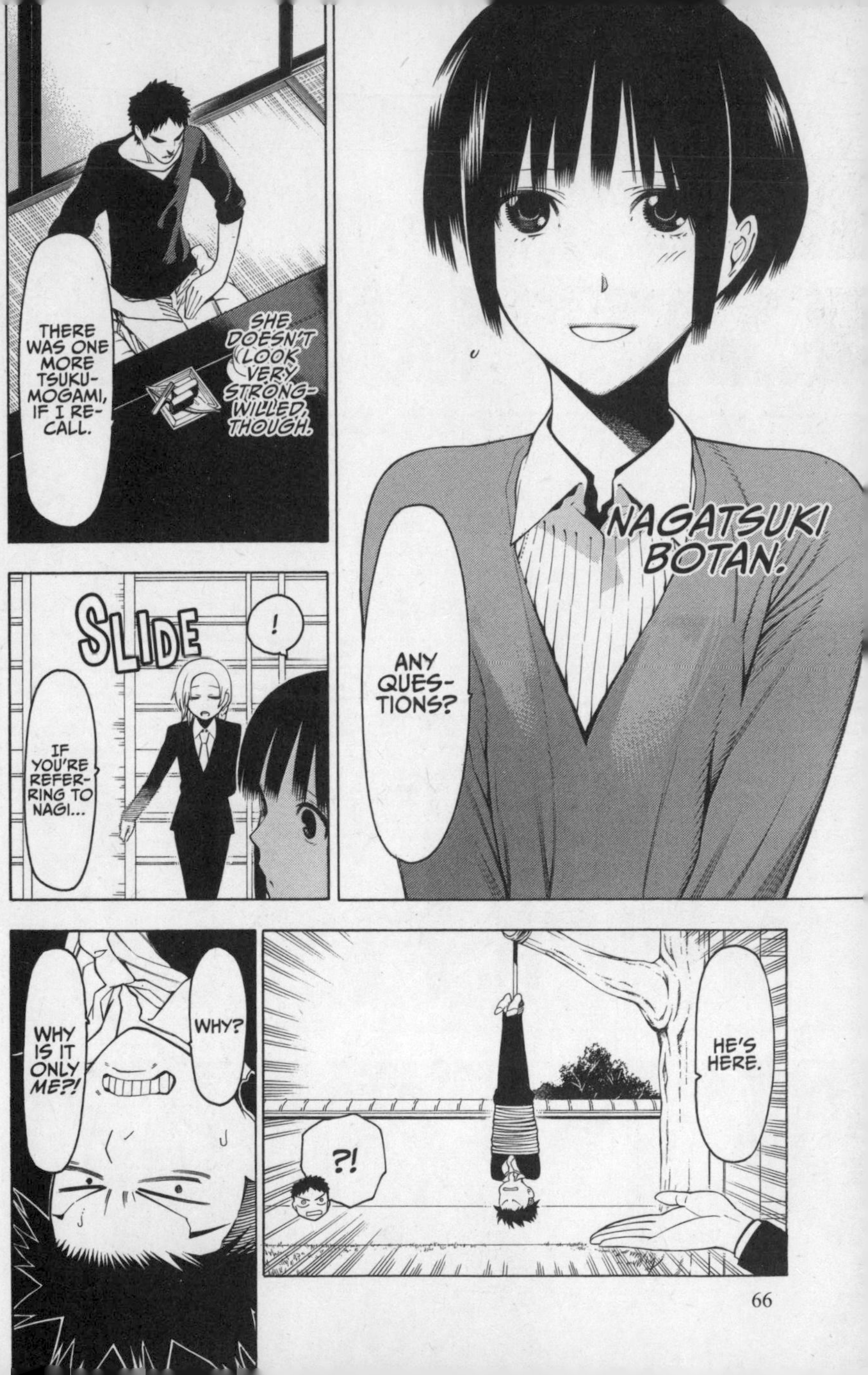

NAGATSUKI BOTAN.
ANY QUESTIONS?
SHE DOESN'T LOOK VERY STRONG-WILLED, THOUGH.
THERE WAS ONE MORE TSUKUMOGAMI, IF I RECALL.
SLIDE
!
IF YOU'RE REFERRING TO NAGI...
HE'S HERE.
?!
WHY?
WHY IS IT ONLY ME?!

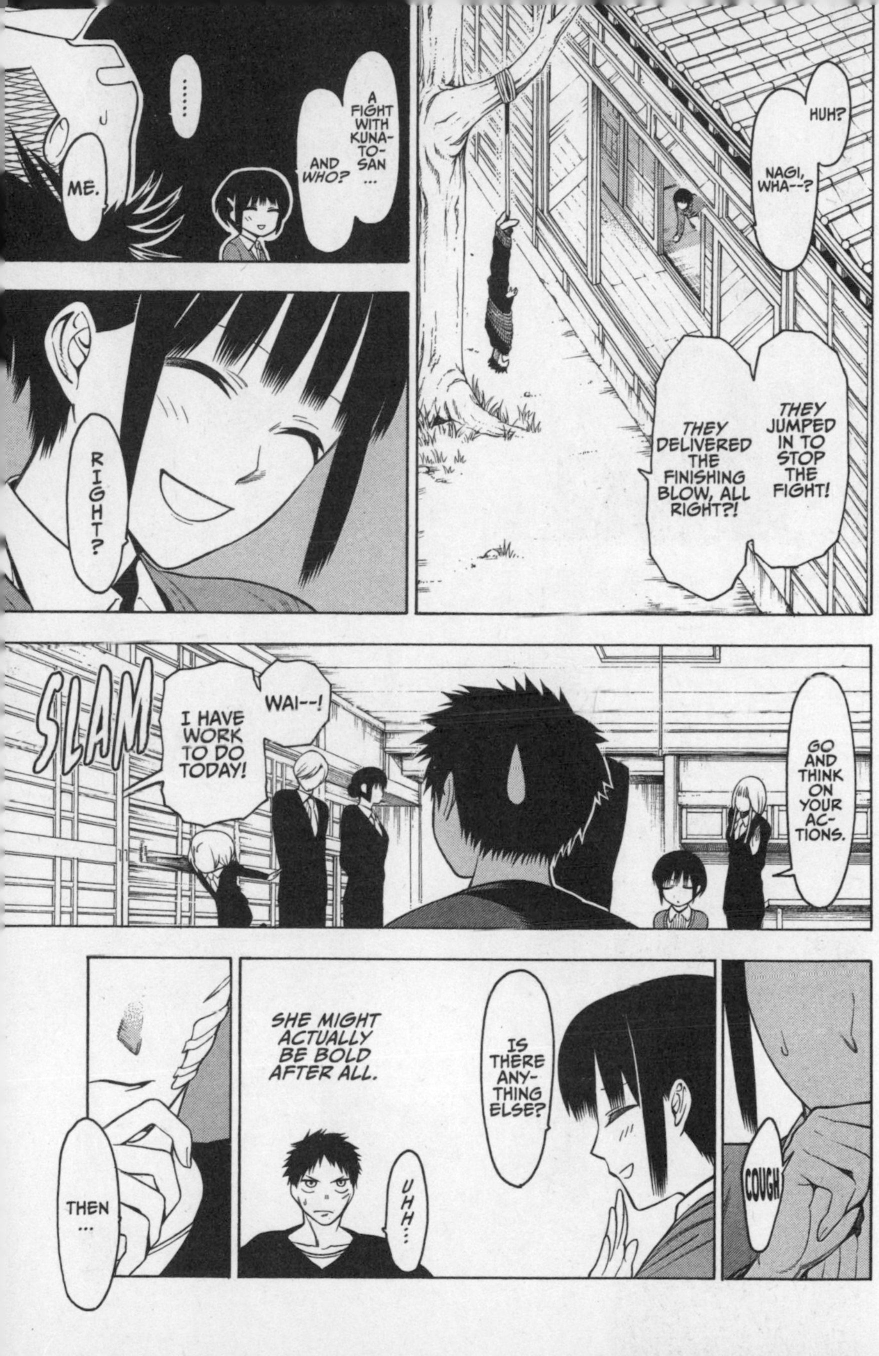
HUH?
NAGI, WHA--?
THEY JUMPED IN TO STOP THE FIGHT!
THEY DELIVERED THE FINISHING BLOW, ALL RIGHT?!
A FIGHT WITH KUNA-TO-SAN...
AND WHO?
......
ME.
RIGHT?
GO AND THINK ON YOUR ACTIONS.
WAI--!
I HAVE WORK TO DO TODAY!
SLAM
COUGH
IS THERE ANYTHING ELSE?
SHE MIGHT ACTUALLY BE BOLD AFTER ALL.
UHH...
THEN...

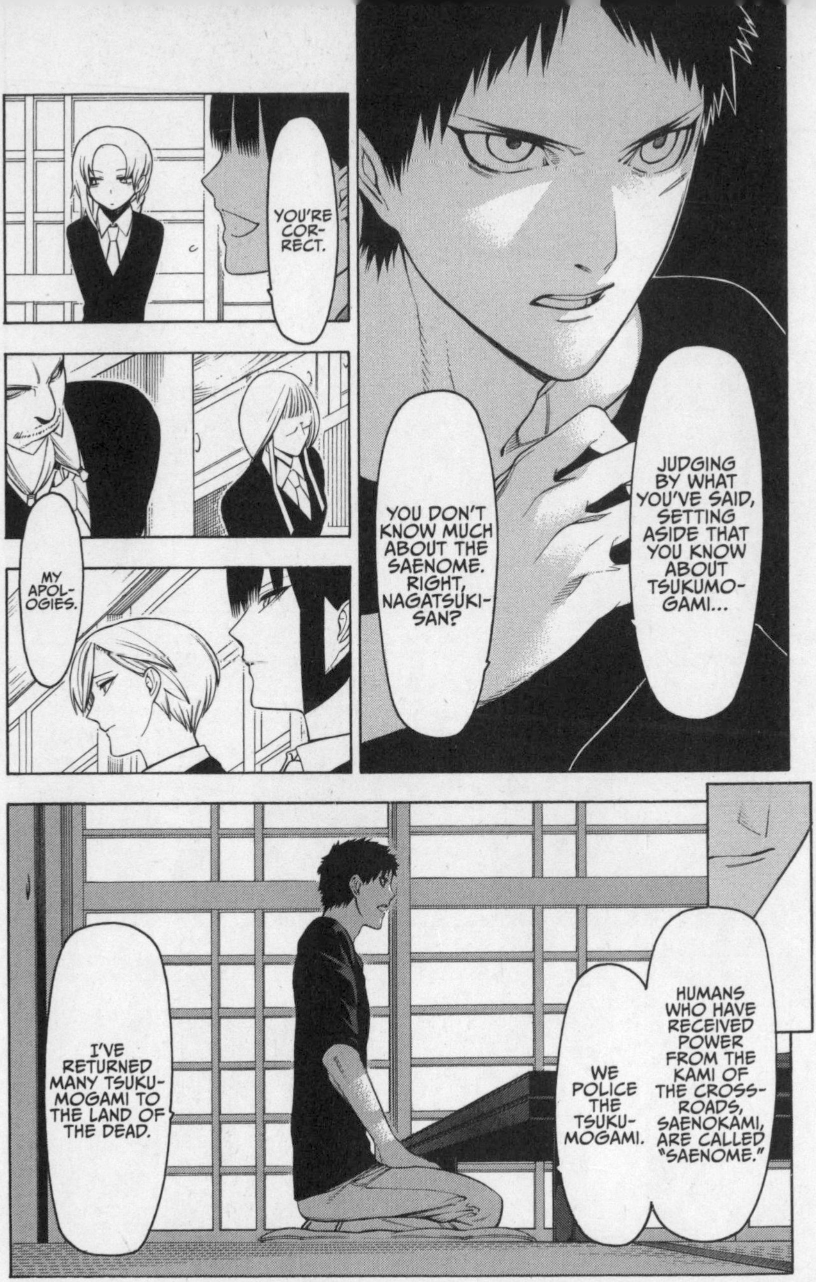
JUDGING BY WHAT YOU'VE SAID, SETTING ASIDE THAT YOU KNOW ABOUT TSUKUMO-GAMI...
YOU DON'T KNOW MUCH ABOUT THE SAENOME. RIGHT, NAGATSUKI-SAN?
YOU'RE COR-RECT.
MY APOL-OGIES.
HUMANS WHO HAVE RECEIVED POWER FROM THE KAMI OF THE CROSS-ROADS, SAENOKAMI, ARE CALLED "SAENOME."
WE POLICE THE TSUKU-MOGAMI.
I'VE RETURNED MANY TSUKU-MOGAMI TO THE LAND OF THE DEAD.

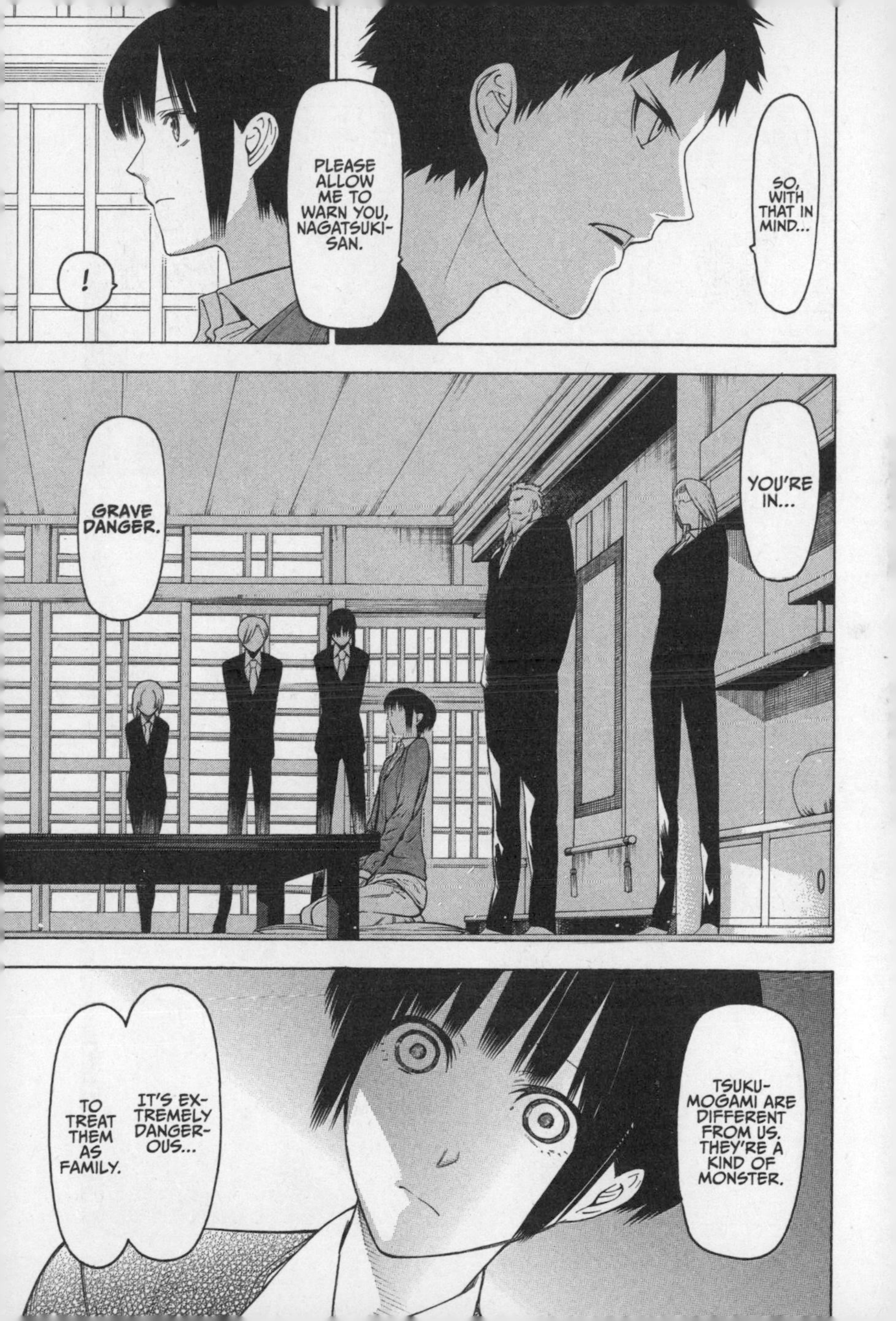
SO, WITH THAT IN MIND...
PLEASE ALLOW ME TO WARN YOU, NAGATSUKI-SAN.
!
YOU'RE IN...
GRAVE DANGER.
TSUKU-MOGAMI ARE DIFFERENT FROM US. THEY'RE A KIND OF MONSTER.
IT'S EX-TREMELY DANGER-OUS...
TO TREAT THEM AS FAMILY.

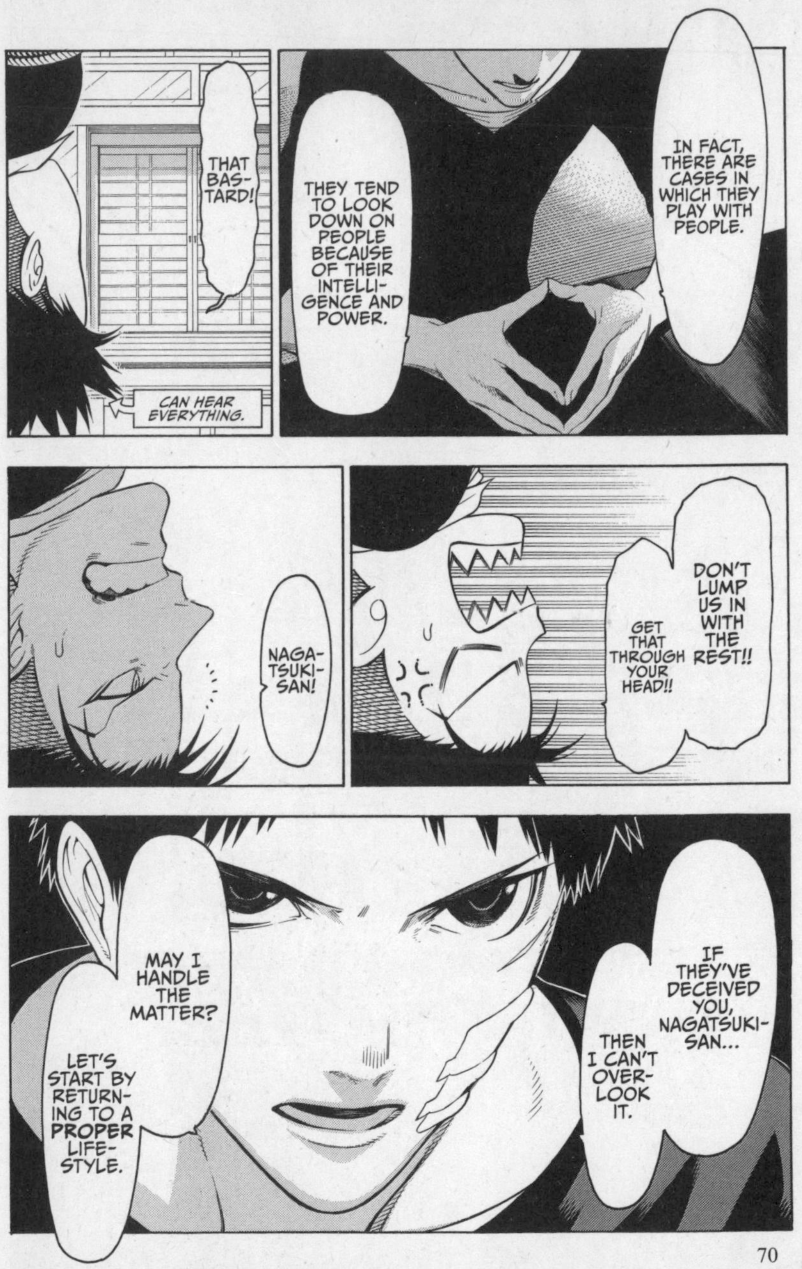
IN FACT, THERE ARE CASES IN WHICH THEY PLAY WITH PEOPLE.
THEY TEND TO LOOK DOWN ON PEOPLE BECAUSE OF THEIR INTELLIGENCE AND POWER.
THAT BASTARD!
CAN HEAR EVERYTHING.
DON'T LUMP US IN WITH THE REST!!
GET THAT THROUGH YOUR HEAD!!
NAGATSUKI-SAN!
IF THEY'VE DECEIVED YOU, NAGATSUKI-SAN...
THEN I CAN'T OVERLOOK IT.
MAY I HANDLE THE MATTER?
LET'S START BY RETURNING TO A **PROPER** LIFESTYLE.

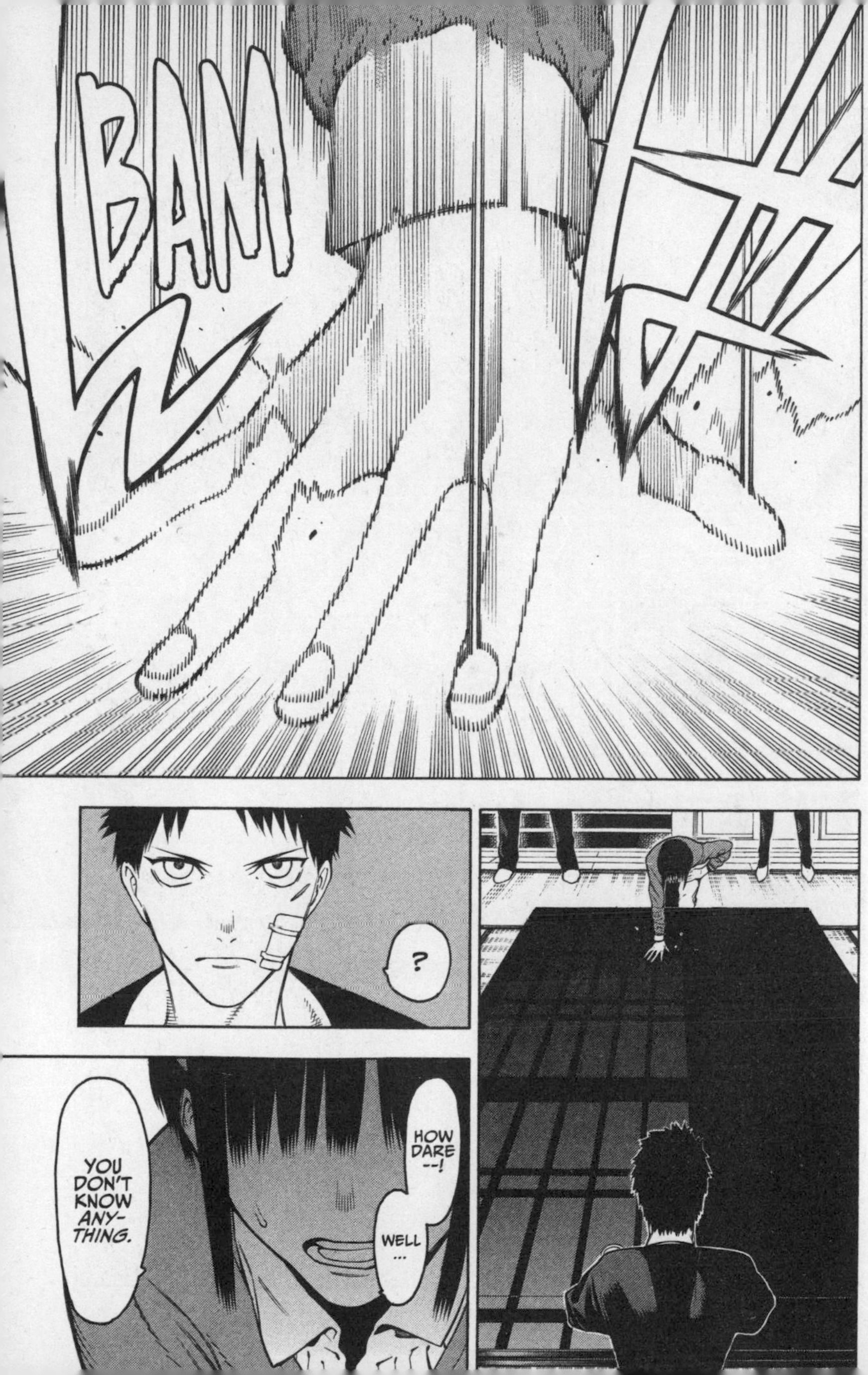
BAM
?
HOW DARE--!
WELL ...
YOU DON'T KNOW ANY-THING.

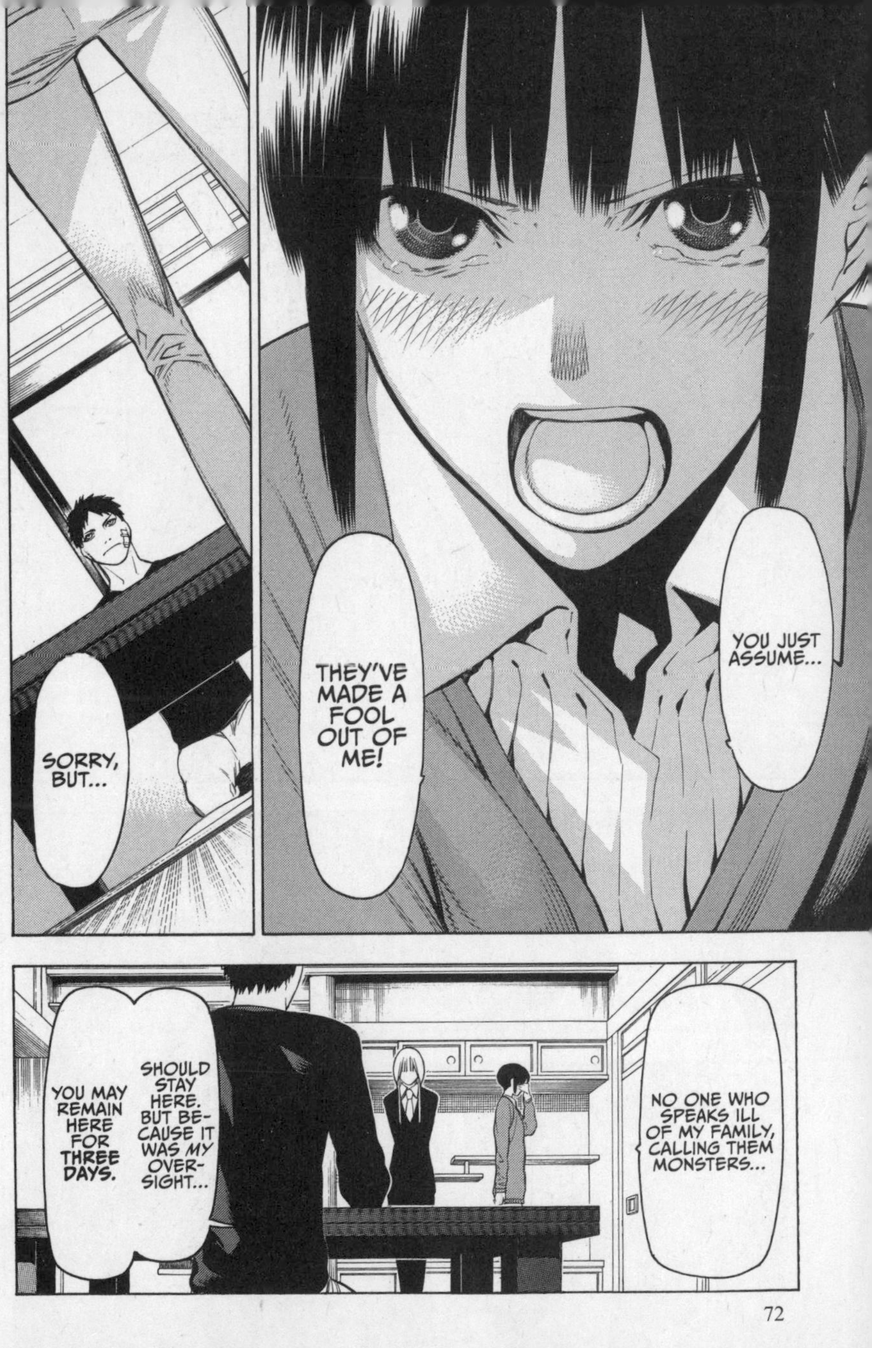
YOU JUST ASSUME...
THEY'VE MADE A FOOL OUT OF ME!
SORRY, BUT...
NO ONE WHO SPEAKS ILL OF MY FAMILY, CALLING THEM MONSTERS...
SHOULD STAY HERE. BUT BE-CAUSE IT WAS MY OVER-SIGHT...
YOU MAY REMAIN HERE FOR THREE DAYS.

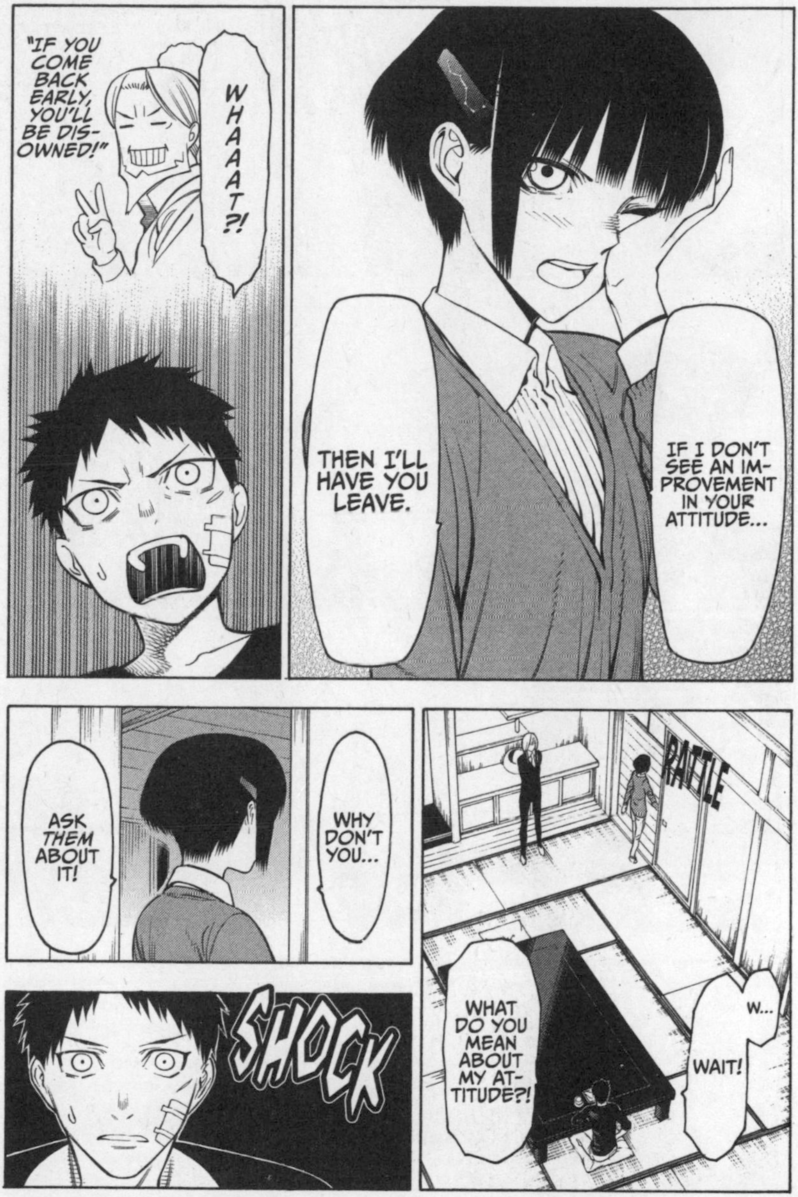
IF I DON'T SEE AN IMPROVEMENT IN YOUR ATTITUDE...
THEN I'LL HAVE YOU LEAVE.
WHAAAAT?!
"IF YOU COME BACK EARLY, YOU'LL BE DISOWNED!"
RATTLE
W... WAIT!
WHAT DO YOU MEAN ABOUT MY ATTITUDE?!
WHY DON'T YOU...
ASK THEM ABOUT IT!
SHOCK

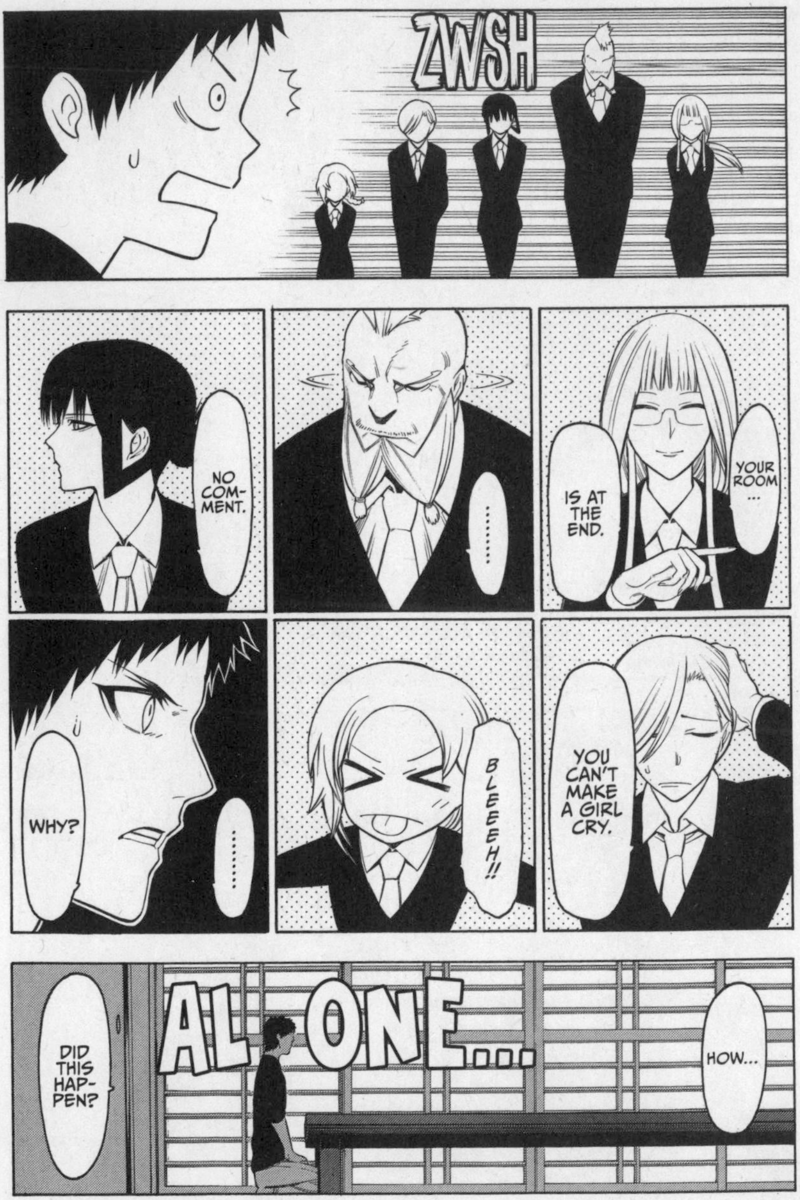
ZWSH
YOUR ROOM...
IS AT THE END.
......
NO COM-MENT.
YOU CAN'T MAKE A GIRL CRY.
BLEEEH!!
......
WHY?
HOW...
AL ONE...
DID THIS HAP-PEN?

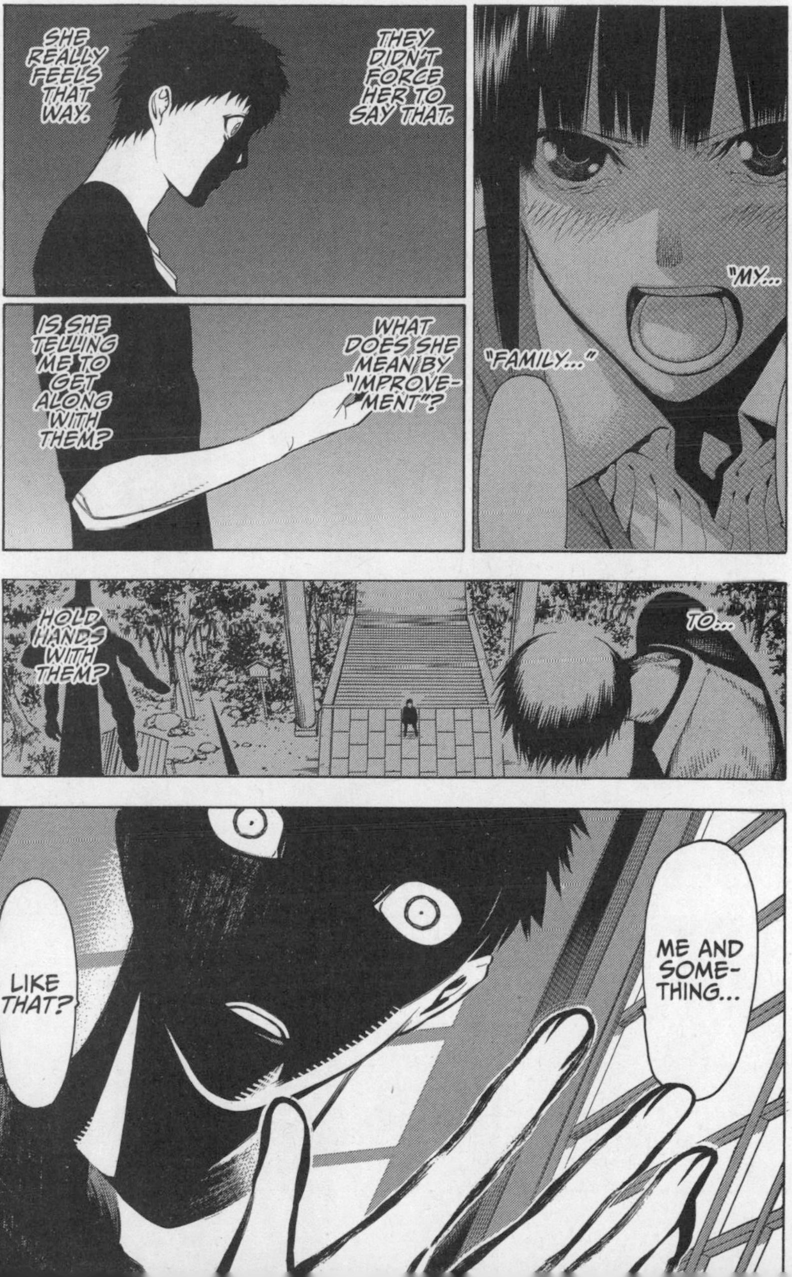
"MY...
"FAMILY..."
THEY DIDN'T FORCE HER TO SAY THAT.
SHE REALLY FEELS THAT WAY.
WHAT DOES SHE MEAN BY "IMPROVEMENT"?
IS SHE TELLING ME TO GET ALONG WITH THEM?
TO...
HOLD HANDS WITH THEM?
ME AND SOME-THING...
LIKE THAT?

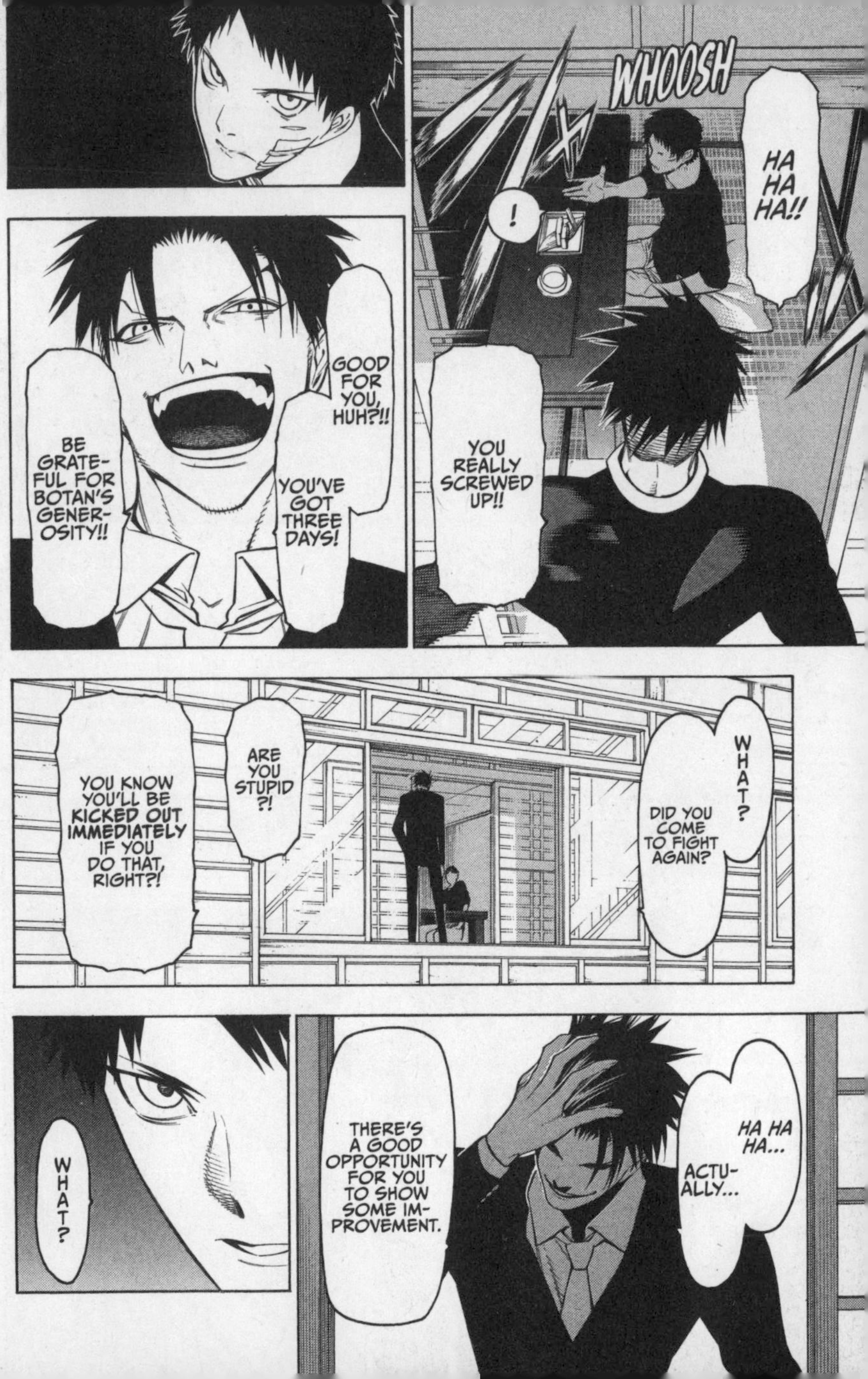
WHOOSH
HA HA HA!!
!
YOU REALLY SCREWED UP!!
GOOD FOR YOU, HUH?!!
YOU'VE GOT THREE DAYS!
BE GRATEFUL FOR BOTAN'S GENEROSITY!!
WHAT?
DID YOU COME TO FIGHT AGAIN?
ARE YOU STUPID?!
YOU KNOW YOU'LL BE KICKED OUT IMMEDIATELY IF YOU DO THAT, RIGHT?!
HA HA HA...
ACTUALLY...
THERE'S A GOOD OPPORTUNITY FOR YOU TO SHOW SOME IMPROVEMENT.
WHAT?

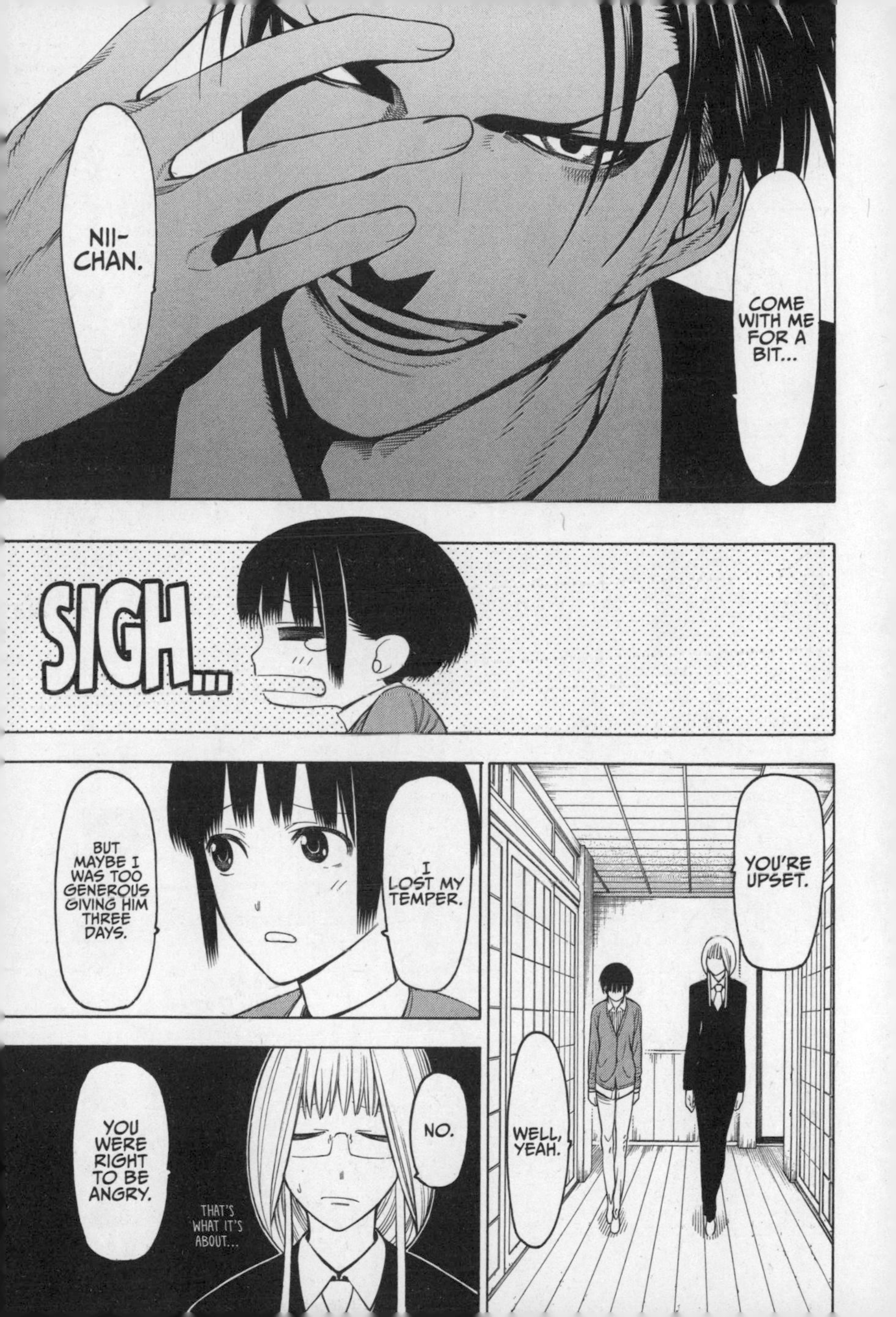
COME WITH ME FOR A BIT...
NII-CHAN.
SIGH...
YOU'RE UPSET.
WELL, YEAH.
I LOST MY TEMPER.
BUT MAYBE I WAS TOO GENEROUS GIVING HIM THREE DAYS.
NO.
YOU WERE RIGHT TO BE ANGRY.
THAT'S WHAT IT'S ABOUT...

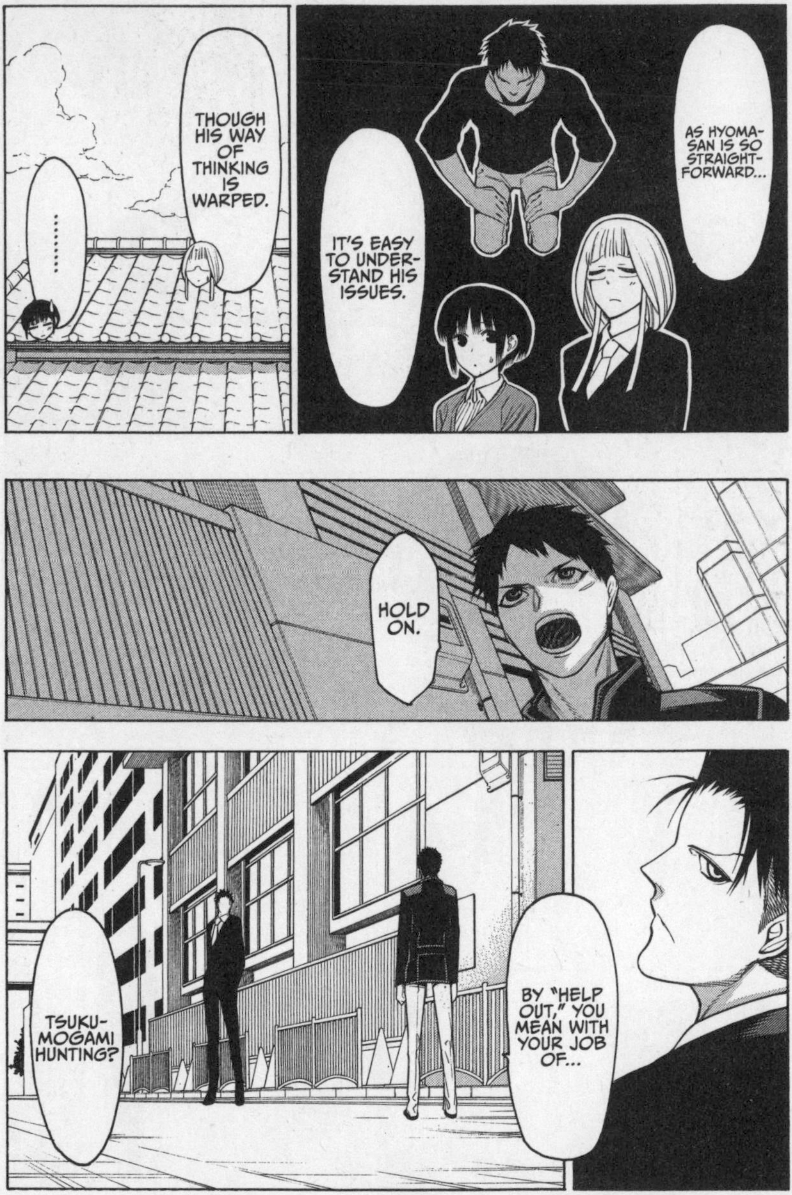
AS HYOMA-SAN IS SO STRAIGHT-FORWARD...
IT'S EASY TO UNDER-STAND HIS ISSUES.
THOUGH HIS WAY OF THINKING IS WARPED.
......
HOLD ON.
BY "HELP OUT," YOU MEAN WITH YOUR JOB OF...
TSUKU-MOGAMI HUNTING?

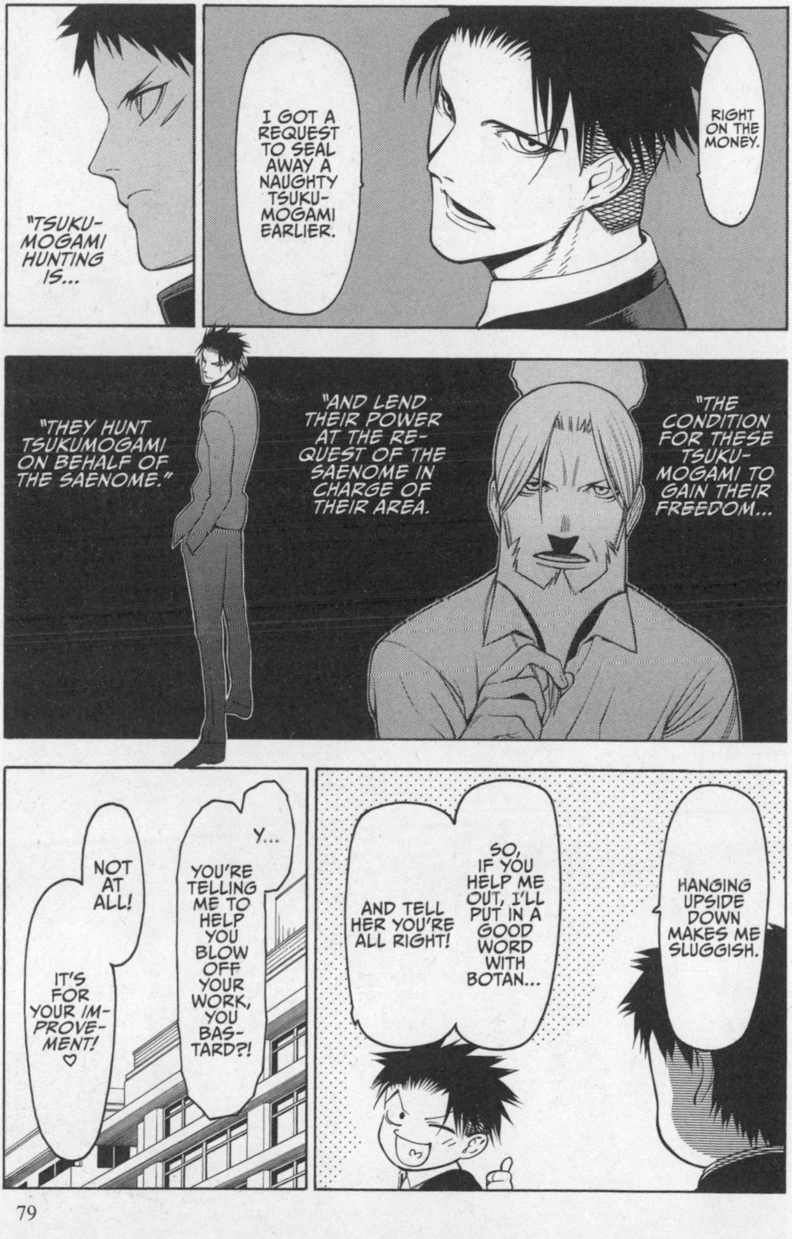
RIGHT ON THE MONEY.
I GOT A REQUEST TO SEAL AWAY A NAUGHTY TSUKU-MOGAMI EARLIER.
"TSUKU-MOGAMI HUNTING IS...
"THE CONDITION FOR THESE TSUKU-MOGAMI TO GAIN THEIR FREEDOM...
"AND LEND THEIR POWER AT THE RE-QUEST OF THE SAENOME IN CHARGE OF THEIR AREA.
"THEY HUNT TSUKUMOGAMI ON BEHALF OF THE SAENOME."
HANGING UPSIDE DOWN MAKES ME SLUGGISH.
SO, IF YOU HELP ME OUT, I'LL PUT IN A GOOD WORD WITH BOTAN...
AND TELL HER YOU'RE ALL RIGHT!
Y...
YOU'RE TELLING ME TO HELP YOU BLOW OFF YOUR WORK, YOU BAS-TARD?!
NOT AT ALL!
IT'S FOR YOUR IM-PROVE-MENT! ♡

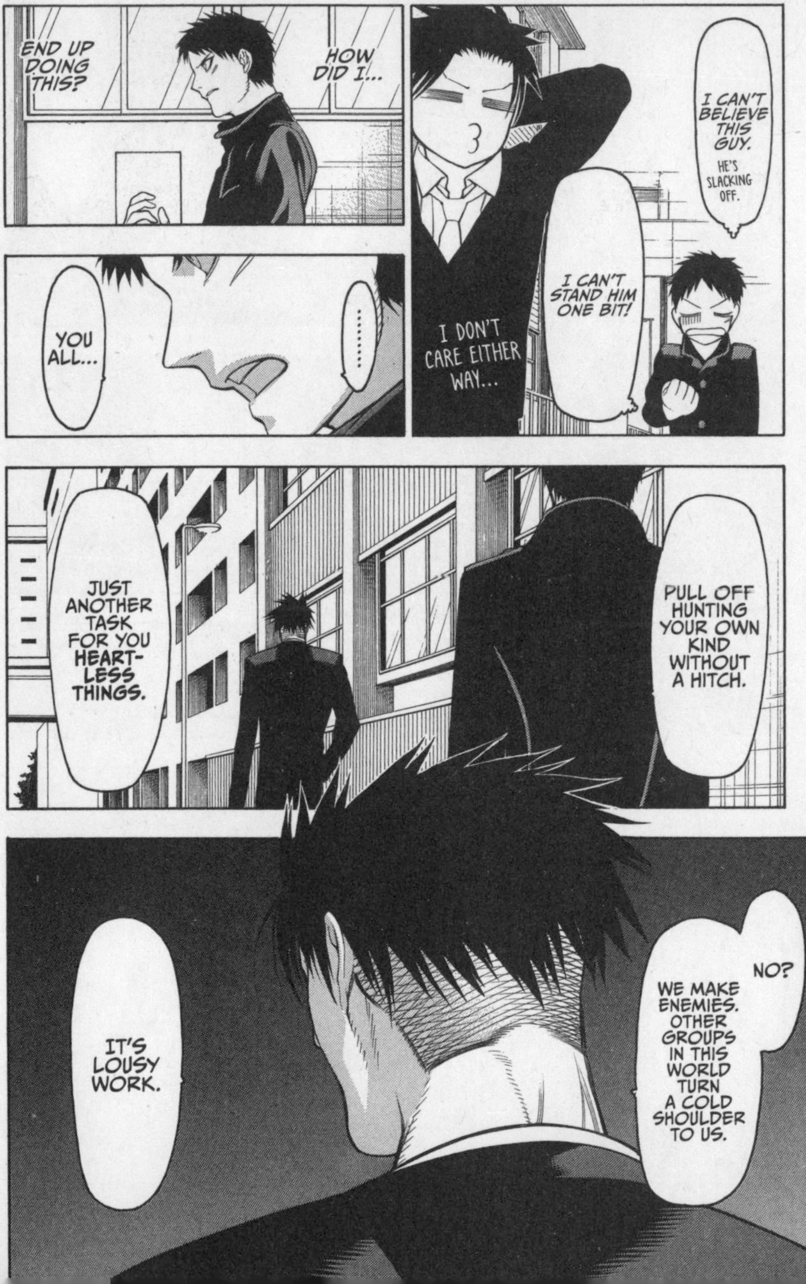
I CAN'T BELIEVE THIS GUY.
HE'S SLACKING OFF.
I CAN'T STAND HIM ONE BIT!
I DON'T CARE EITHER WAY...
HOW DID I...
END UP DOING THIS?
......
YOU ALL...
PULL OFF HUNTING YOUR OWN KIND WITHOUT A HITCH.
JUST ANOTHER TASK FOR YOU HEARTLESS THINGS.
NO?
WE MAKE ENEMIES. OTHER GROUPS IN THIS WORLD TURN A COLD SHOULDER TO US.
IT'S LOUSY WORK.

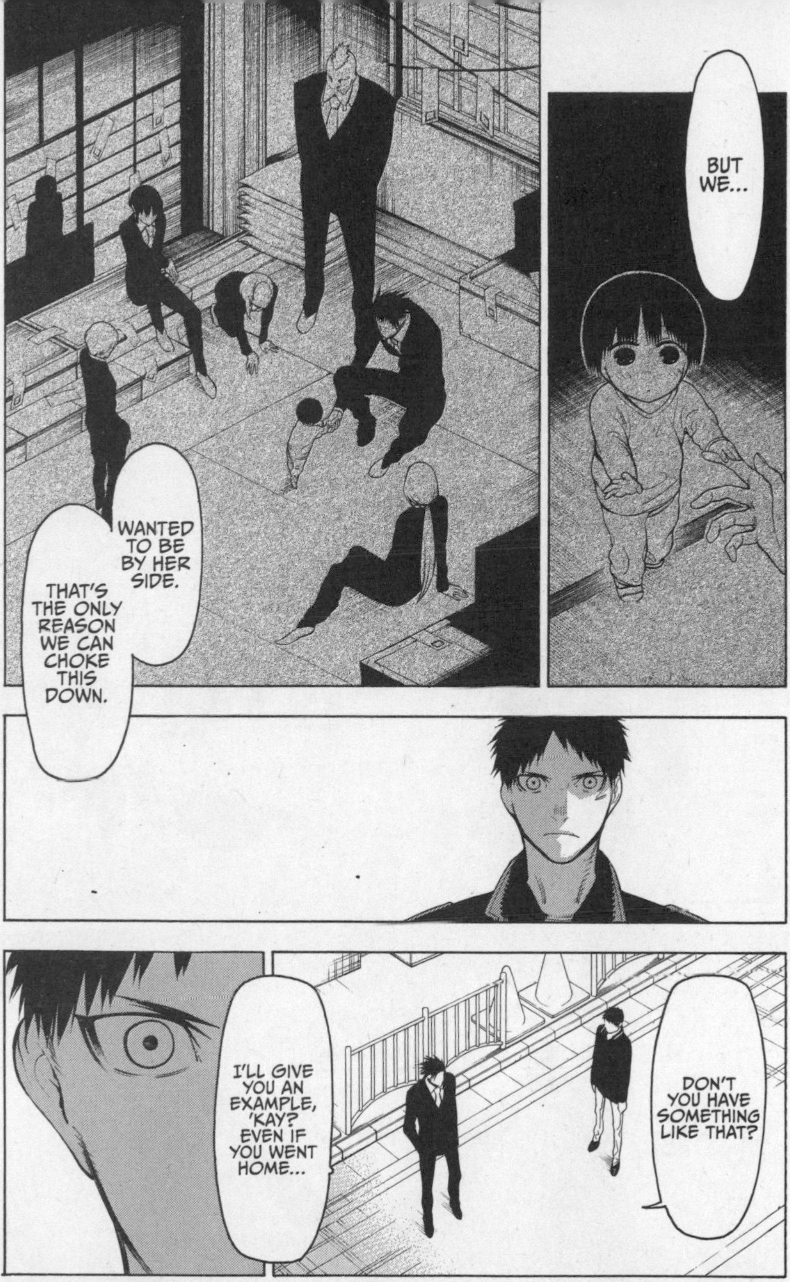
BUT WE...
WANTED TO BE BY HER SIDE.
THAT'S THE ONLY REASON WE CAN CHOKE THIS DOWN.
DON'T YOU HAVE SOMETHING LIKE THAT?
I'LL GIVE YOU AN EXAMPLE, 'KAY? EVEN IF YOU WENT HOME...

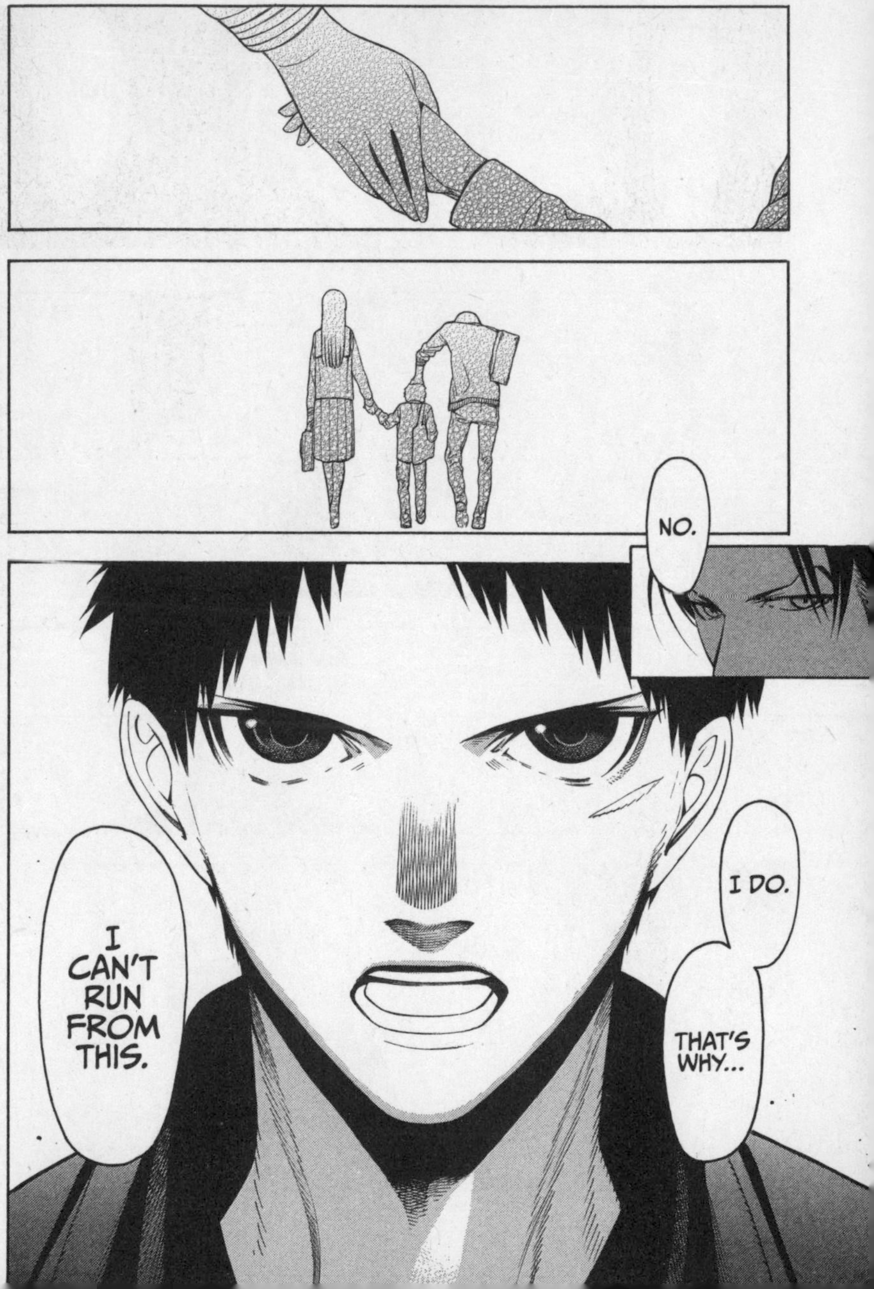
NO.
I DO.
THAT'S WHY...
I CAN'T RUN FROM THIS.

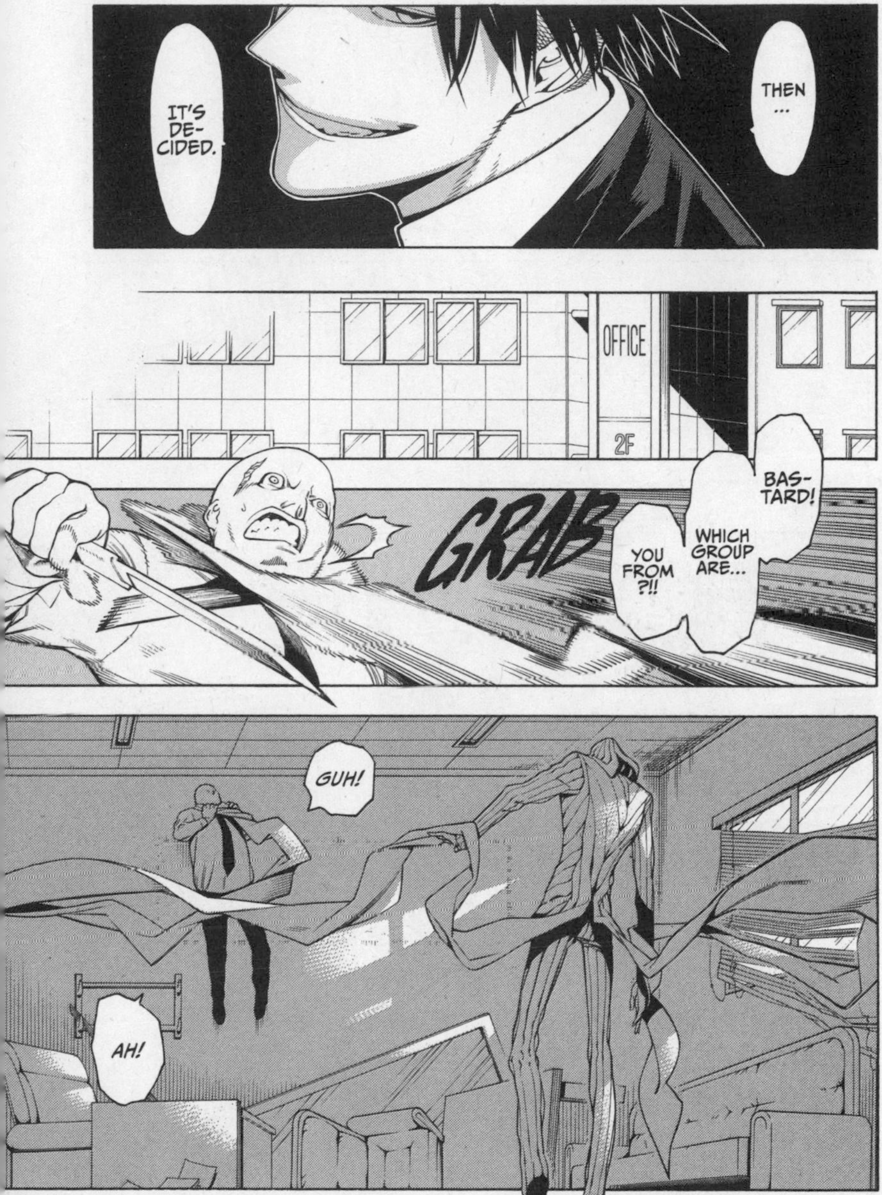
THEN ...
IT'S DE-CIDED.
OFFICE
2F
BAS-TARD!
WHICH GROUP ARE...
YOU FROM ?!!
GRAB
GUH!
AH!

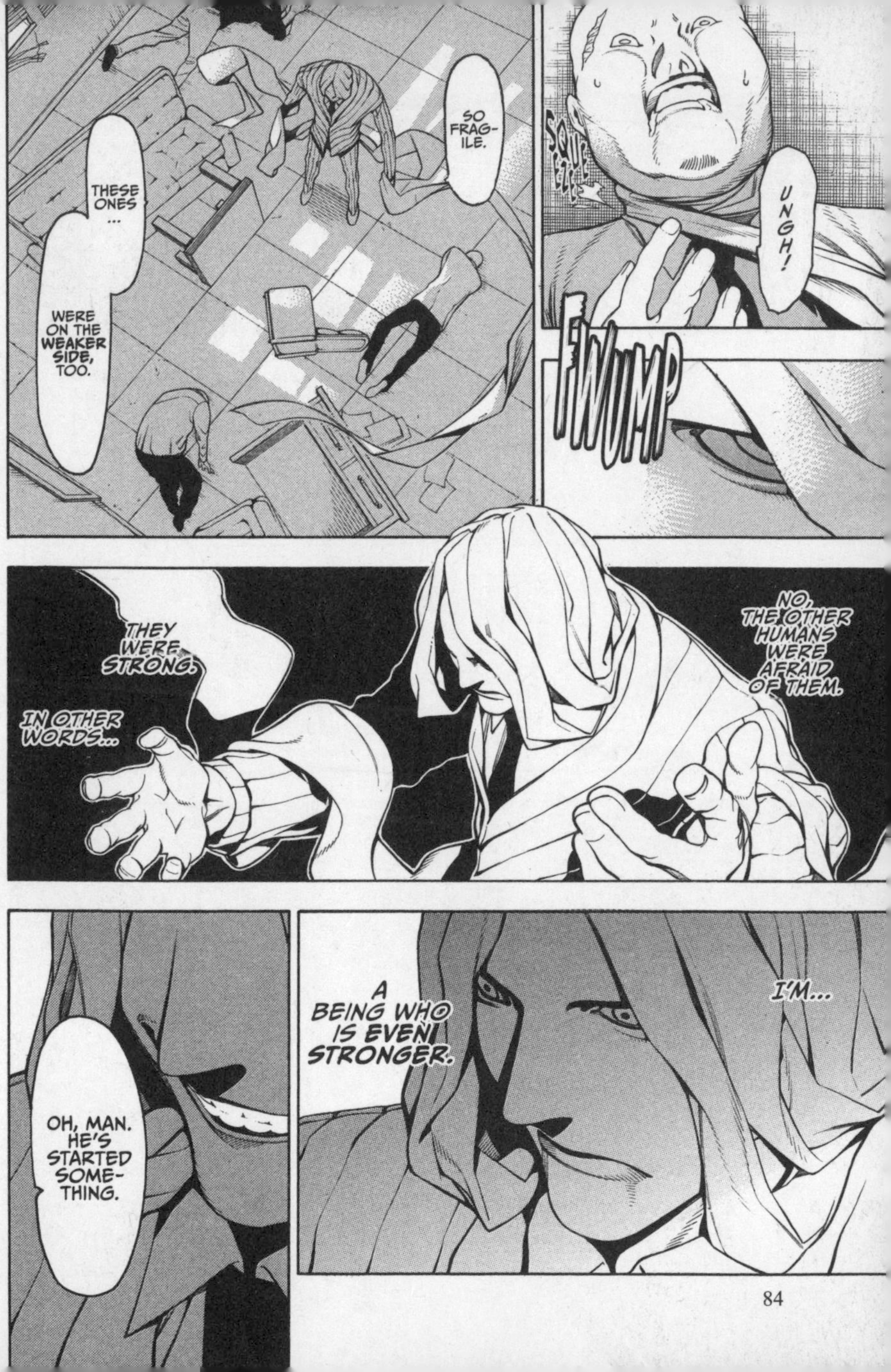
SQUEEZE
UNGH!
FWUMP
SO FRAGILE.
THESE ONES...
WERE ON THE WEAKER SIDE, TOO.
NO, THE OTHER HUMANS WERE AFRAID OF THEM.
THEY WERE STRONG.
IN OTHER WORDS...
I'M...
A BEING WHO IS EVEN STRONGER.
OH, MAN. HE'S STARTED SOMETHING.

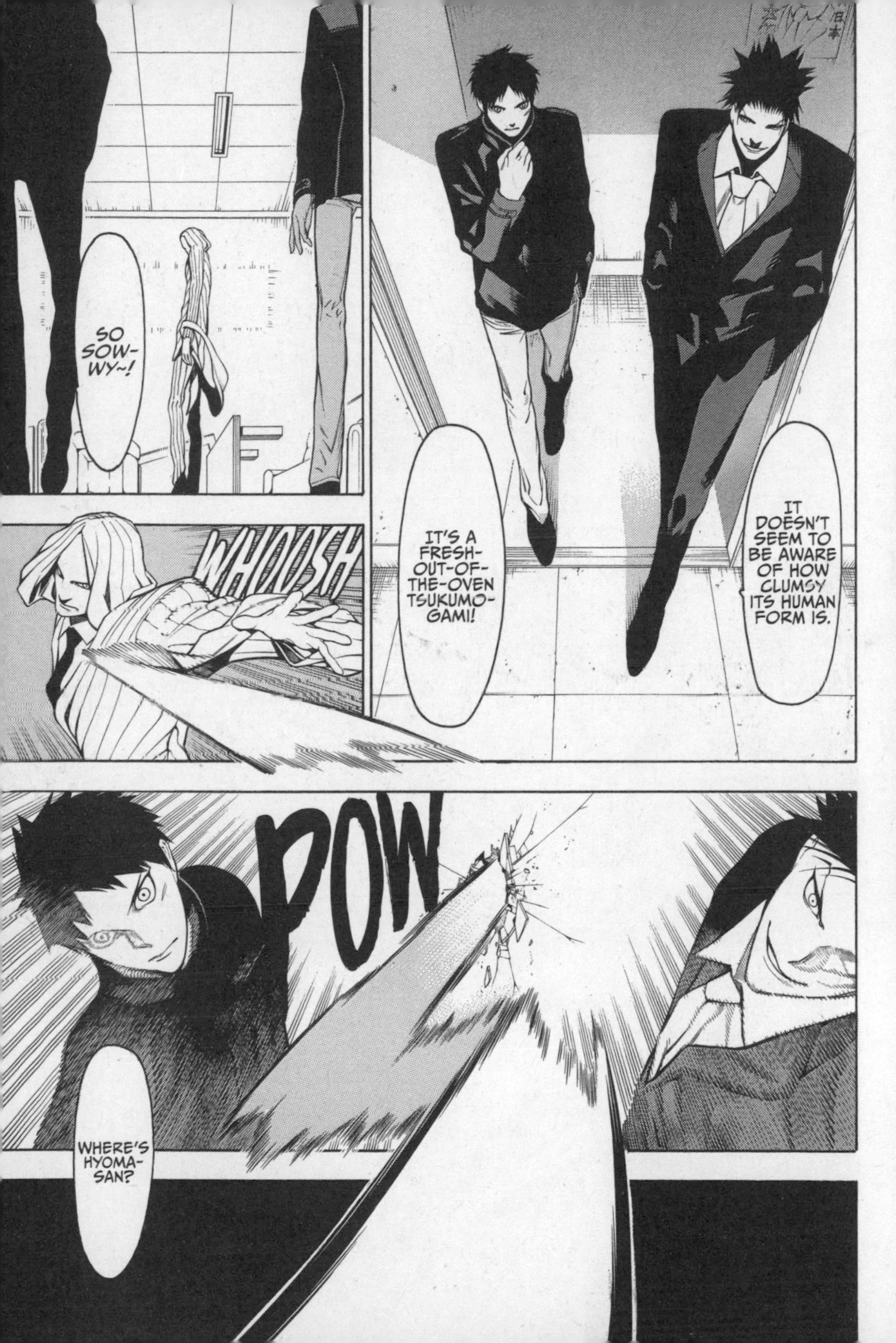
IT DOESN'T SEEM TO BE AWARE OF HOW CLUMSY ITS HUMAN FORM IS.
IT'S A FRESH-OUT-OF-THE-OVEN TSUKUMO-GAMI!
SO SOW-WY~!
WHOOSH
POW
WHERE'S HYOMA-SAN?

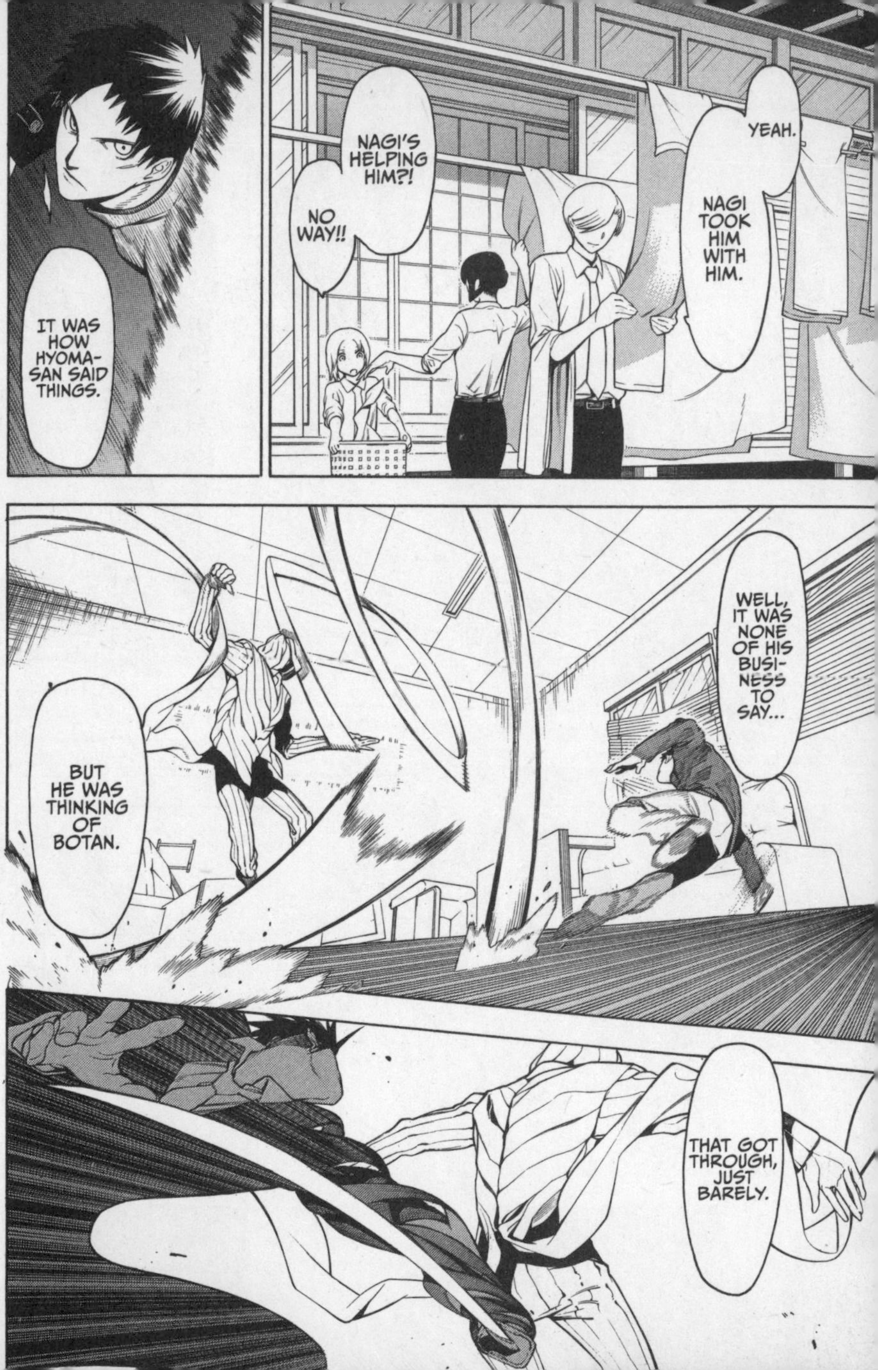
YEAH.
NAGI TOOK HIM WITH HIM.
NAGI'S HELPING HIM?!
NO WAY!!
IT WAS HOW HYOMA-SAN SAID THINGS.
WELL, IT WAS NONE OF HIS BUSI-NESS TO SAY...
BUT HE WAS THINKING OF BOTAN.
THAT GOT THROUGH, JUST BARELY.

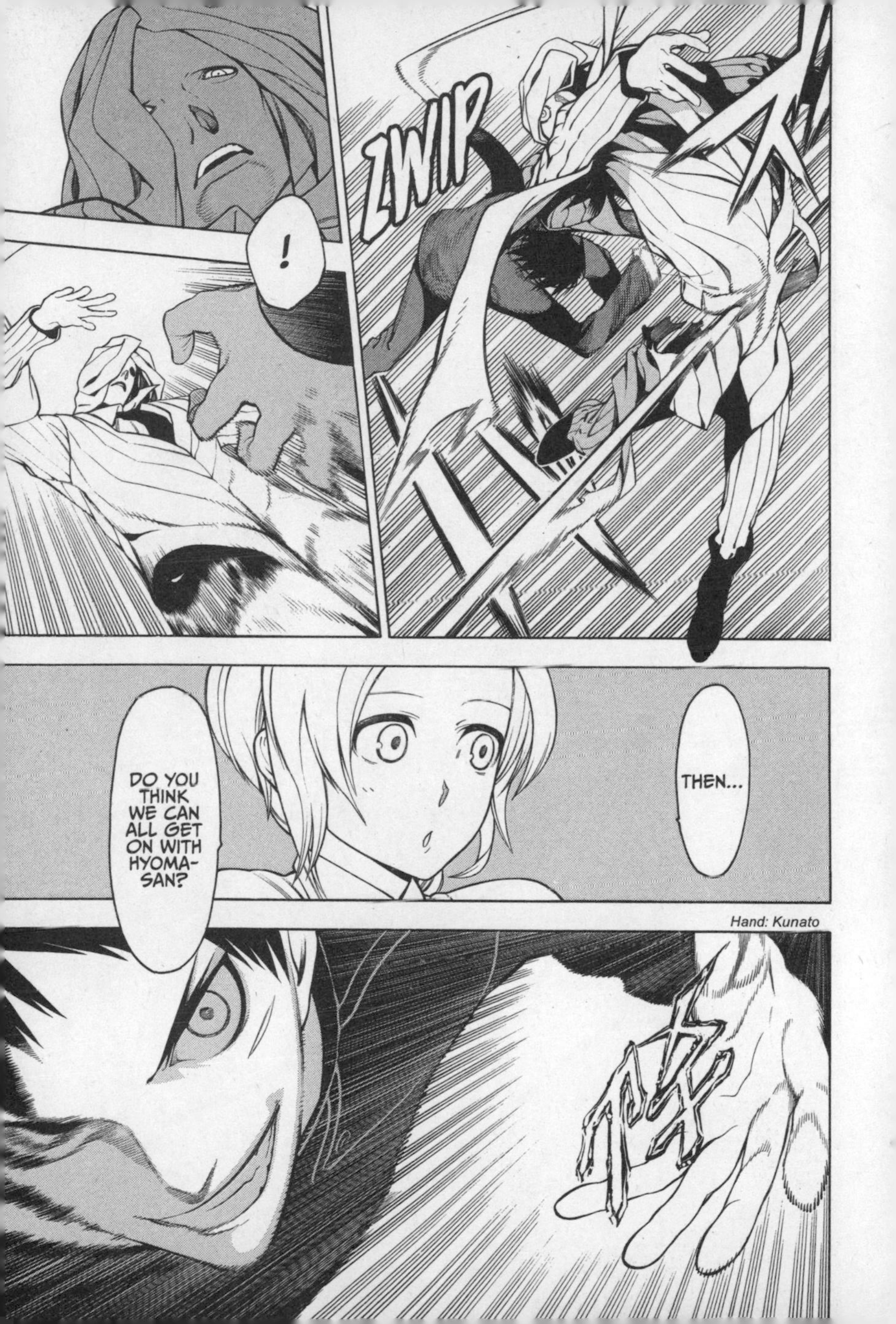
ZWIP
!
THEN...
DO YOU THINK WE CAN ALL GET ON WITH HYOMA-SAN?
Hand: Kunato

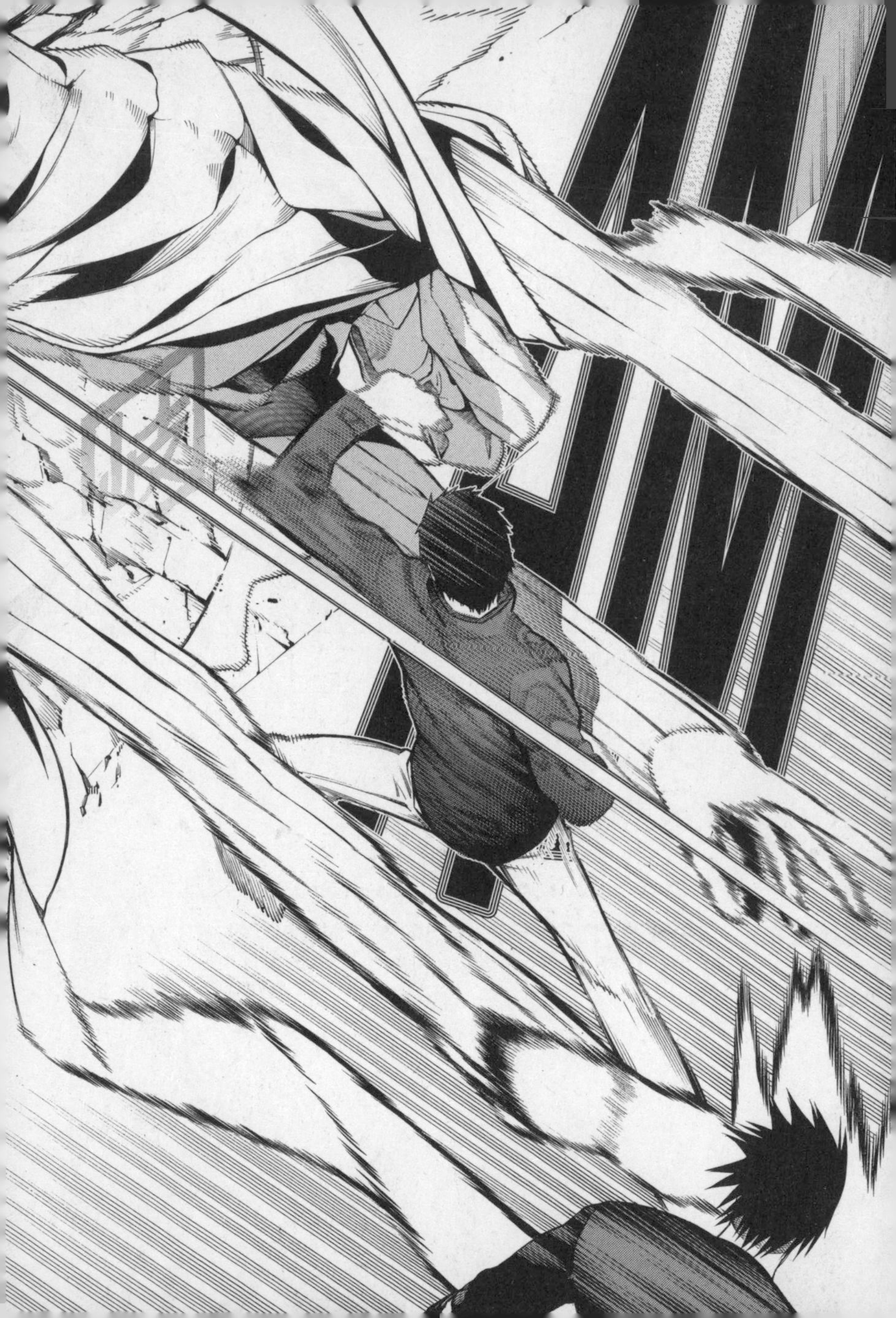

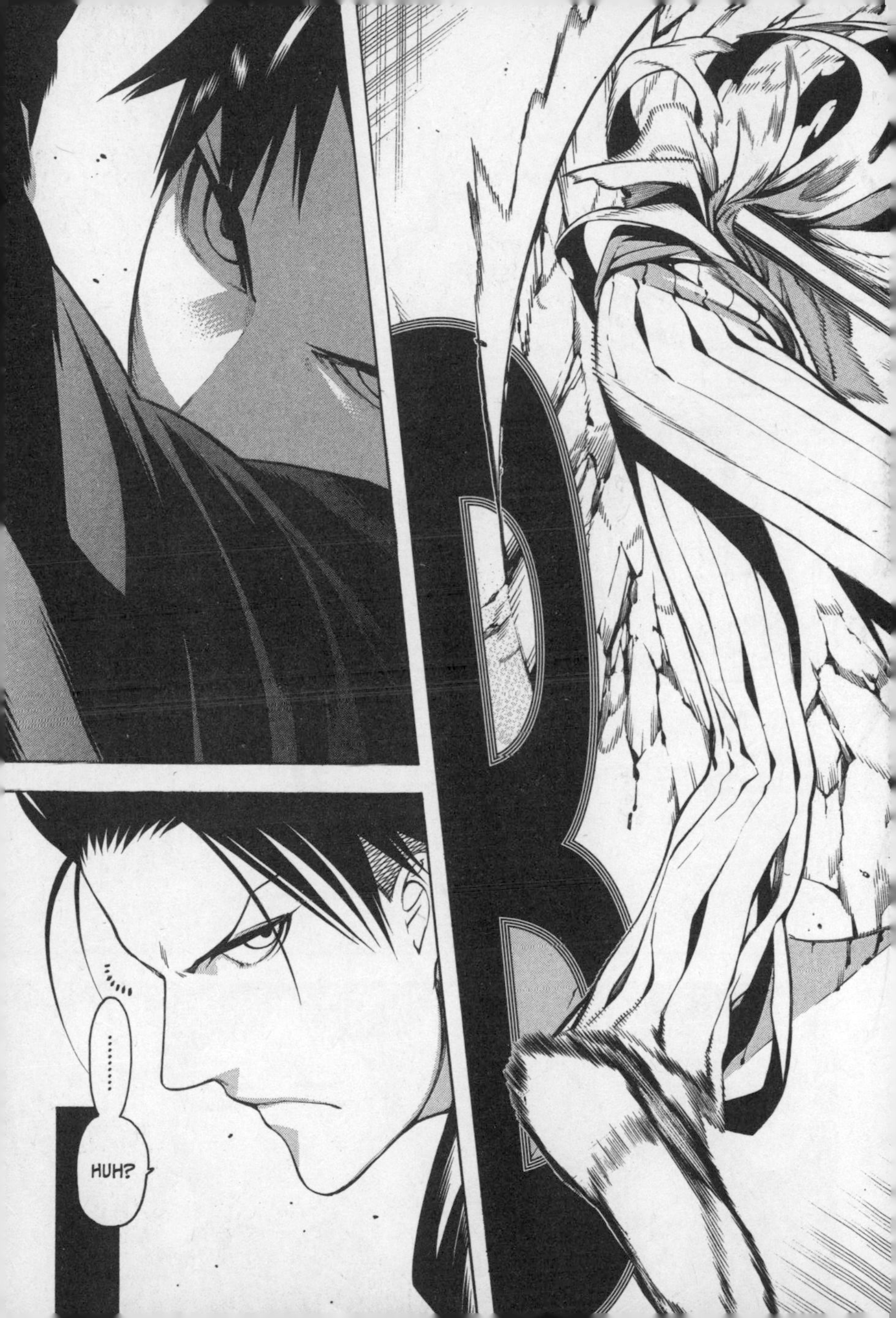

......
HUH?

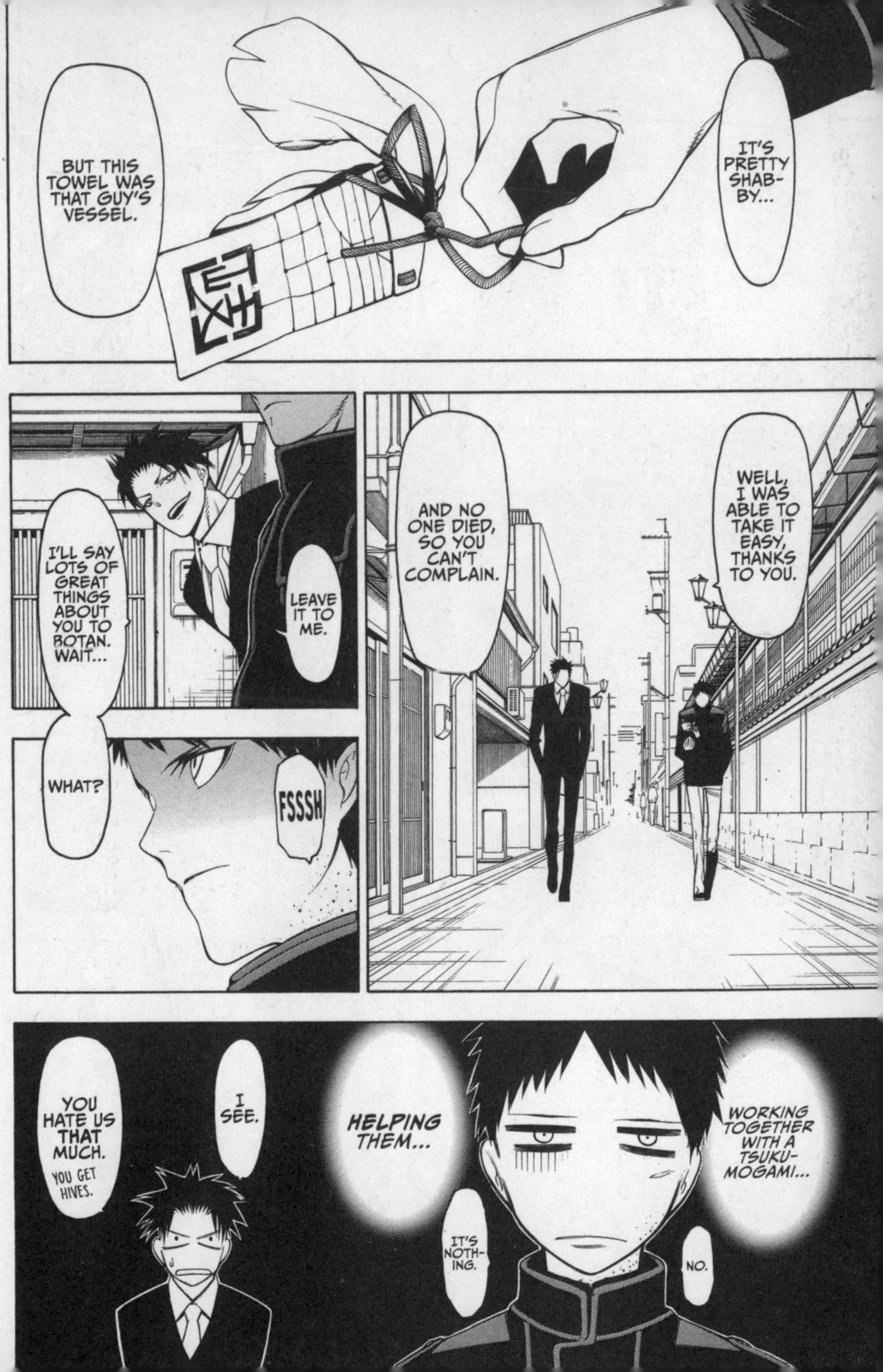
IT'S PRETTY SHABBY...
BUT THIS TOWEL WAS THAT GUY'S VESSEL.
WELL, I WAS ABLE TO TAKE IT EASY, THANKS TO YOU.
AND NO ONE DIED, SO YOU CAN'T COMPLAIN.
LEAVE IT TO ME.
I'LL SAY LOTS OF GREAT THINGS ABOUT YOU TO BOTAN. WAIT...
FSSSH
WHAT?
WORKING TOGETHER WITH A TSUKUMOGAMI...
HELPING THEM...
I SEE.
YOU HATE US THAT MUCH.
YOU GET HIVES.
NO.
IT'S NOTHING.

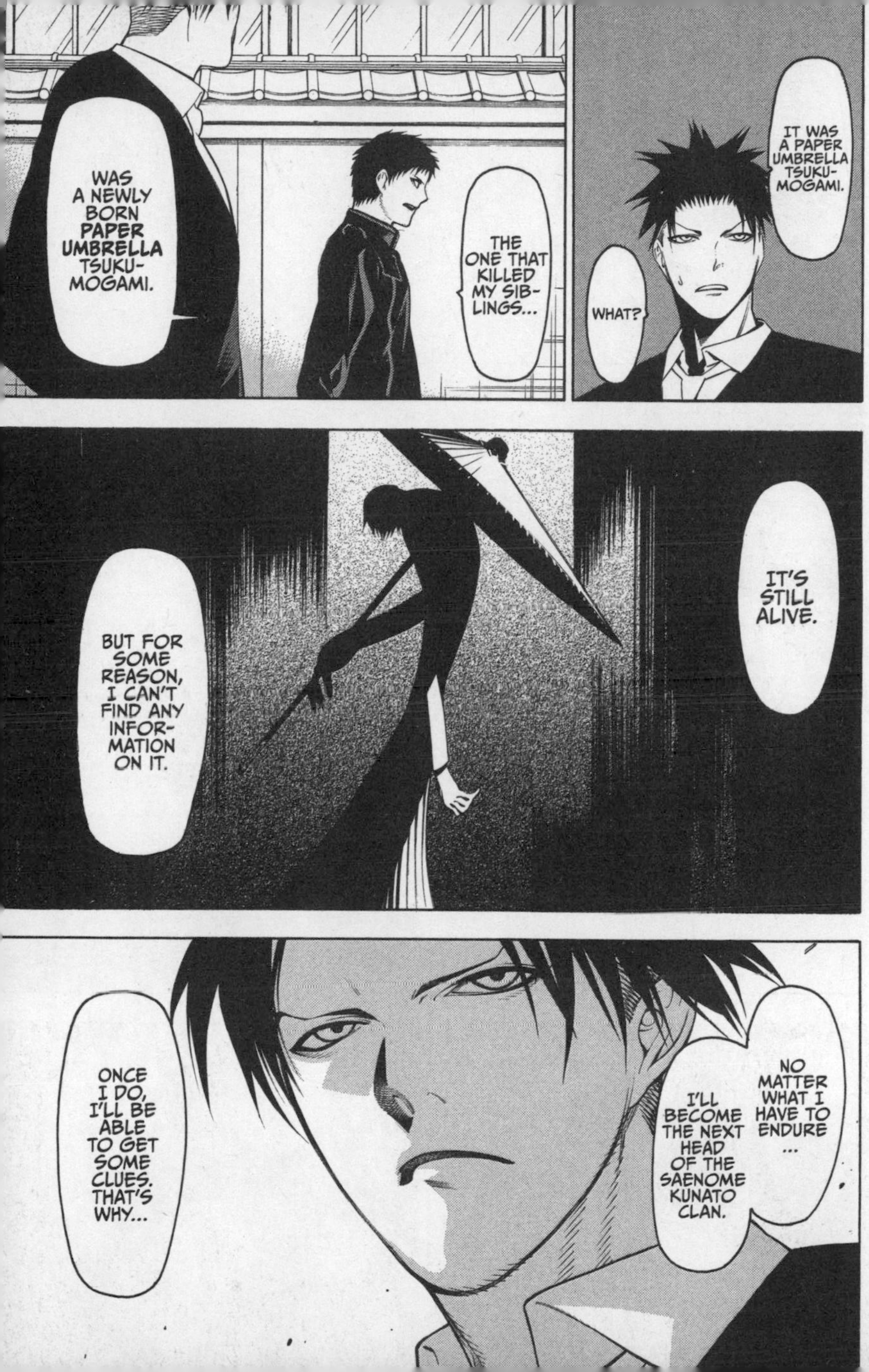
IT WAS A PAPER UMBRELLA TSUKU-MOGAMI.
WHAT?
THE ONE THAT KILLED MY SIB-LINGS...
WAS A NEWLY BORN PAPER UMBRELLA TSUKU-MOGAMI.
IT'S STILL ALIVE.
BUT FOR SOME REASON, I CAN'T FIND ANY INFOR-MATION ON IT.
NO MATTER WHAT I HAVE TO ENDURE...
I'LL BECOME THE NEXT HEAD OF THE SAENOME KUNATO CLAN.
ONCE I DO, I'LL BE ABLE TO GET SOME CLUES. THAT'S WHY...

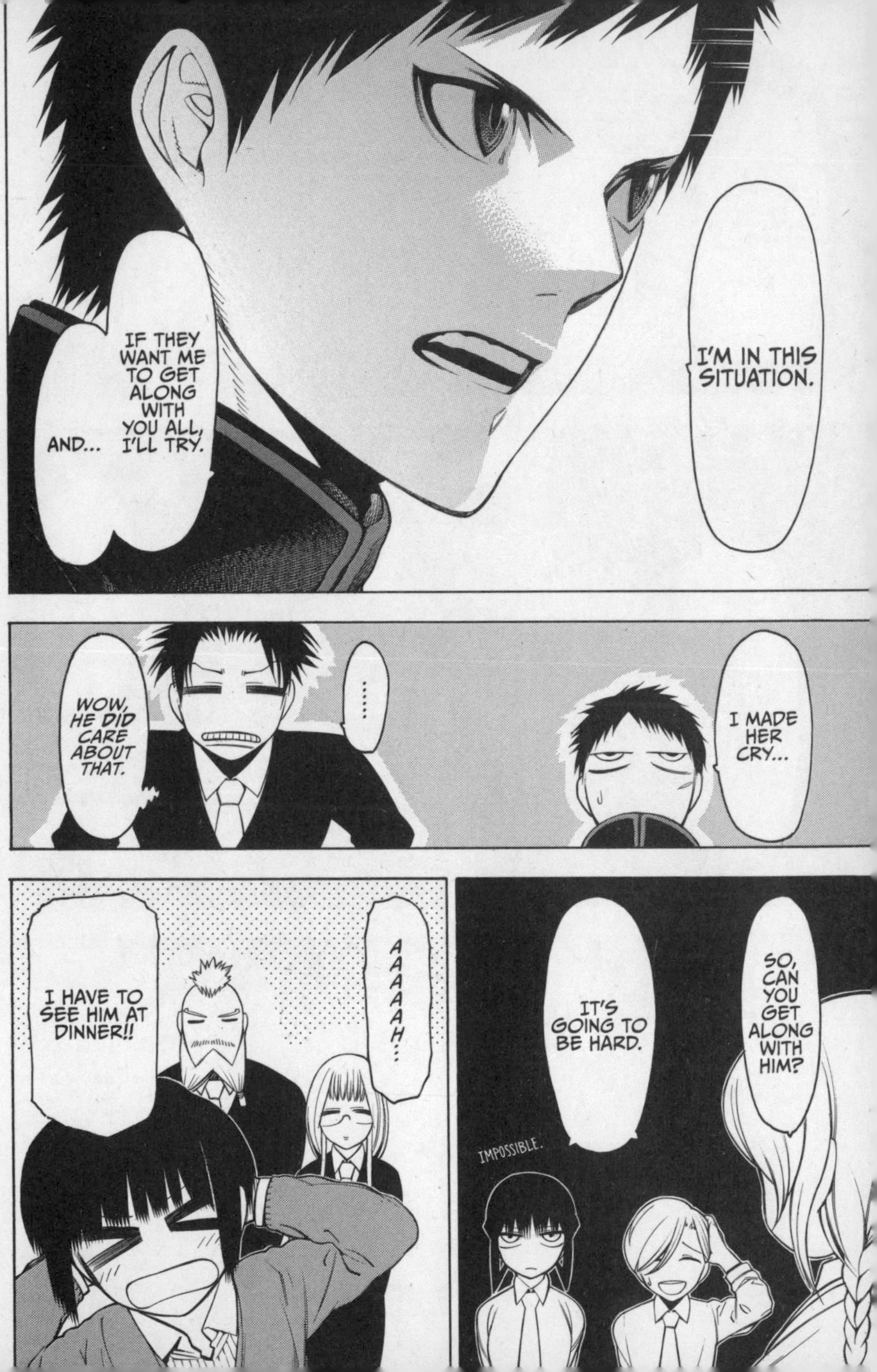
I'M IN THIS SITUATION.
IF THEY WANT ME TO GET ALONG WITH YOU ALL, I'LL TRY.
AND...
I MADE HER CRY...
......
WOW, HE DID CARE ABOUT THAT.
SO, CAN YOU GET ALONG WITH HIM?
IT'S GOING TO BE HARD.
IMPOSSIBLE.
AAAAAAH...
I HAVE TO SEE HIM AT DINNER!!

MONONOGATARI

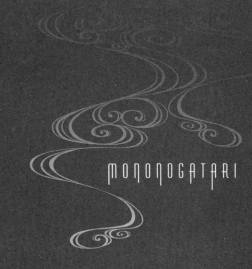

CHAPTER 3 | SHORELINE

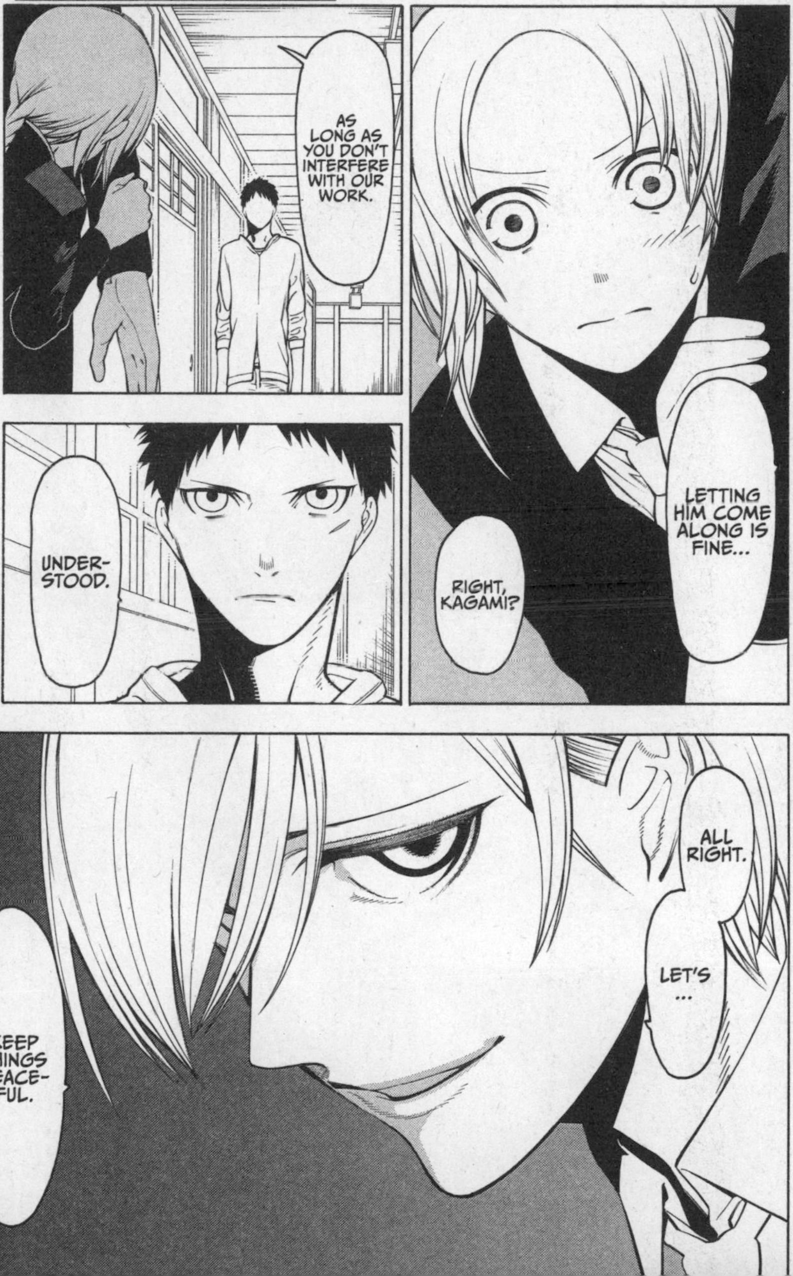
LETTING HIM COME ALONG IS FINE...
RIGHT, KAGAMI?
AS LONG AS YOU DON'T INTERFERE WITH OUR WORK.
UNDER-STOOD.
ALL RIGHT.
LET'S...
KEEP THINGS PEACE-FUL.

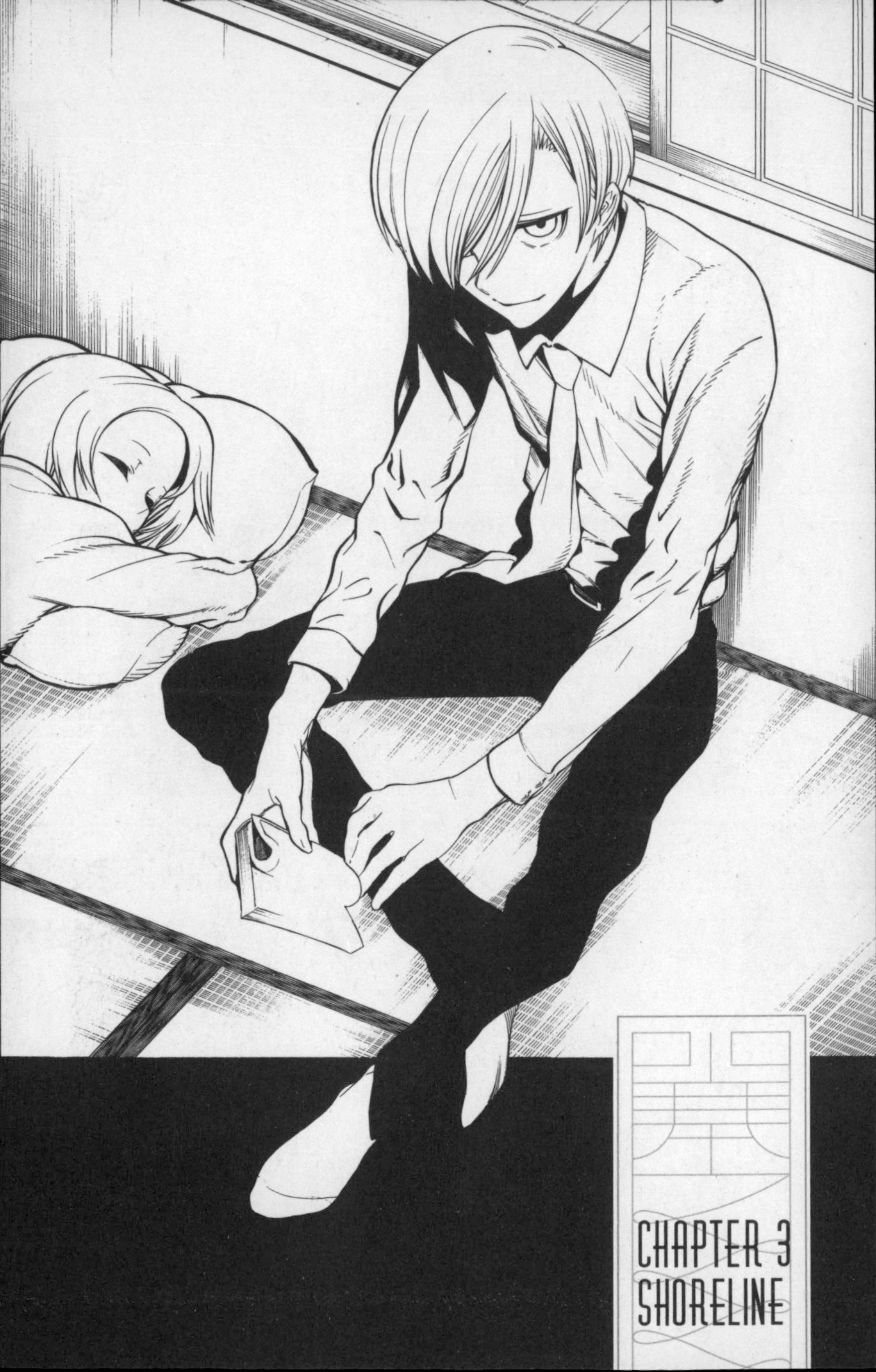
CHAPTER 3
SHORELINE

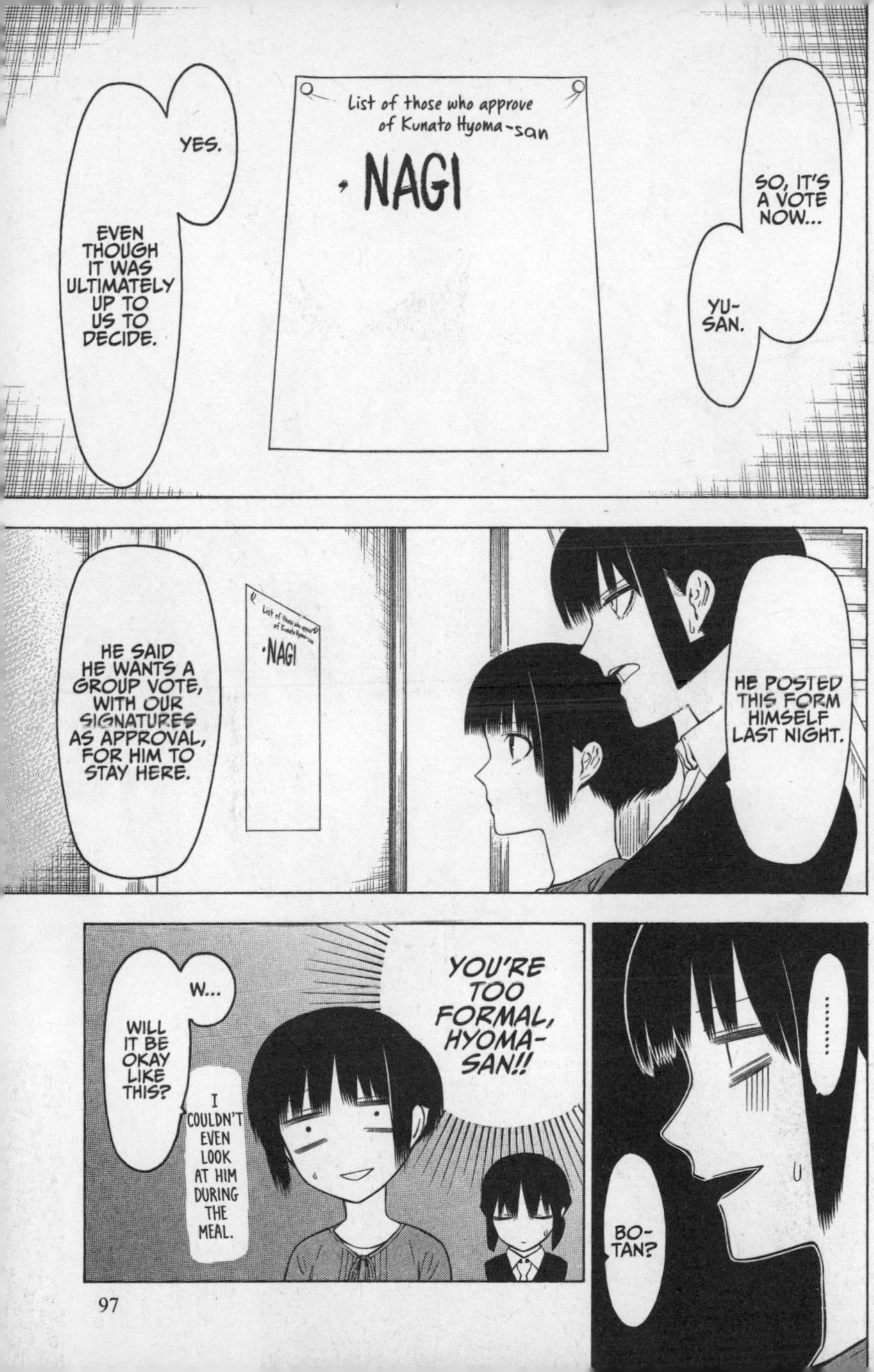
SO, IT'S A VOTE NOW...
YU-SAN.
List of those who approve of Kunato Hyoma-san
・NAGI
YES.
EVEN THOUGH IT WAS ULTIMATELY UP TO US TO DECIDE.
HE POSTED THIS FORM HIMSELF LAST NIGHT.
HE SAID HE WANTS A GROUP VOTE, WITH OUR SIGNATURES AS APPROVAL, FOR HIM TO STAY HERE.
......
BO-TAN?
YOU'RE TOO FORMAL, HYOMA-SAN!!
W...
WILL IT BE OKAY LIKE THIS?
I COULDN'T EVEN LOOK AT HIM DURING THE MEAL.

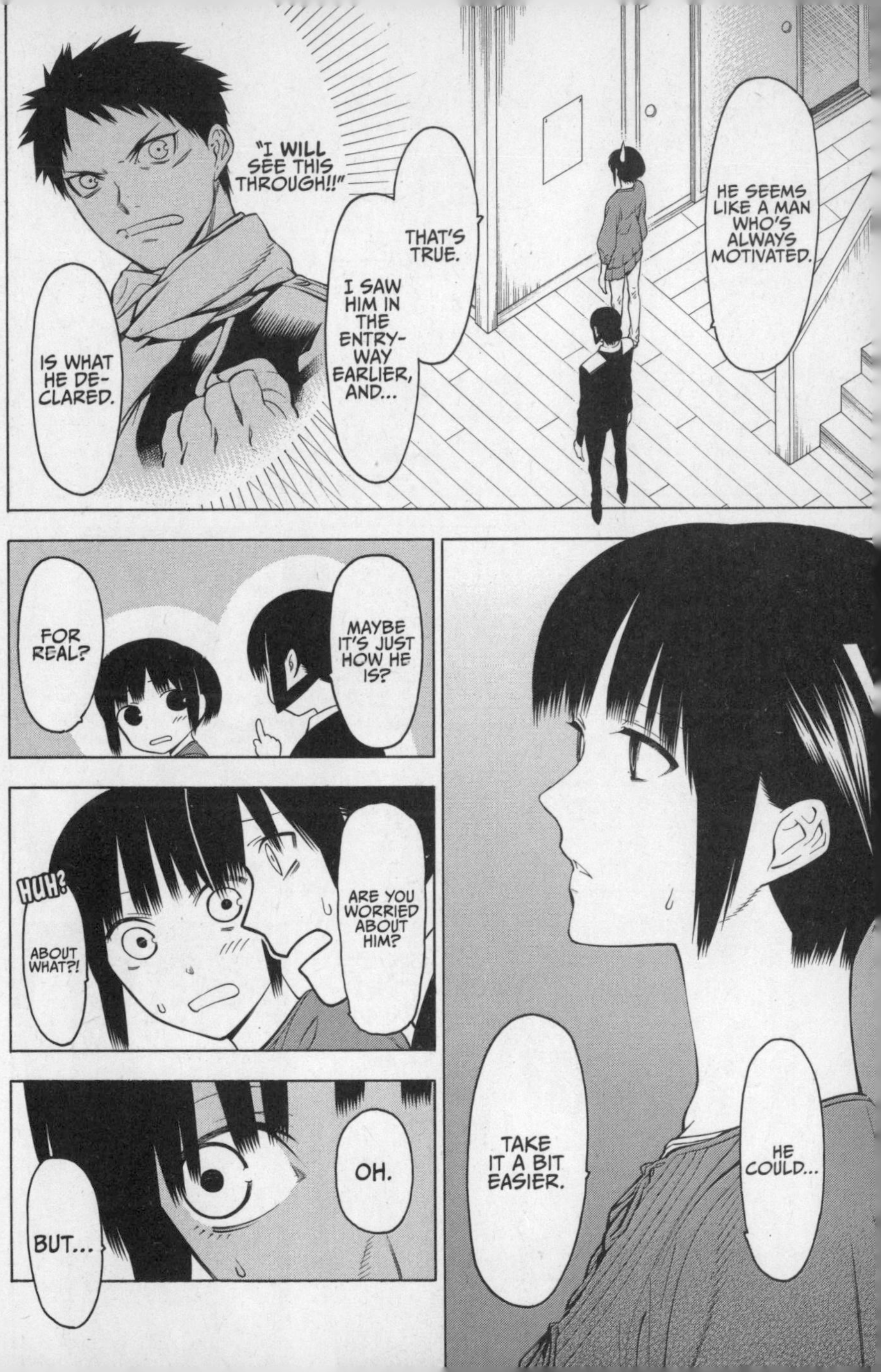
HE SEEMS LIKE A MAN WHO'S ALWAYS MOTIVATED.
THAT'S TRUE.
I SAW HIM IN THE ENTRY-WAY EARLIER, AND...
"I WILL SEE THIS THROUGH!!"
IS WHAT HE DE-CLARED.
HE COULD...
TAKE IT A BIT EASIER.
MAYBE IT'S JUST HOW HE IS?
FOR REAL?
ARE YOU WORRIED ABOUT HIM?
HUH?
ABOUT WHAT?!
OH.
BUT...

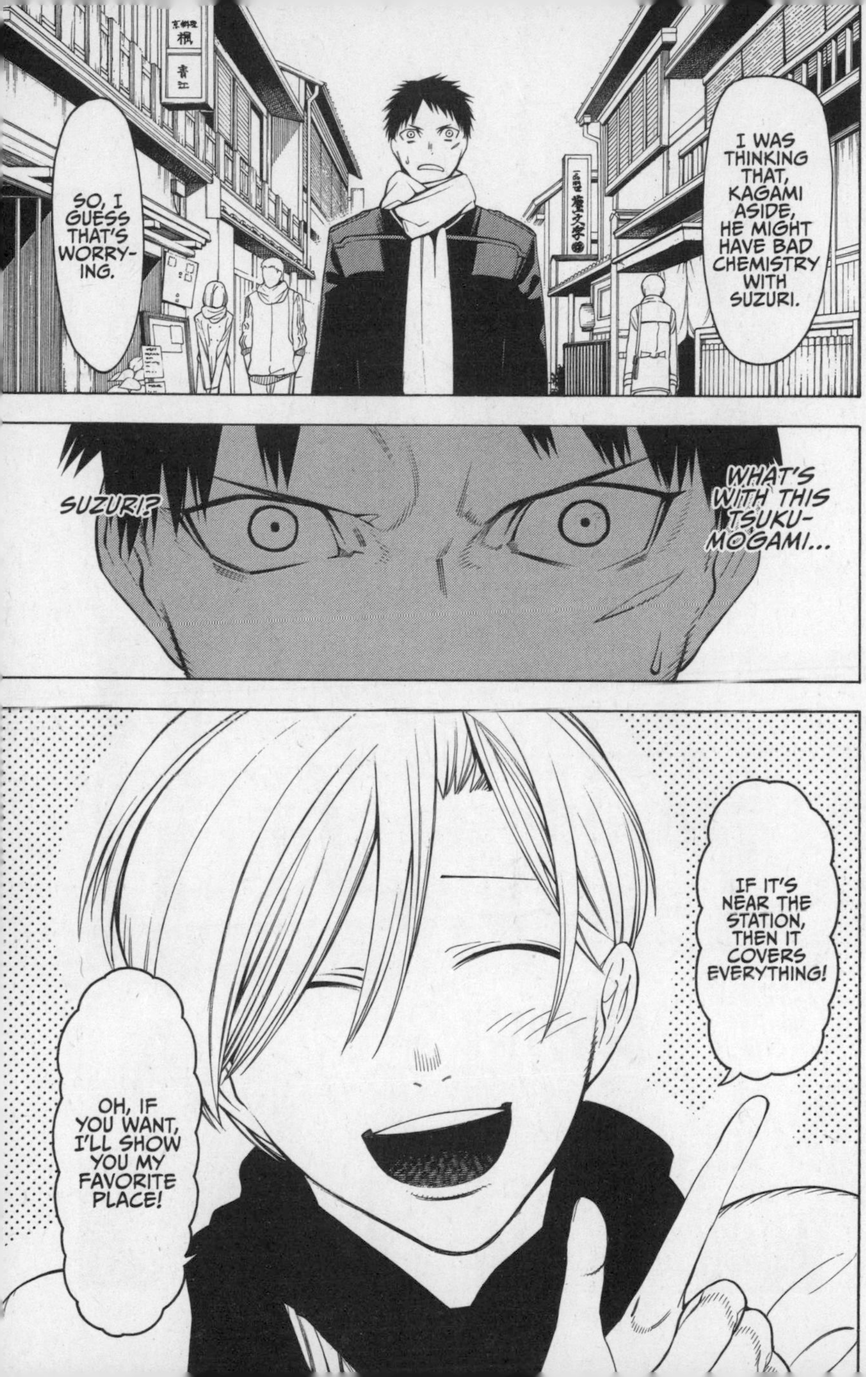
I WAS THINKING THAT, KAGAMI ASIDE, HE MIGHT HAVE BAD CHEMISTRY WITH SUZURI.
SO, I GUESS THAT'S WORRY-ING.
WHAT'S WITH THIS TSUKU-MOGAMI...
SUZURI?
IF IT'S NEAR THE STATION, THEN IT COVERS EVERYTHING!
OH, IF YOU WANT, I'LL SHOW YOU MY FAVORITE PLACE!

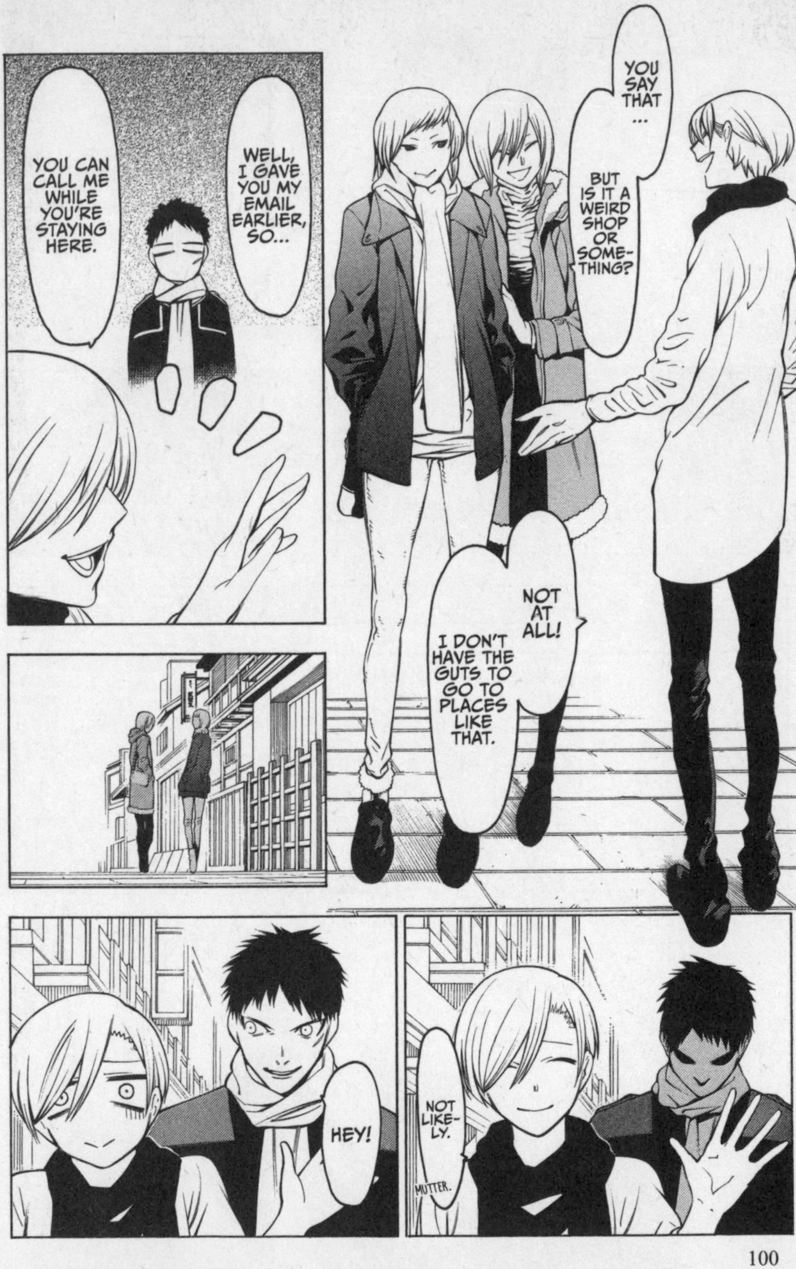
YOU SAY THAT ...
BUT IS IT A WEIRD SHOP OR SOME-THING?
NOT AT ALL!
I DON'T HAVE THE GUTS TO GO TO PLACES LIKE THAT.
WELL, I GAVE YOU MY EMAIL EARLIER, SO...
YOU CAN CALL ME WHILE YOU'RE STAYING HERE.
NOT LIKE-LY.
MUTTER.
HEY!

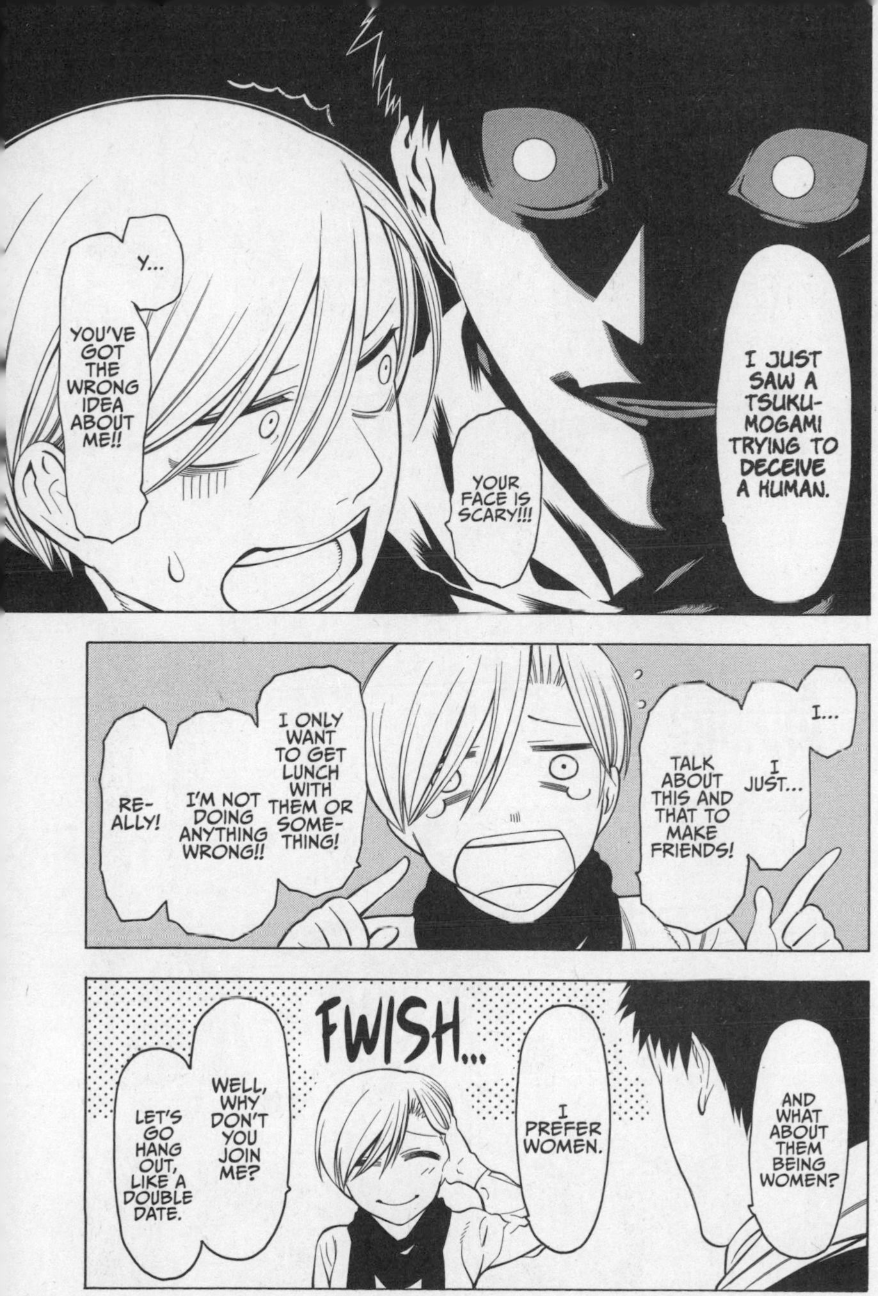
I JUST SAW A TSUKU-MOGAMI TRYING TO DECEIVE A HUMAN.
YOUR FACE IS SCARY!!!
Y...
YOU'VE GOT THE WRONG IDEA ABOUT ME!!
I...
I JUST...
TALK ABOUT THIS AND THAT TO MAKE FRIENDS!
I ONLY WANT TO GET LUNCH WITH THEM OR SOME-THING!
I'M NOT DOING ANYTHING WRONG!!
RE-ALLY!
AND WHAT ABOUT THEM BEING WOMEN?
I PREFER WOMEN.
FWISH...
WELL, WHY DON'T YOU JOIN ME?
LET'S GO HANG OUT, LIKE A DOUBLE DATE.

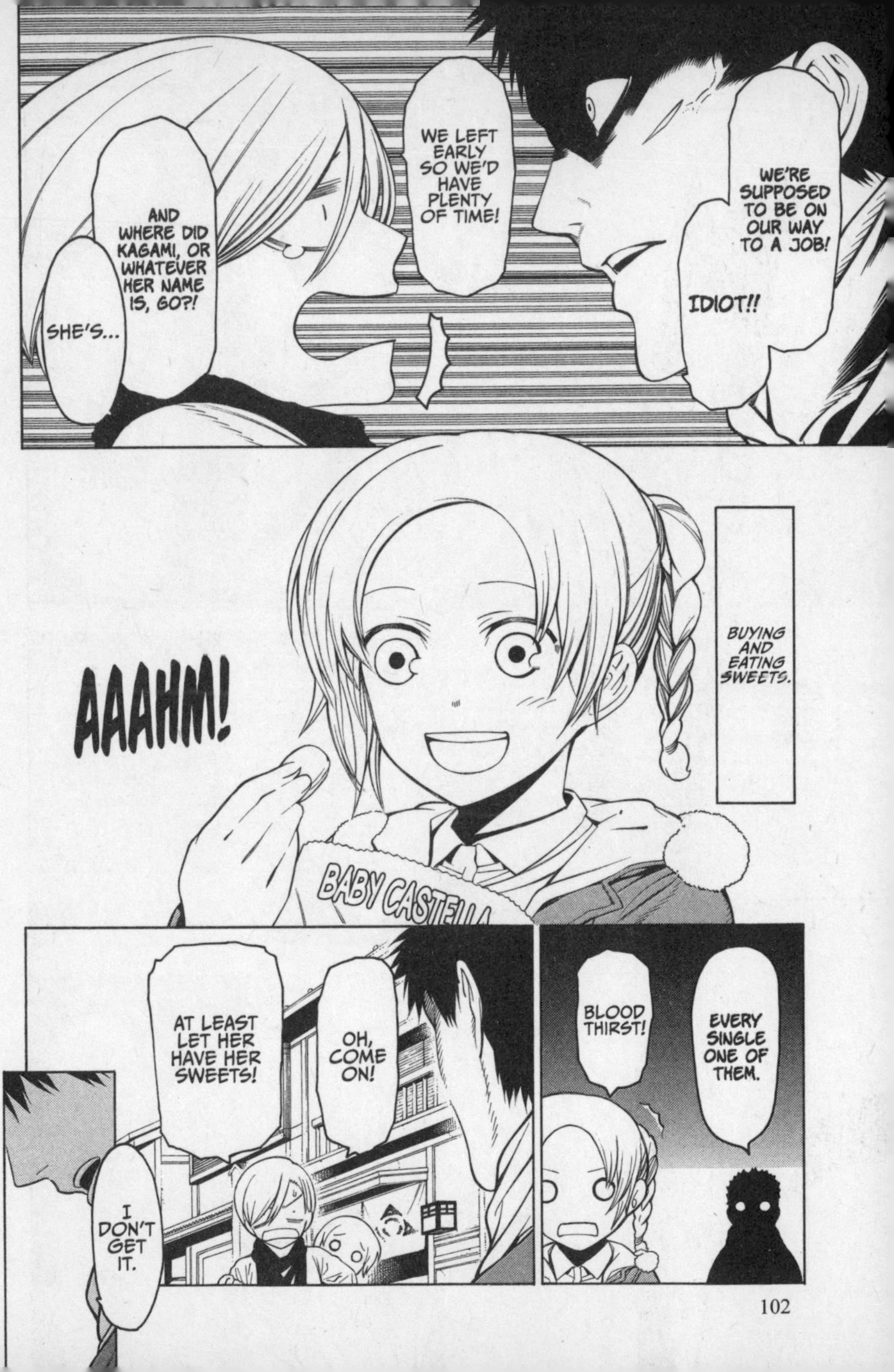
WE'RE SUPPOSED TO BE ON OUR WAY TO A JOB!
IDIOT!!
WE LEFT EARLY SO WE'D HAVE PLENTY OF TIME!
AND WHERE DID KAGAMI, OR WHATEVER HER NAME IS, GO?!
SHE'S...
BUYING AND EATING SWEETS.
AAAHM!
BABY CASTELLA
EVERY SINGLE ONE OF THEM.
BLOOD THIRST!
OH, COME ON!
AT LEAST LET HER HAVE HER SWEETS!
I DON'T GET IT.

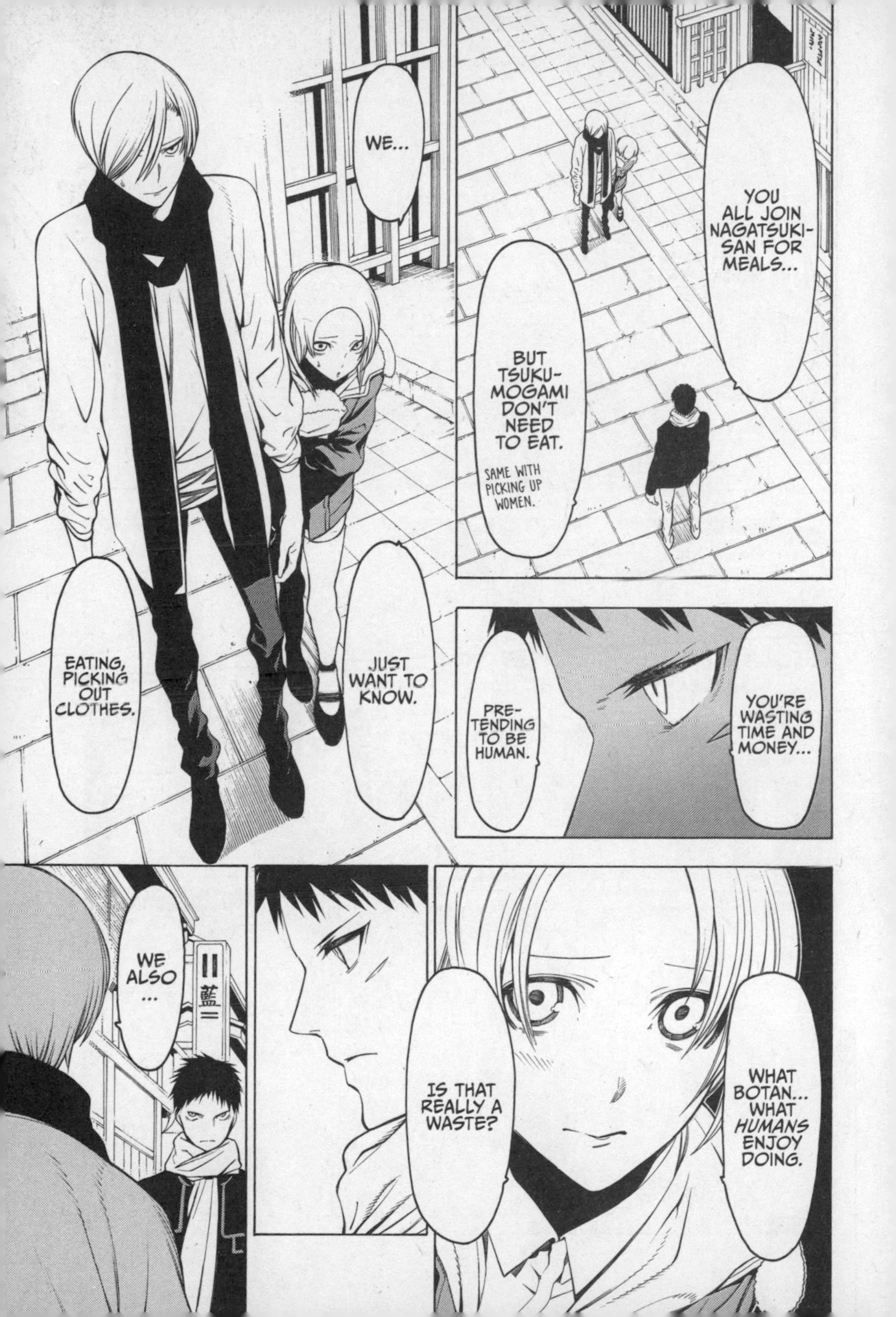

YOU ALL JOIN NAGATSUKI-SAN FOR MEALS...
BUT TSUKU-MOGAMI DON'T NEED TO EAT.
SAME WITH PICKING UP WOMEN.
YOU'RE WASTING TIME AND MONEY...
PRE-TENDING TO BE HUMAN.
WE...
JUST WANT TO KNOW.
EATING, PICKING OUT CLOTHES.
WHAT BOTAN... WHAT *HUMANS* ENJOY DOING.
IS THAT REALLY A WASTE?
WE ALSO ...
藍

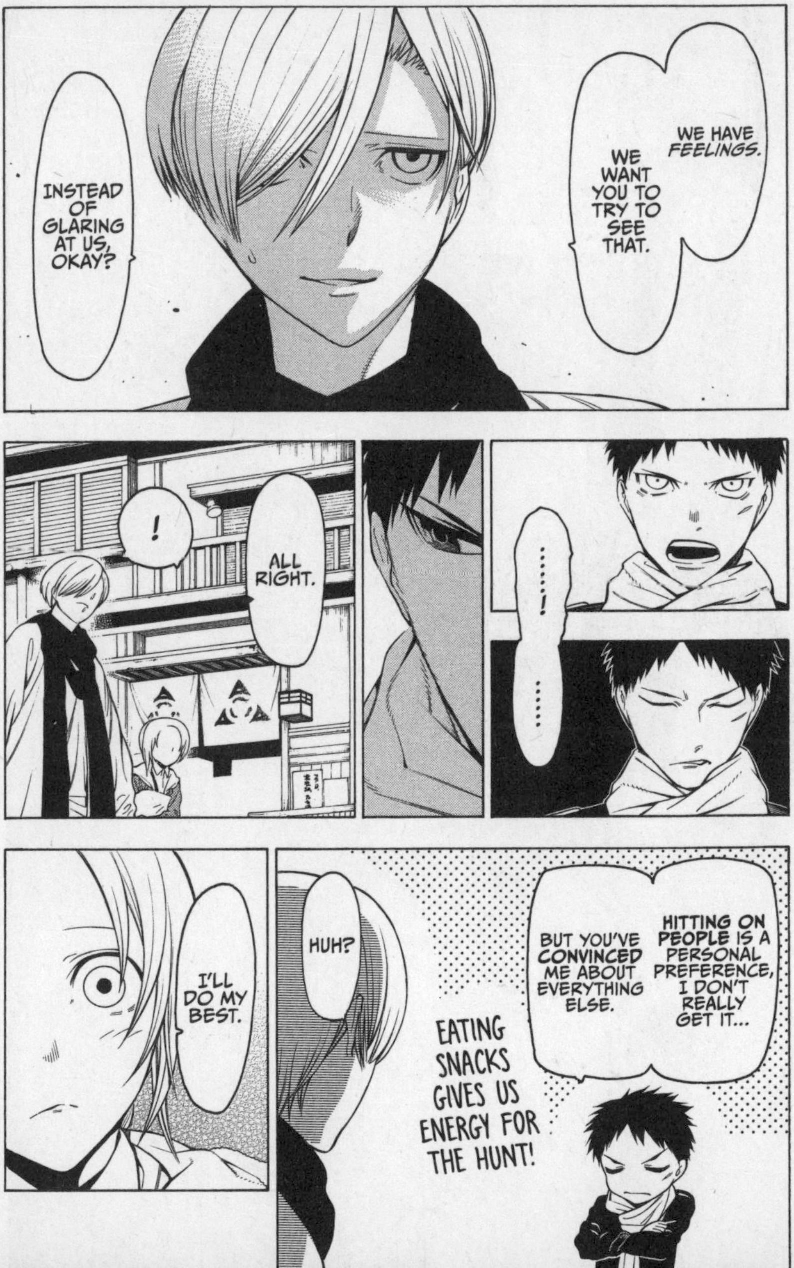
WE HAVE FEELINGS.
WE WANT YOU TO TRY TO SEE THAT.
INSTEAD OF GLARING AT US, OKAY?
......!
......
ALL RIGHT.
!
HITTING ON PEOPLE IS A PERSONAL PREFERENCE, I DON'T REALLY GET IT...
BUT YOU'VE CONVINCED ME ABOUT EVERYTHING ELSE.
EATING SNACKS GIVES US ENERGY FOR THE HUNT!
HUH?
I'LL DO MY BEST.

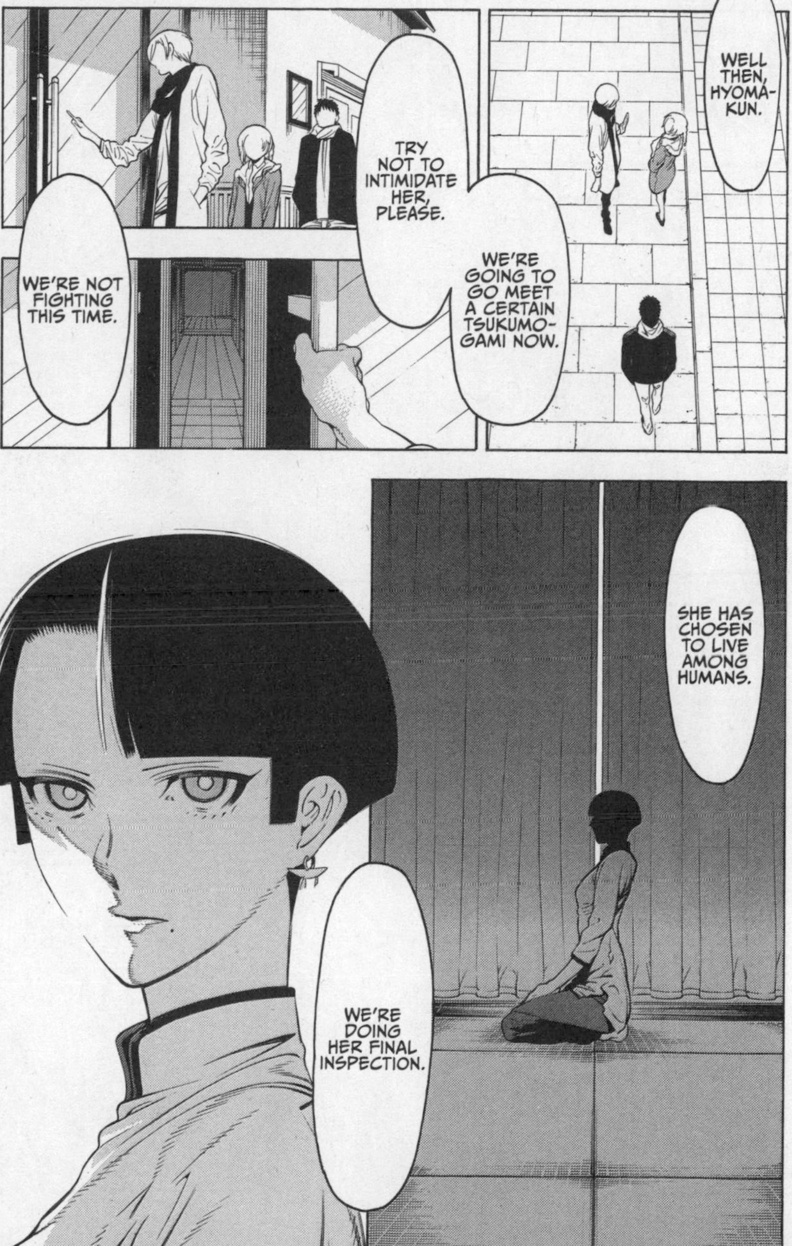
WELL THEN, HYOMA-KUN.
WE'RE GOING TO GO MEET A CERTAIN TSUKUMOGAMI NOW.
TRY NOT TO INTIMIDATE HER, PLEASE.
WE'RE NOT FIGHTING THIS TIME.
SHE HAS CHOSEN TO LIVE AMONG HUMANS.
WE'RE DOING HER FINAL INSPECTION.

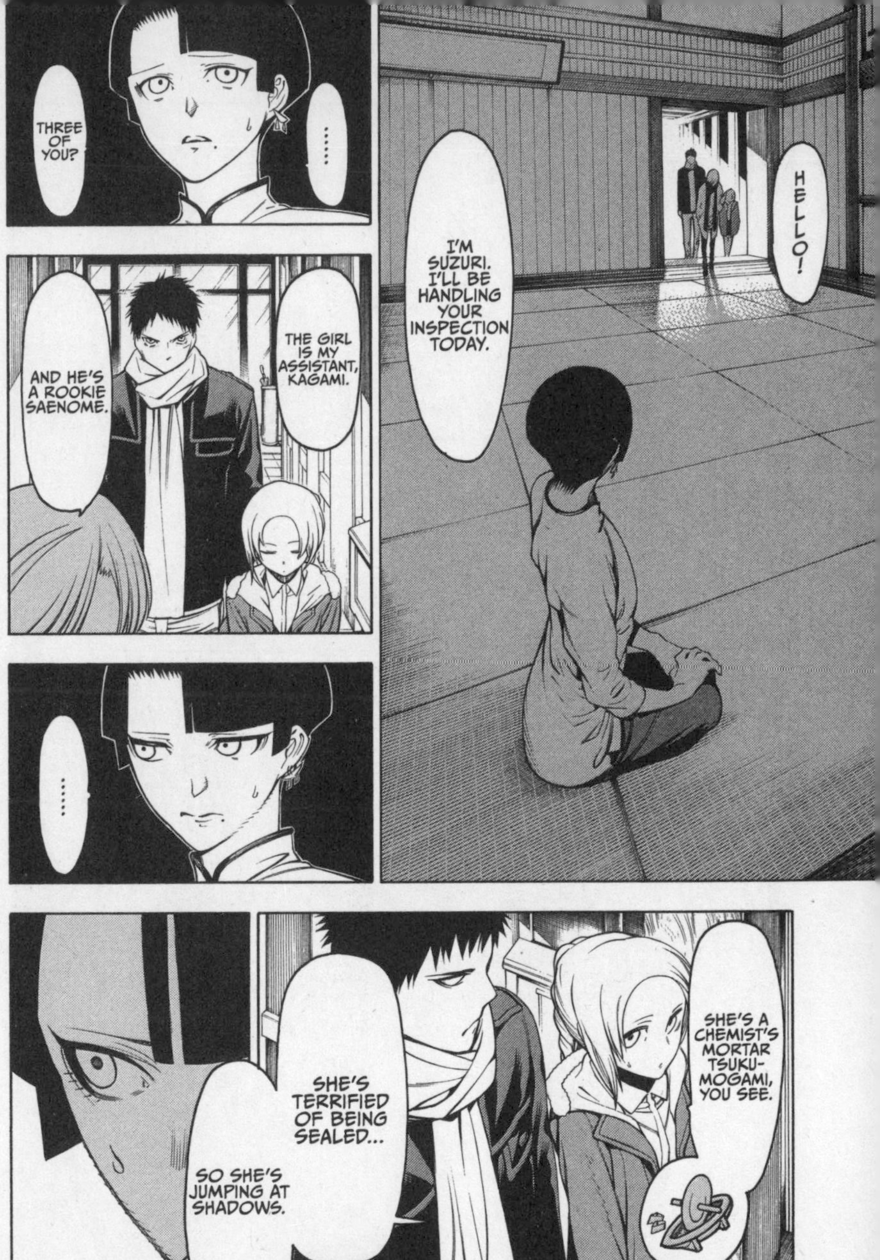
HELLO!
I'M SUZURI. I'LL BE HANDLING YOUR INSPECTION TODAY.
......
THREE OF YOU?
THE GIRL IS MY ASSISTANT, KAGAMI.
AND HE'S A ROOKIE SAENOME.
......
SHE'S A CHEMIST'S MORTAR TSUKU-MOGAMI, YOU SEE.
SHE'S TERRIFIED OF BEING SEALED...
SO SHE'S JUMPING AT SHADOWS.

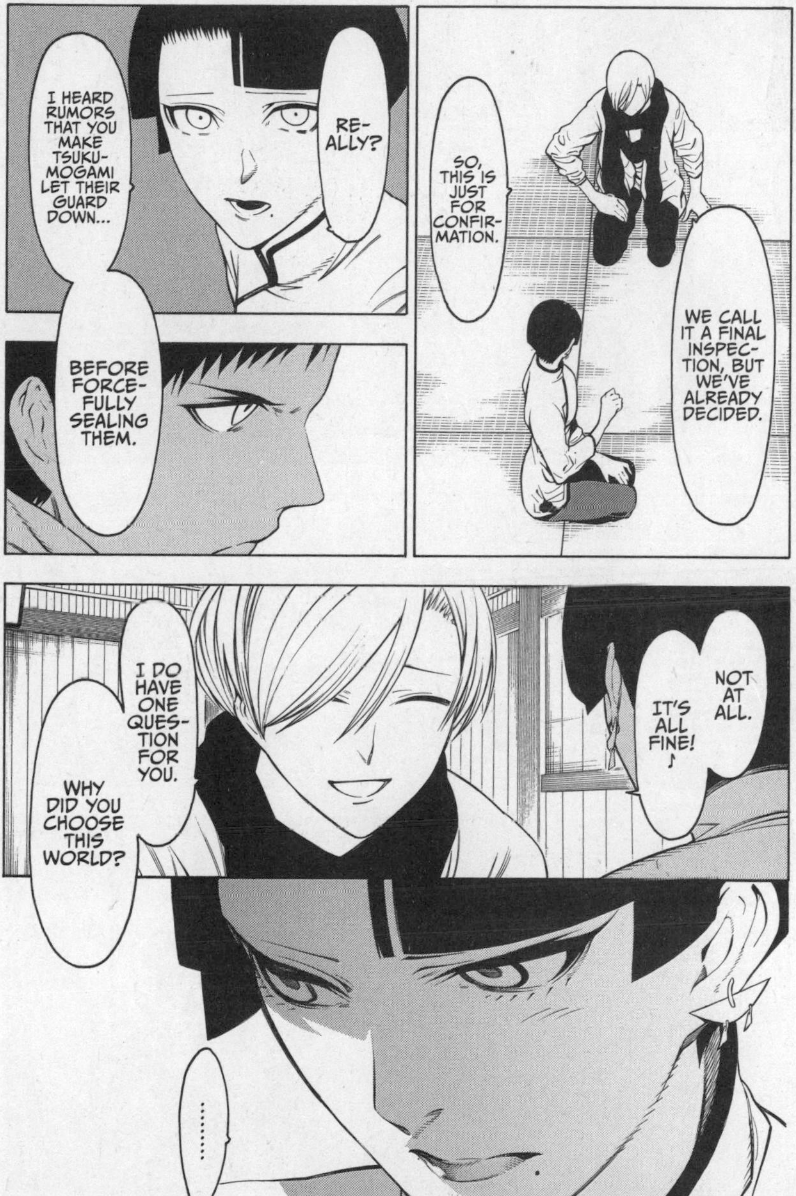
WE CALL IT A FINAL INSPECTION, BUT WE'VE ALREADY DECIDED.
SO, THIS IS JUST FOR CONFIRMATION.
RE-ALLY?
I HEARD RUMORS THAT YOU MAKE TSUKUMOGAMI LET THEIR GUARD DOWN...
BEFORE FORCEFULLY SEALING THEM.
NOT AT ALL.
IT'S ALL FINE! ♪
I DO HAVE ONE QUESTION FOR YOU.
WHY DID YOU CHOOSE THIS WORLD?
......

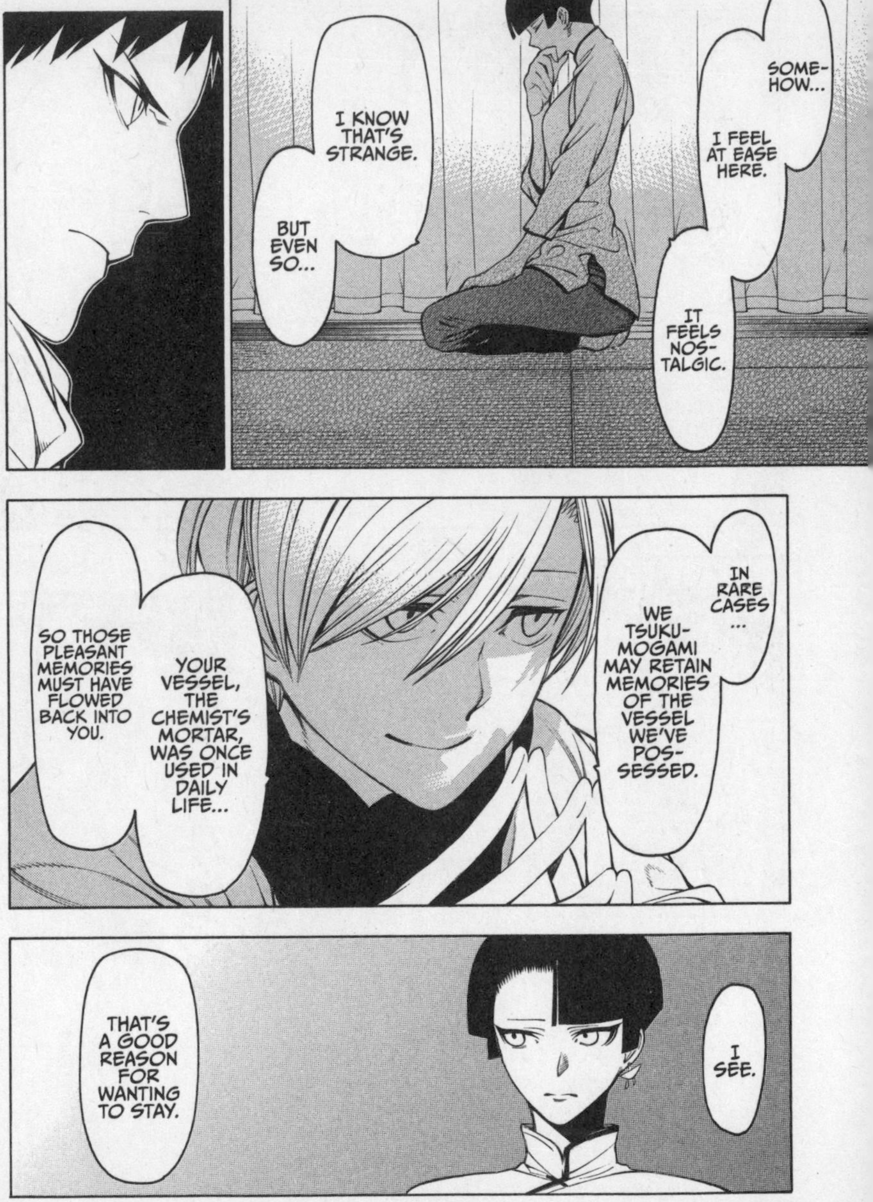
SOMEHOW...
I FEEL AT EASE HERE.
IT FEELS NOSTALGIC.
I KNOW THAT'S STRANGE.
BUT EVEN SO...
IN RARE CASES...
WE TSUKUMOGAMI MAY RETAIN MEMORIES OF THE VESSEL WE'VE POSSESSED.
YOUR VESSEL, THE CHEMIST'S MORTAR, WAS ONCE USED IN DAILY LIFE...
SO THOSE PLEASANT MEMORIES MUST HAVE FLOWED BACK INTO YOU.
I SEE.
THAT'S A GOOD REASON FOR WANTING TO STAY.

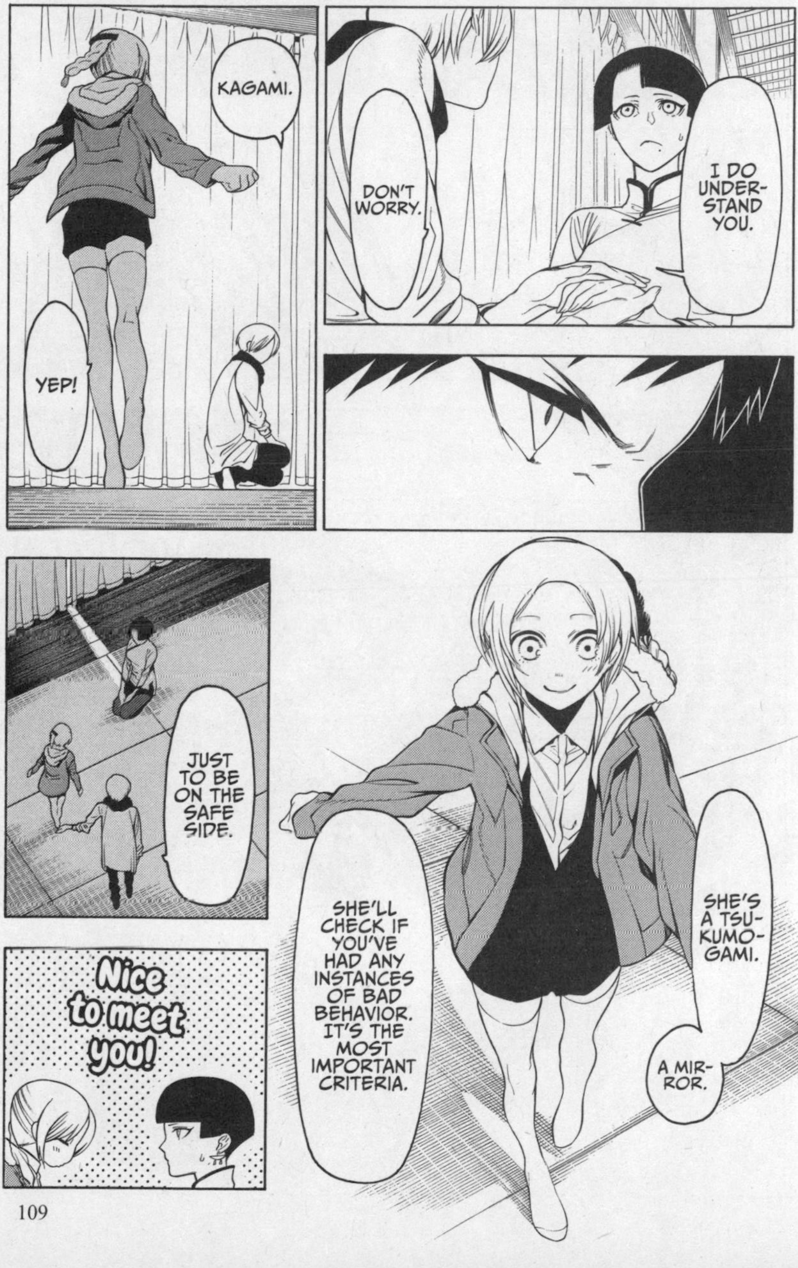
I DO UNDERSTAND YOU.
DON'T WORRY.
KAGAMI.
YEP!
SHE'S A TSUKUMOGAMI.
A MIRROR.
SHE'LL CHECK IF YOU'VE HAD ANY INSTANCES OF BAD BEHAVIOR. IT'S THE MOST IMPORTANT CRITERIA.
JUST TO BE ON THE SAFE SIDE.
Nice to meet you!

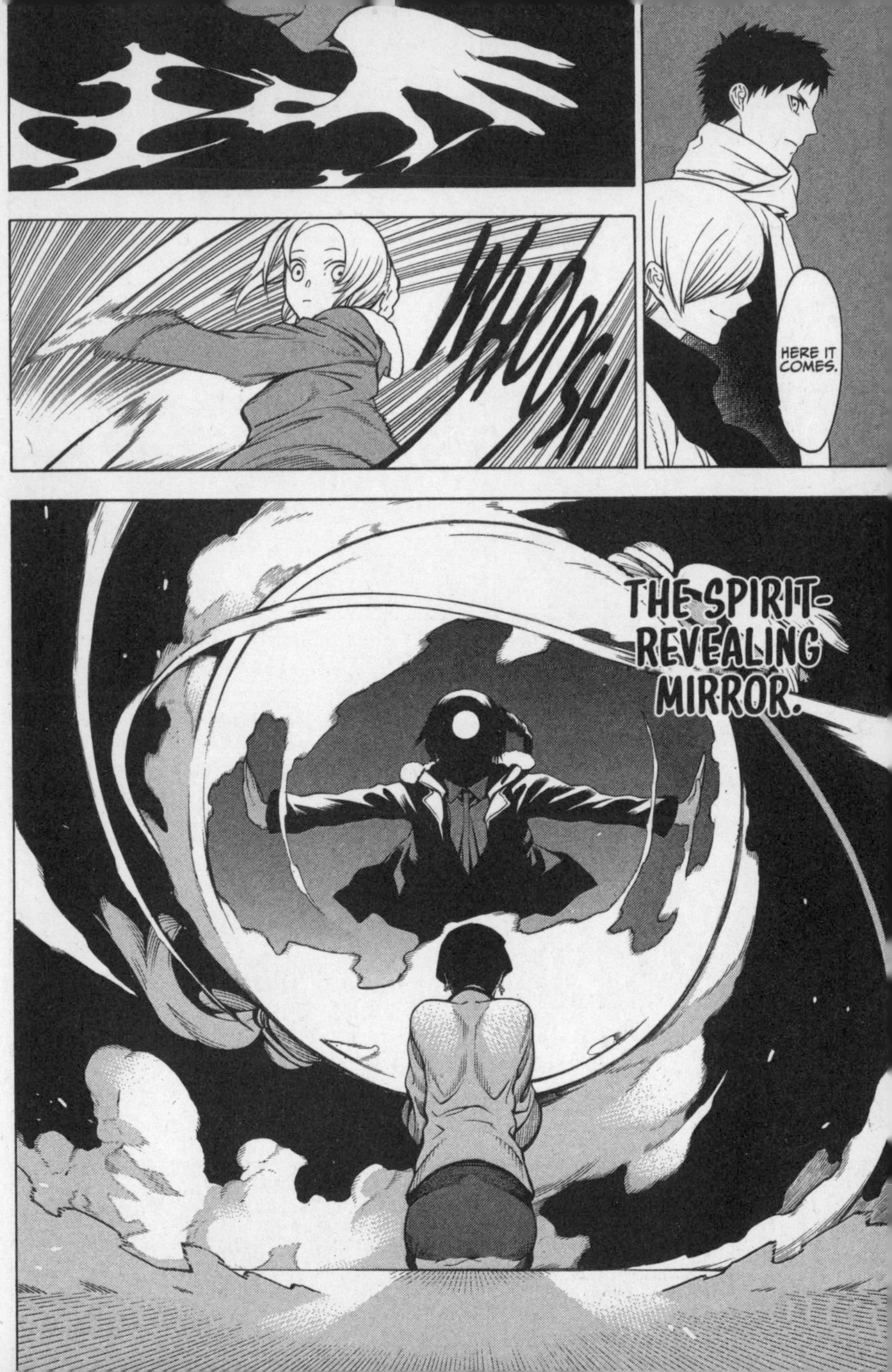
HERE IT COMES.
WHOOSH
THE SPIRIT-REVEALING MIRROR.

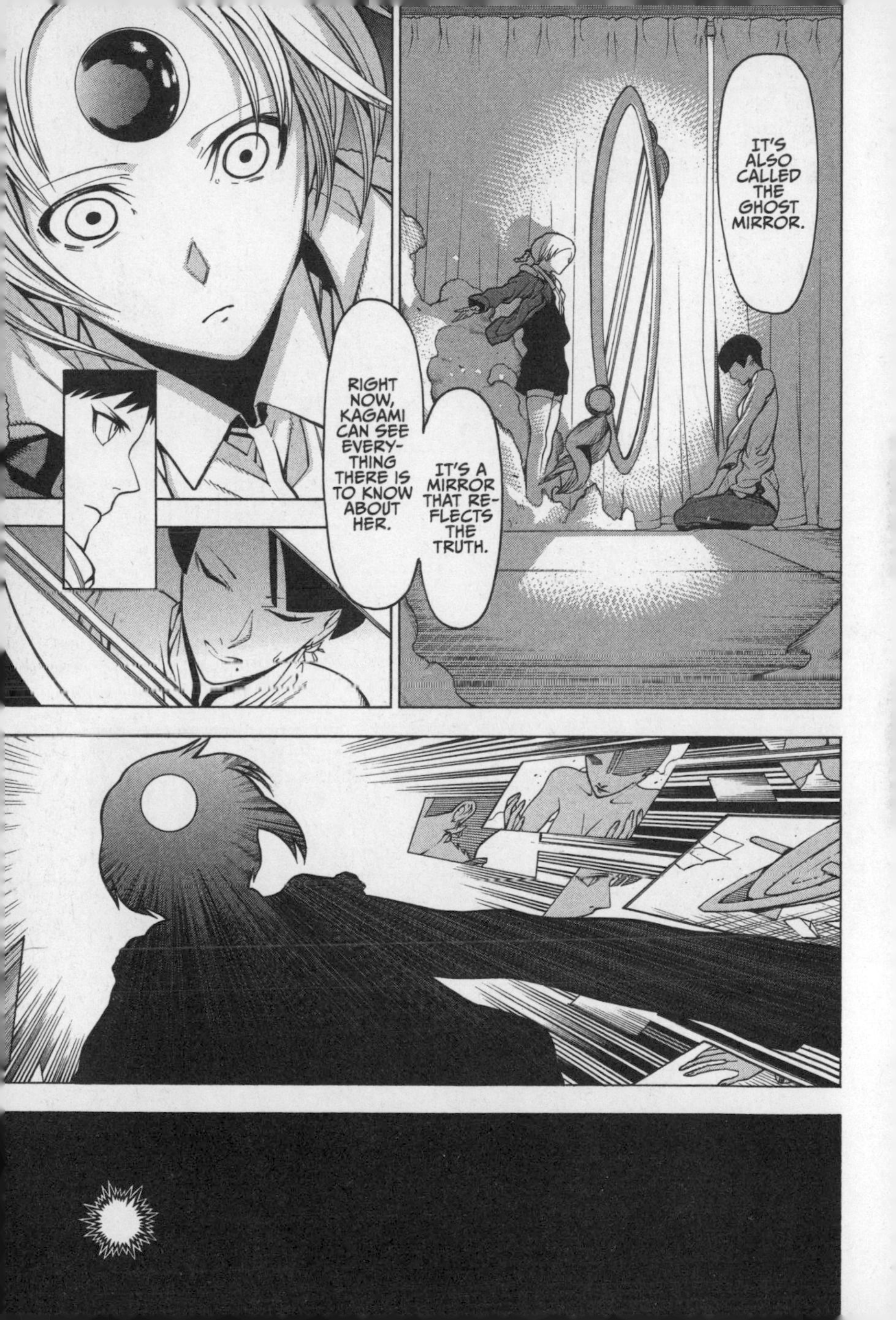
IT'S ALSO CALLED THE GHOST MIRROR.
IT'S A MIRROR THAT RE-FLECTS THE TRUTH.
RIGHT NOW, KAGAMI CAN SEE EVERY-THING THERE IS TO KNOW ABOUT HER.

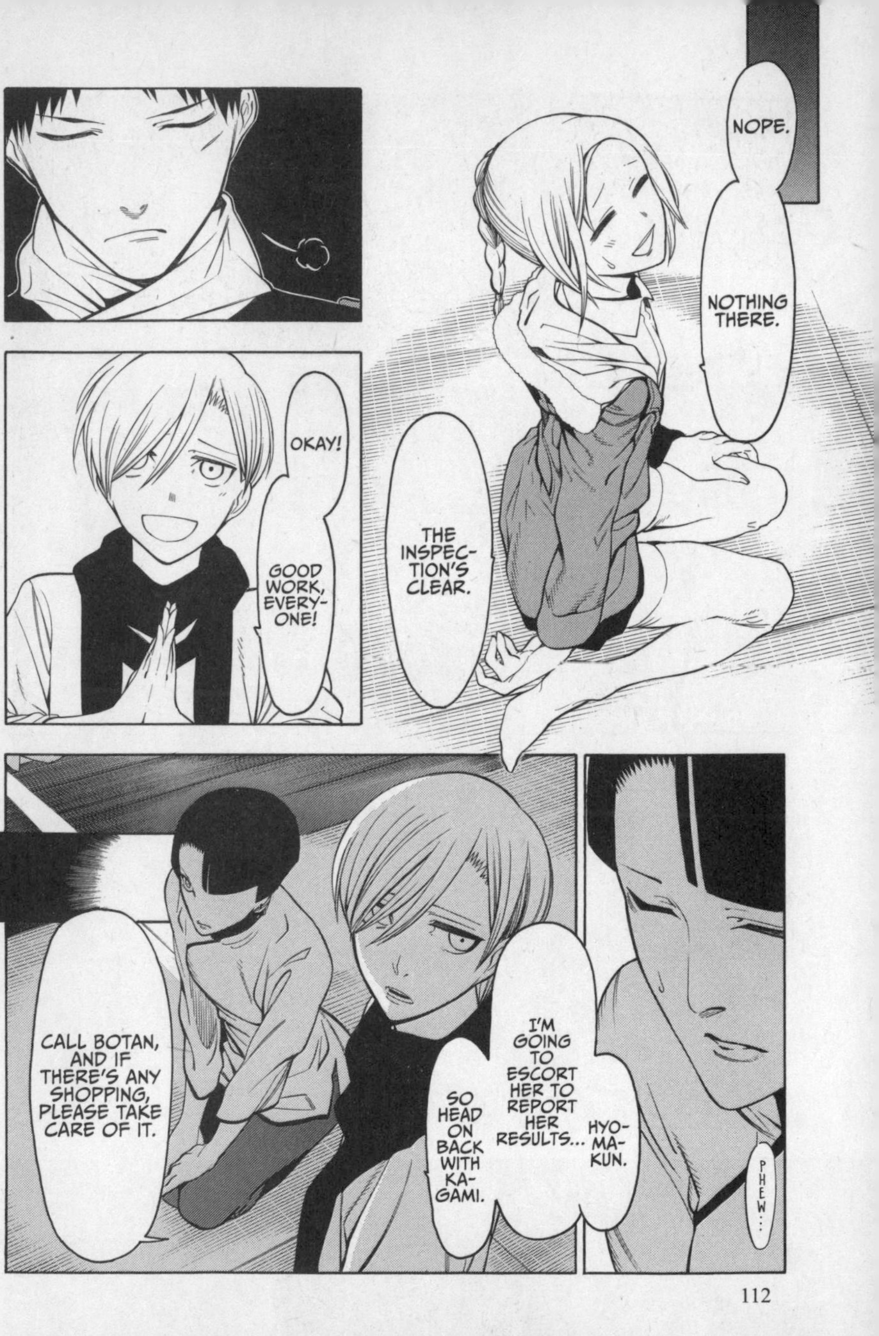
NOPE.
NOTHING THERE.
THE INSPECTION'S CLEAR.
OKAY!
GOOD WORK, EVERYONE!
PHEW...
HYOMA-KUN.
I'M GOING TO ESCORT HER TO REPORT HER RESULTS...
SO HEAD ON BACK WITH KAGAMI.
CALL BOTAN, AND IF THERE'S ANY SHOPPING, PLEASE TAKE CARE OF IT.

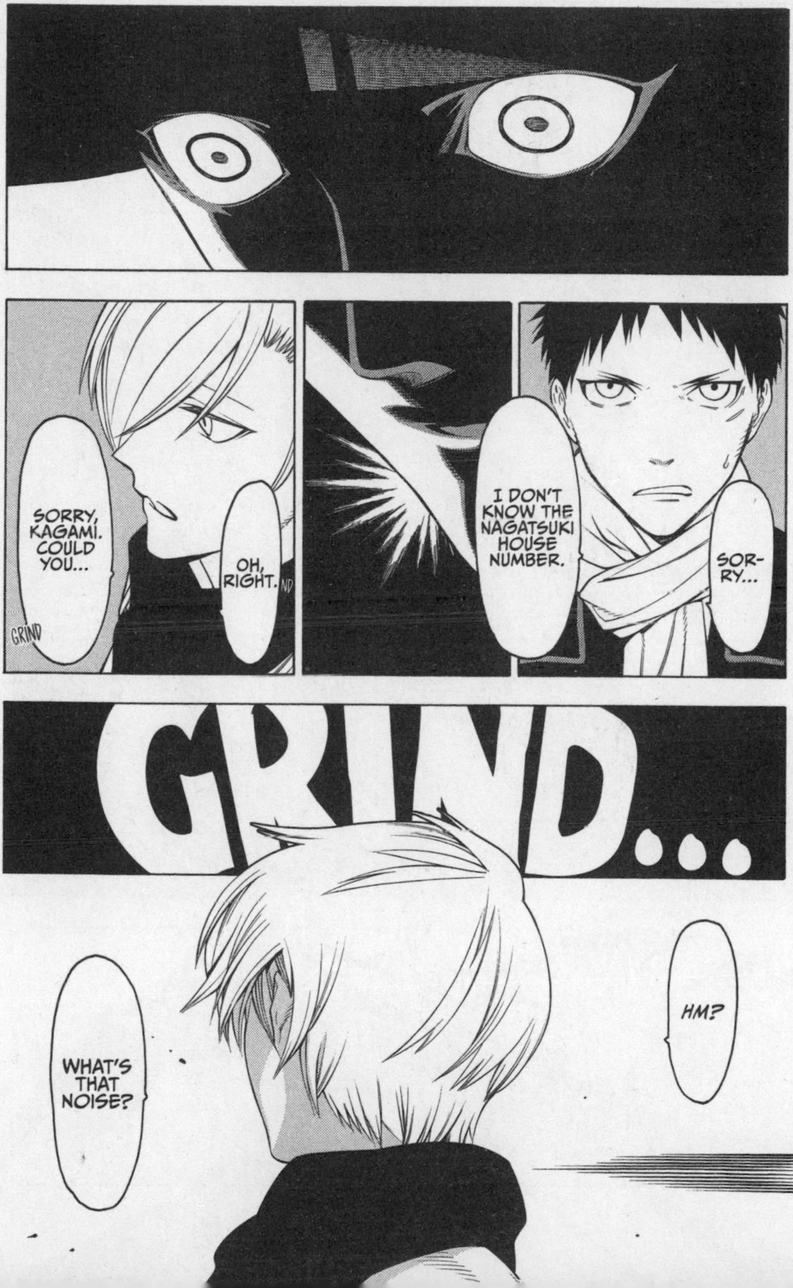
SORRY...
I DON'T KNOW THE NAGATSUKI HOUSE NUMBER.
OH, RIGHT.
SORRY, KAGAMI. COULD YOU...
GRIND
GRIND...
HM?
WHAT'S THAT NOISE?

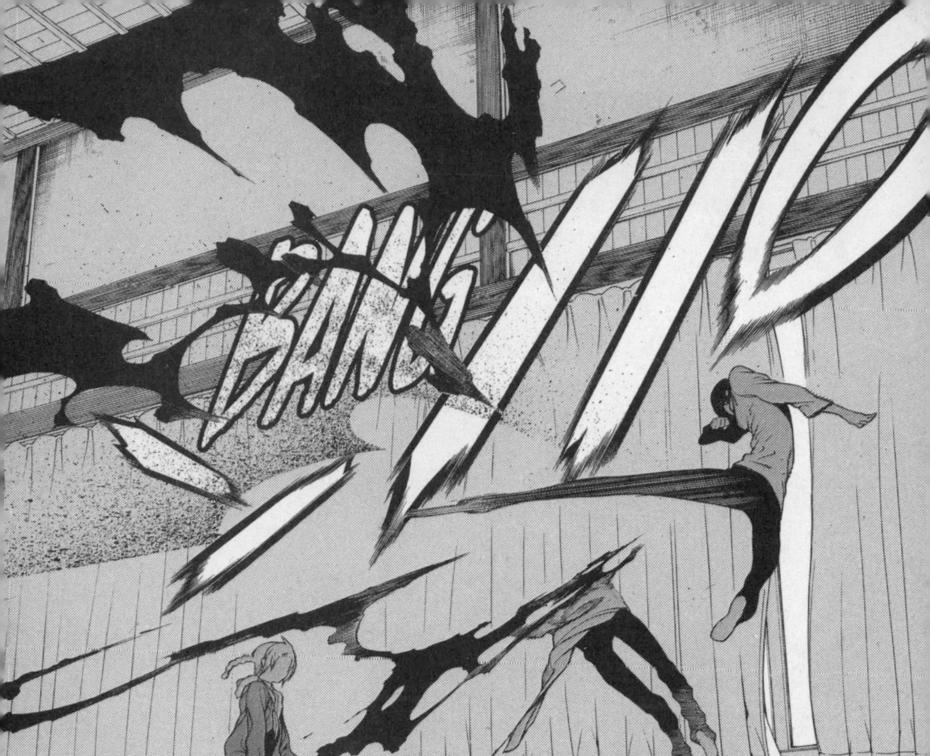
BANG

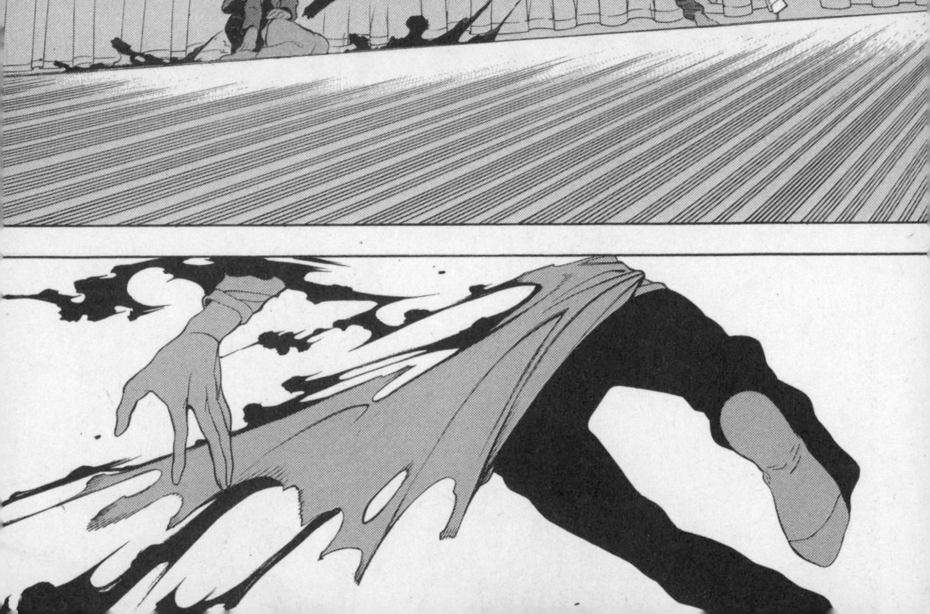

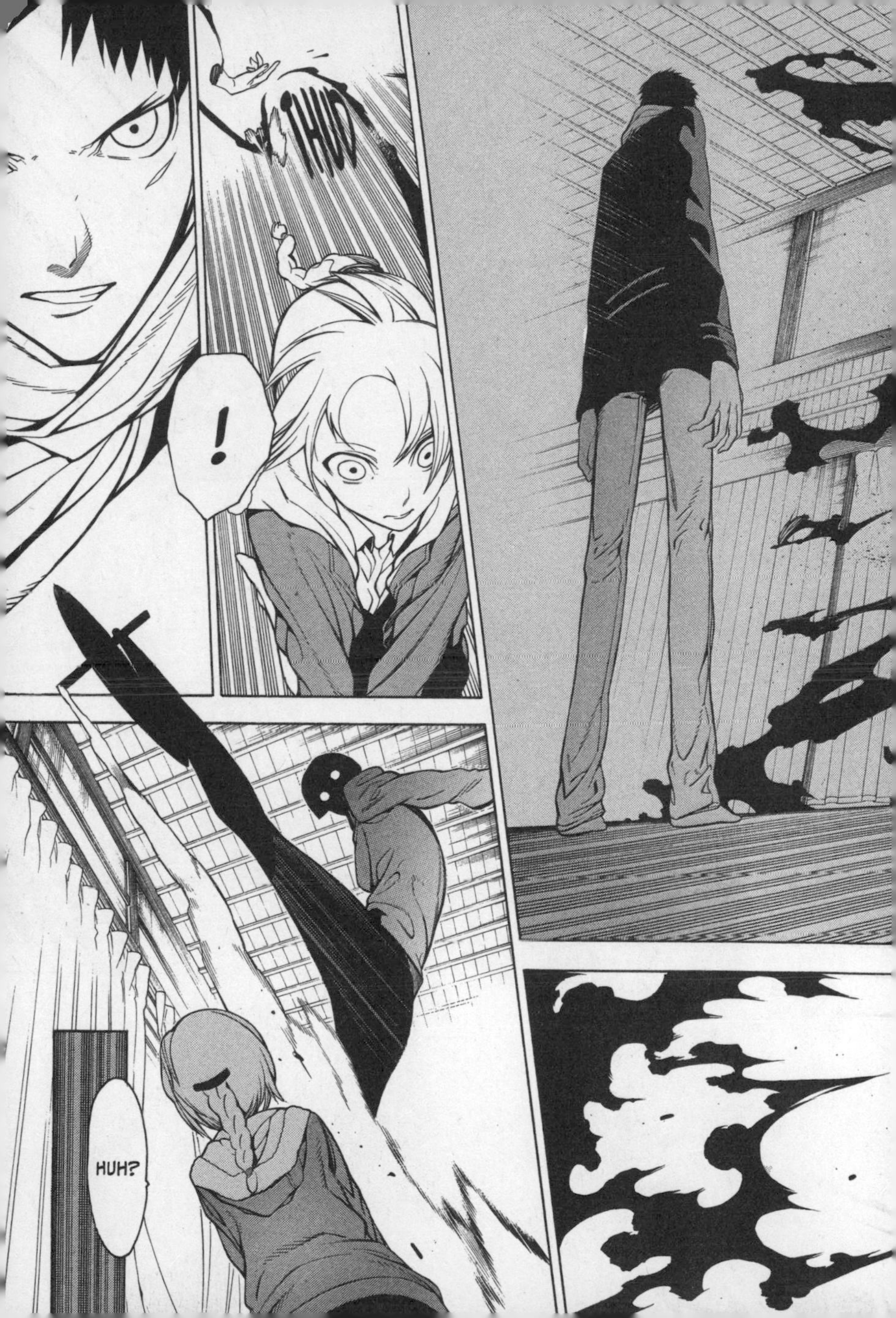
THUD
!
HUH?

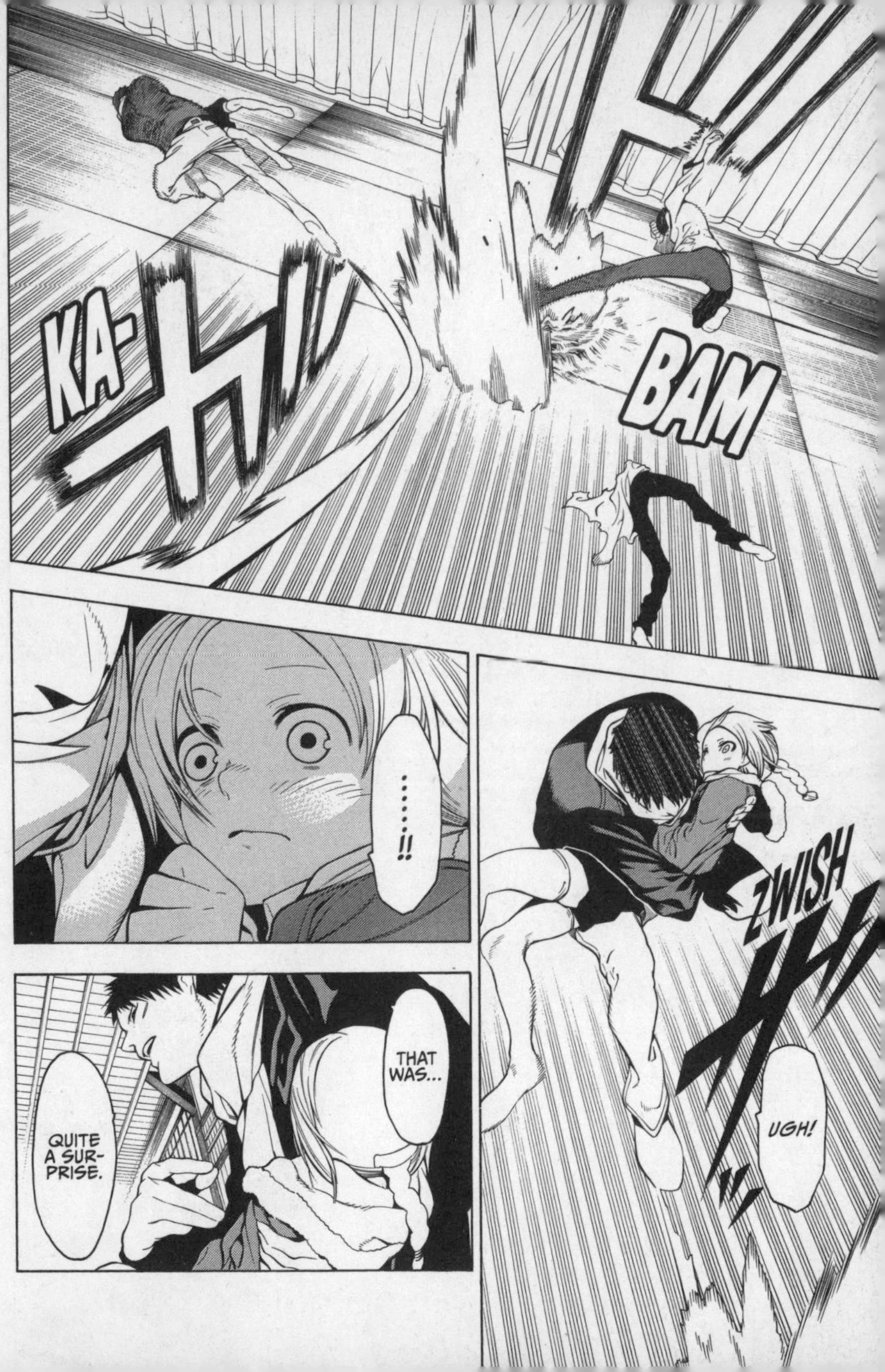
BAM
KA-
ZWISH
UGH!
......!!
THAT WAS...
QUITE A SUR-PRISE.

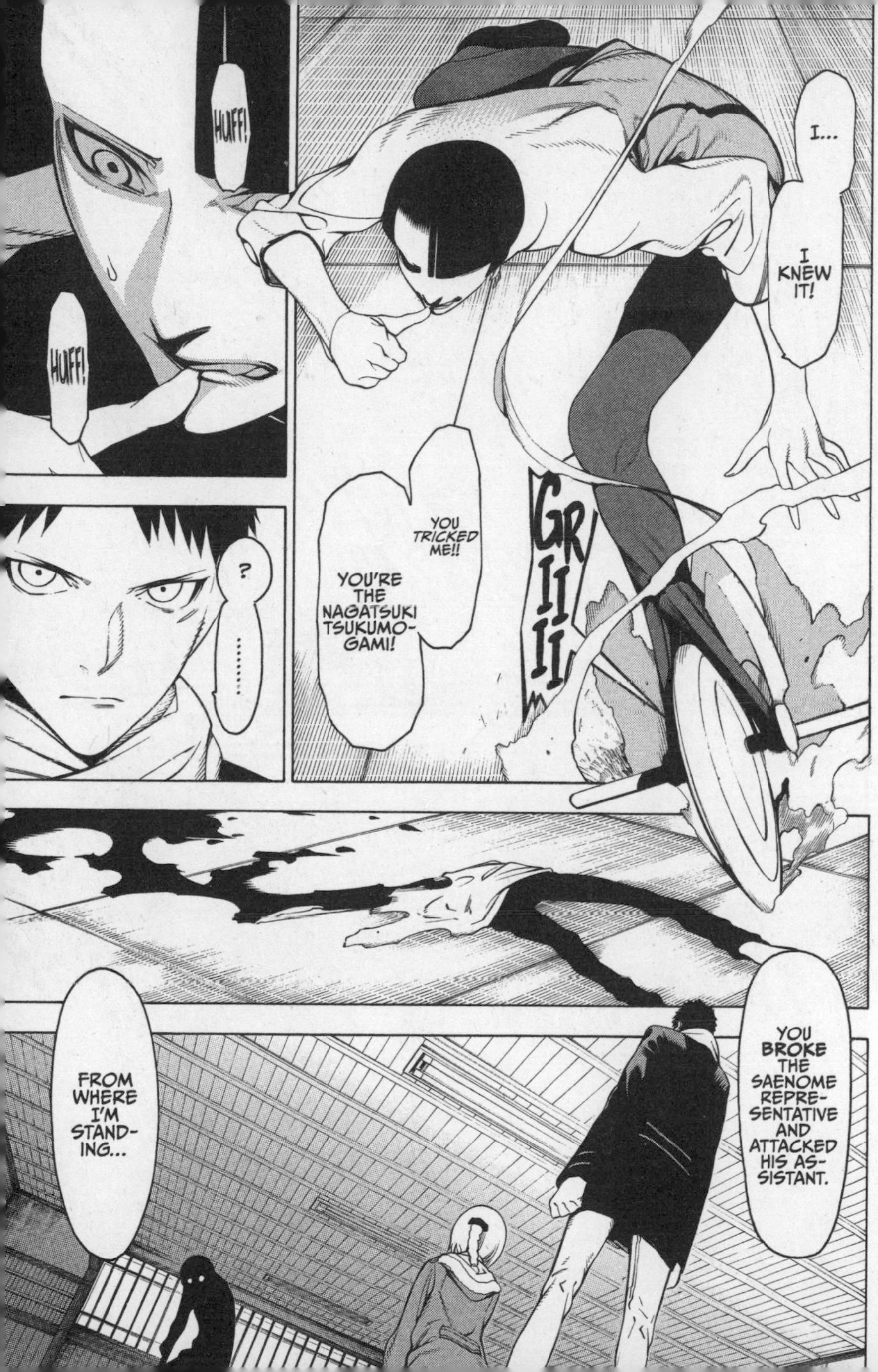
I...
I KNEW IT!
GRIIII
YOU TRICKED ME!!
YOU'RE THE NAGATSUKI TSUKUMO-GAMI!
HUFF!
HUFF!
?
......
YOU BROKE THE SAENOME REPRE-SENTATIVE AND ATTACKED HIS AS-SISTANT.
FROM WHERE I'M STAND-ING...

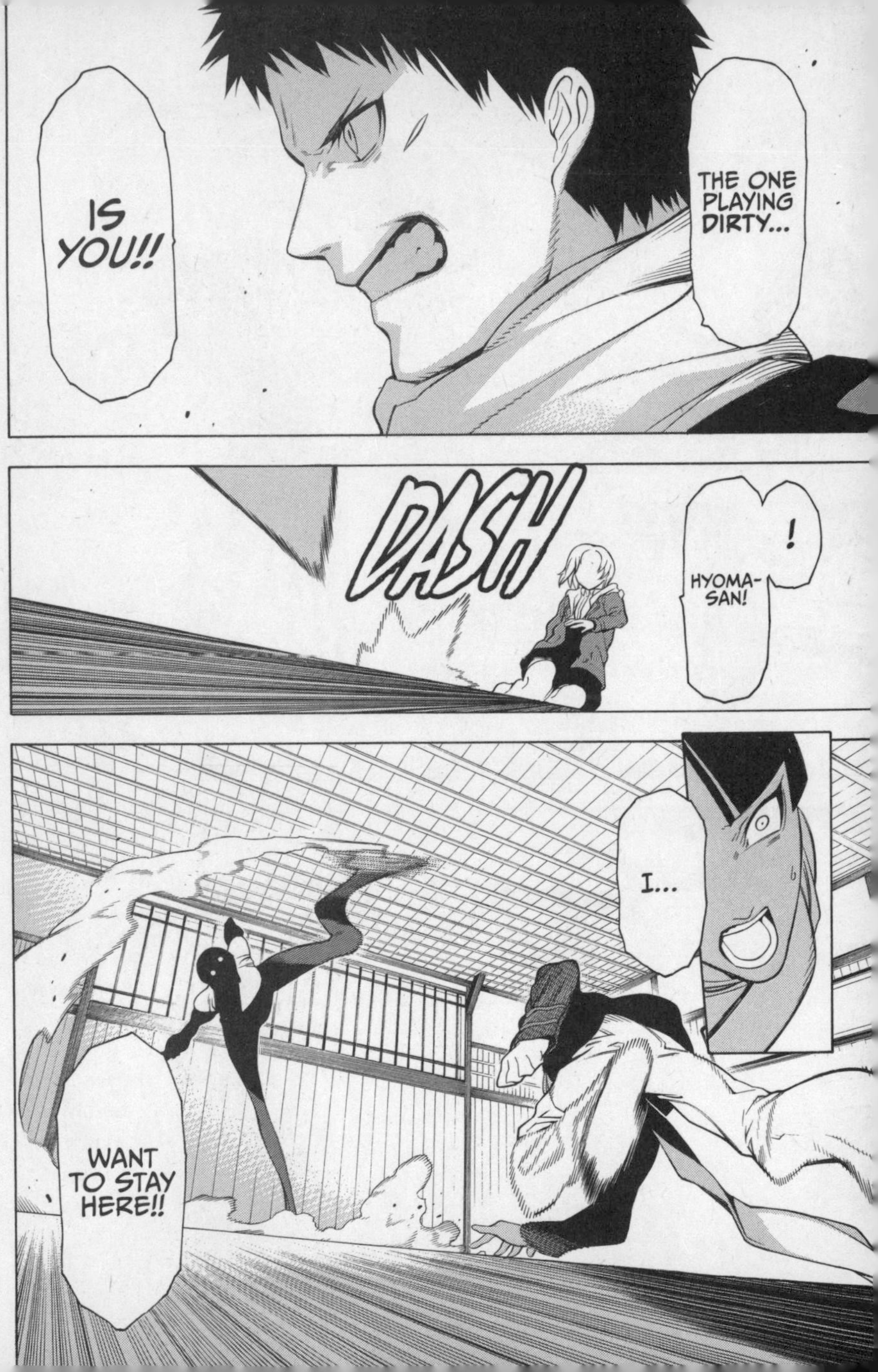
THE ONE PLAYING DIRTY...
IS YOU!!
!
HYOMA-SAN!
DASH
I...
WANT TO STAY HERE!!

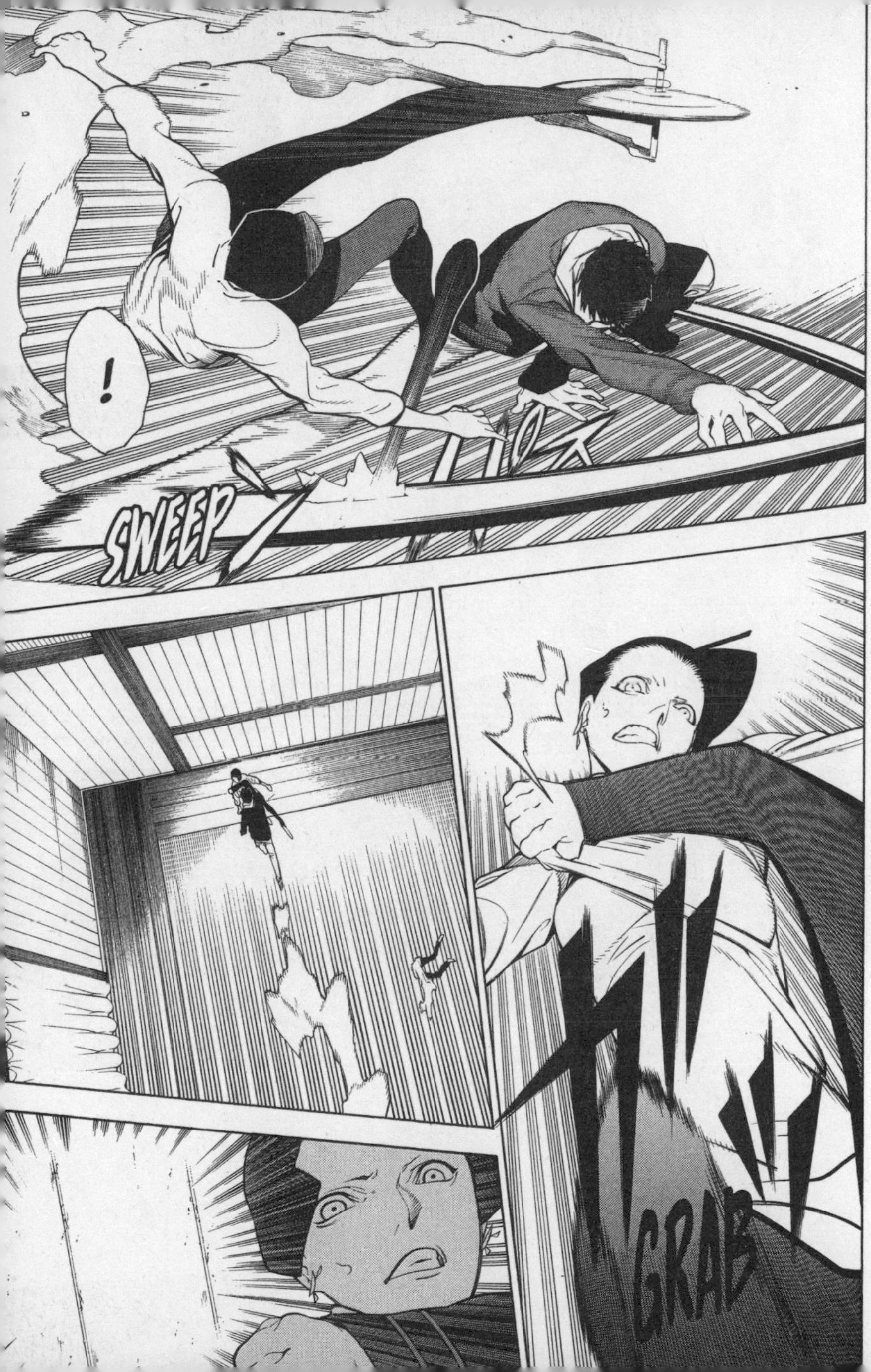
!
SWEEP
GRAB

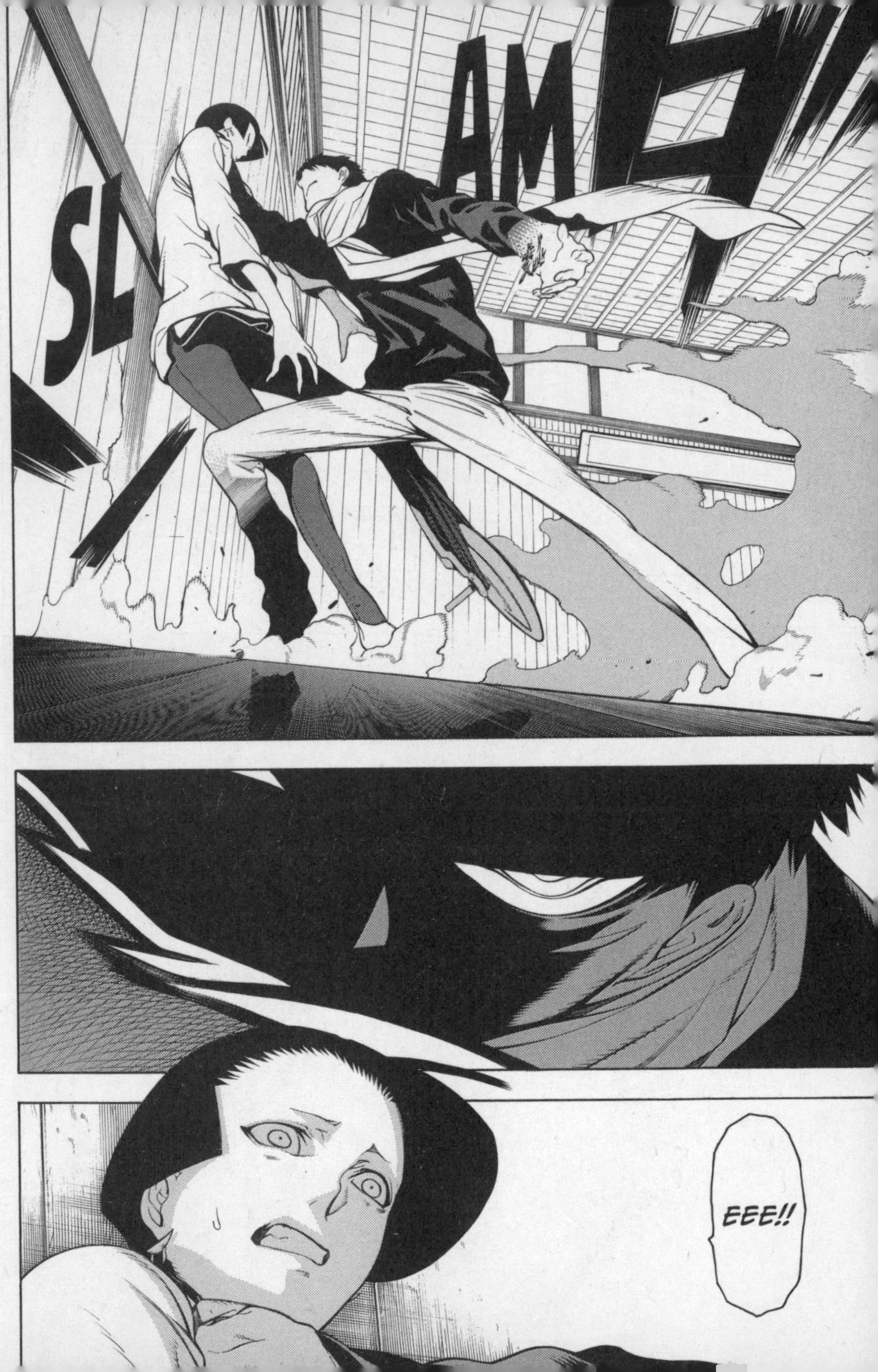
SLAM
EEE!!

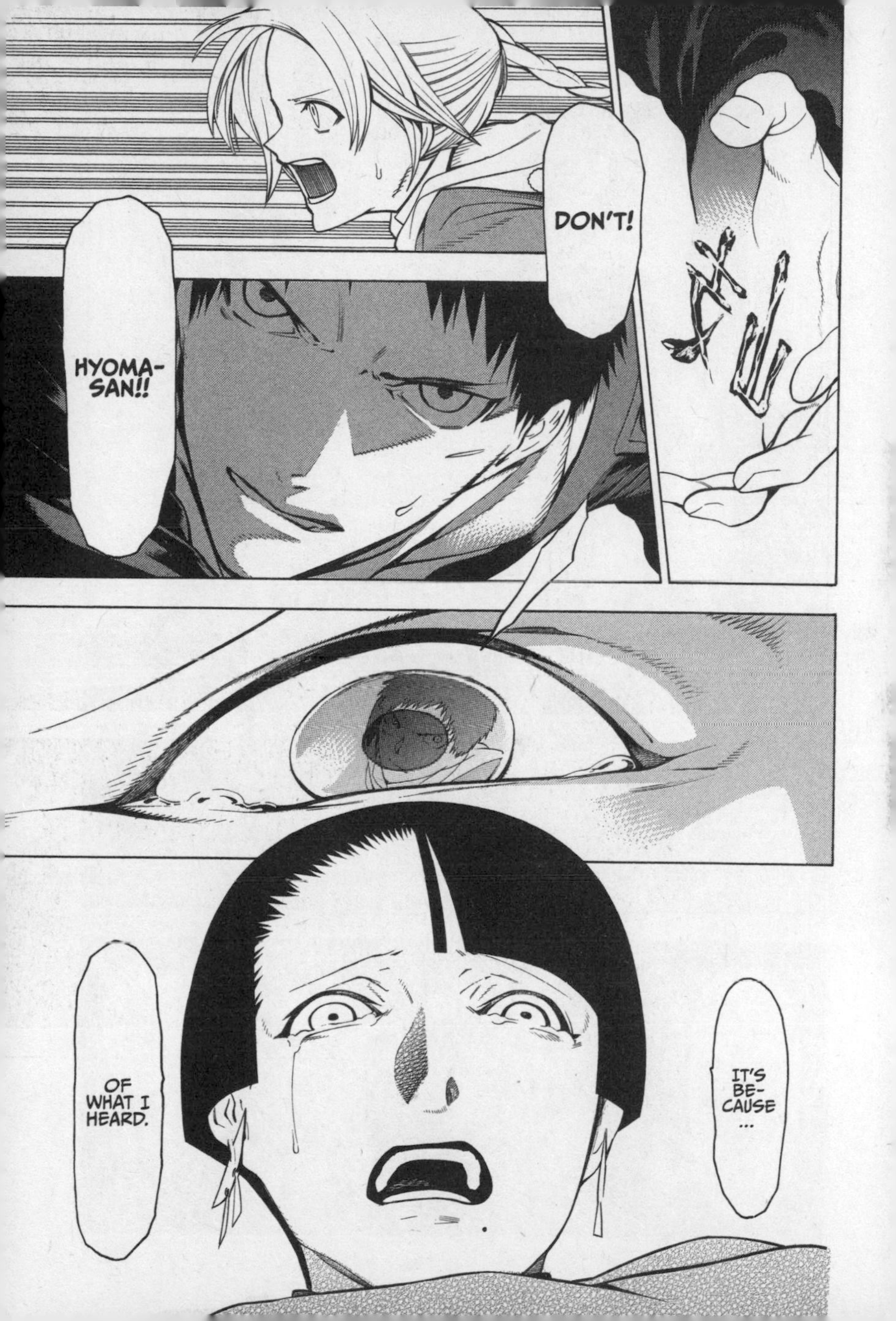
DON'T!
HYOMA-SAN!!
IT'S BE-CAUSE ...
OF WHAT I HEARD.

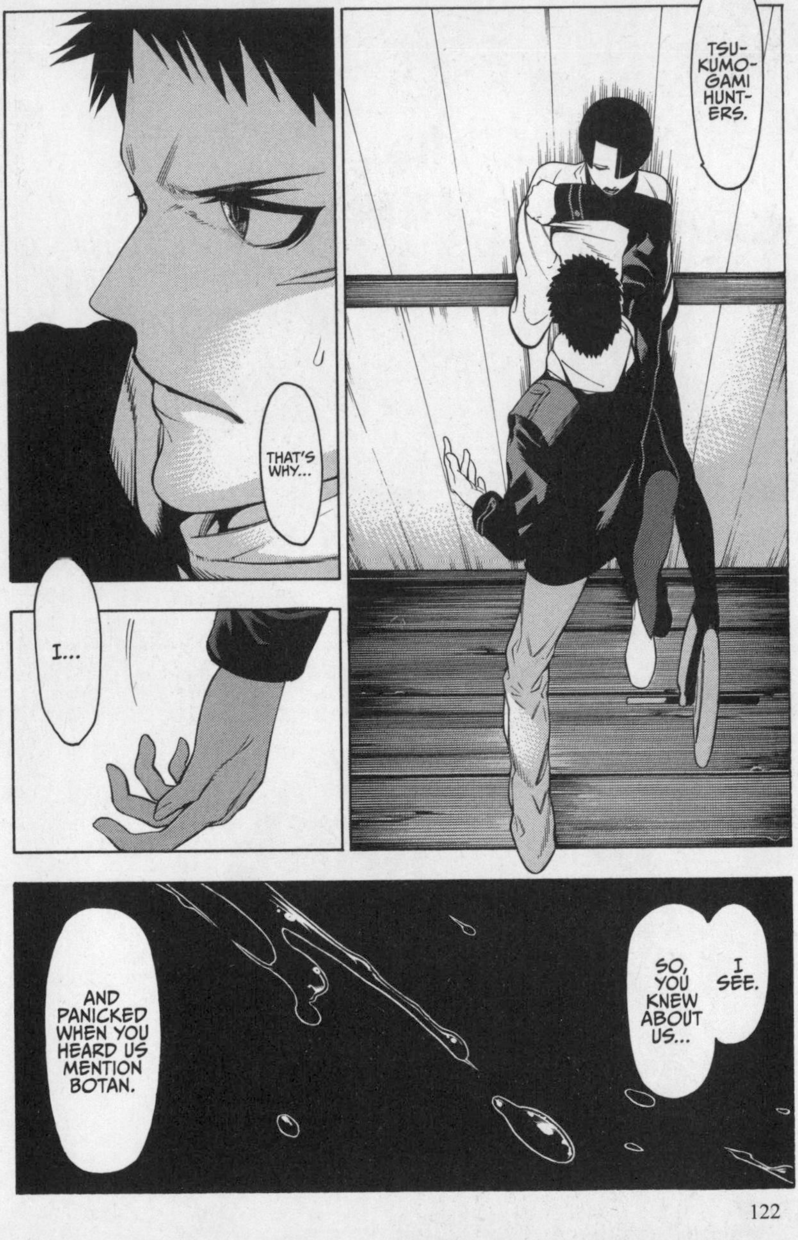
TSU-KUMO-GAMI HUNT-ERS.
THAT'S WHY...
I...
I SEE.
SO, YOU KNEW ABOUT US...
AND PANICKED WHEN YOU HEARD US MENTION BOTAN.

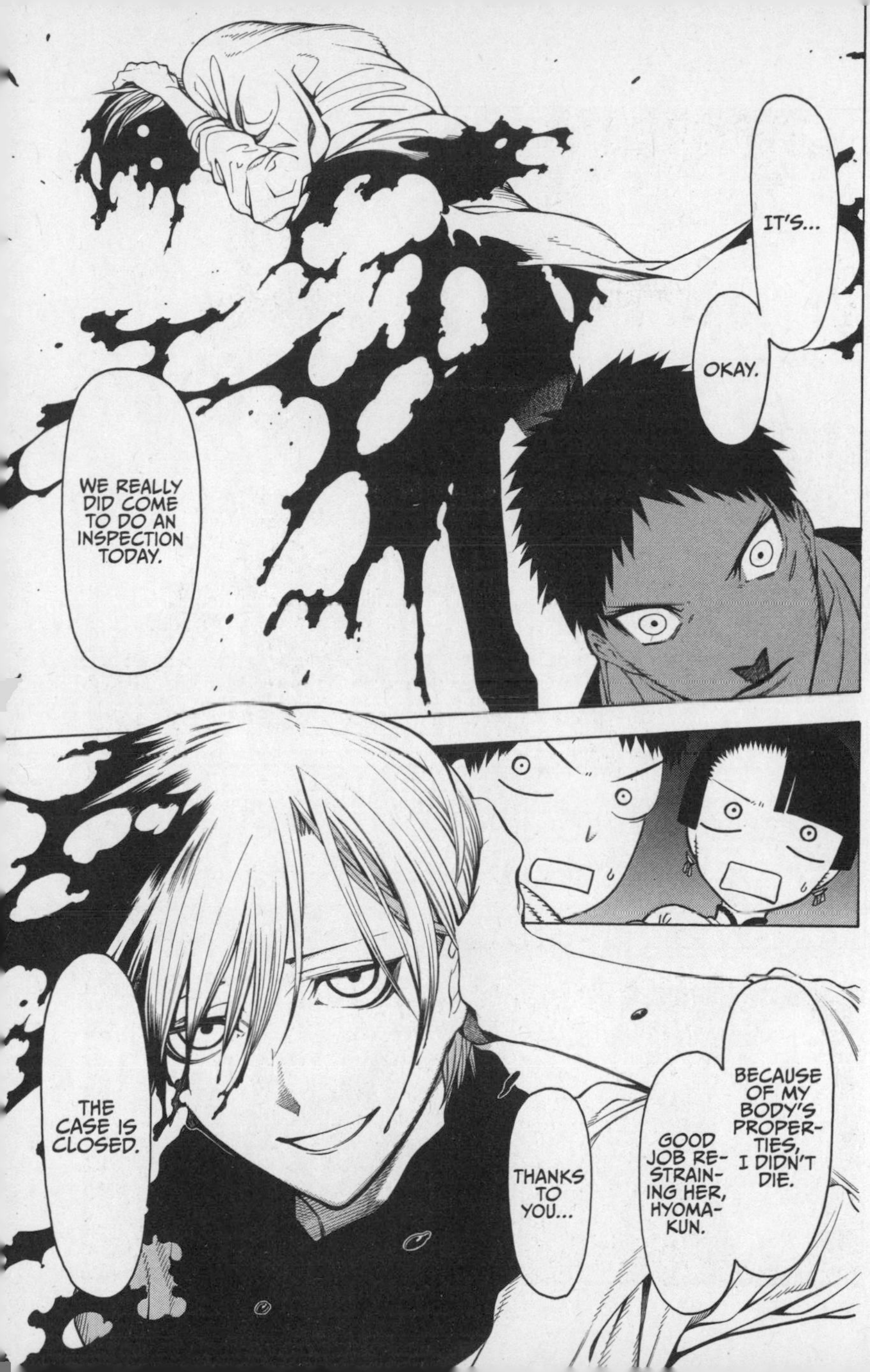
IT'S...
OKAY.
WE REALLY DID COME TO DO AN INSPECTION TODAY.
BECAUSE OF MY BODY'S PROPER-TIES, I DIDN'T DIE.
GOOD JOB RE-STRAIN-ING HER, HYOMA-KUN.
THANKS TO YOU...
THE CASE IS CLOSED.

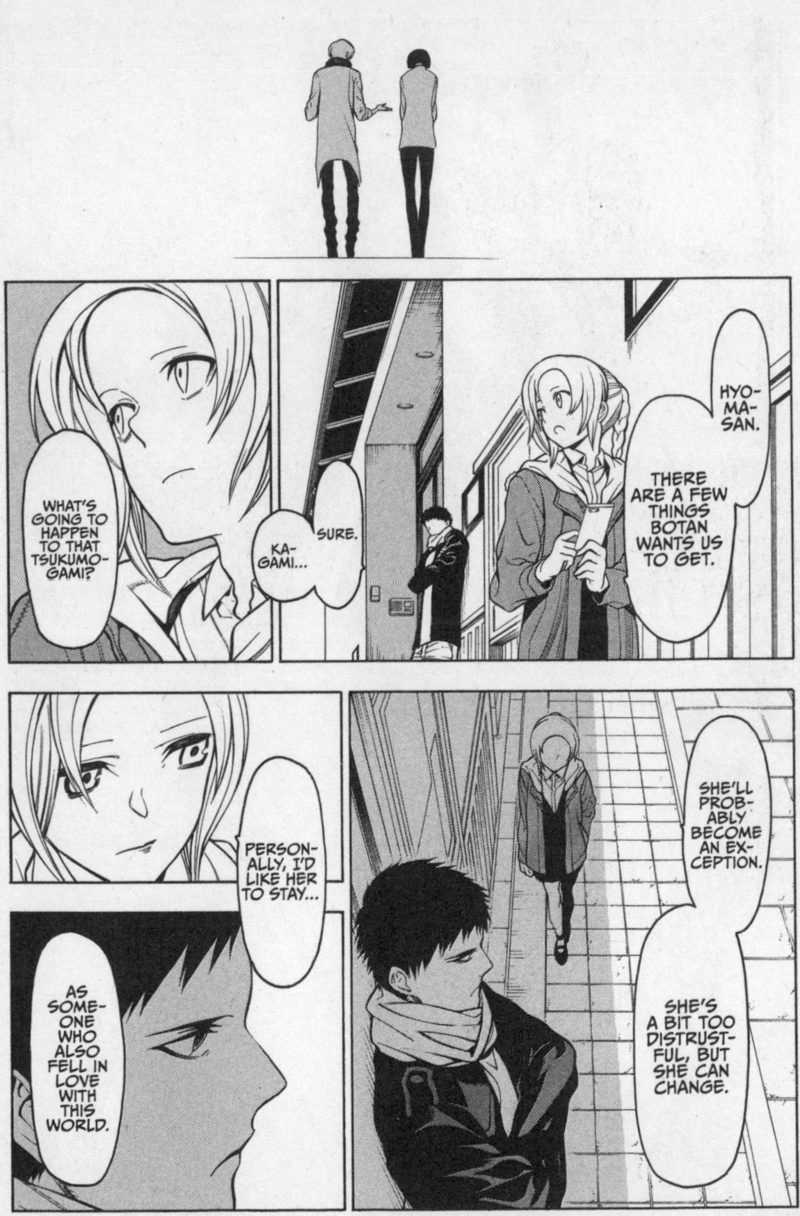
HYO-MA-SAN.
THERE ARE A FEW THINGS BOTAN WANTS US TO GET.
SURE.
KA-GAMI...
WHAT'S GOING TO HAPPEN TO THAT TSUKUMO-GAMI?
SHE'LL PROB-ABLY BECOME AN EX-CEPTION.
SHE'S A BIT TOO DISTRUST-FUL, BUT SHE CAN CHANGE.
PERSON-ALLY, I'D LIKE HER TO STAY...
AS SOME-ONE WHO ALSO FELL IN LOVE WITH THIS WORLD.

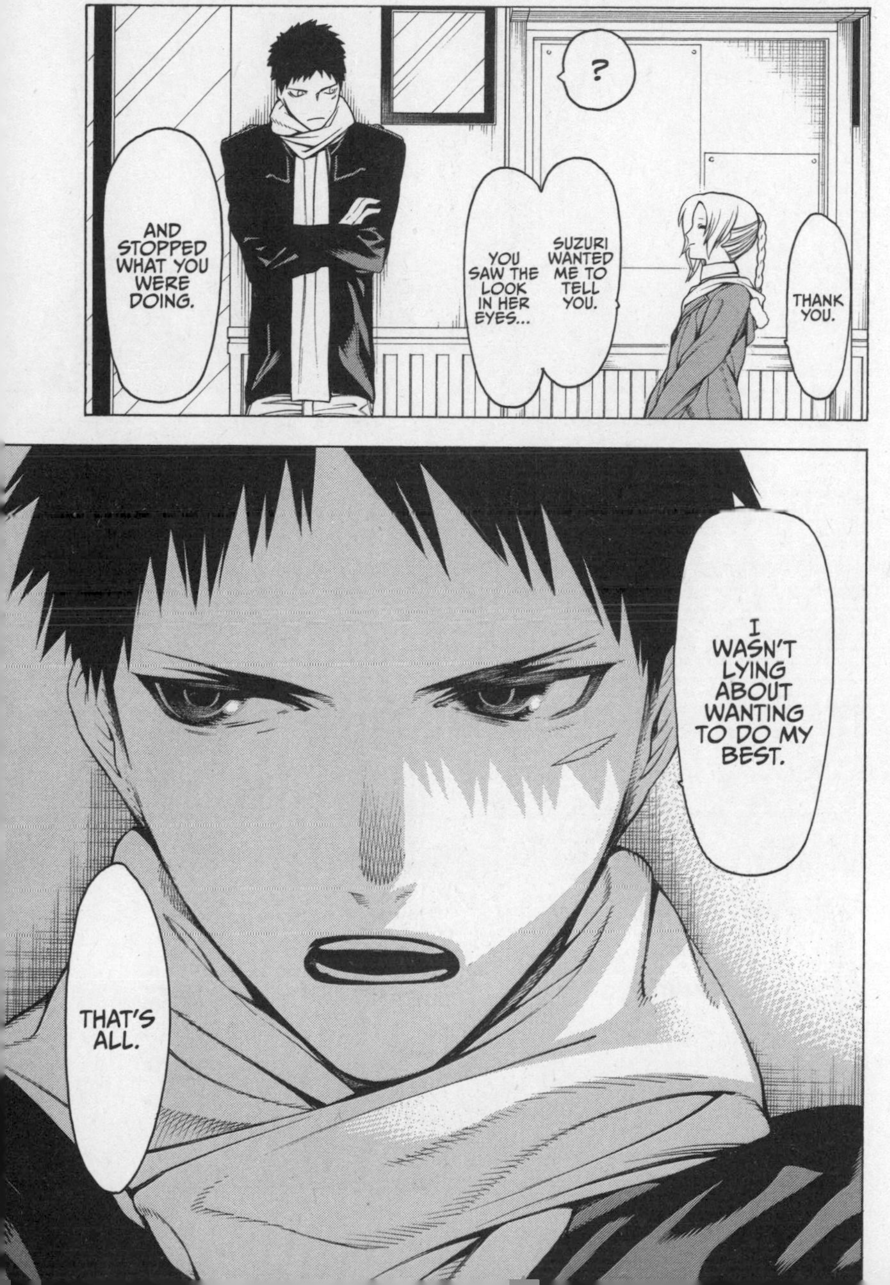
THANK YOU.
?
SUZURI WANTED ME TO TELL YOU.
YOU SAW THE LOOK IN HER EYES...
AND STOPPED WHAT YOU WERE DOING.
I WASN'T LYING ABOUT WANTING TO DO MY BEST.
THAT'S ALL.

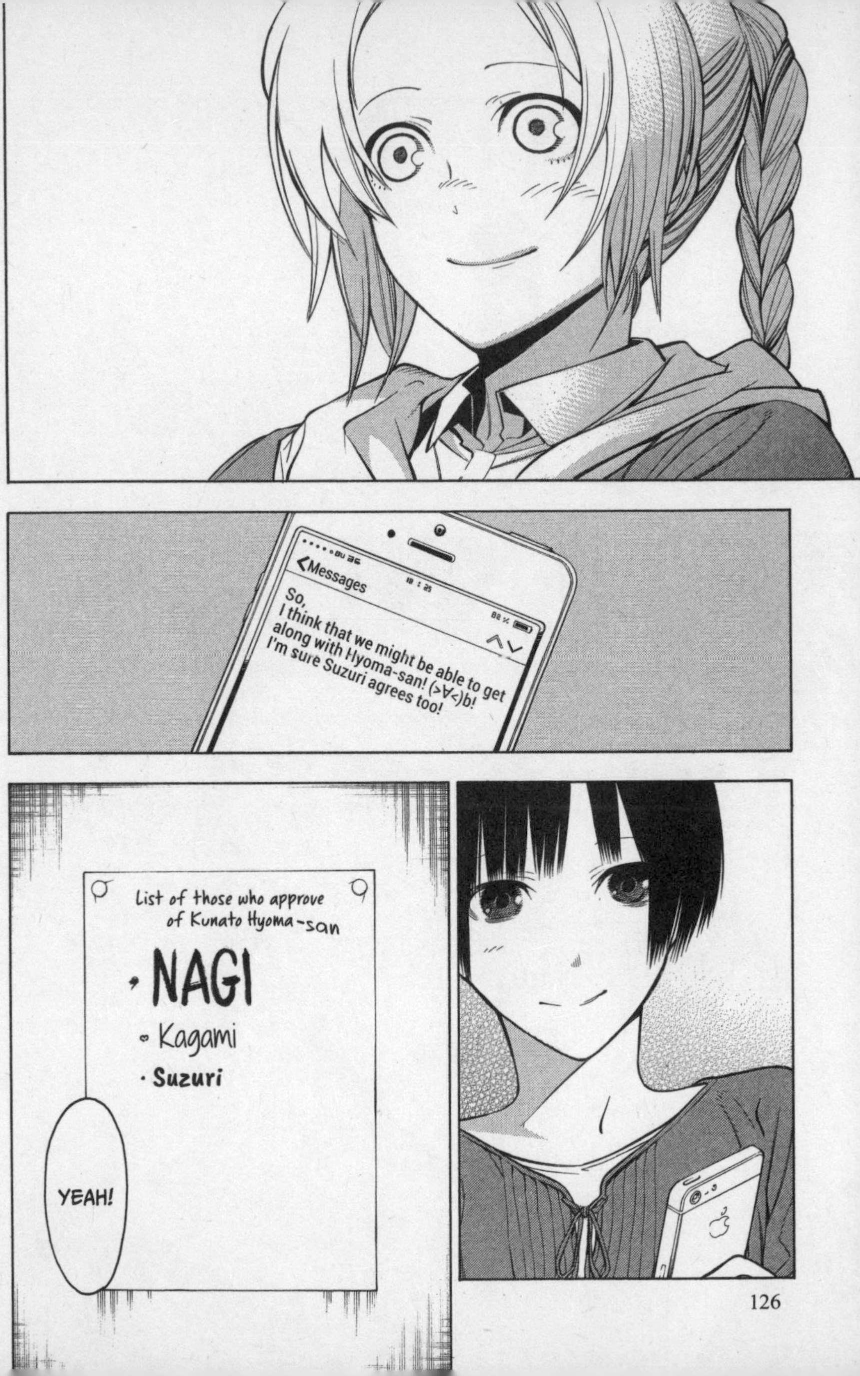
<Messages
So,
I think that we might be able to get along with Hyoma-san! (>∀<)b!
I'm sure Suzuri agrees too!
List of those who approve of Kunato Hyoma-san
NAGI
Kagami
Suzuri
YEAH!

MONONOGATARI

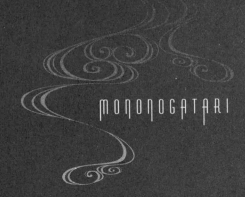

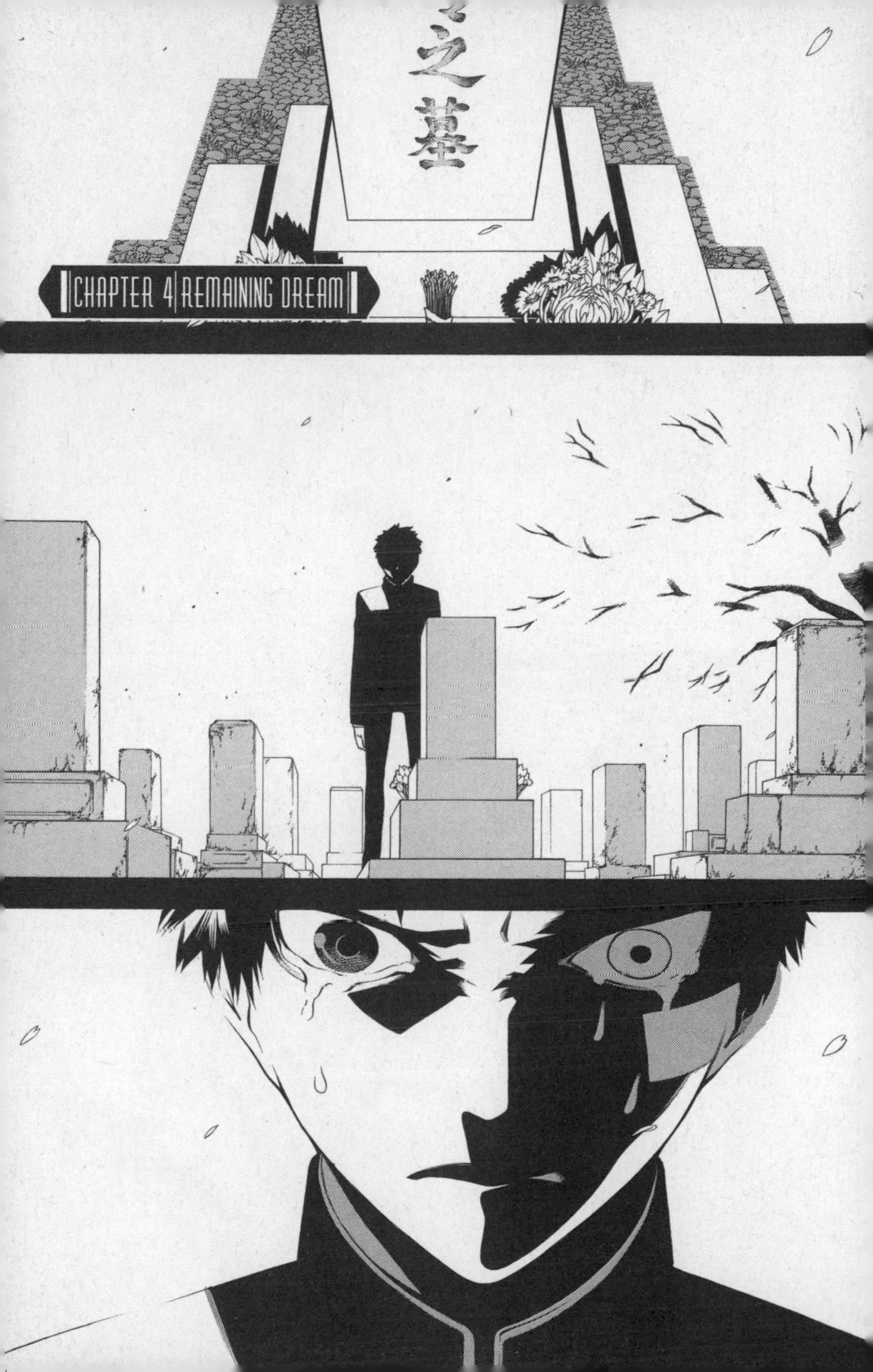
之墓
CHAPTER 4 | REMAINING DREAM

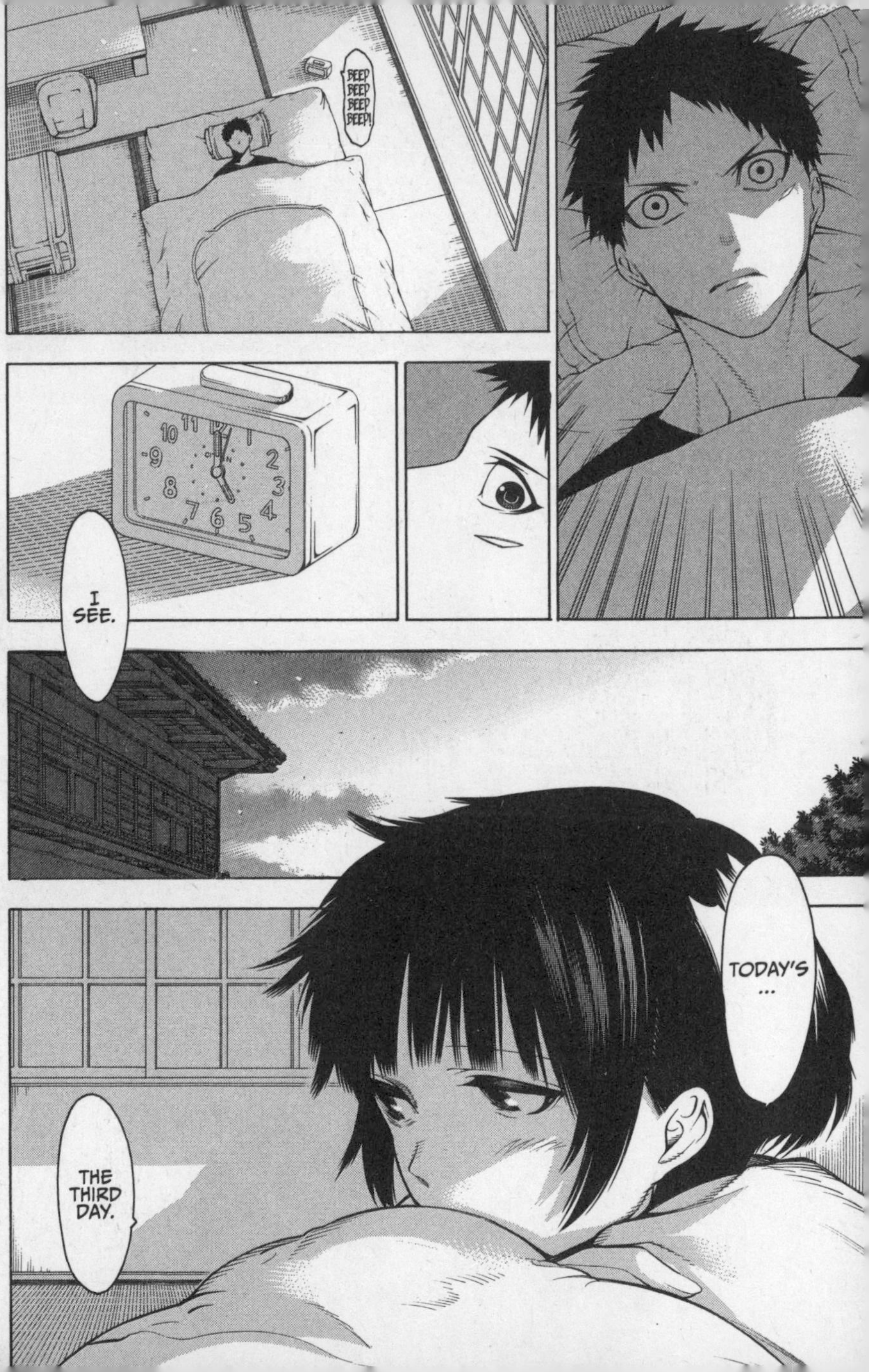
BEEP BEEP BEEP BEEP!
I SEE.
TODAY'S ...
THE THIRD DAY.

CHAPTER 4 REMAINING DREAM

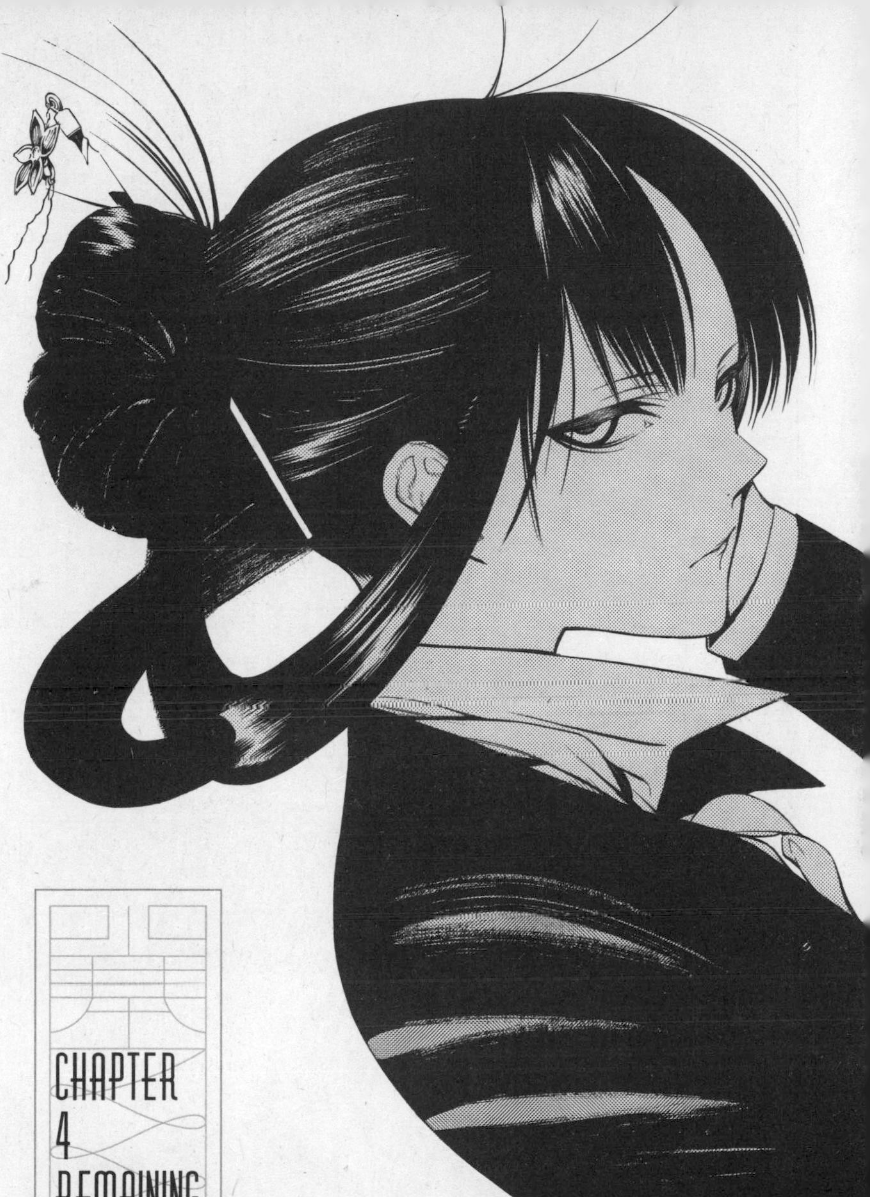

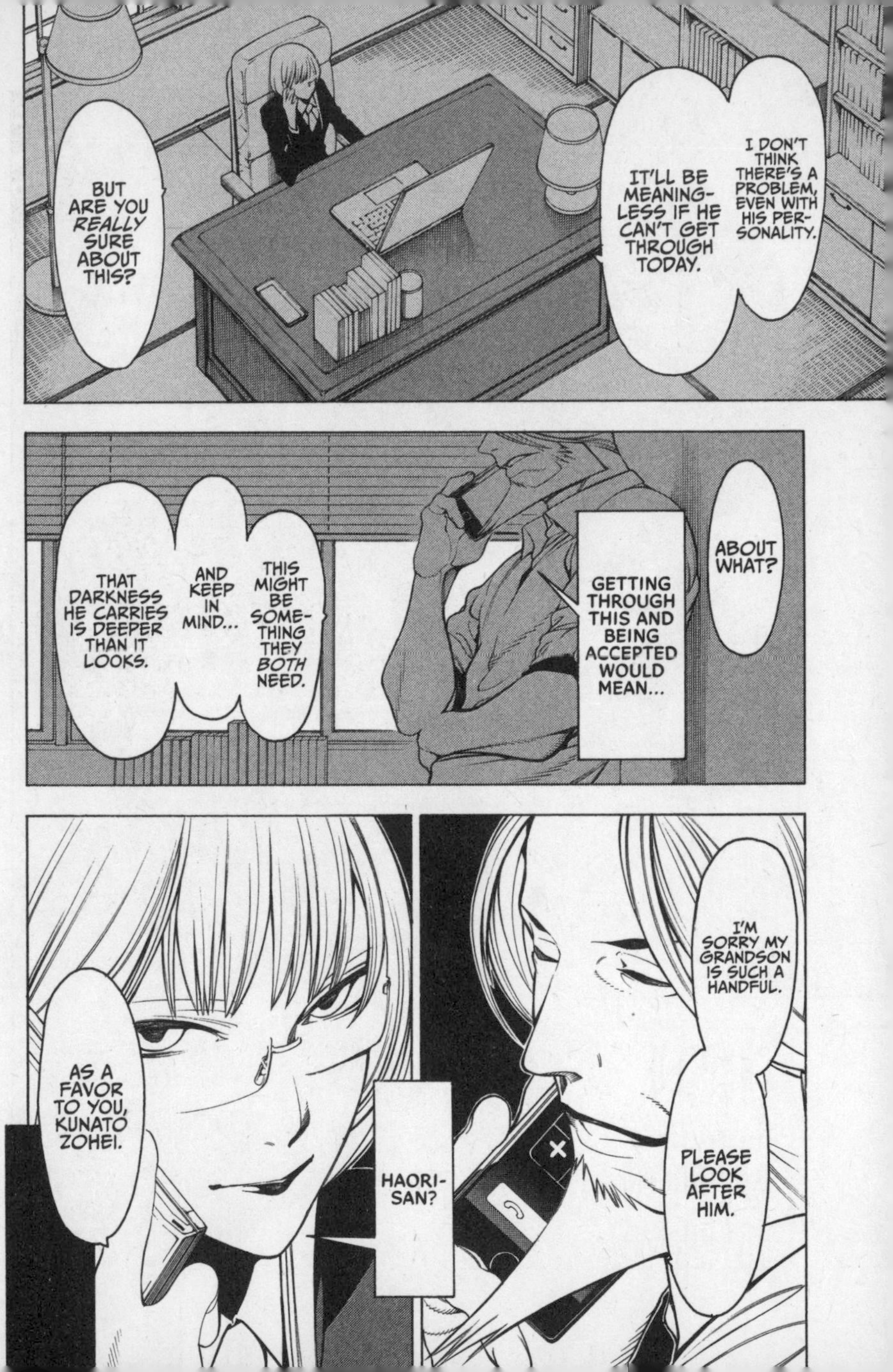
I DON'T THINK THERE'S A PROBLEM, EVEN WITH HIS PERSONALITY.
IT'LL BE MEANINGLESS IF HE CAN'T GET THROUGH TODAY.
BUT ARE YOU *REALLY* SURE ABOUT THIS?
ABOUT WHAT?
GETTING THROUGH THIS AND BEING ACCEPTED WOULD MEAN...
THIS MIGHT BE SOMETHING THEY *BOTH* NEED.
AND KEEP IN MIND...
THAT DARKNESS HE CARRIES IS DEEPER THAN IT LOOKS.
I'M SORRY MY GRANDSON IS SUCH A HANDFUL.
PLEASE LOOK AFTER HIM.
HAORI-SAN?
AS A FAVOR TO YOU, KUNATO ZOHEI.

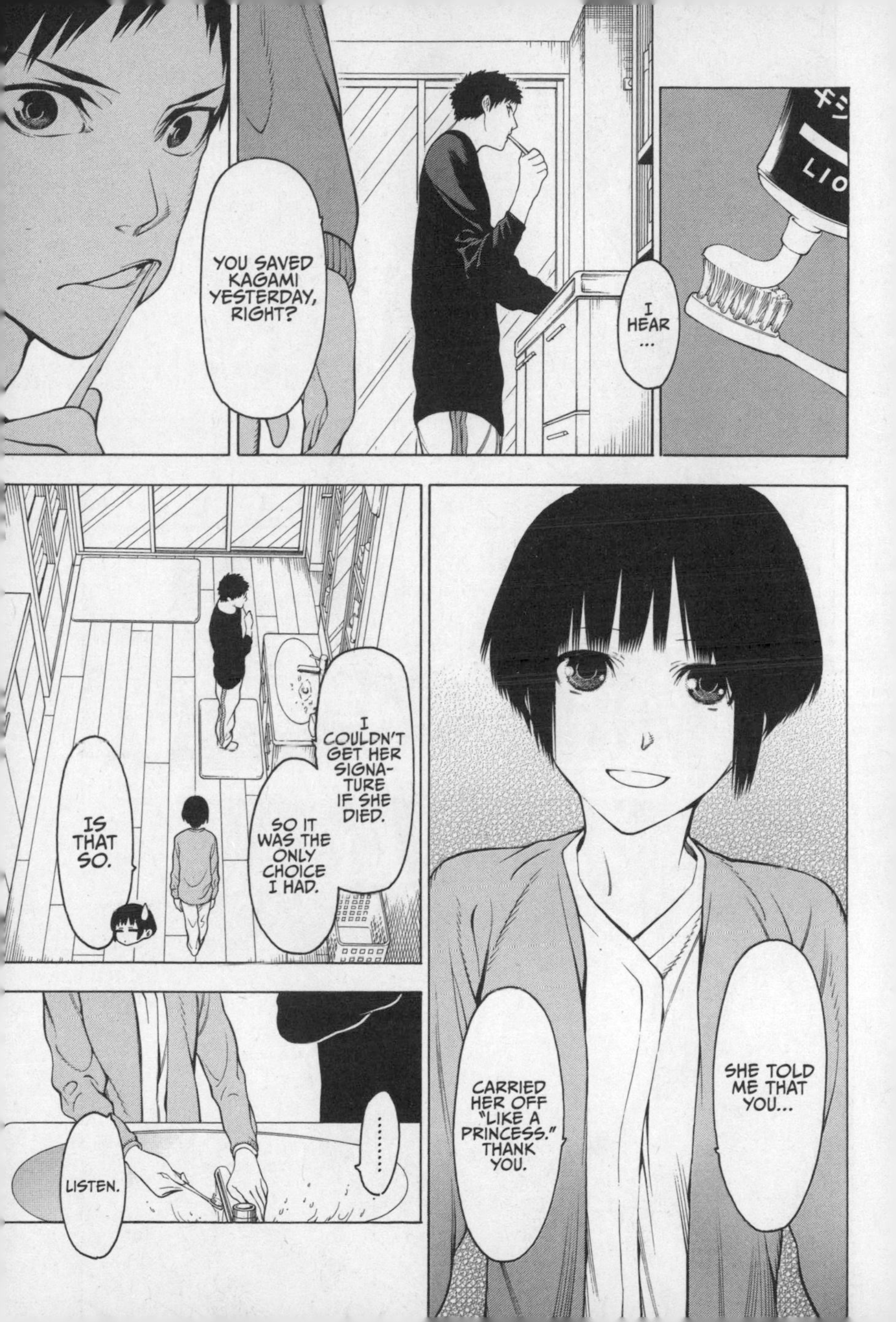
I HEAR ...
YOU SAVED KAGAMI YESTERDAY, RIGHT?
SHE TOLD ME THAT YOU...
CARRIED HER OFF "LIKE A PRINCESS." THANK YOU.
I COULDN'T GET HER SIGNA-TURE IF SHE DIED.
SO IT WAS THE ONLY CHOICE I HAD.
IS THAT SO.
......
LISTEN.

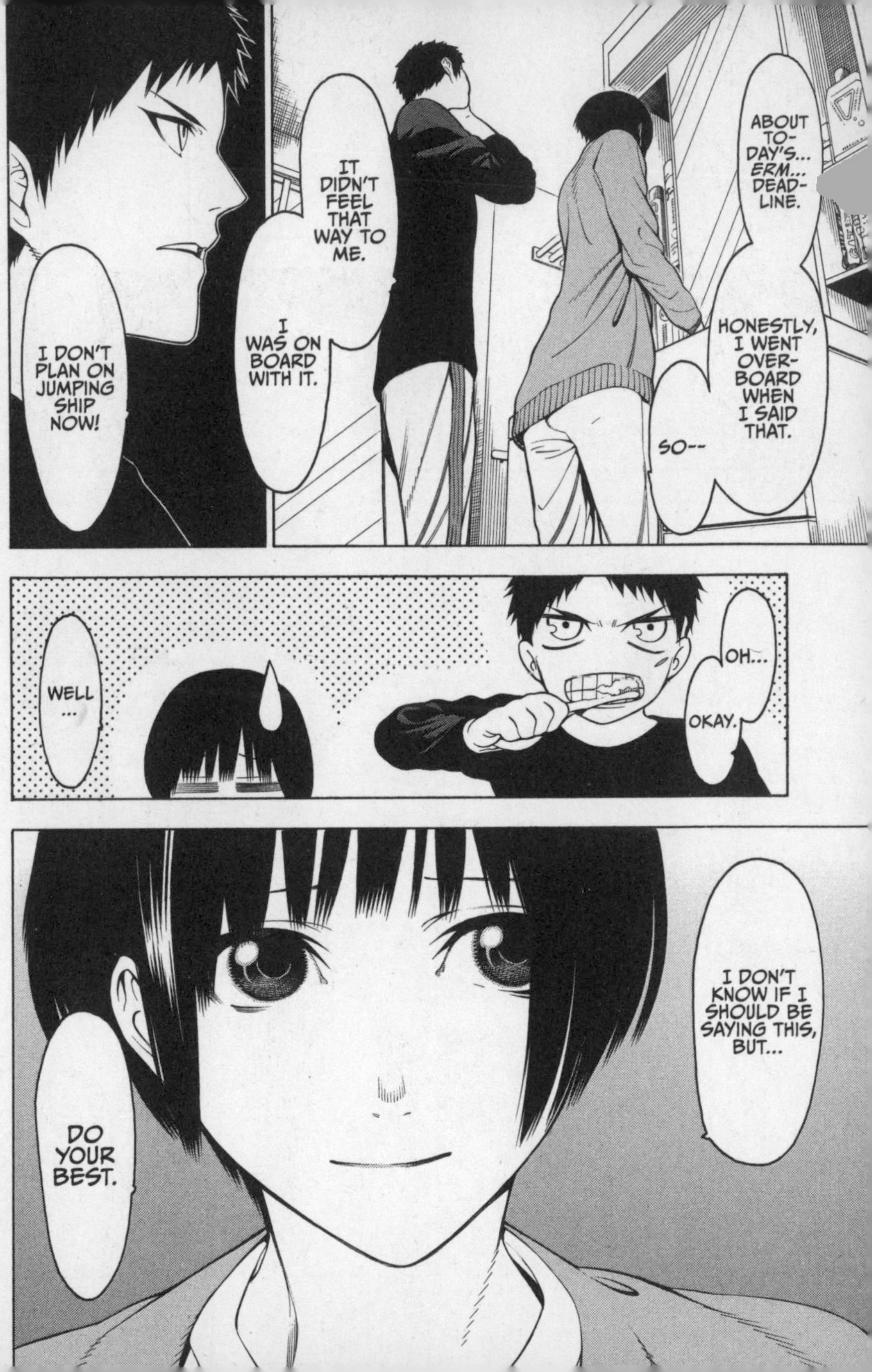
ABOUT TO-DAY'S... ERM... DEAD-LINE.
HONESTLY, I WENT OVER-BOARD WHEN I SAID THAT.
SO--
IT DIDN'T FEEL THAT WAY TO ME.
I WAS ON BOARD WITH IT.
I DON'T PLAN ON JUMPING SHIP NOW!
OH...
OKAY.
WELL ...
I DON'T KNOW IF I SHOULD BE SAYING THIS, BUT...
DO YOUR BEST.

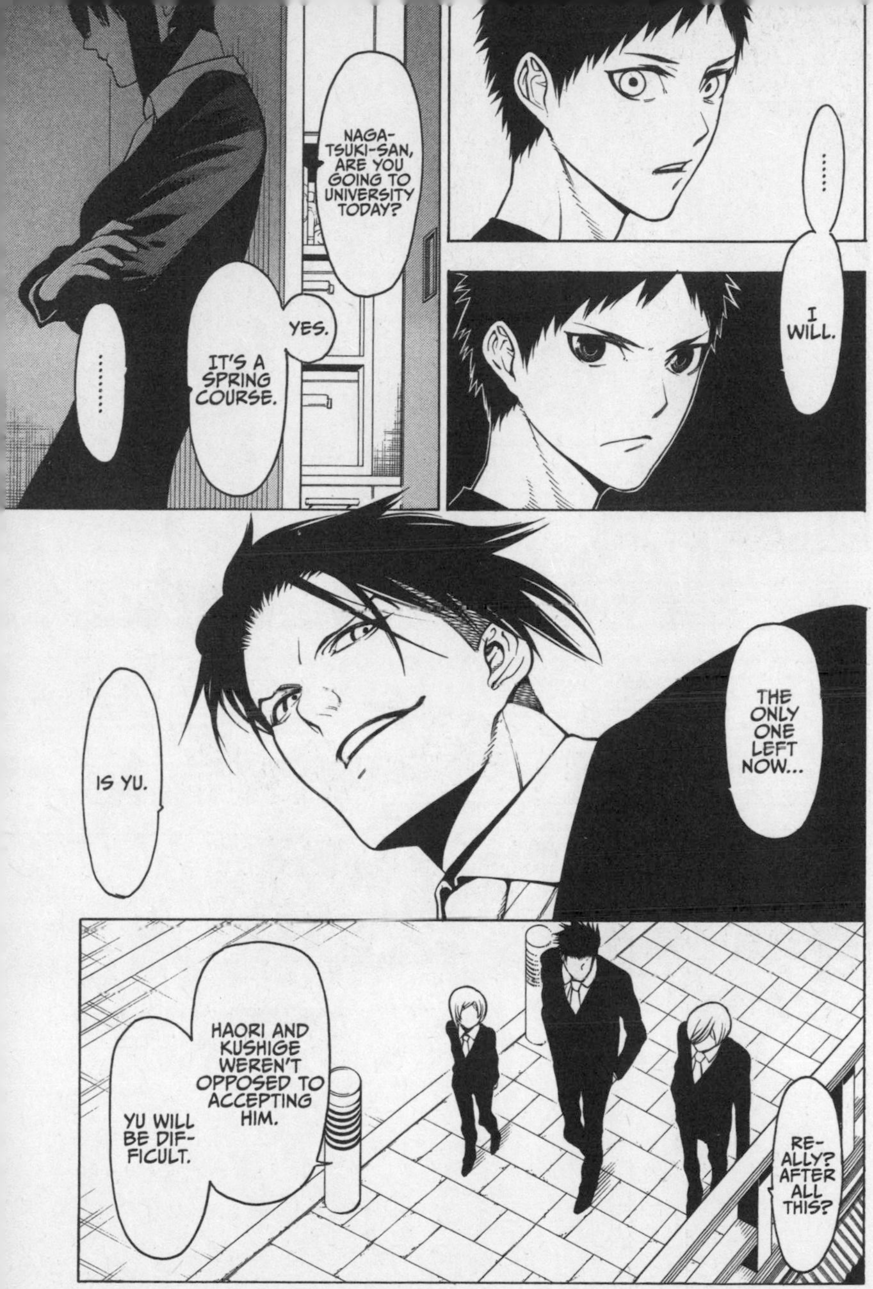
......
I WILL.
NAGA-TSUKI-SAN, ARE YOU GOING TO UNIVERSITY TODAY?
YES.
IT'S A SPRING COURSE.
......
THE ONLY ONE LEFT NOW...
IS YU.
RE-ALLY? AFTER ALL THIS?
HAORI AND KUSHIGE WEREN'T OPPOSED TO ACCEPTING HIM.
YU WILL BE DIF-FICULT.

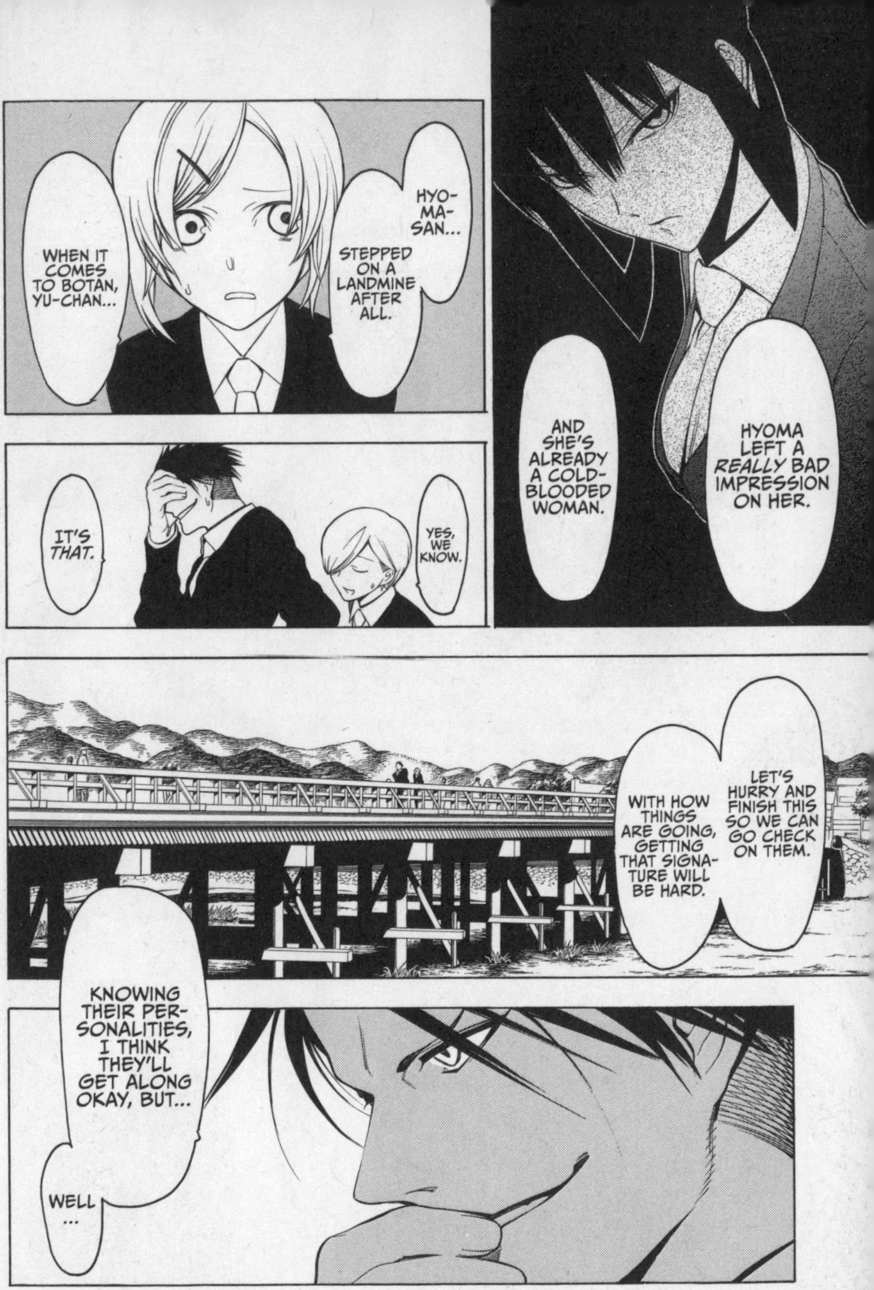
HYOMA LEFT A *REALLY* BAD IMPRESSION ON HER.
AND SHE'S ALREADY A COLD-BLOODED WOMAN.
HYOMA-SAN... STEPPED ON A LANDMINE AFTER ALL.
WHEN IT COMES TO BOTAN, YU-CHAN...
YES, WE KNOW.
IT'S *THAT*.
LET'S HURRY AND FINISH THIS SO WE CAN GO CHECK ON THEM.
WITH HOW THINGS ARE GOING, GETTING THAT SIGNATURE WILL BE HARD.
KNOWING THEIR PERSONALITIES, I THINK THEY'LL GET ALONG OKAY, BUT...
WELL ...

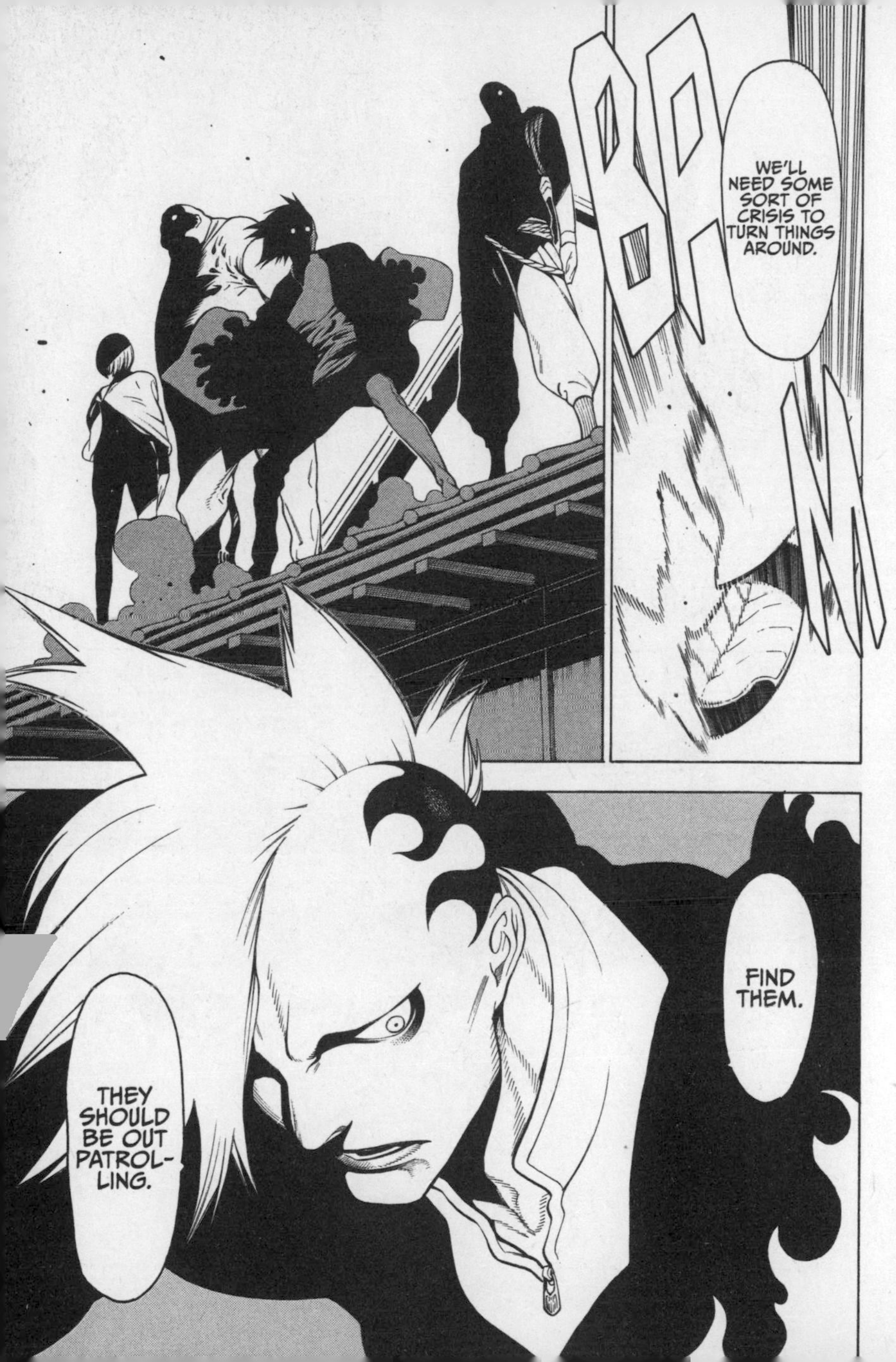
BAM
WE'LL NEED SOME SORT OF CRISIS TO TURN THINGS AROUND.
FIND THEM.
THEY SHOULD BE OUT PATROL-LING.

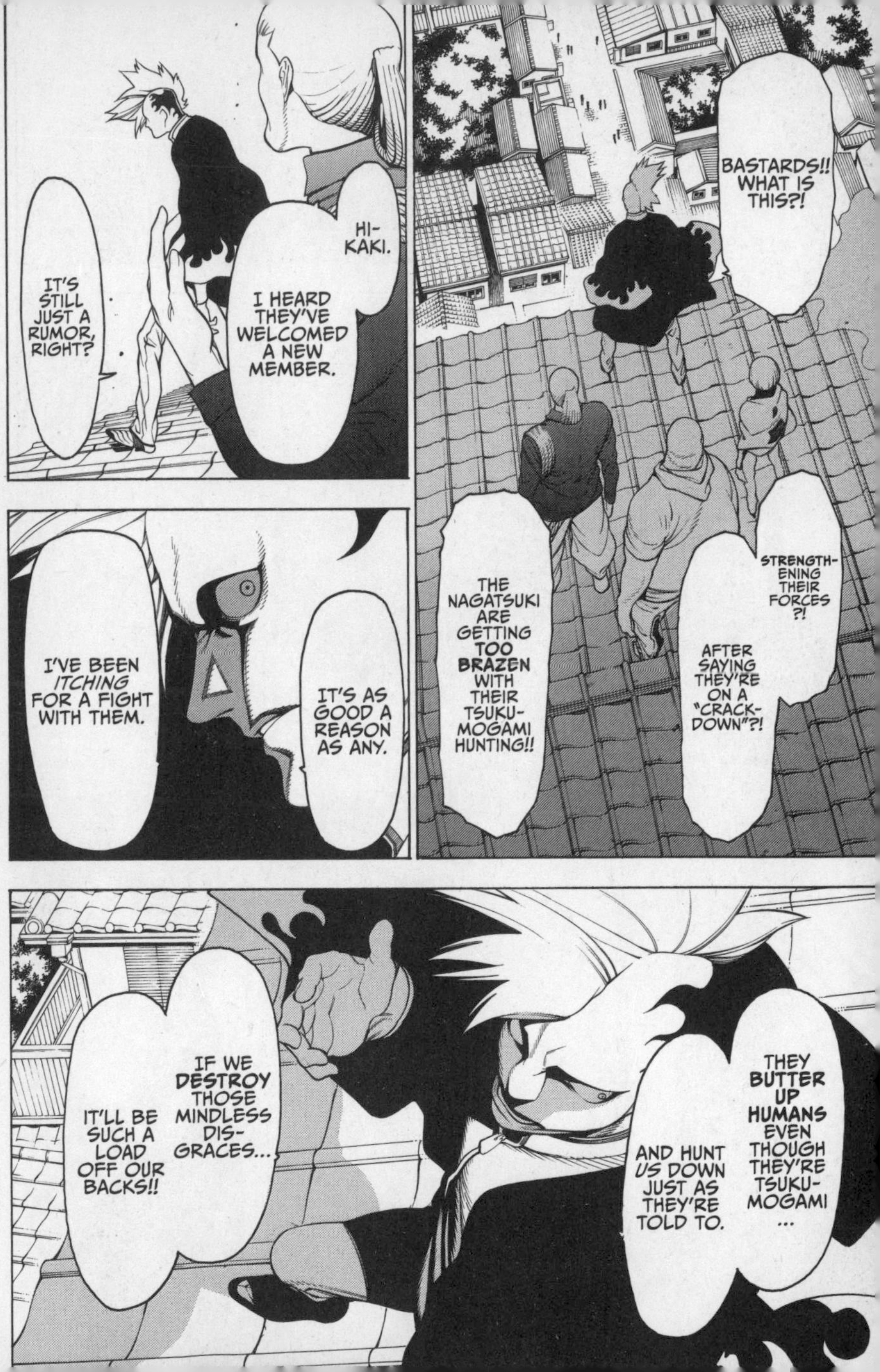
BASTARDS!! WHAT IS THIS?!
STRENGTHENING THEIR FORCES?!
AFTER SAYING THEY'RE ON A "CRACKDOWN"?!
THE NAGATSUKI ARE GETTING **TOO BRAZEN** WITH THEIR TSUKUMOGAMI HUNTING!!
HI-KAKI.
I HEARD THEY'VE WELCOMED A NEW MEMBER.
IT'S STILL JUST A RUMOR, RIGHT?
IT'S AS GOOD A REASON AS ANY.
I'VE BEEN *ITCHING* FOR A FIGHT WITH THEM.
THEY **BUTTER UP HUMANS** EVEN THOUGH THEY'RE TSUKUMOGAMI...
AND HUNT *US* DOWN JUST AS THEY'RE TOLD TO.
IF WE **DESTROY** THOSE MINDLESS DISGRACES...
IT'LL BE SUCH A LOAD OFF OUR BACKS!!

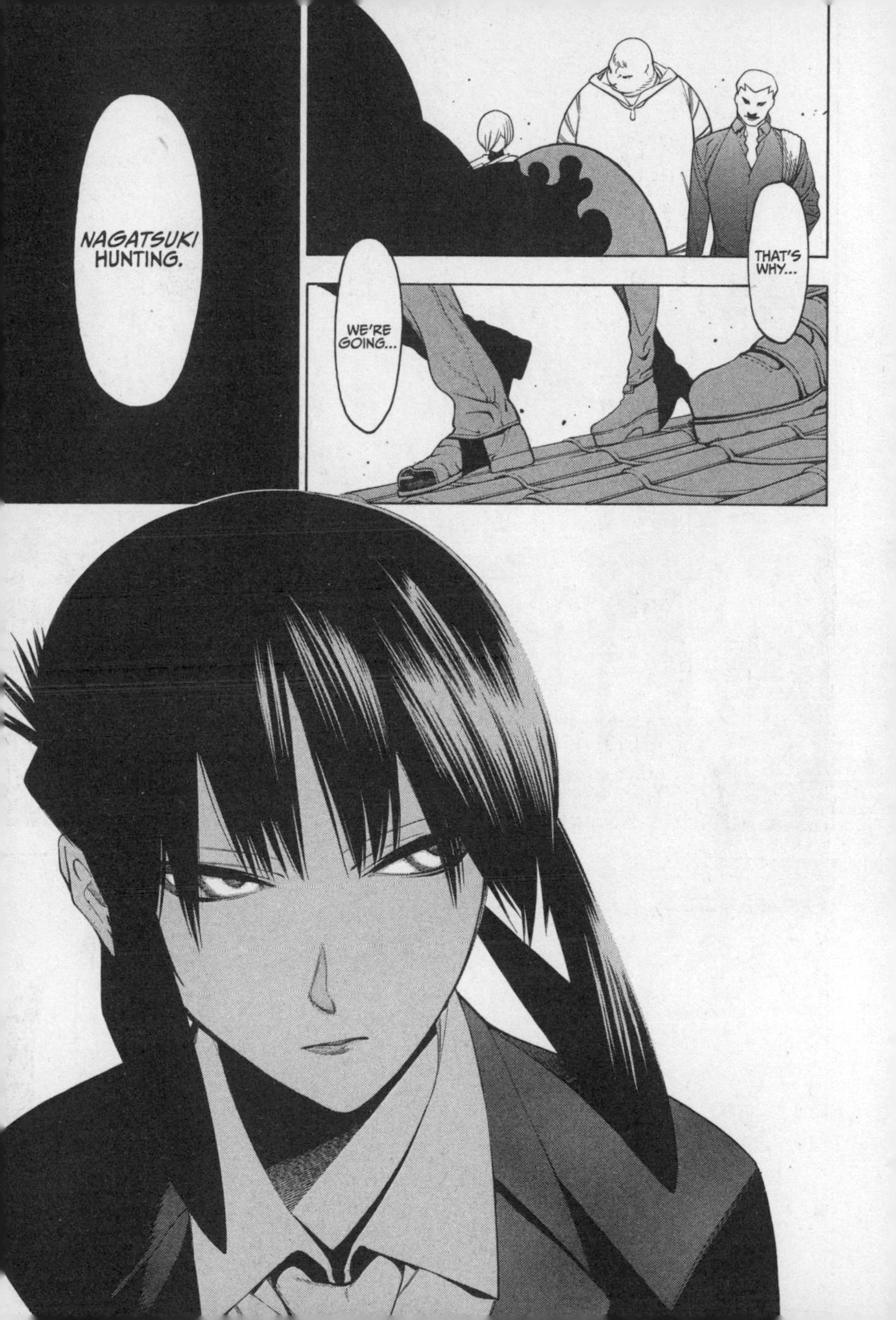
THAT'S WHY...
WE'RE GOING...
NAGATSUKI HUNTING.

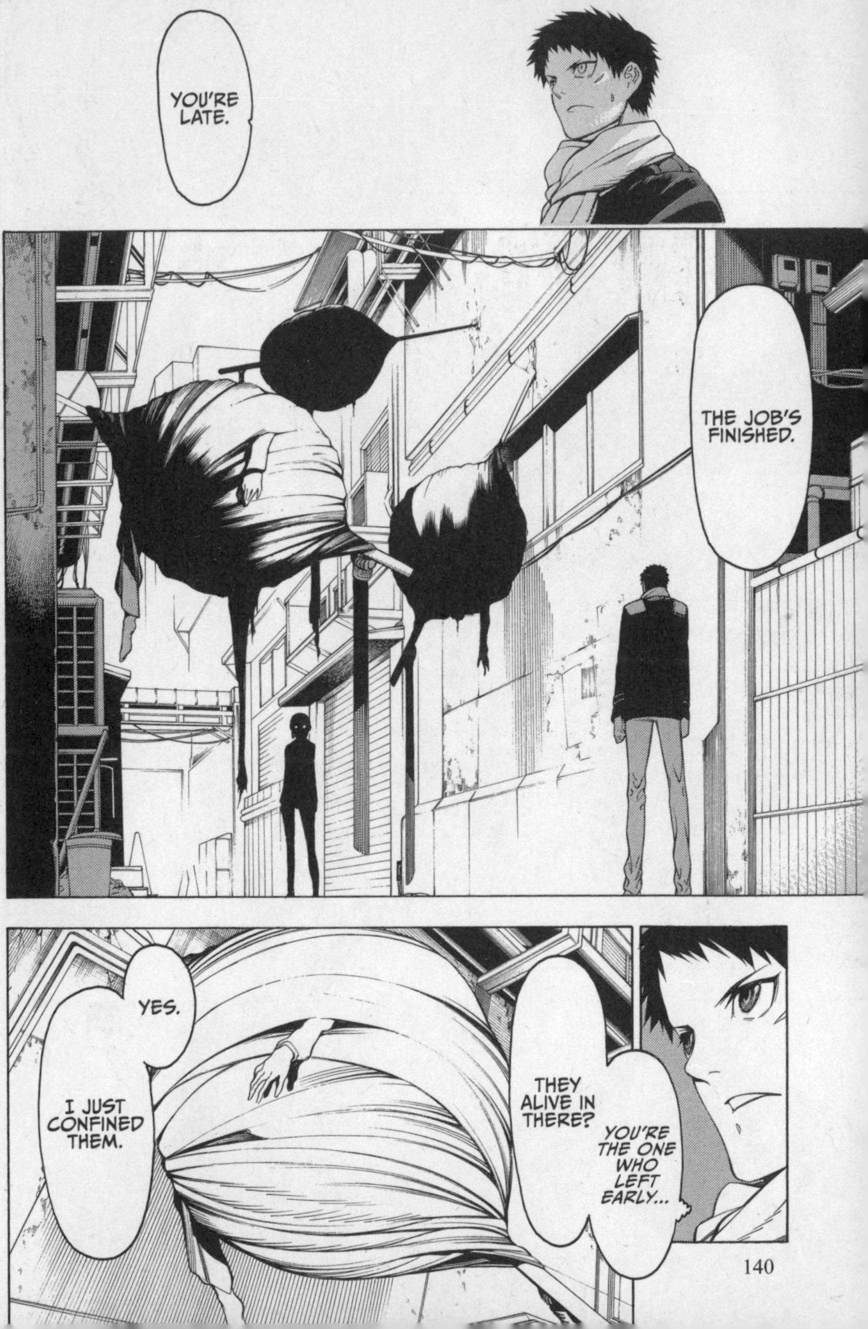
YOU'RE LATE.
THE JOB'S FINISHED.
YOU'RE THE ONE WHO LEFT EARLY...
THEY ALIVE IN THERE?
YES.
I JUST CONFINED THEM.

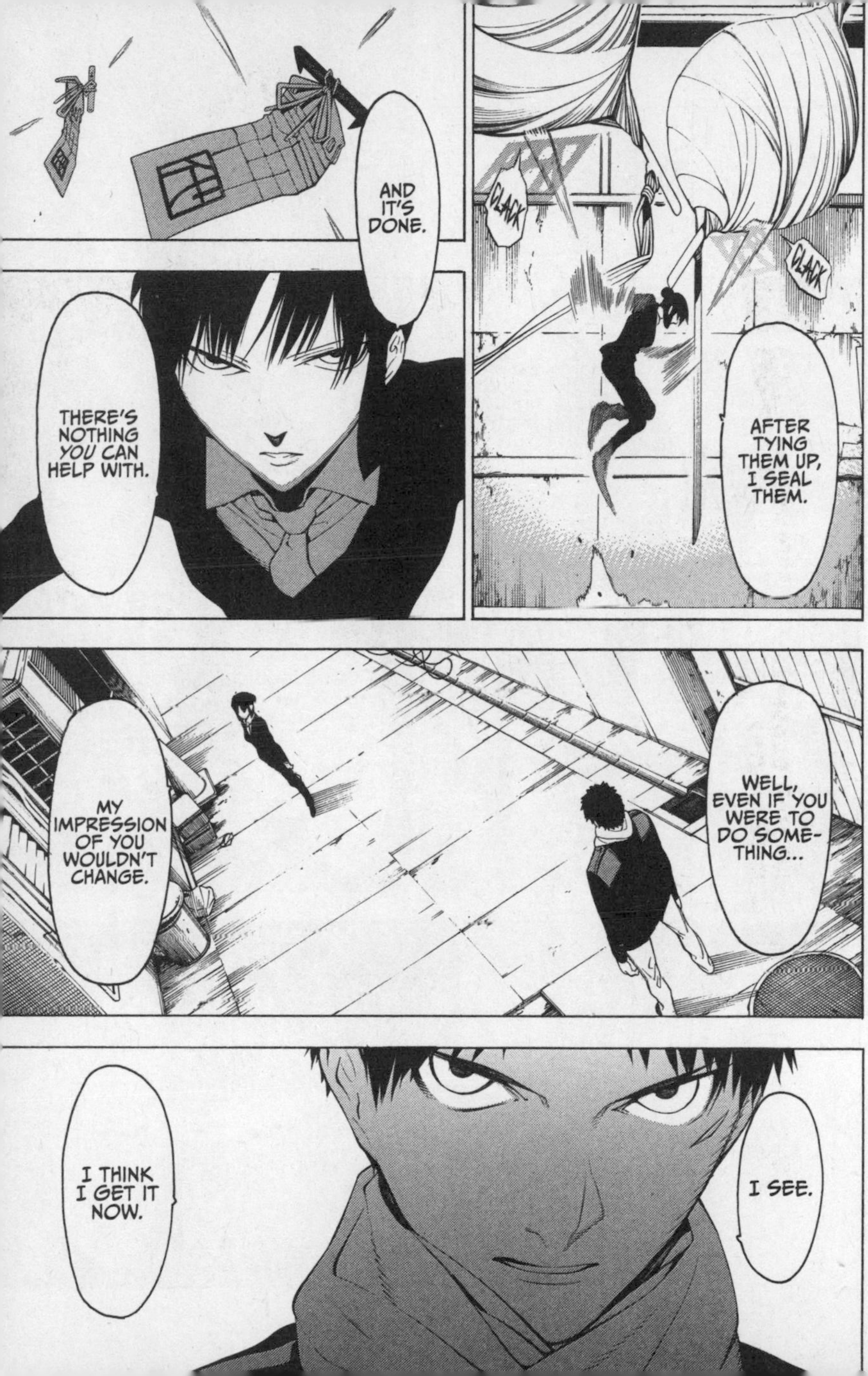
CLACK
CLACK
AFTER TYING THEM UP, I SEAL THEM.
AND IT'S DONE.
THERE'S NOTHING YOU CAN HELP WITH.
WELL, EVEN IF YOU WERE TO DO SOME-THING...
MY IMPRESSION OF YOU WOULDN'T CHANGE.
I SEE.
I THINK I GET IT NOW.

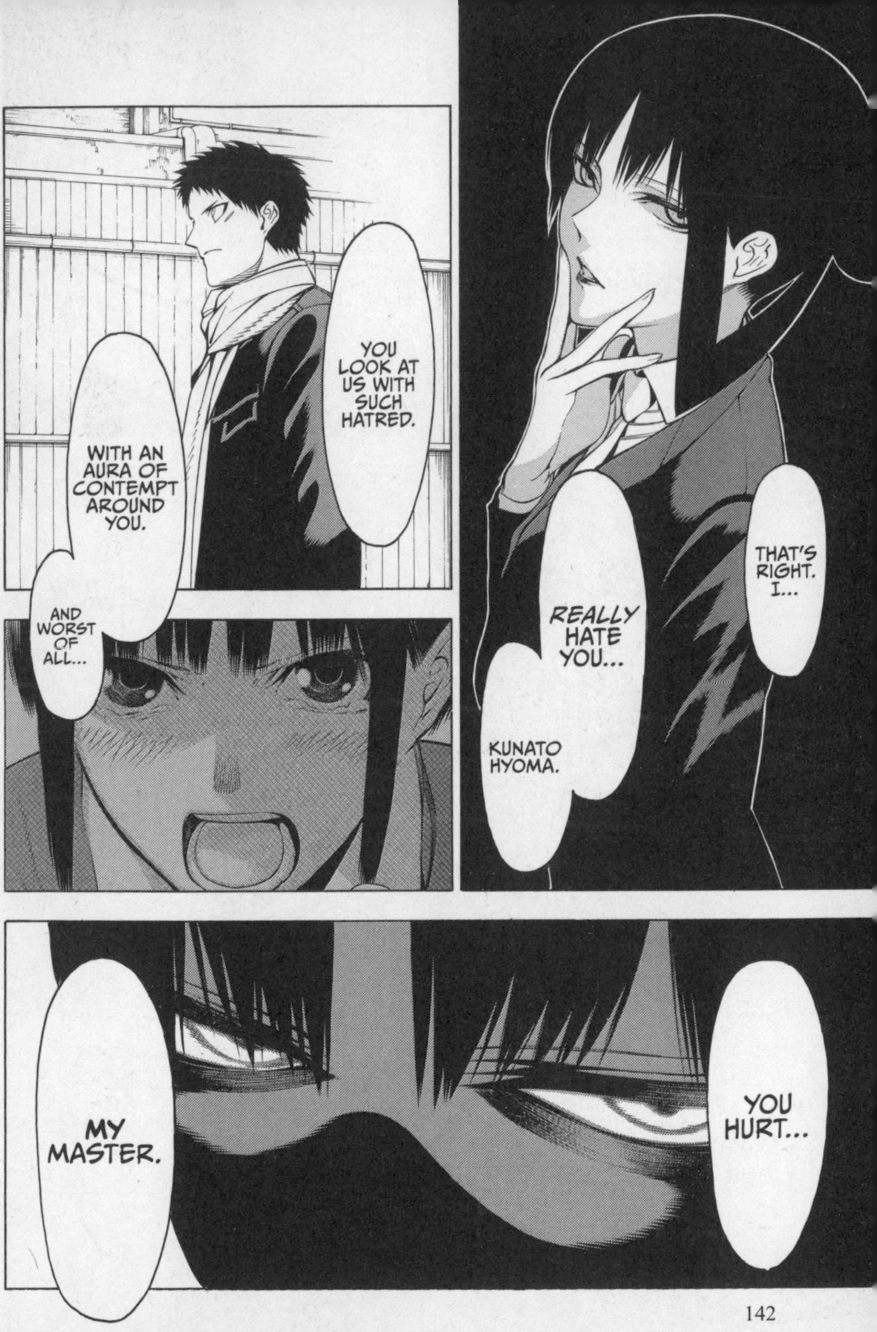
THAT'S RIGHT. I...
REALLY HATE YOU...
KUNATO HYOMA.
YOU LOOK AT US WITH SUCH HATRED.
WITH AN AURA OF CONTEMPT AROUND YOU.
AND WORST OF ALL...
YOU HURT...
MY MASTER.

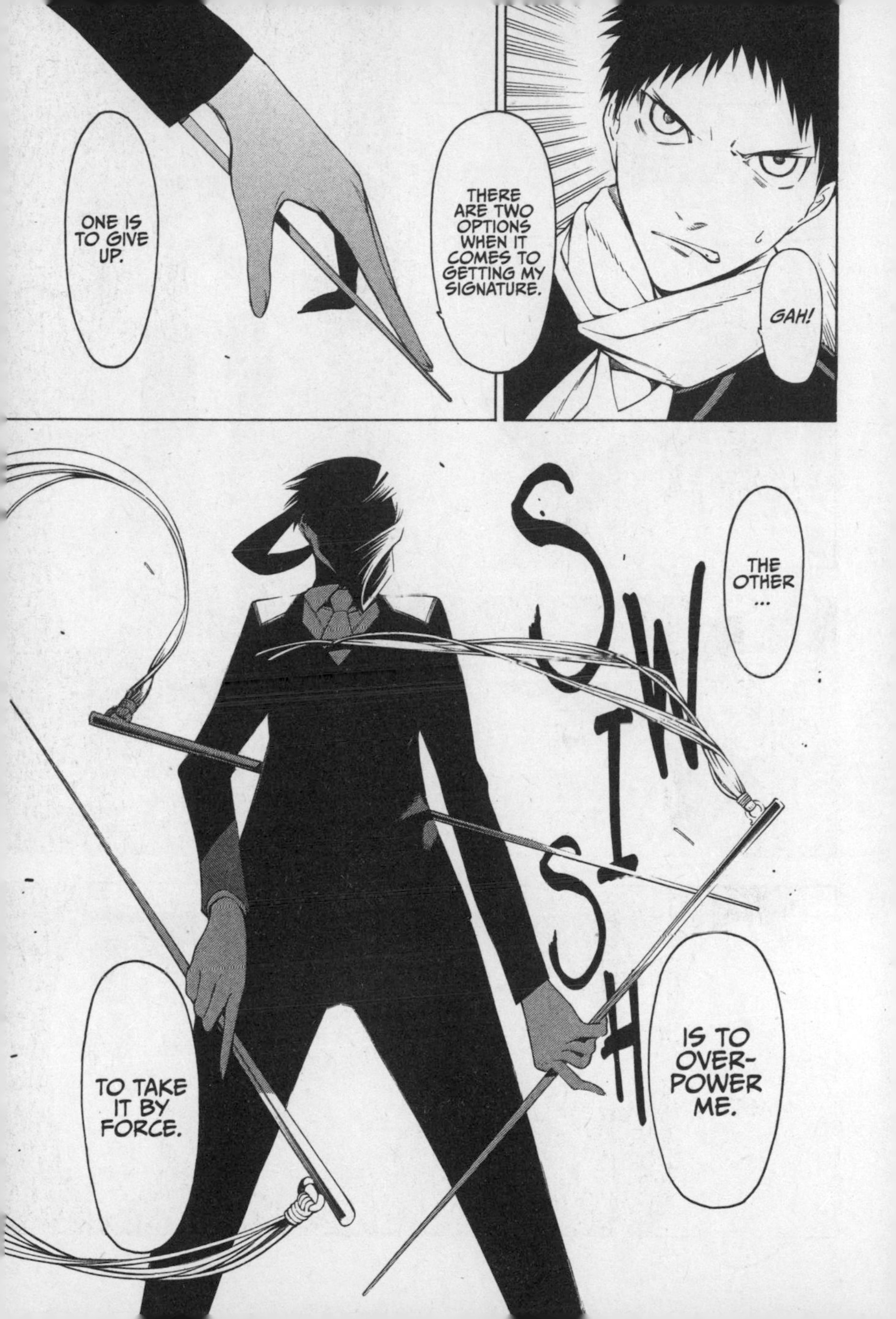
GAH!
THERE ARE TWO OPTIONS WHEN IT COMES TO GETTING MY SIGNATURE.
ONE IS TO GIVE UP.
THE OTHER ...
SWISH
IS TO OVER-POWER ME.
TO TAKE IT BY FORCE.

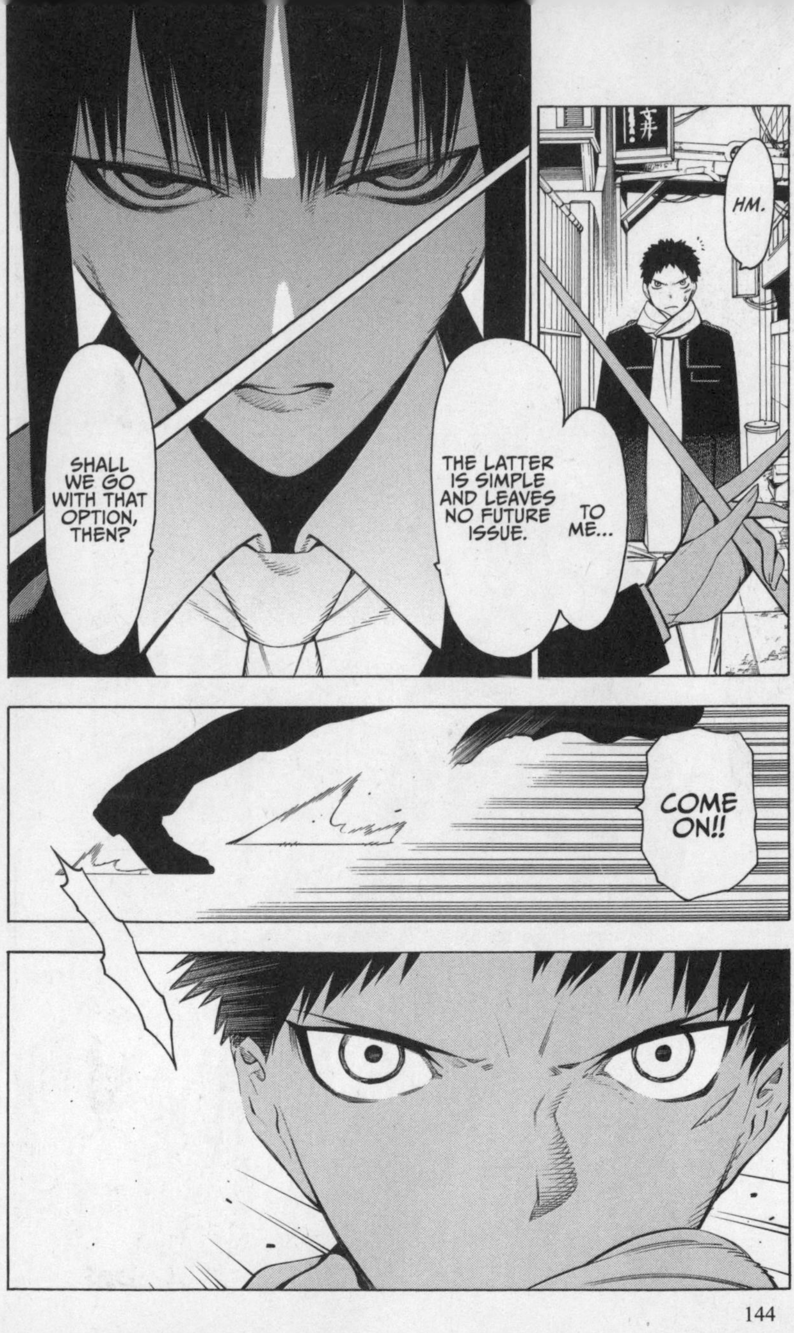
HM.
TO ME...
THE LATTER IS SIMPLE AND LEAVES NO FUTURE ISSUE.
SHALL WE GO WITH THAT OPTION, THEN?
COME ON!!

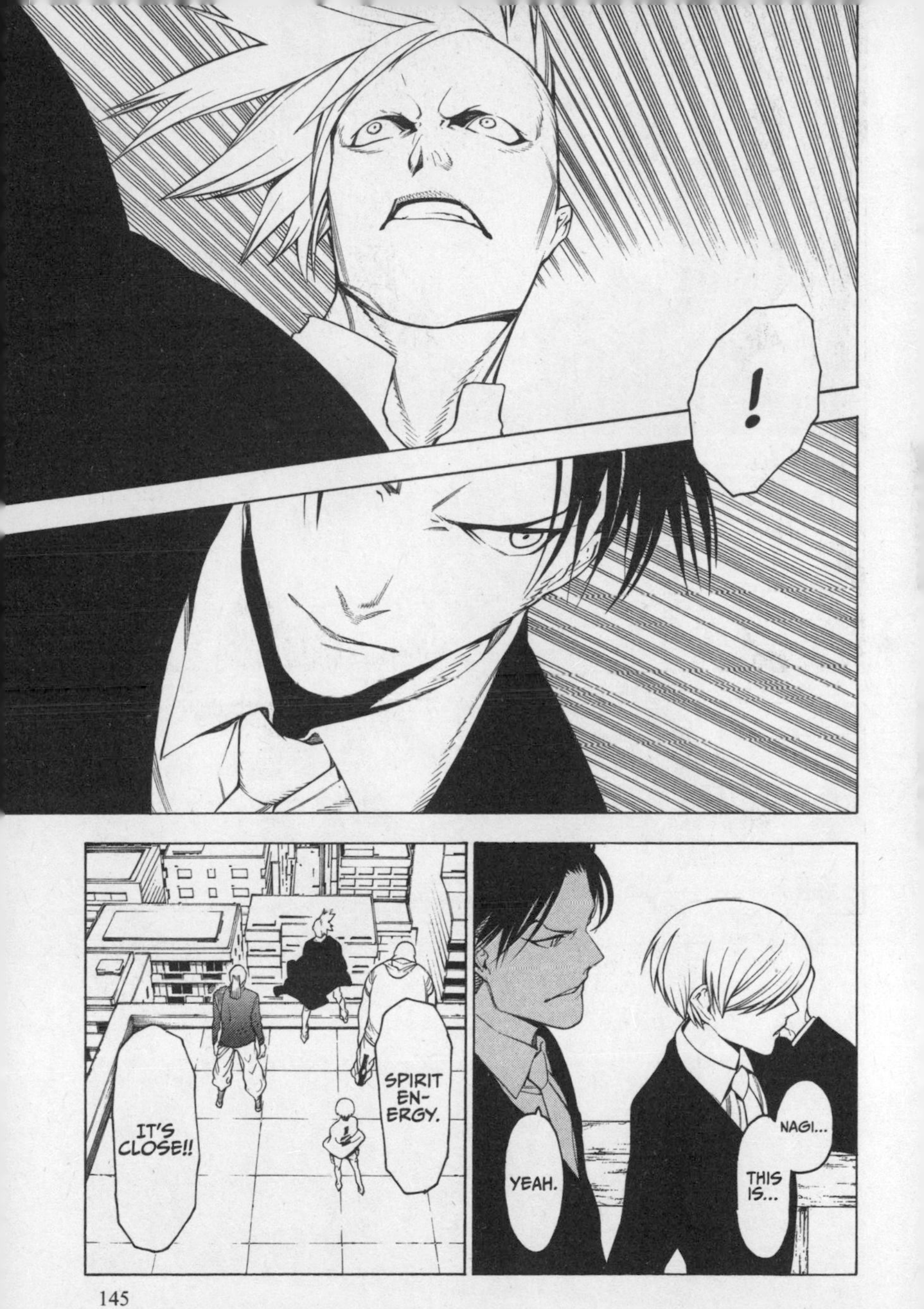
!
NAGI... THIS IS...
YEAH.
SPIRIT EN-ERGY.
IT'S CLOSE!!

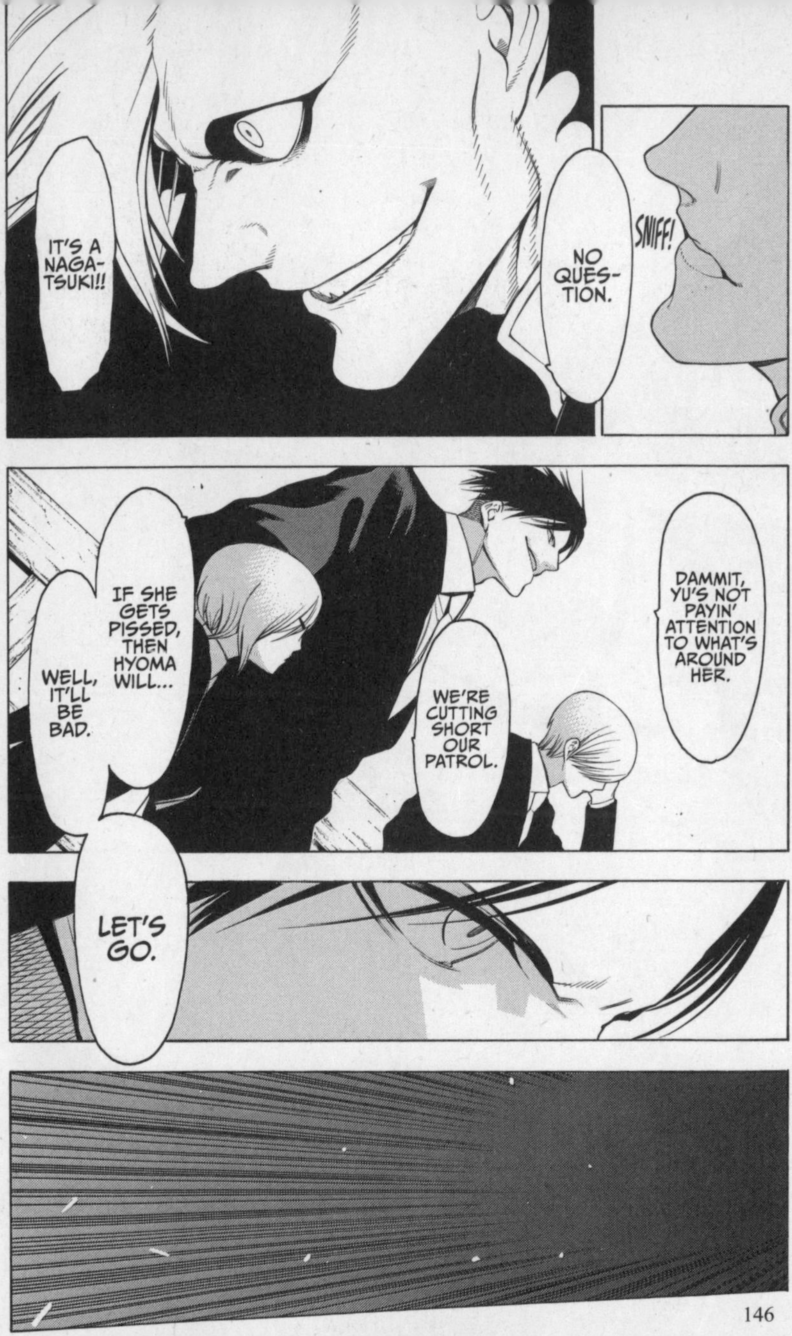
SNIFF!
NO QUES-TION.
IT'S A NAGA-TSUKI!!
DAMMIT, YU'S NOT PAYIN' ATTENTION TO WHAT'S AROUND HER.
WE'RE CUTTING SHORT OUR PATROL.
IF SHE GETS PISSED, THEN HYOMA WILL...
WELL, IT'LL BE BAD.
LET'S GO.

CLACK

CLACK

TUG

WHOOSH

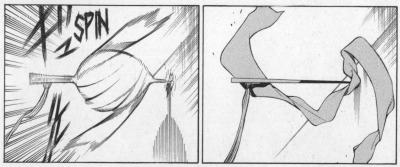

SPIN

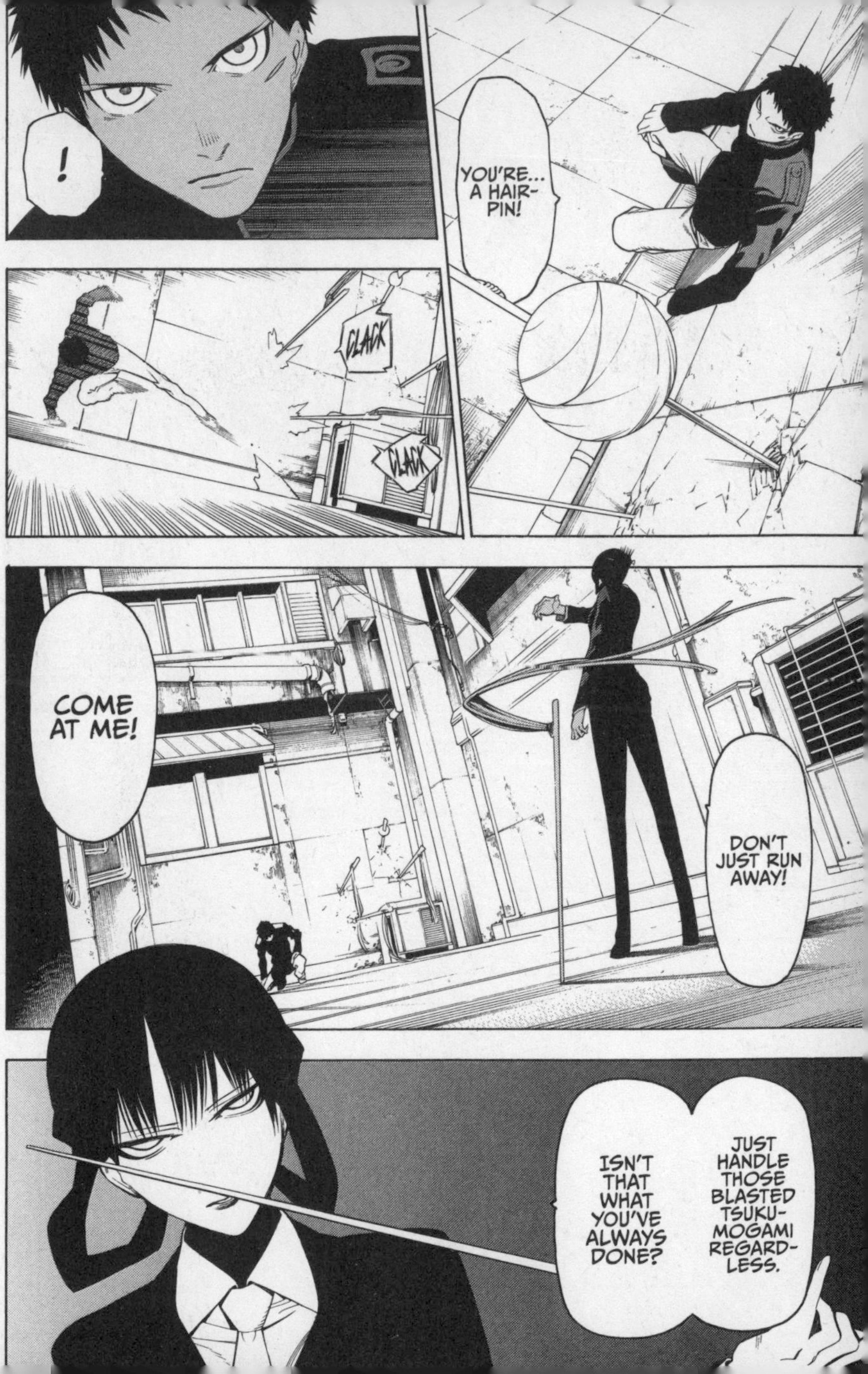
YOU'RE... A HAIR-PIN!
!
CLACK
CLACK
DON'T JUST RUN AWAY!
COME AT ME!
JUST HANDLE THOSE BLASTED TSUKU-MOGAMI REGARD-LESS.
ISN'T THAT WHAT YOU'VE ALWAYS DONE?

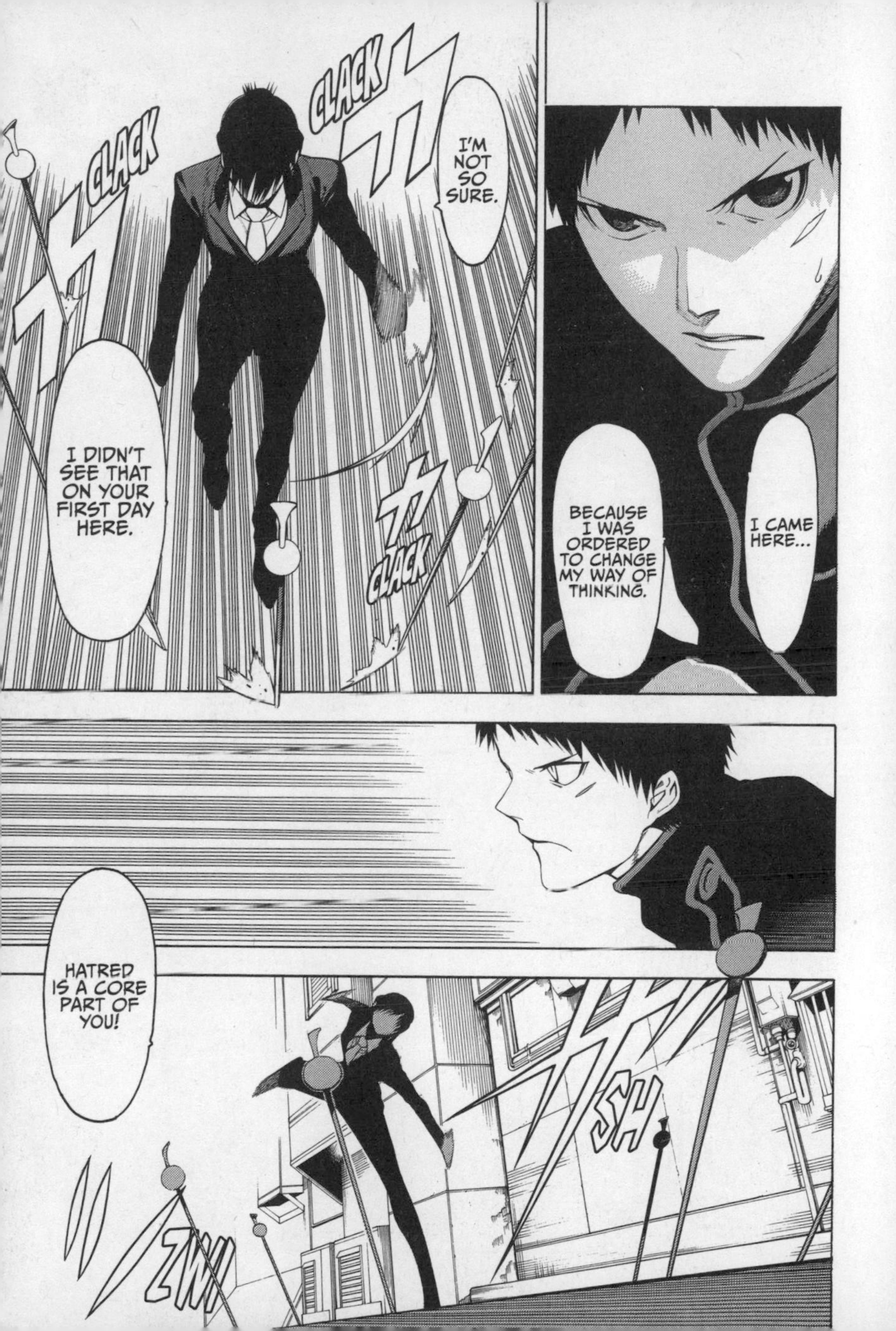
I CAME HERE...
BECAUSE I WAS ORDERED TO CHANGE MY WAY OF THINKING.
CLACK
I'M NOT SO SURE.
CLACK
CLACK
CLACK
I DIDN'T SEE THAT ON YOUR FIRST DAY HERE.
HATRED IS A CORE PART OF YOU!
SH
ZWI

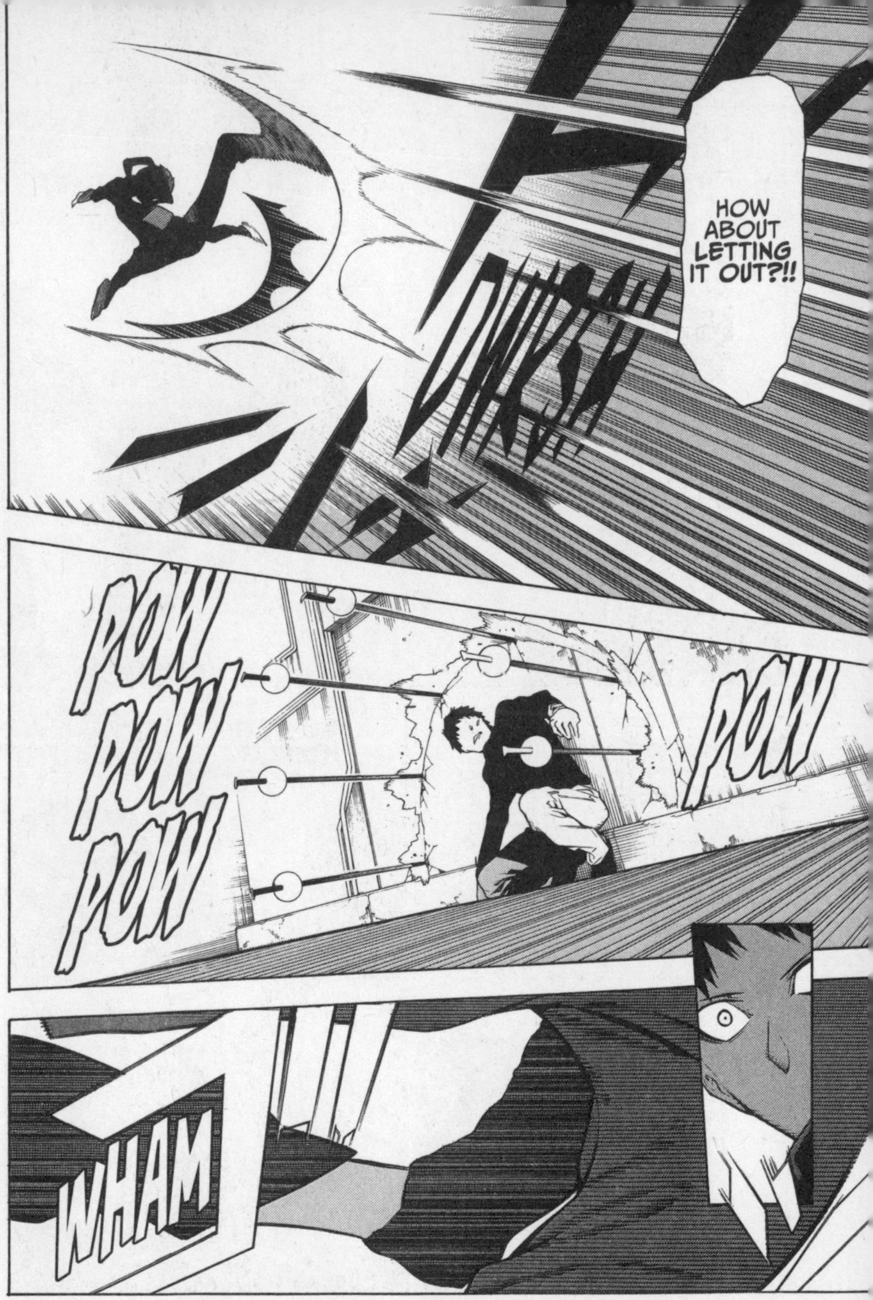
HOW ABOUT LETTING IT OUT?!!
POW
POW POW POW
WHAM

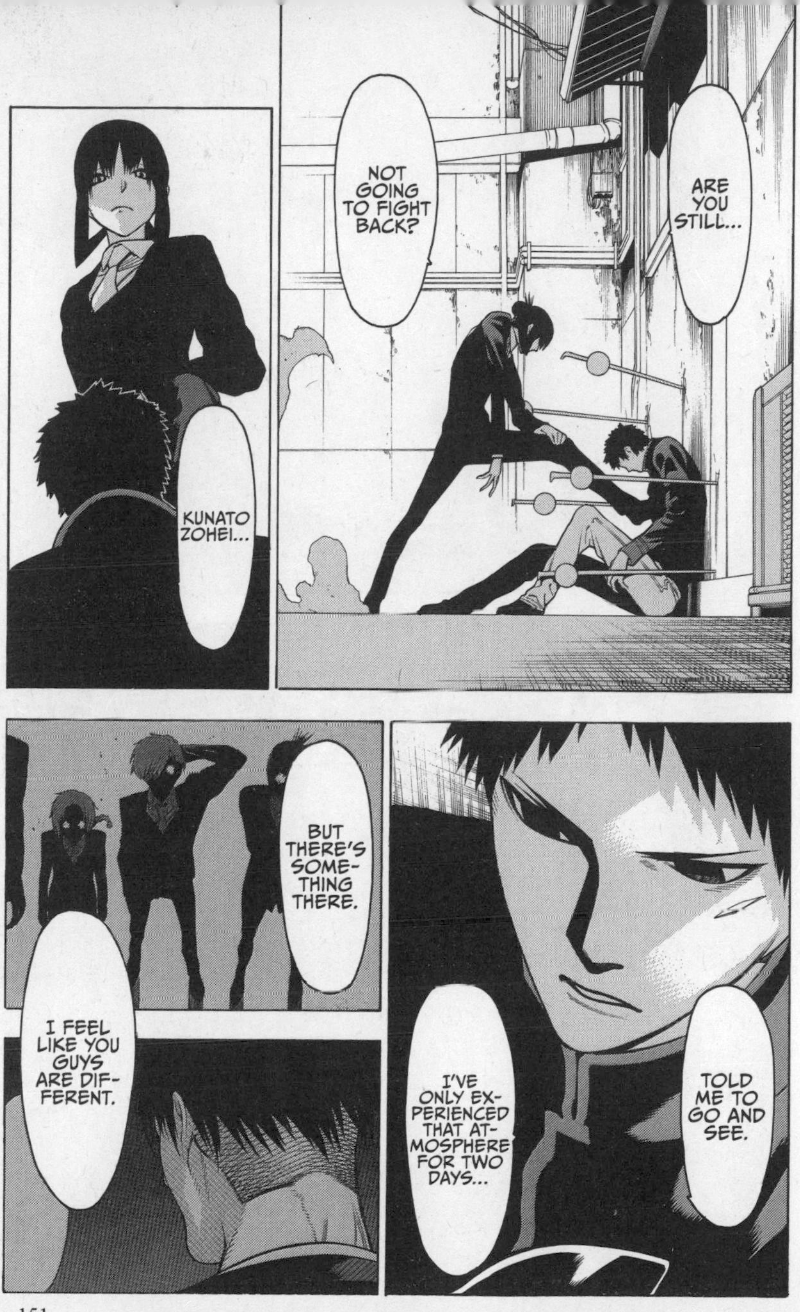
ARE YOU STILL...
NOT GOING TO FIGHT BACK?
KUNATO ZOHEI...
TOLD ME TO GO AND SEE.
I'VE ONLY EXPERIENCED THAT ATMOSPHERE FOR TWO DAYS...
BUT THERE'S SOMETHING THERE.
I FEEL LIKE YOU GUYS ARE DIFFERENT.

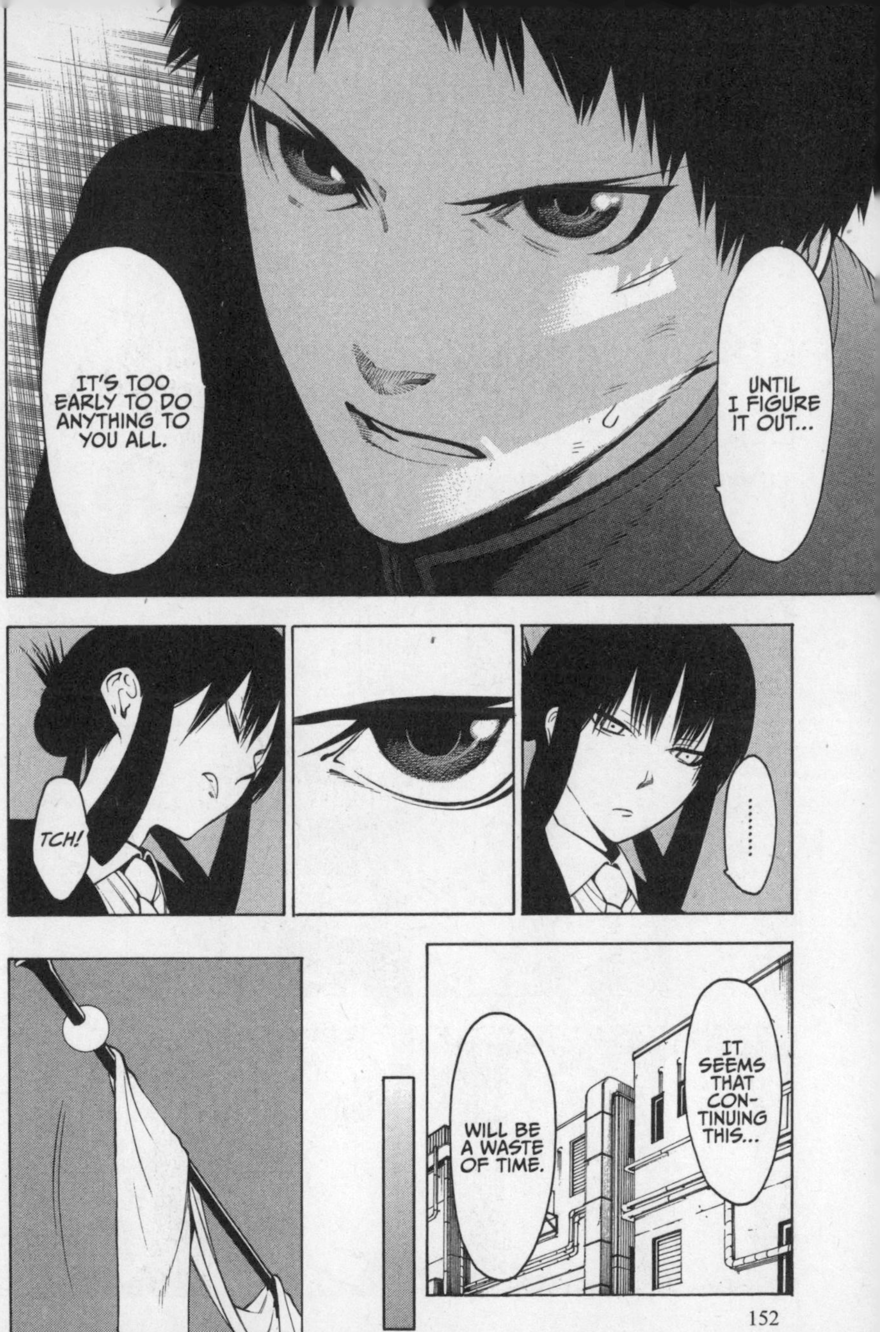
UNTIL I FIGURE IT OUT...
IT'S TOO EARLY TO DO ANYTHING TO YOU ALL.
......
TCH!
IT SEEMS THAT CON-TINUING THIS...
WILL BE A WASTE OF TIME.

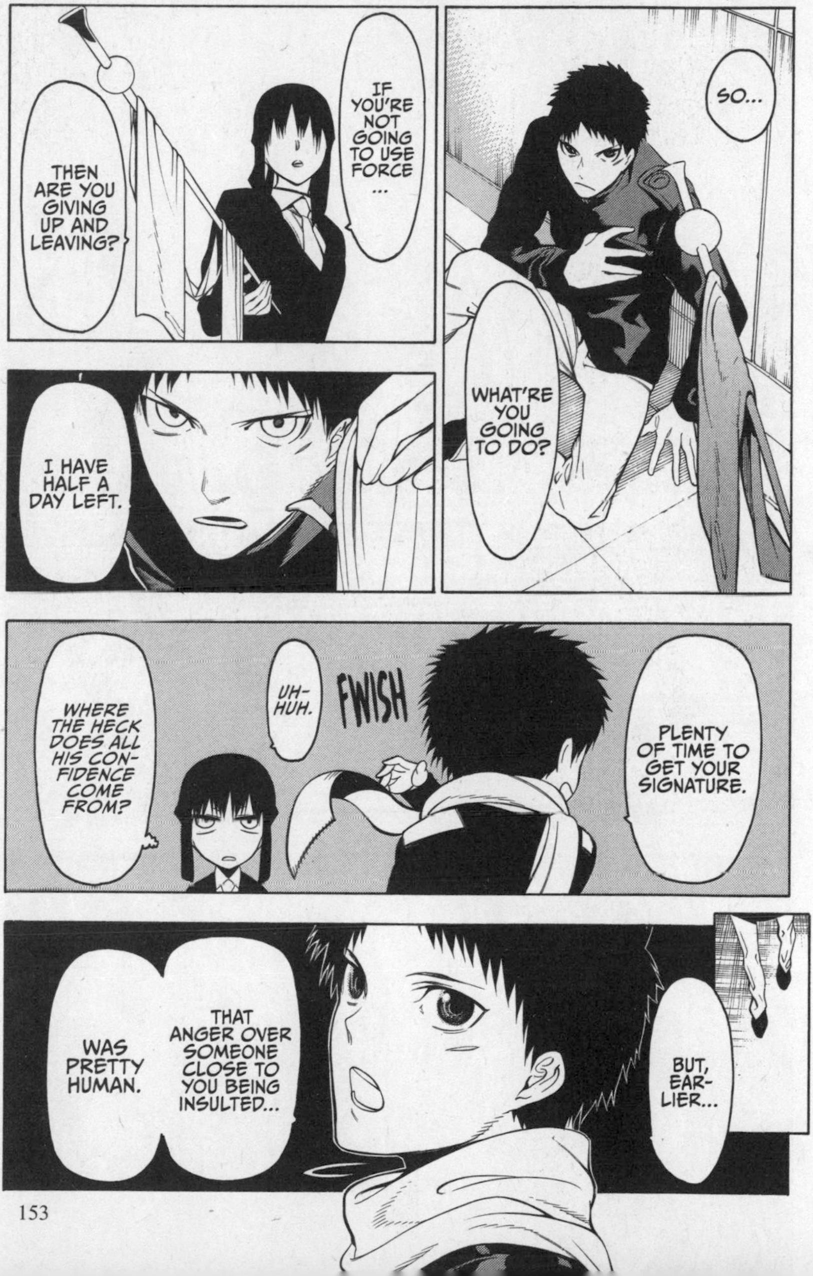
SO...
WHAT'RE YOU GOING TO DO?
IF YOU'RE NOT GOING TO USE FORCE ...
THEN ARE YOU GIVING UP AND LEAVING?
I HAVE HALF A DAY LEFT.
PLENTY OF TIME TO GET YOUR SIGNATURE.
FWISH
UH-HUH.
WHERE THE HECK DOES ALL HIS CONFIDENCE COME FROM?
BUT, EARLIER...
THAT ANGER OVER SOMEONE CLOSE TO YOU BEING INSULTED...
WAS PRETTY HUMAN.

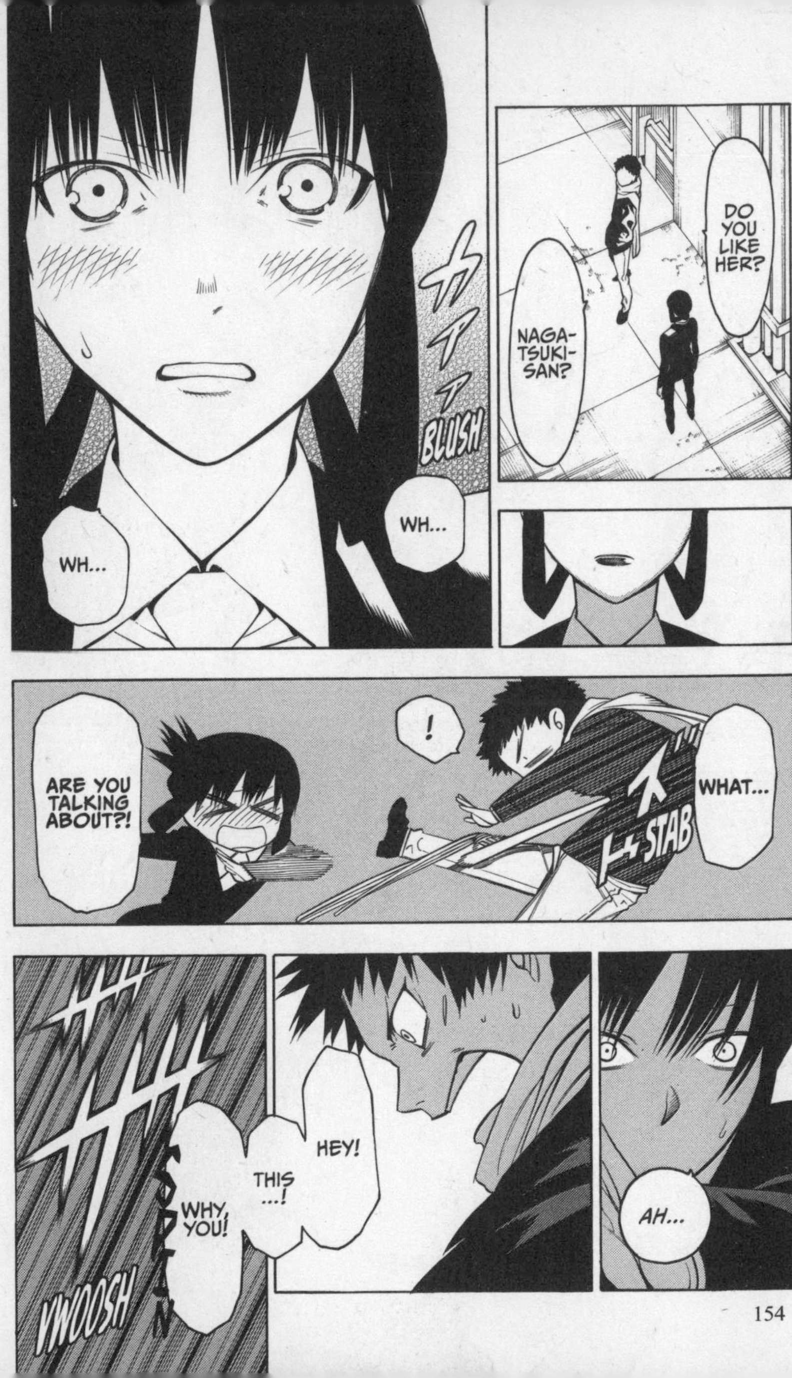
DO YOU LIKE HER?
NAGATSUKI-SAN?
BLUSH
WH...
WH...
WHAT...
STAB
!
ARE YOU TALKING ABOUT?!
AH...
HEY!
THIS ...!
WHY, YOU!
VWOOSH

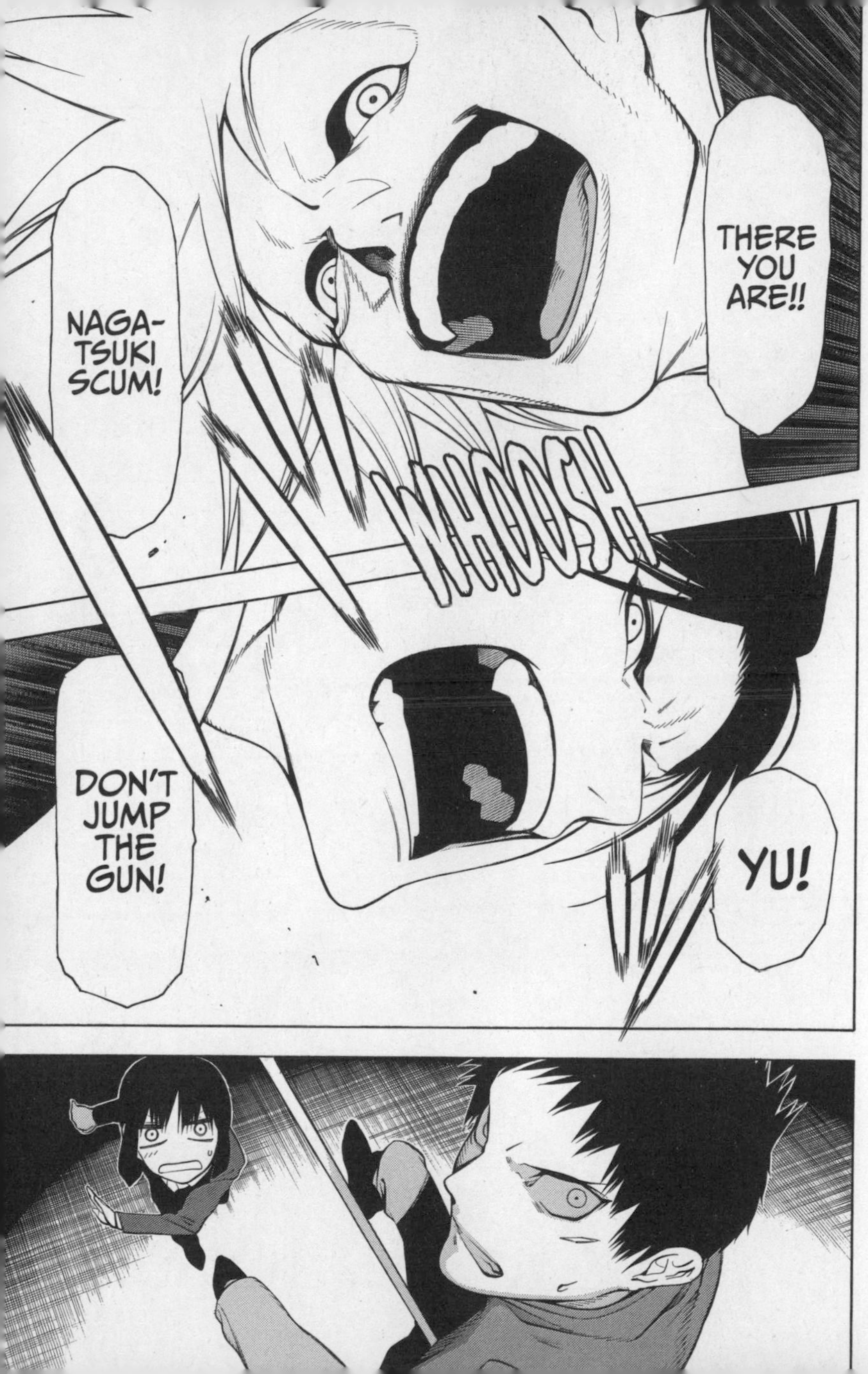
THERE YOU ARE!!
NAGA-TSUKI SCUM!
WHOOSH
YU!
DON'T JUMP THE GUN!

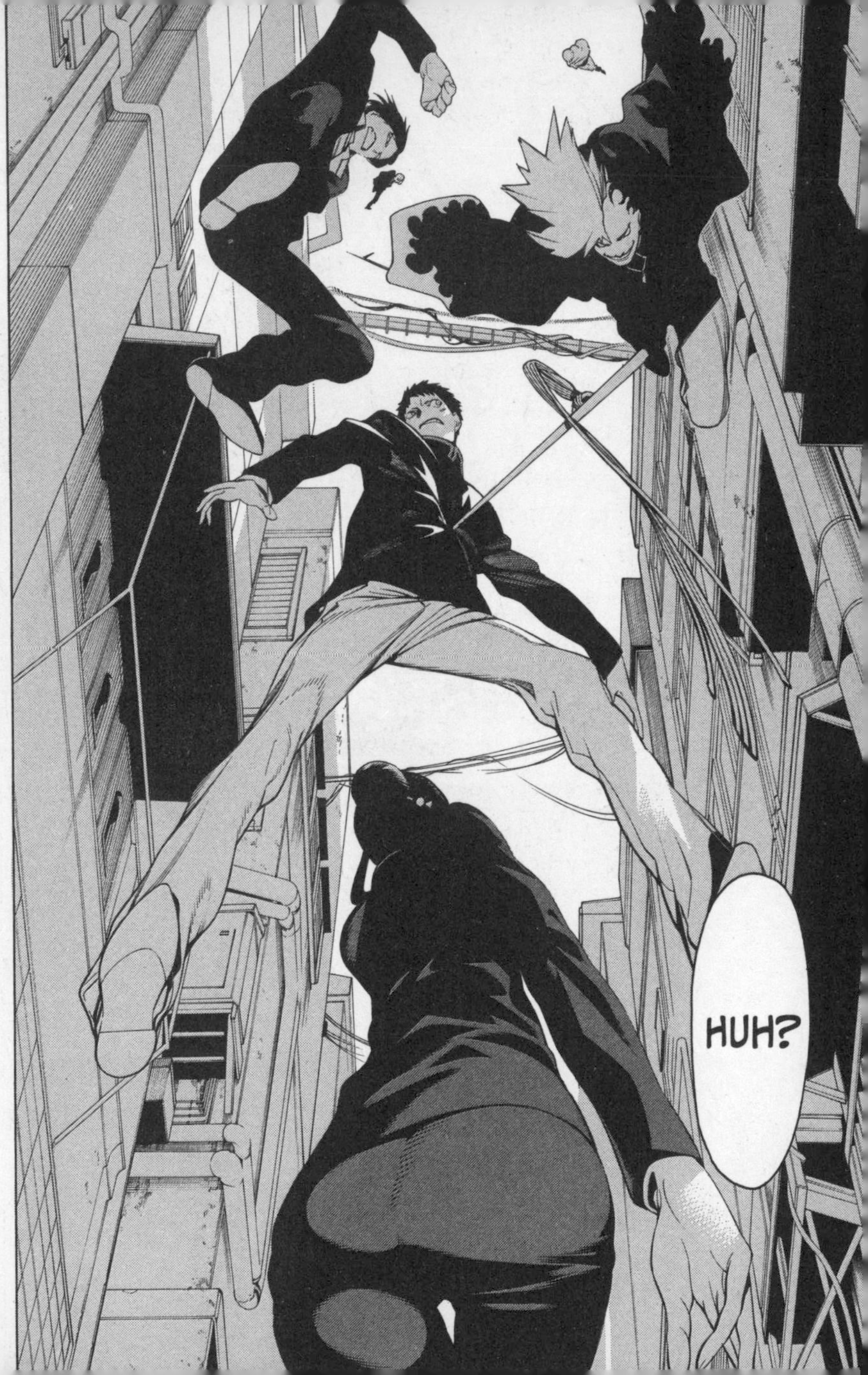
HUH?

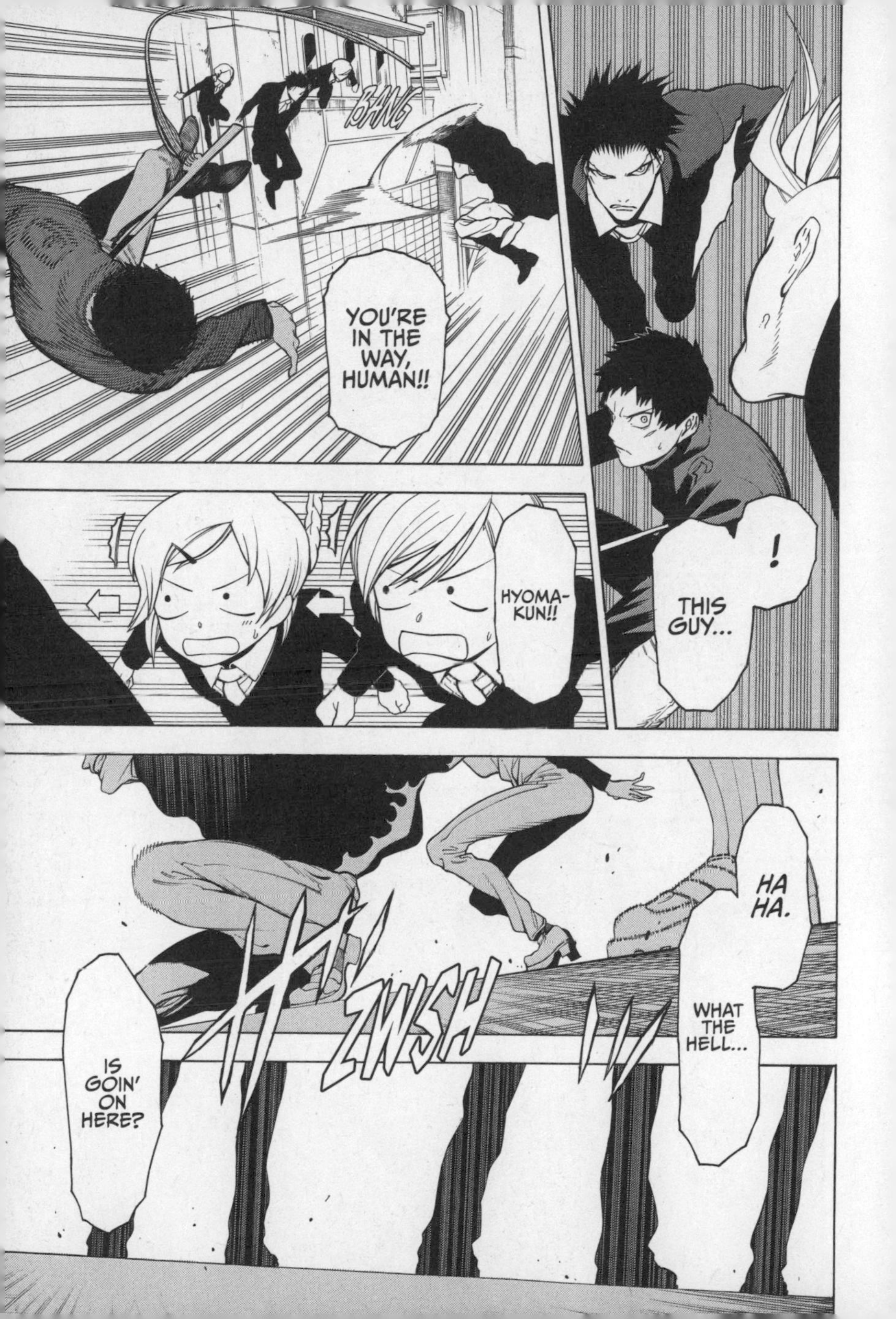
!
THIS GUY...
BANG
YOU'RE IN THE WAY, HUMAN!!
HYOMA-KUN!!
HA HA.
WHAT THE HELL...
ZWISH
IS GOIN' ON HERE?

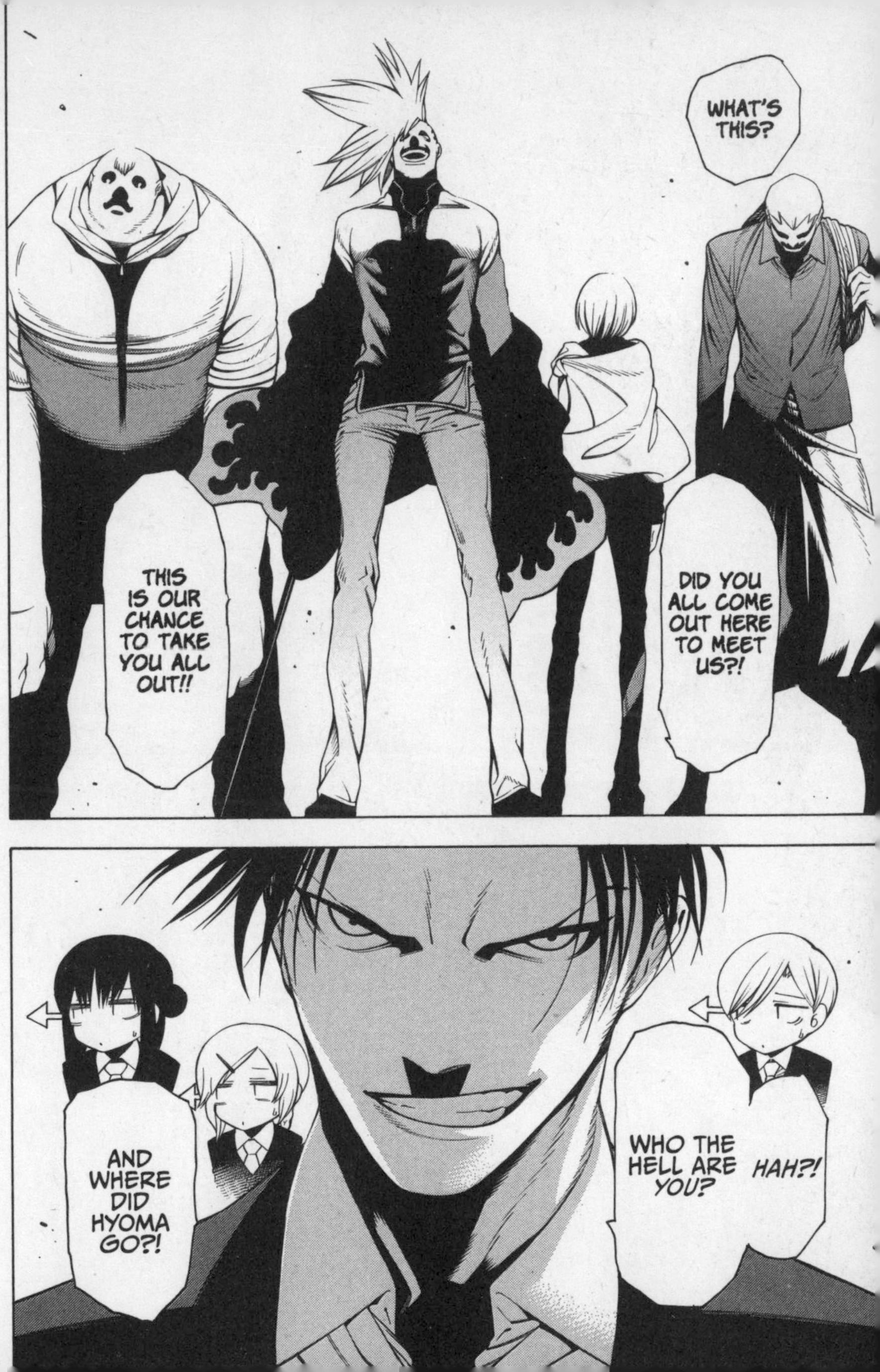
WHAT'S THIS?
DID YOU ALL COME OUT HERE TO MEET US?!
THIS IS OUR CHANCE TO TAKE YOU ALL OUT!!
HAH?!
WHO THE HELL ARE YOU?
AND WHERE DID HYOMA GO?!

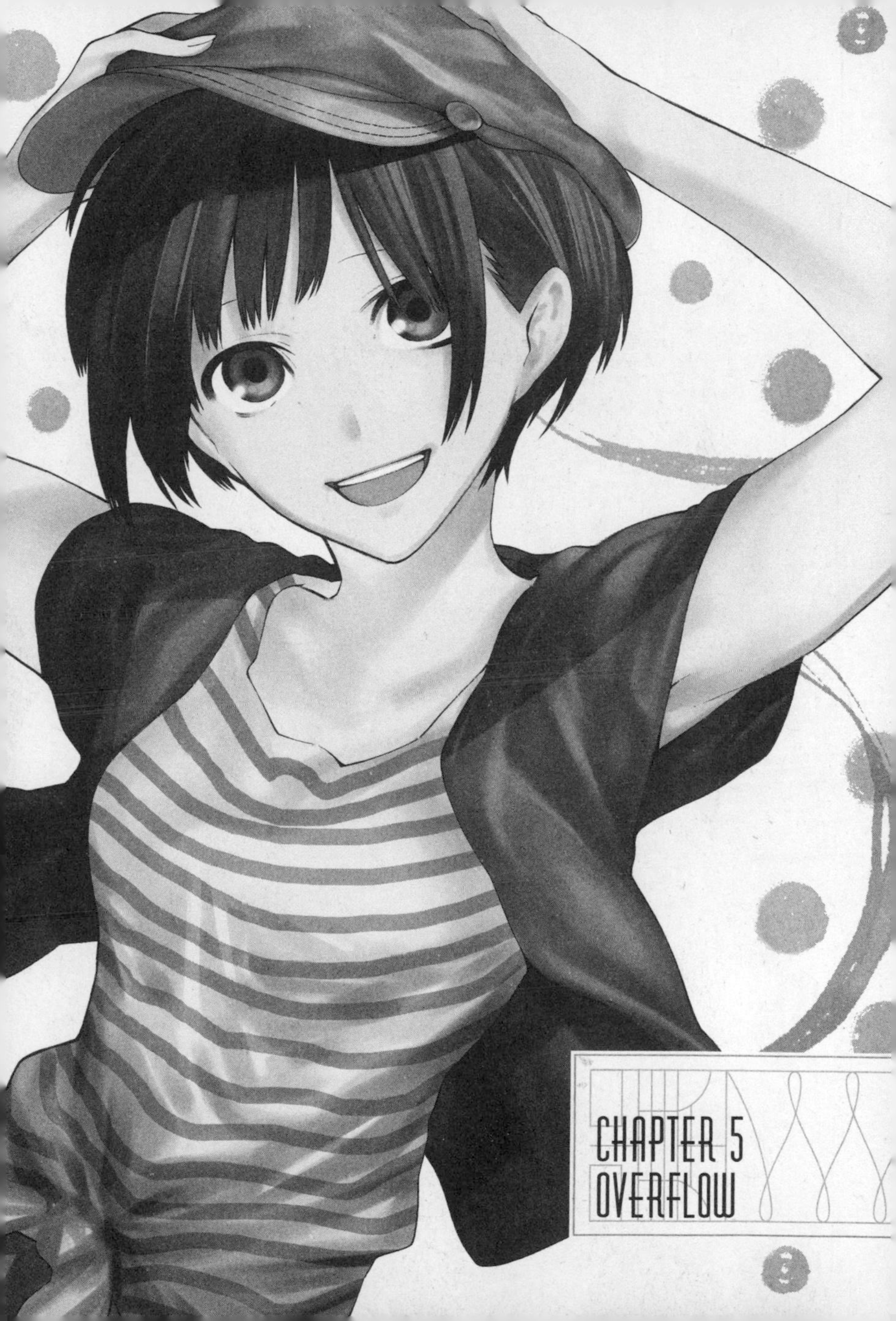
CHAPTER 5
OVERFLOW

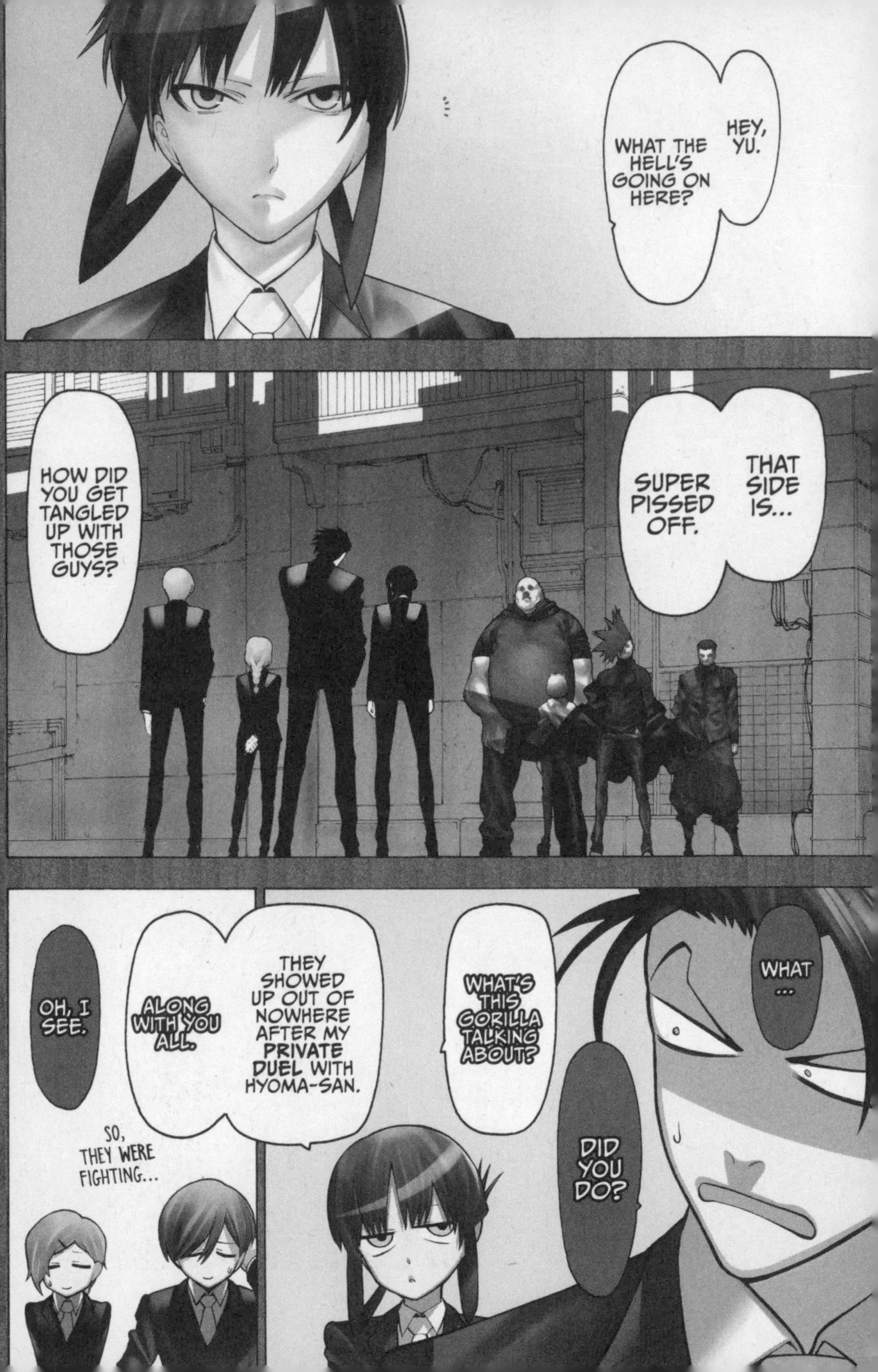
HEY, YU.
WHAT THE HELL'S GOING ON HERE?
THAT SIDE IS...
SUPER PISSED OFF.
HOW DID YOU GET TANGLED UP WITH THOSE GUYS?
WHAT...
DID YOU DO?
WHAT'S THIS GORILLA TALKING ABOUT?
THEY SHOWED UP OUT OF NOWHERE AFTER MY PRIVATE DUEL WITH HYOMA-SAN.
ALONG WITH YOU ALL.
OH, I SEE.
SO, THEY WERE FIGHTING...

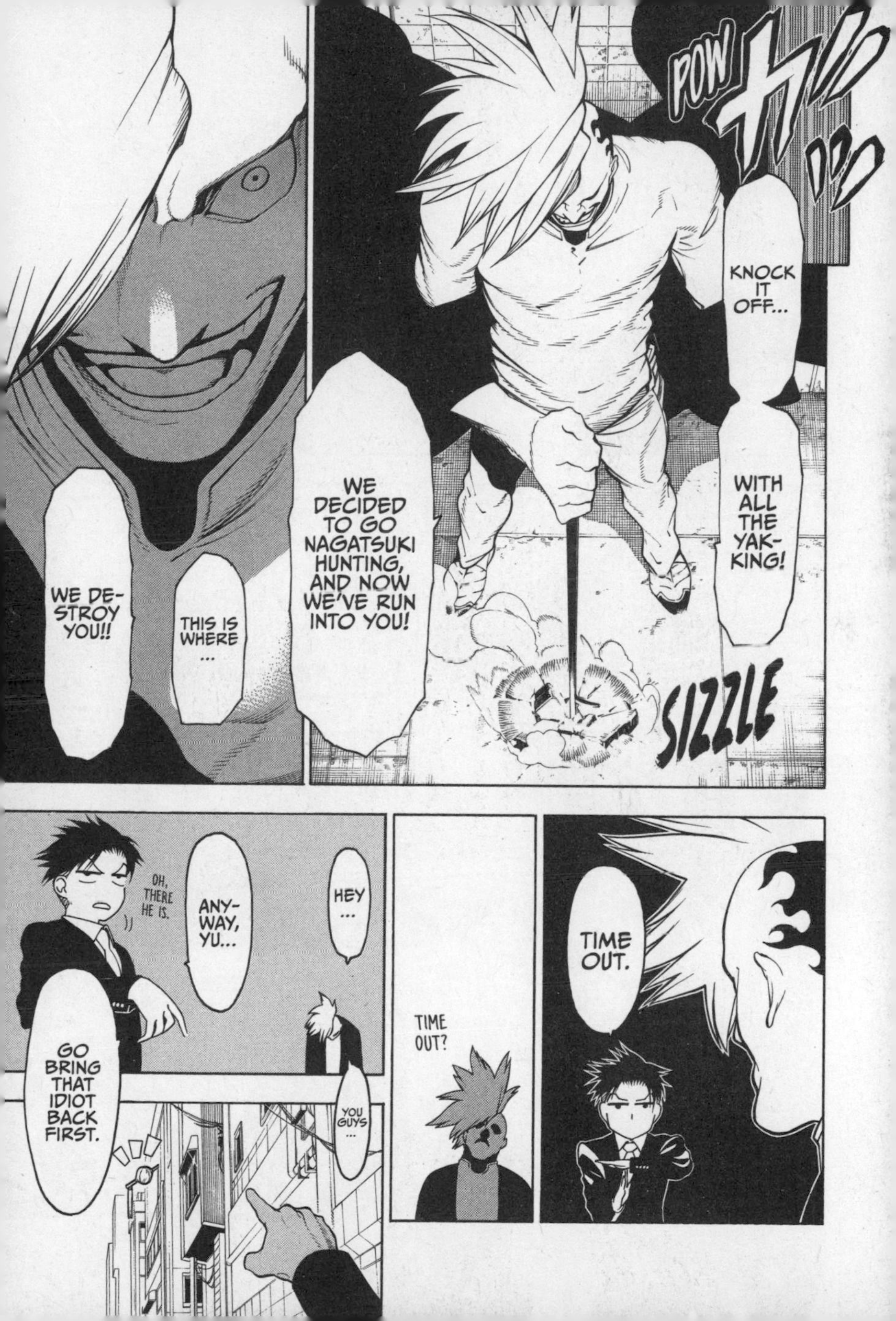
POW
KNOCK IT OFF...
WITH ALL THE YAK-KING!
SIZZLE
WE DECIDED TO GO NAGATSUKI HUNTING, AND NOW WE'VE RUN INTO YOU!
THIS IS WHERE ...
WE DE-STROY YOU!!
TIME OUT.
TIME OUT?
HEY ...
ANY-WAY, YU...
OH, THERE HE IS.
GO BRING THAT IDIOT BACK FIRST.
YOU GUYS ...

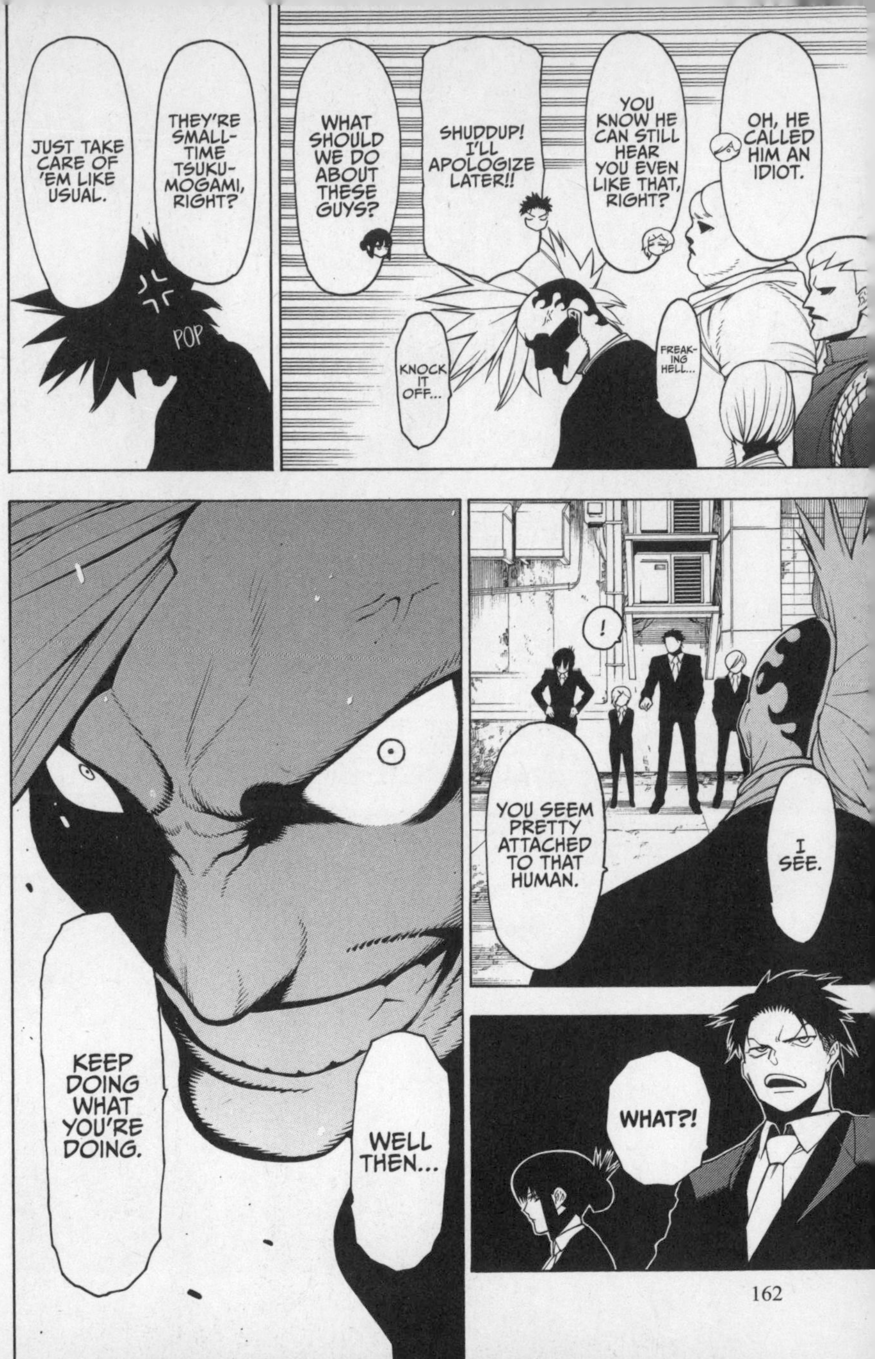
OH, HE CALLED HIM AN IDIOT.
YOU KNOW HE CAN STILL HEAR YOU EVEN LIKE THAT, RIGHT?
FREAKING HELL...
SHUDDUP! I'LL APOLOGIZE LATER!!
KNOCK IT OFF...
WHAT SHOULD WE DO ABOUT THESE GUYS?
THEY'RE SMALL-TIME TSUKUMOGAMI, RIGHT?
JUST TAKE CARE OF 'EM LIKE USUAL.
POP
I SEE.
YOU SEEM PRETTY ATTACHED TO THAT HUMAN.
!
WHAT?!
WELL THEN...
KEEP DOING WHAT YOU'RE DOING.

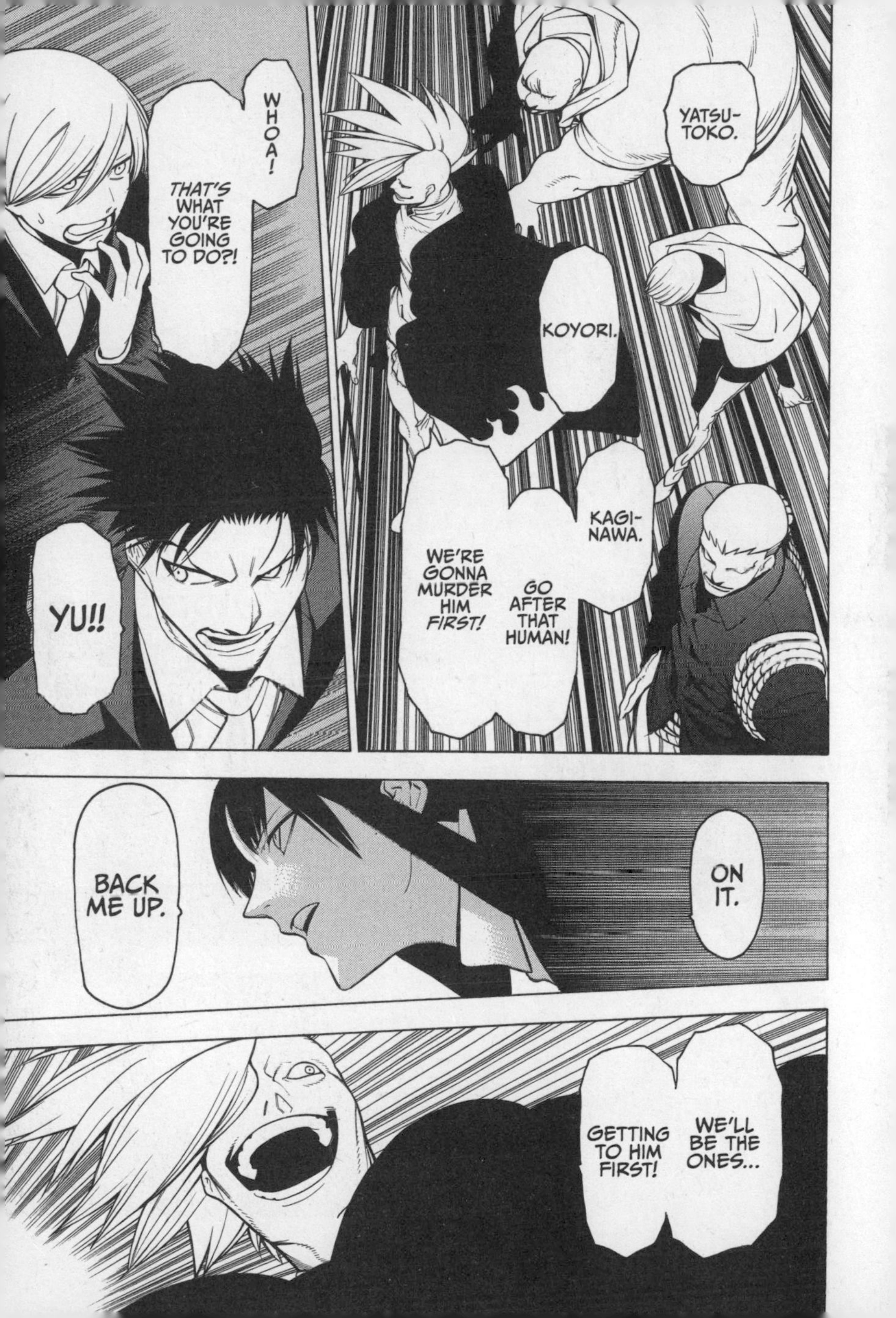
YATSU-TOKO.
KOYORI.
KAGI-NAWA.
GO AFTER THAT HUMAN!
WE'RE GONNA MURDER HIM *FIRST!*
WHOA!
THAT'S WHAT YOU'RE GOING TO DO?!
YU!!
BACK ME UP.
ON IT.
WE'LL BE THE ONES...
GETTING TO HIM FIRST!

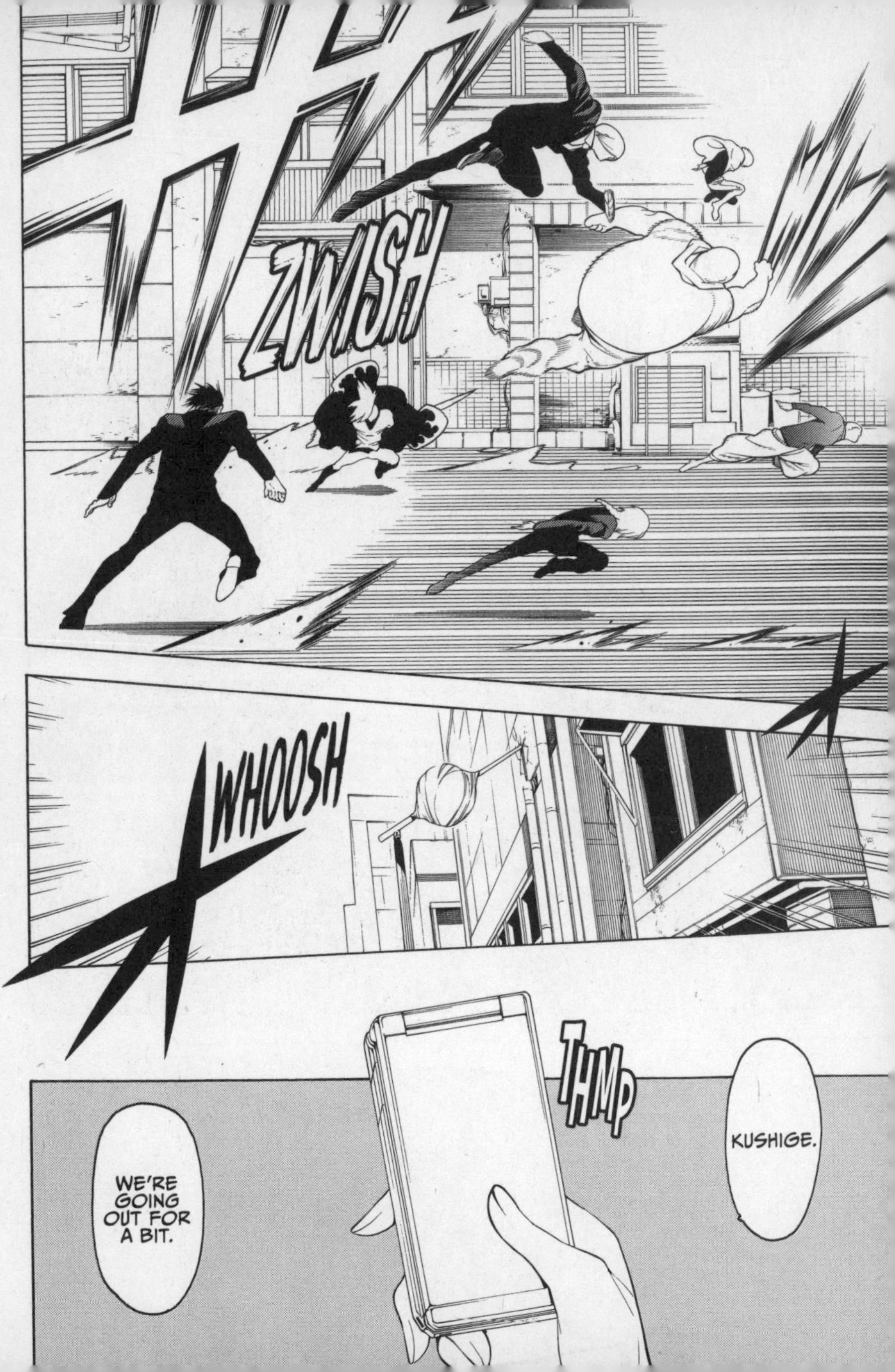
ZWISH
WHOOSH
KUSHIGE.
THMP
WE'RE GOING OUT FOR A BIT.

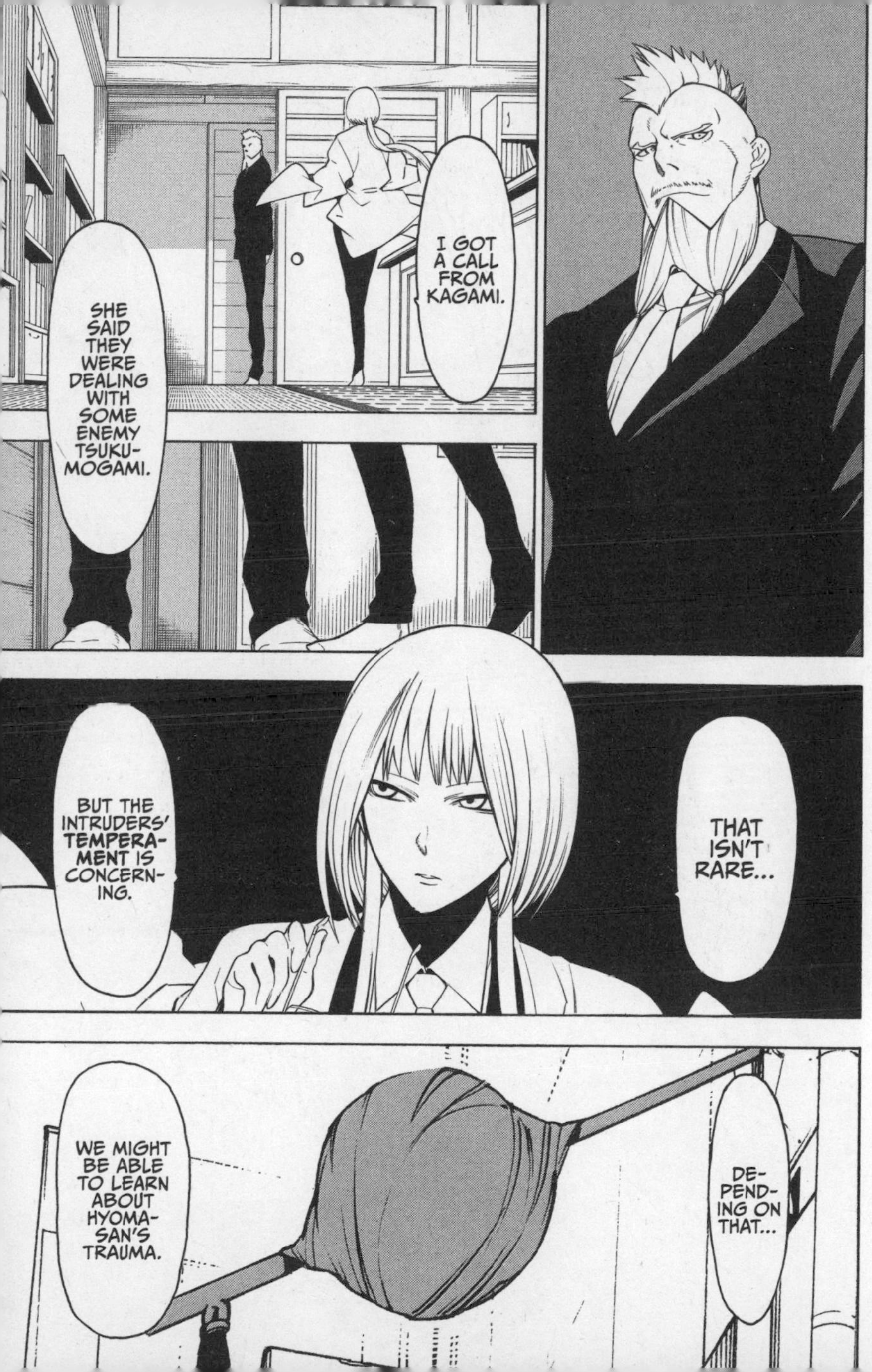
I GOT A CALL FROM KAGAMI.
SHE SAID THEY WERE DEALING WITH SOME ENEMY TSUKU-MOGAMI.
THAT ISN'T RARE...
BUT THE INTRUDERS' TEMPERA-MENT IS CONCERN-ING.
DE-PEND-ING ON THAT...
WE MIGHT BE ABLE TO LEARN ABOUT HYOMA-SAN'S TRAUMA.

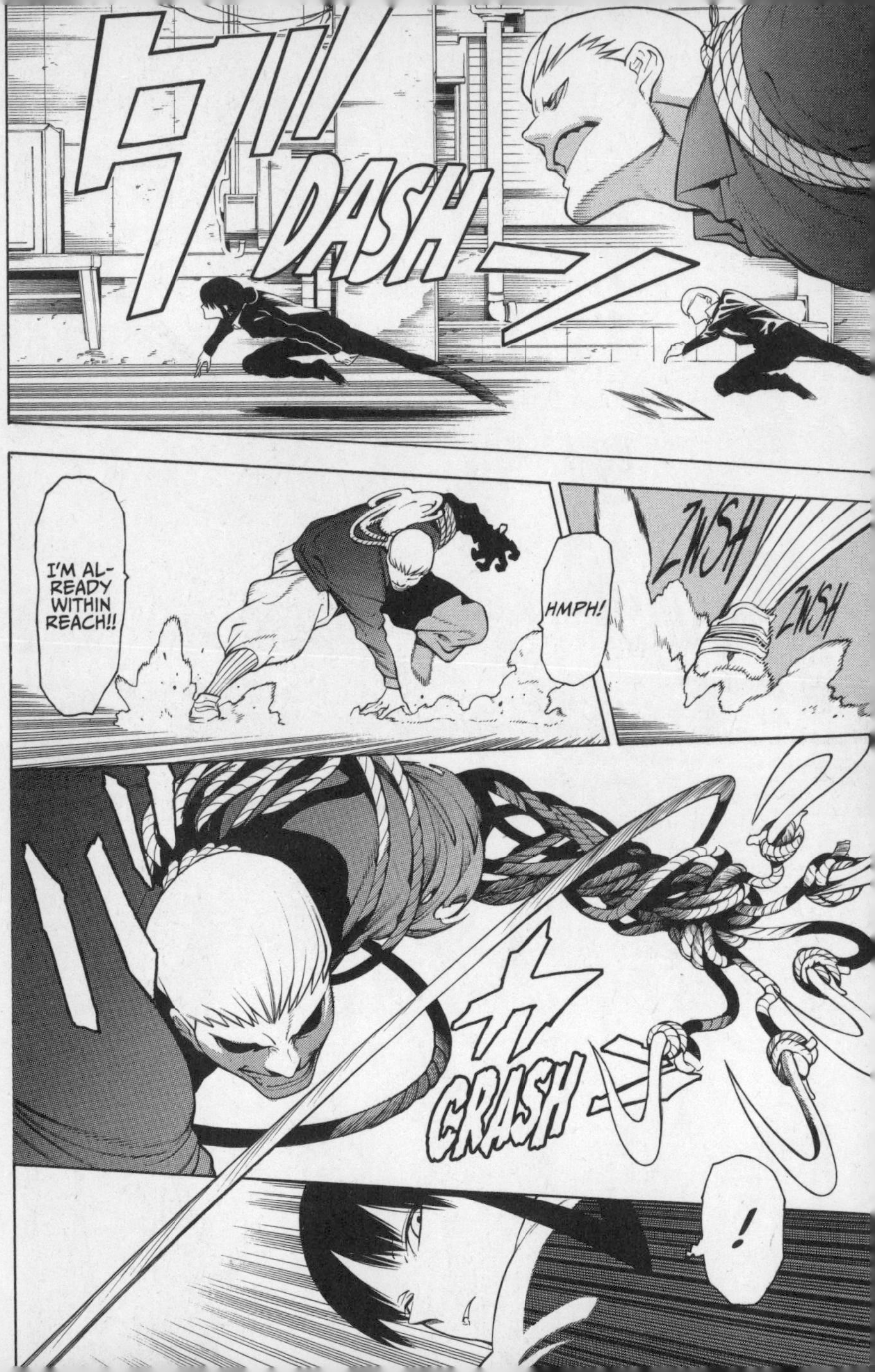
DASH
ZNSH
ZNSH
HMPH!
I'M AL-READY WITHIN REACH!!
CRASH
!

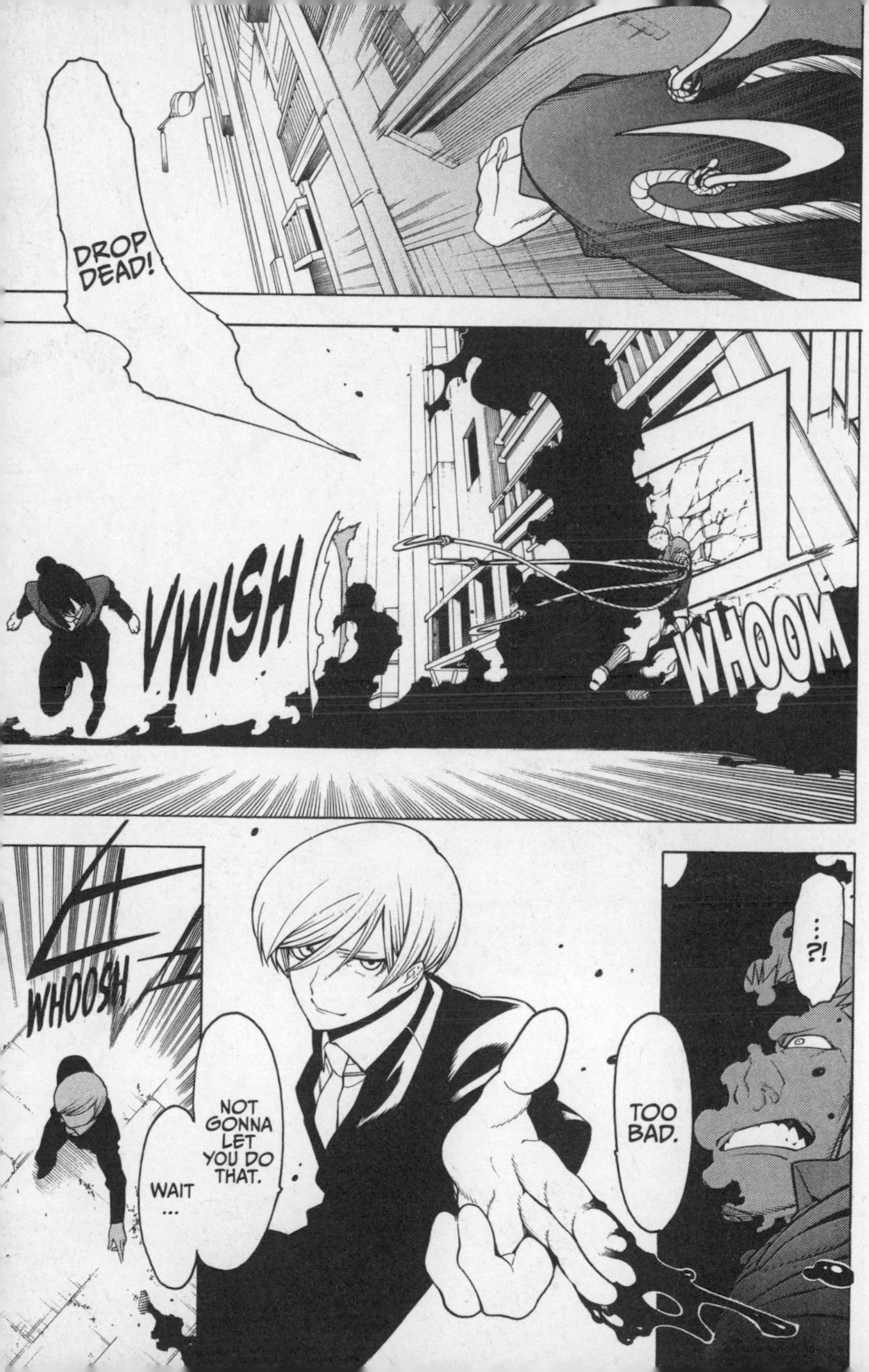
DROP DEAD!
WHOOM
VWISH
...?!
TOO BAD.
NOT GONNA LET YOU DO THAT.
WAIT ...
WHOOSH

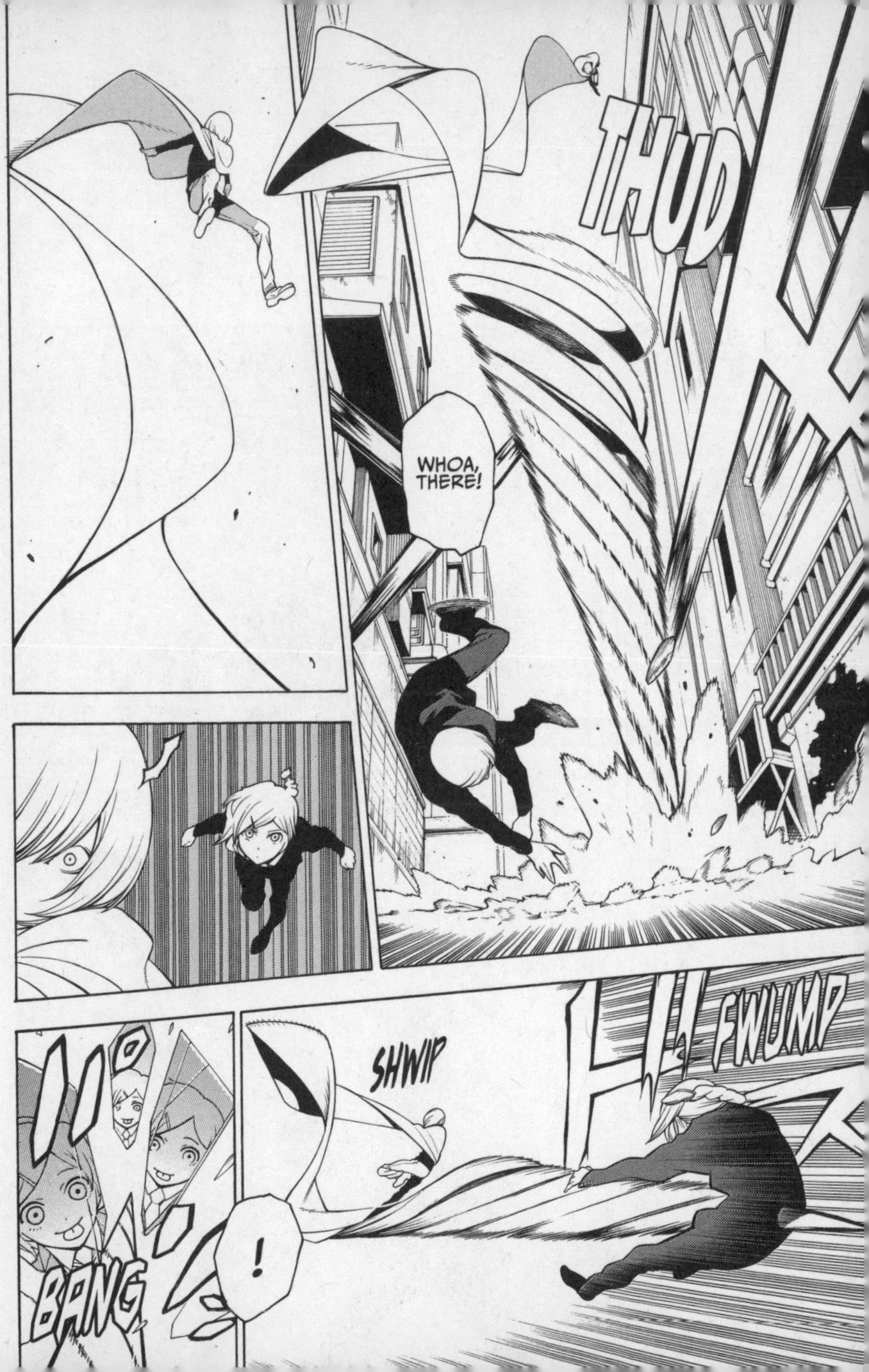
THUD
WHOA, THERE!
FWUMP
SHWIP
!
BANG

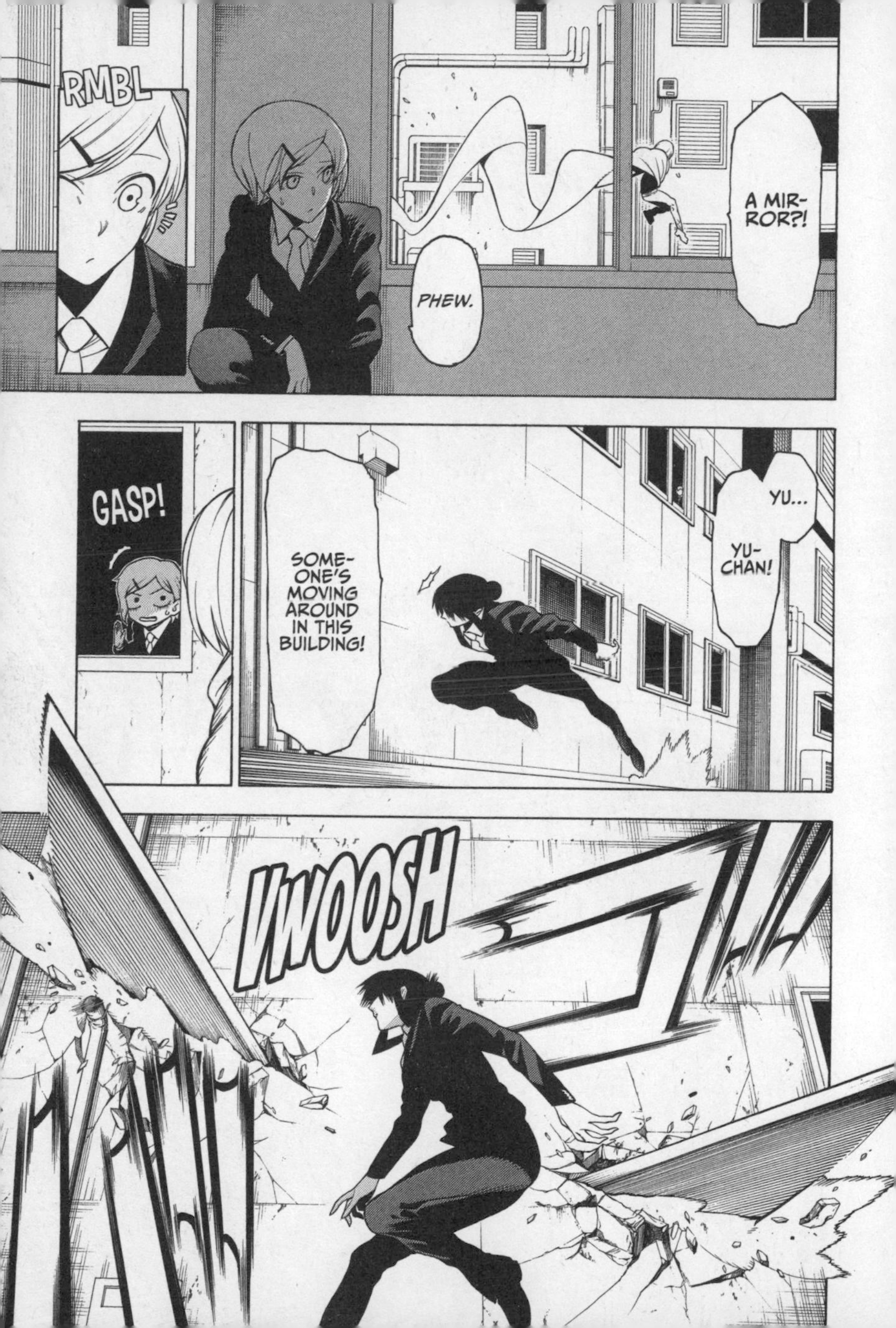

A MIR-ROR?!
PHEW.
RMBL
YU... YU-CHAN!
SOME-ONE'S MOVING AROUND IN THIS BUILDING!
GASP!
VWOOSH

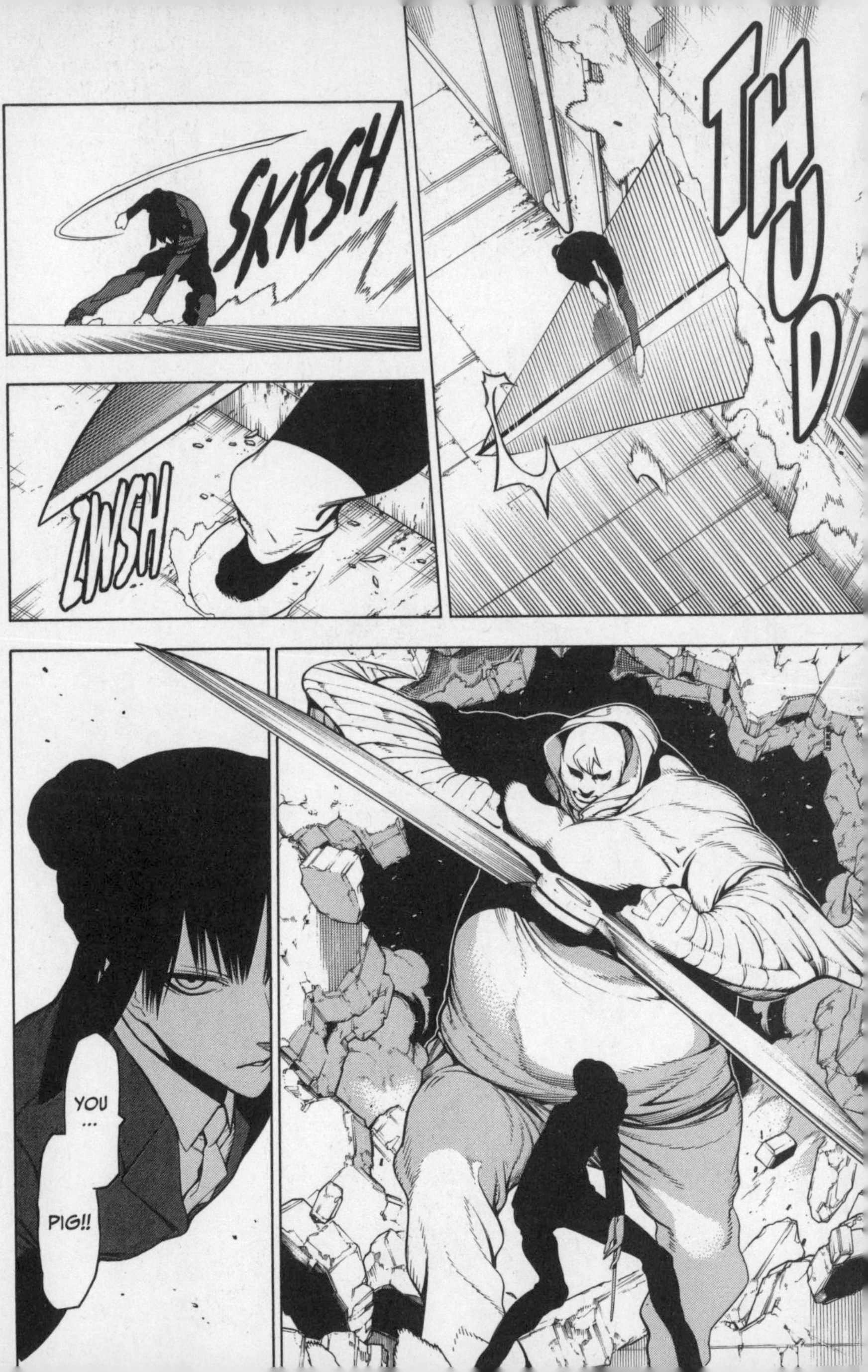
THUD
SKRSH
ZWSH
YOU ...
PIG!!

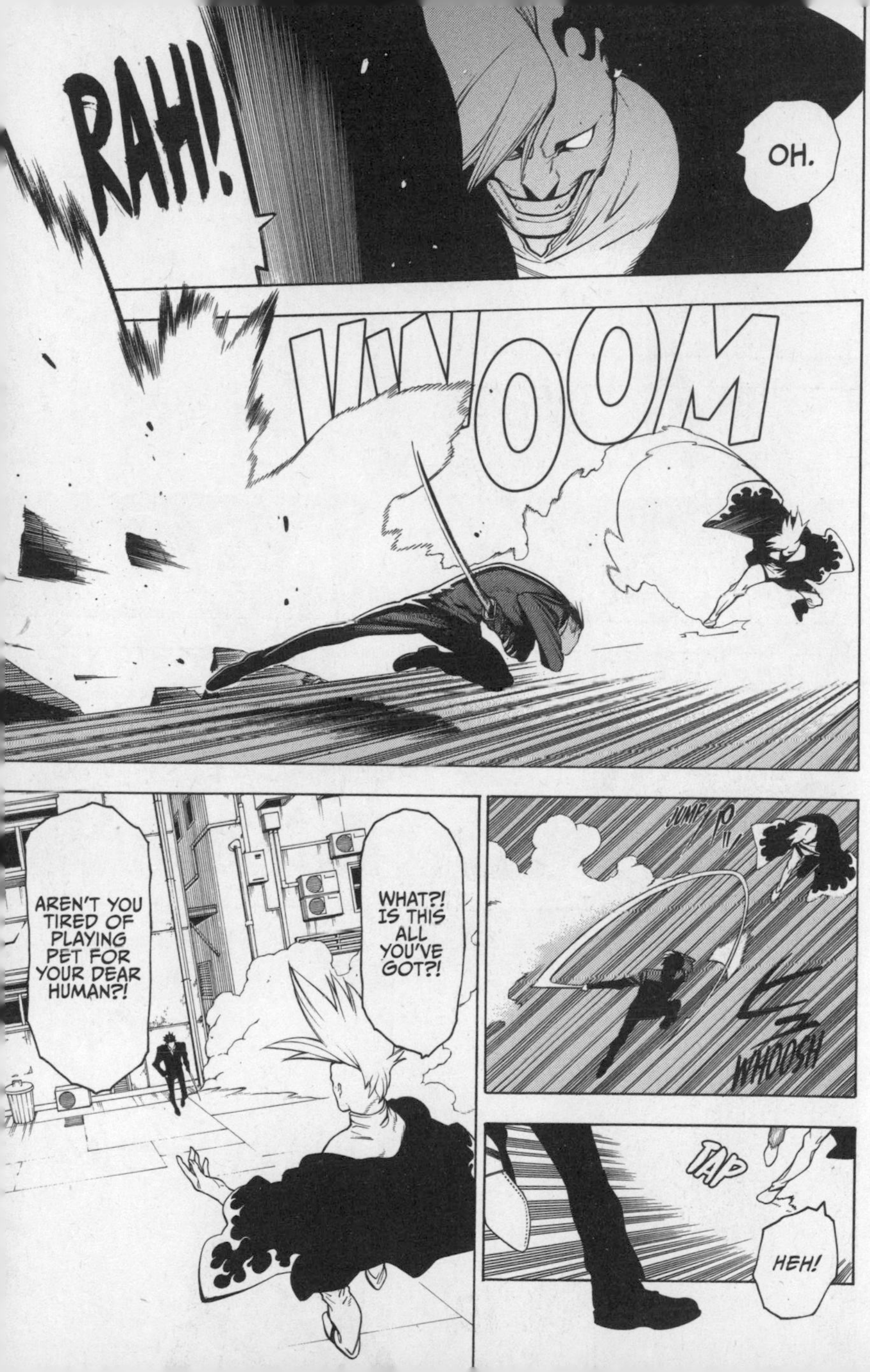
OH.
RAH!
JUMP
WHOOSH
TAP
HEH!
WHAT?! IS THIS ALL YOU'VE GOT?!
AREN'T YOU TIRED OF PLAYING PET FOR YOUR DEAR HUMAN?!

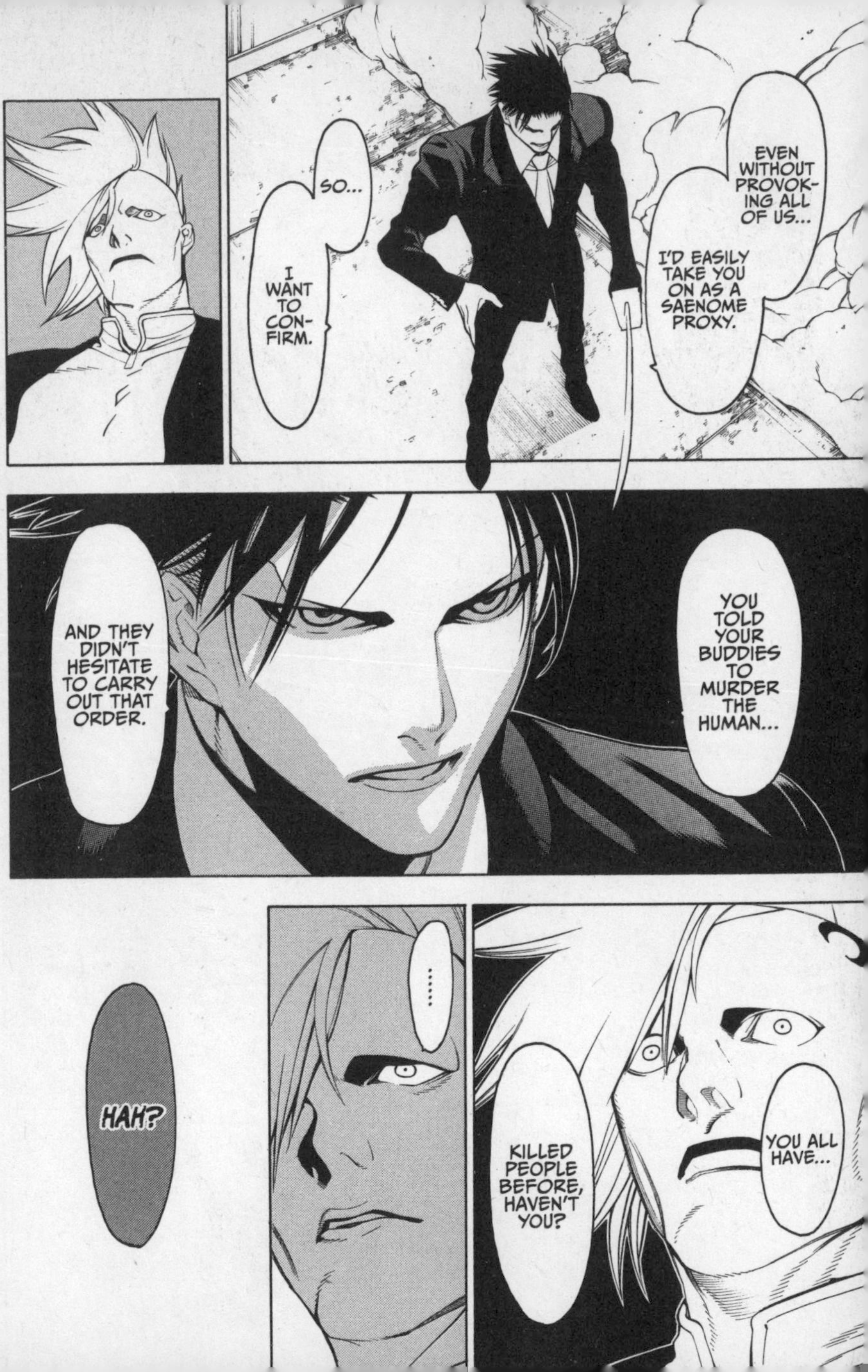
EVEN WITHOUT PROVOKING ALL OF US...
I'D EASILY TAKE YOU ON AS A SAENOME PROXY.
SO...
I WANT TO CONFIRM.
YOU TOLD YOUR BUDDIES TO MURDER THE HUMAN...
AND THEY DIDN'T HESITATE TO CARRY OUT THAT ORDER.
YOU ALL HAVE...
KILLED PEOPLE BEFORE, HAVEN'T YOU?
......
HAH?

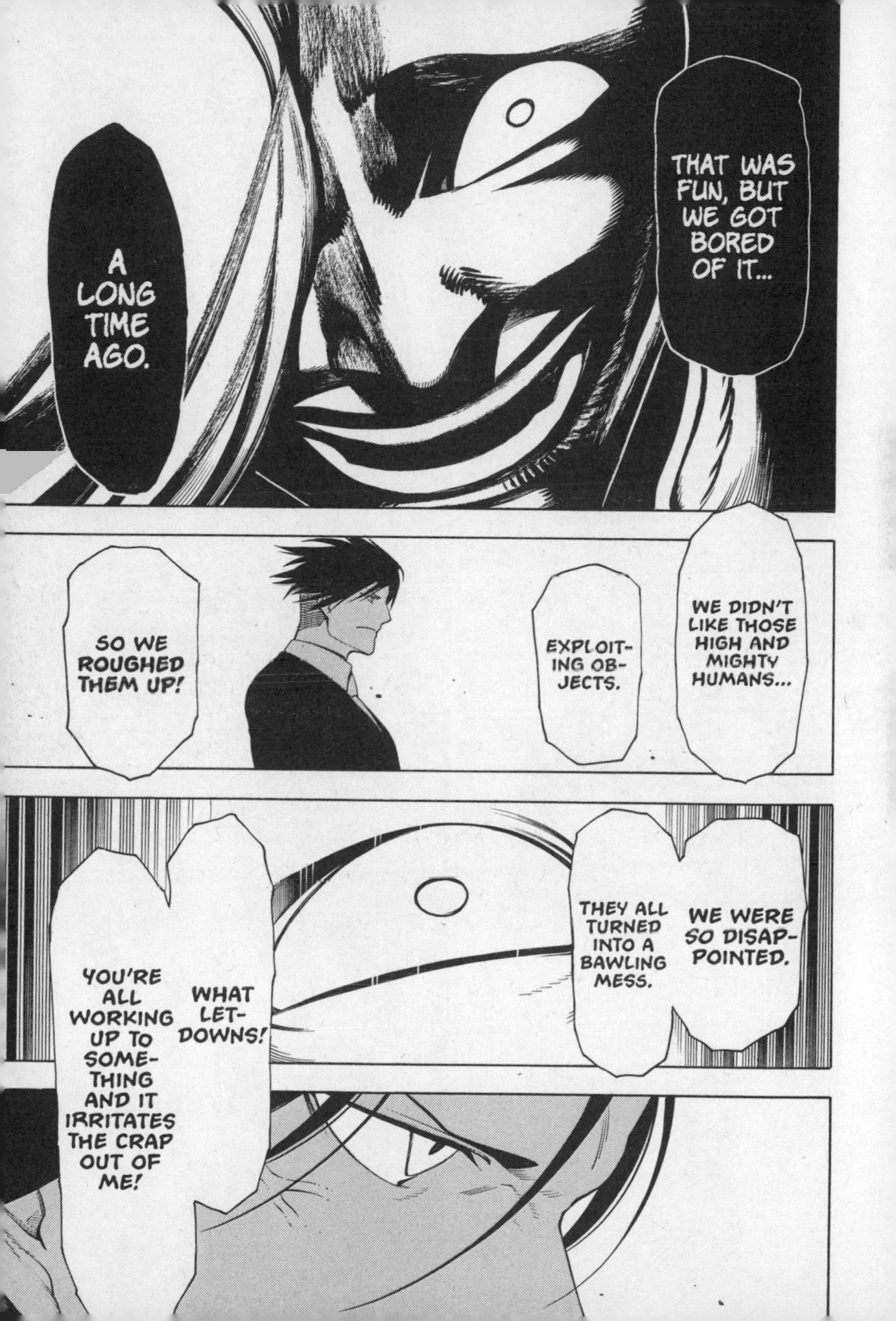
THAT WAS FUN, BUT WE GOT BORED OF IT...
A LONG TIME AGO.
WE DIDN'T LIKE THOSE HIGH AND MIGHTY HUMANS...
EXPLOITING OBJECTS.
SO WE ROUGHED THEM UP!
WE WERE SO DISAPPOINTED.
THEY ALL TURNED INTO A BAWLING MESS.
WHAT LETDOWNS!
YOU'RE ALL WORKING UP TO SOMETHING AND IT IRRITATES THE CRAP OUT OF ME!

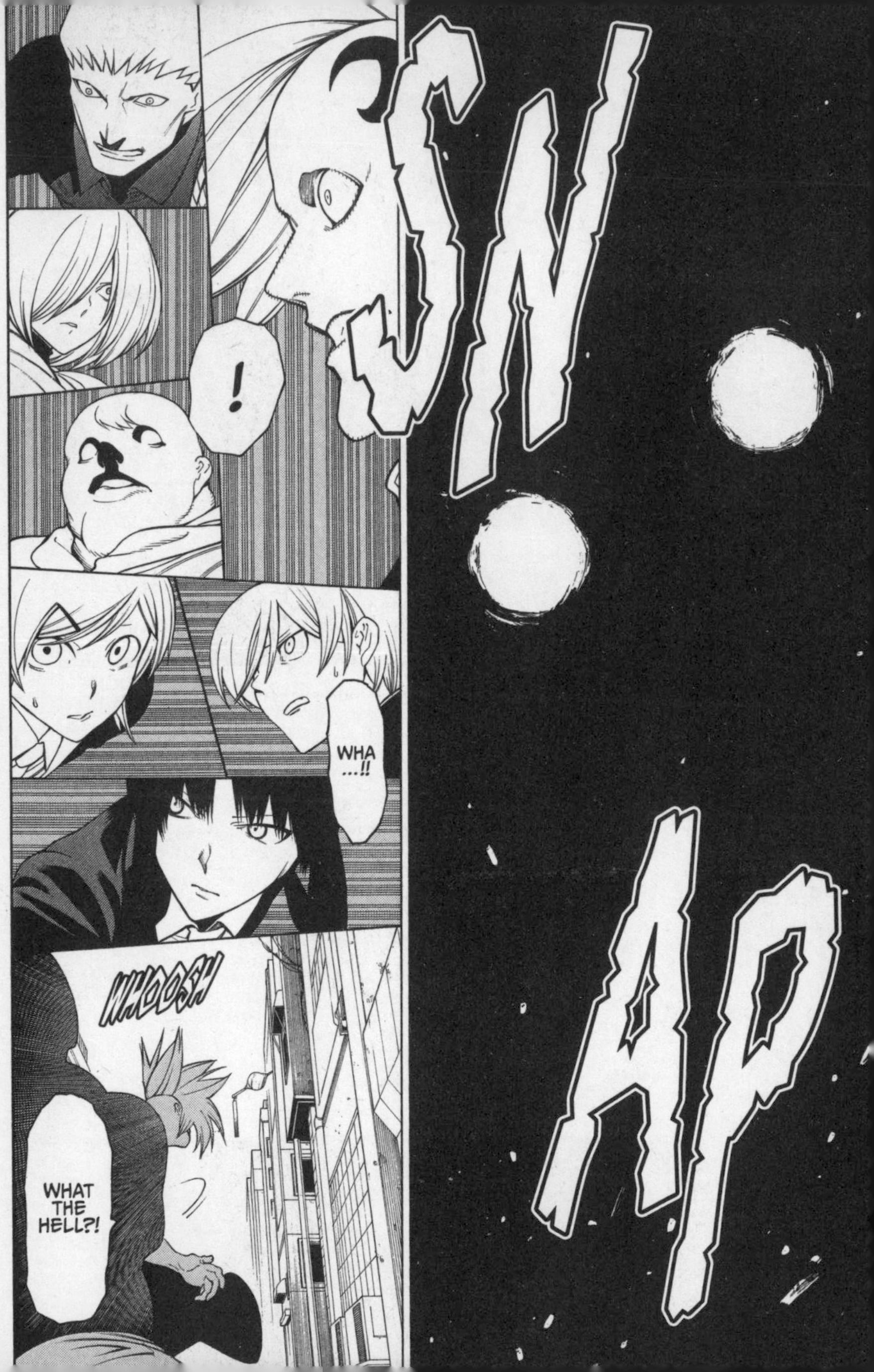
SNAP
!
WHA ...!!
WHOOSH
WHAT THE HELL?!

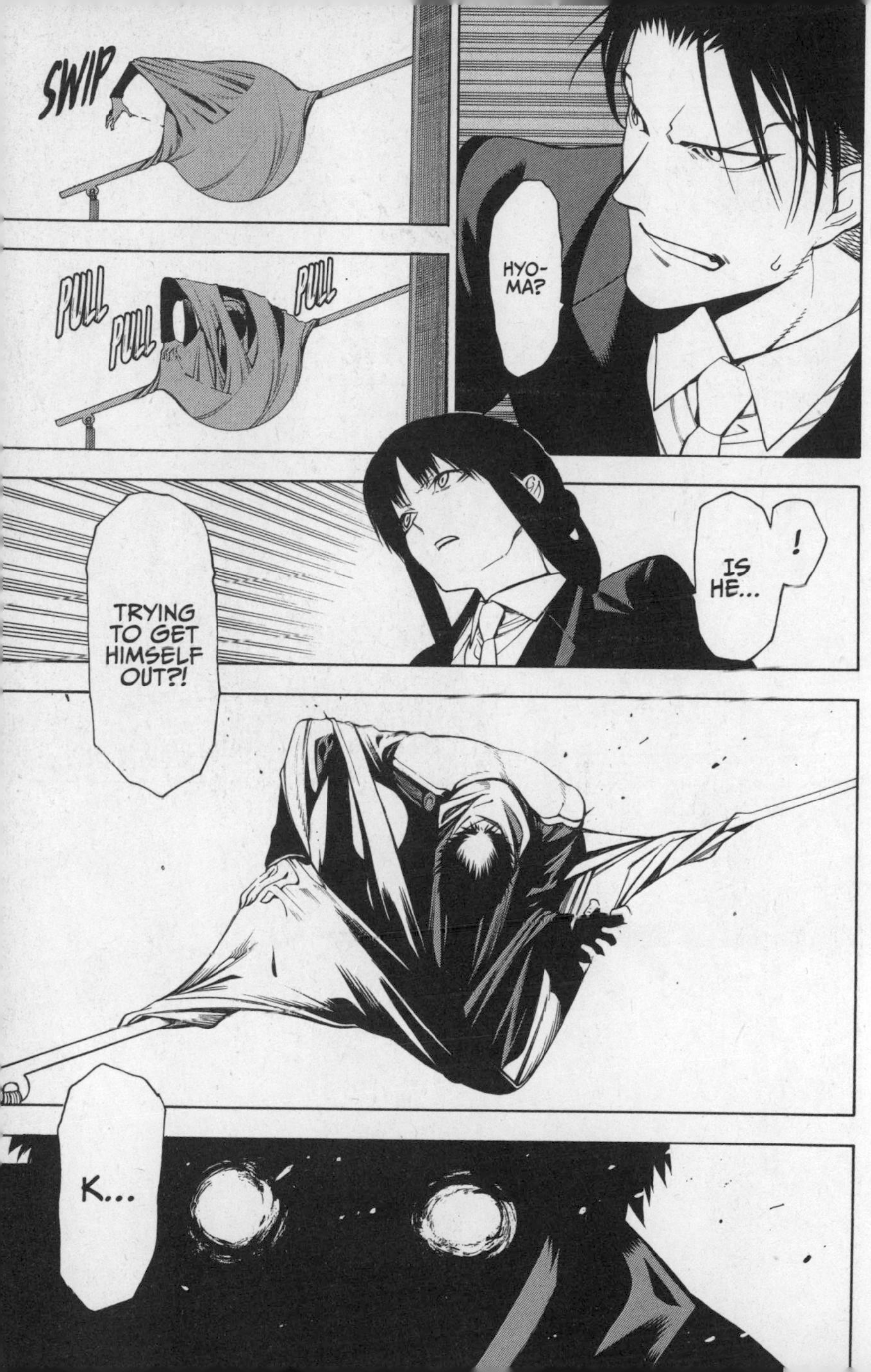
HYO-MA?
SWIP
PULL
PULL
PULL
!
IS HE...
TRYING TO GET HIMSELF OUT?!
K...

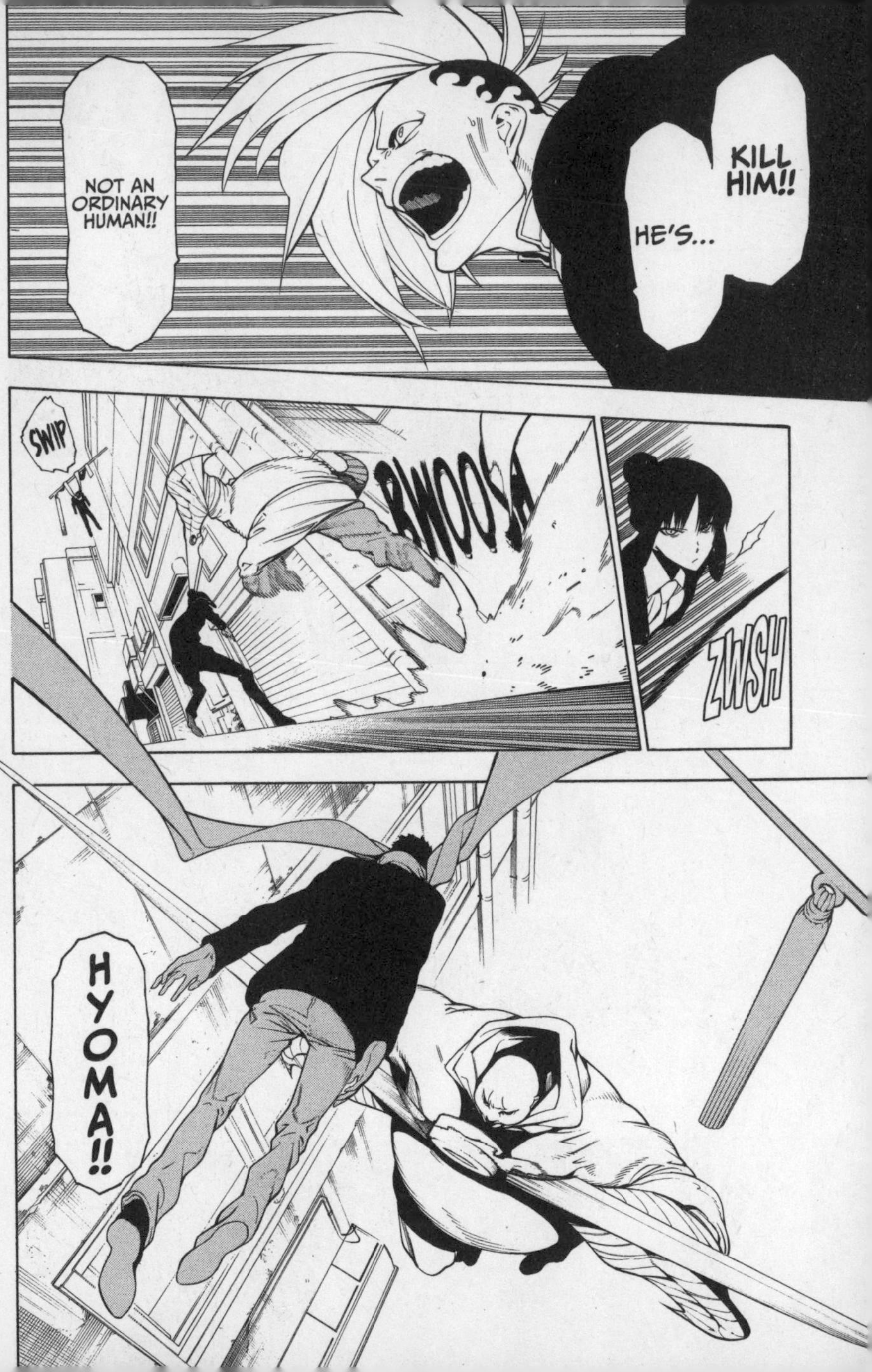
KILL HIM!!
HE'S...
NOT AN ORDINARY HUMAN!!
ZWSH
SWIP
HYOMA!!

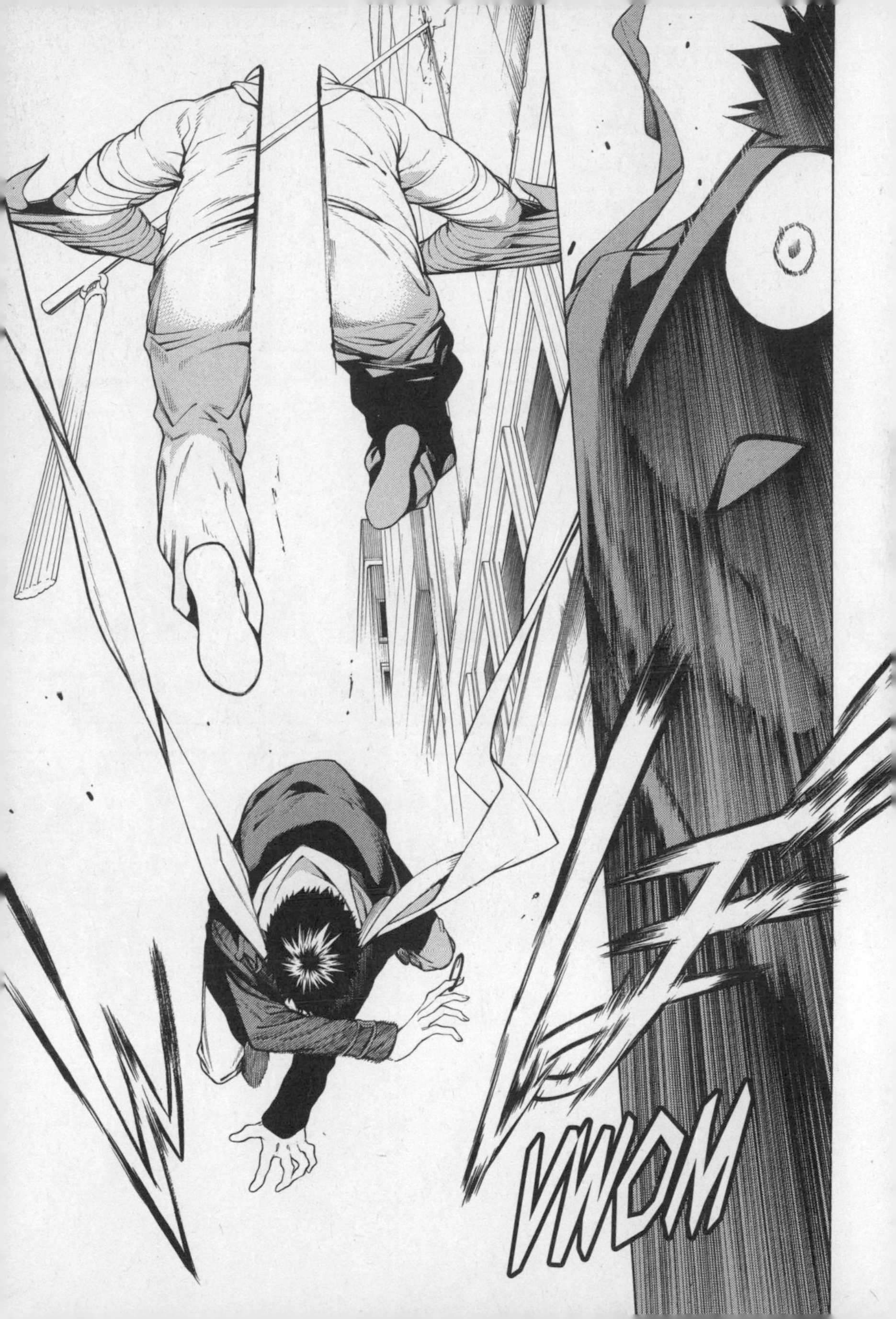
VWOM

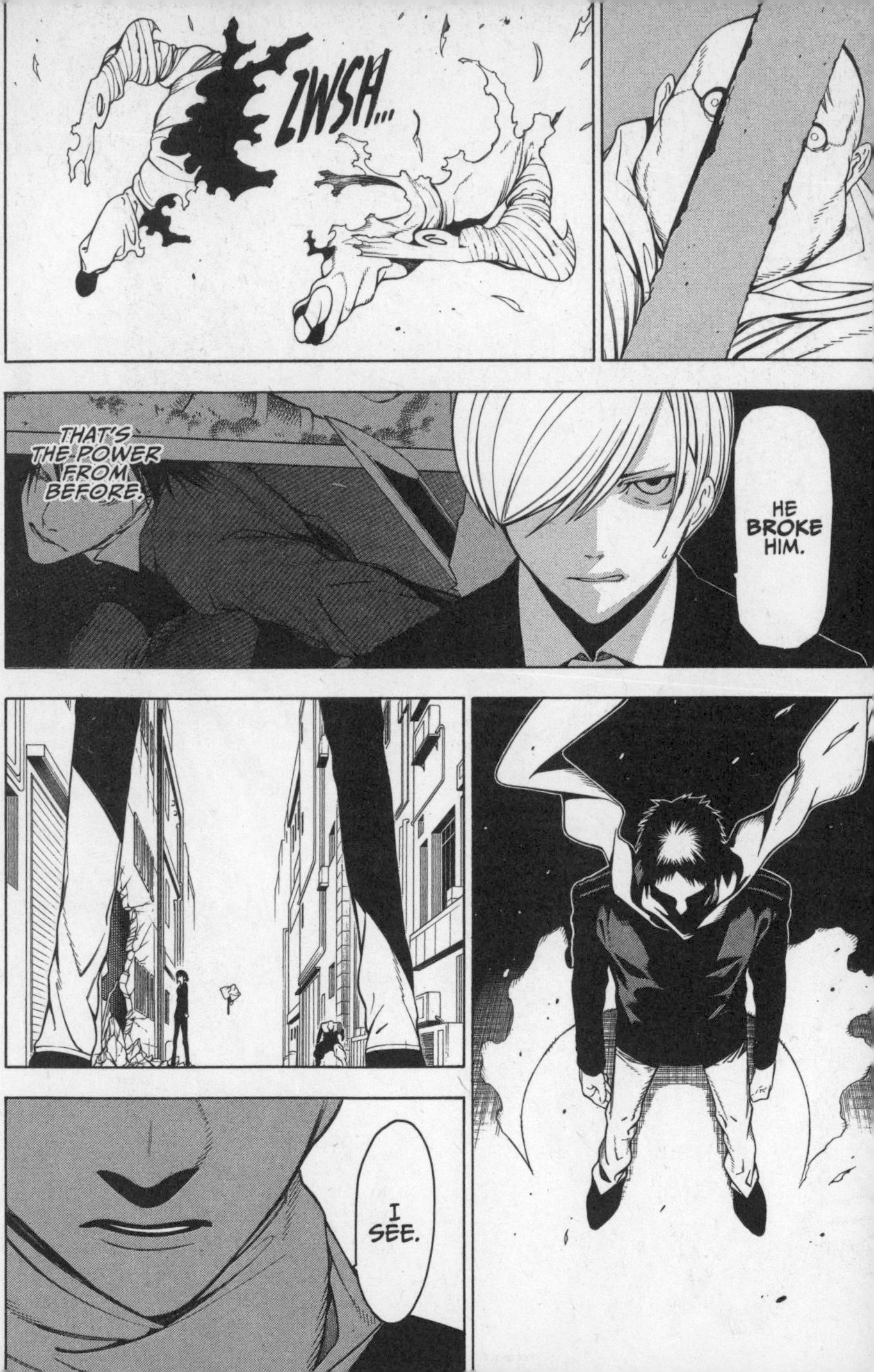
ZWSH...
HE BROKE HIM.
THAT'S THE POWER FROM BEFORE.
I SEE.

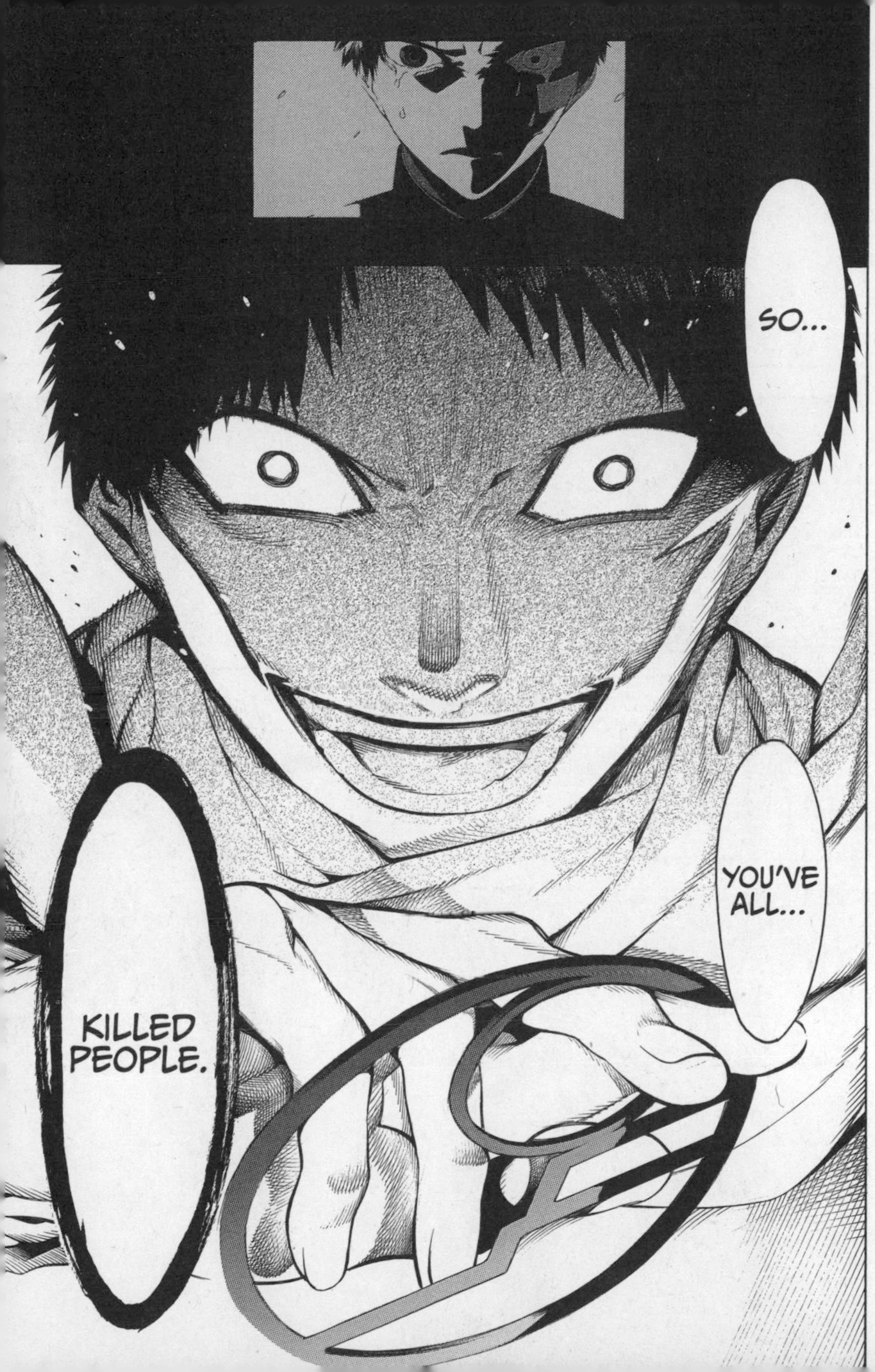
SO...
YOU'VE ALL...
KILLED PEOPLE.

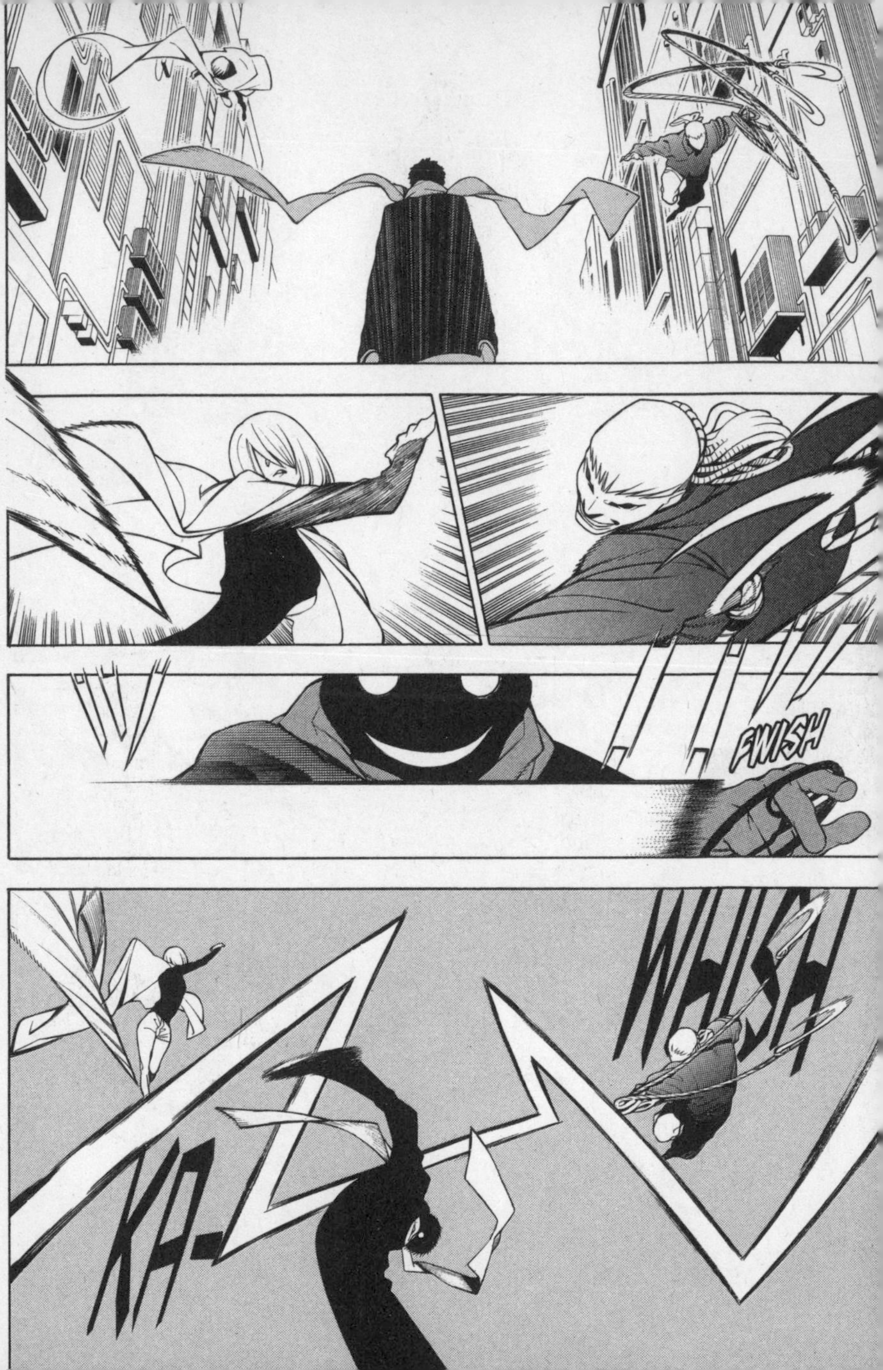
FWISH
WHISH
KA-

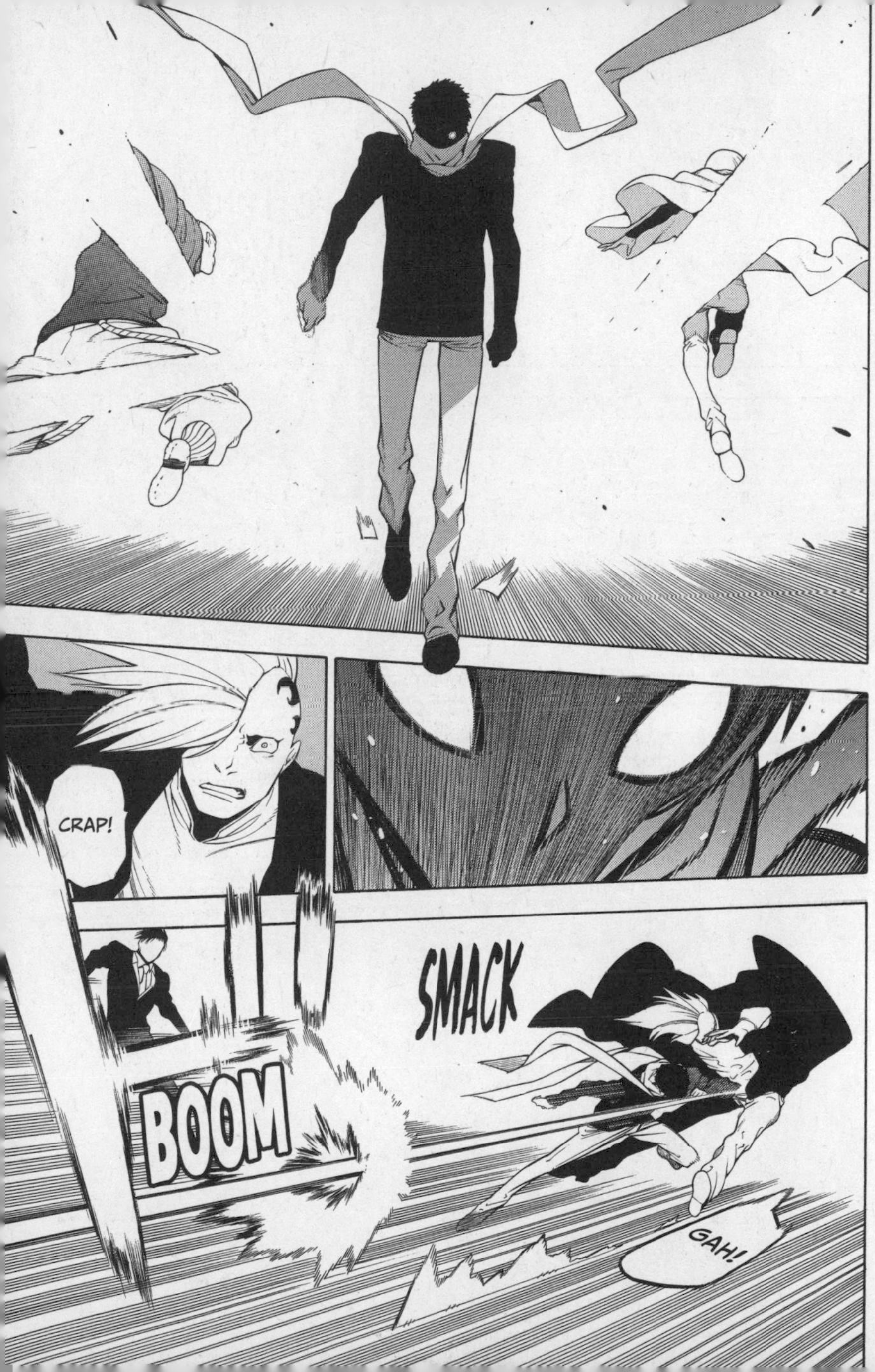
CRAP!
SMACK
GAH!
BOOM

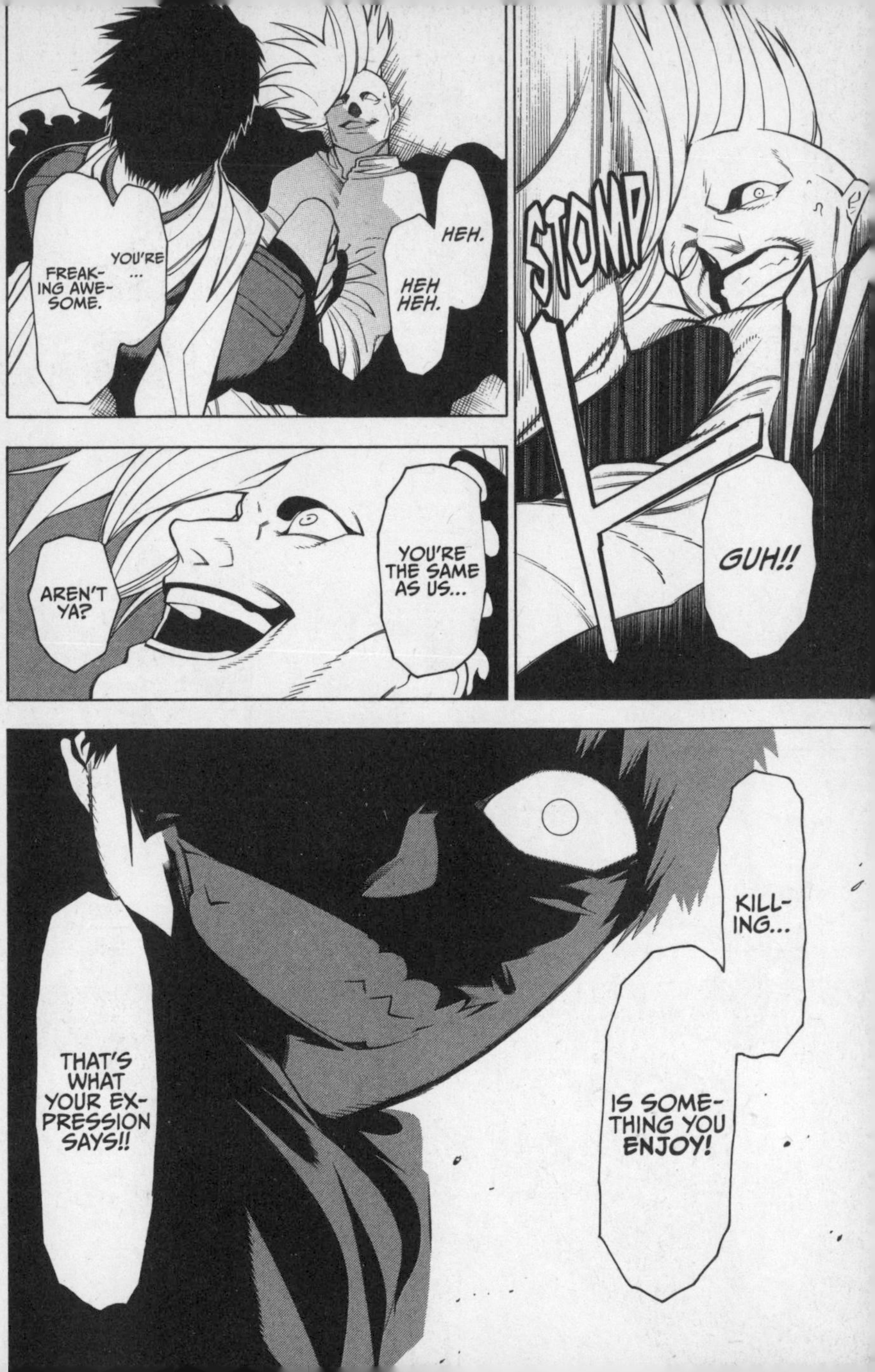
STOMP
GUH!!
HEH.
HEH HEH.
YOU'RE ...
FREAKING AWESOME.
YOU'RE THE SAME AS US...
AREN'T YA?
KILLING...
IS SOMETHING YOU ENJOY!
THAT'S WHAT YOUR EXPRESSION SAYS!!

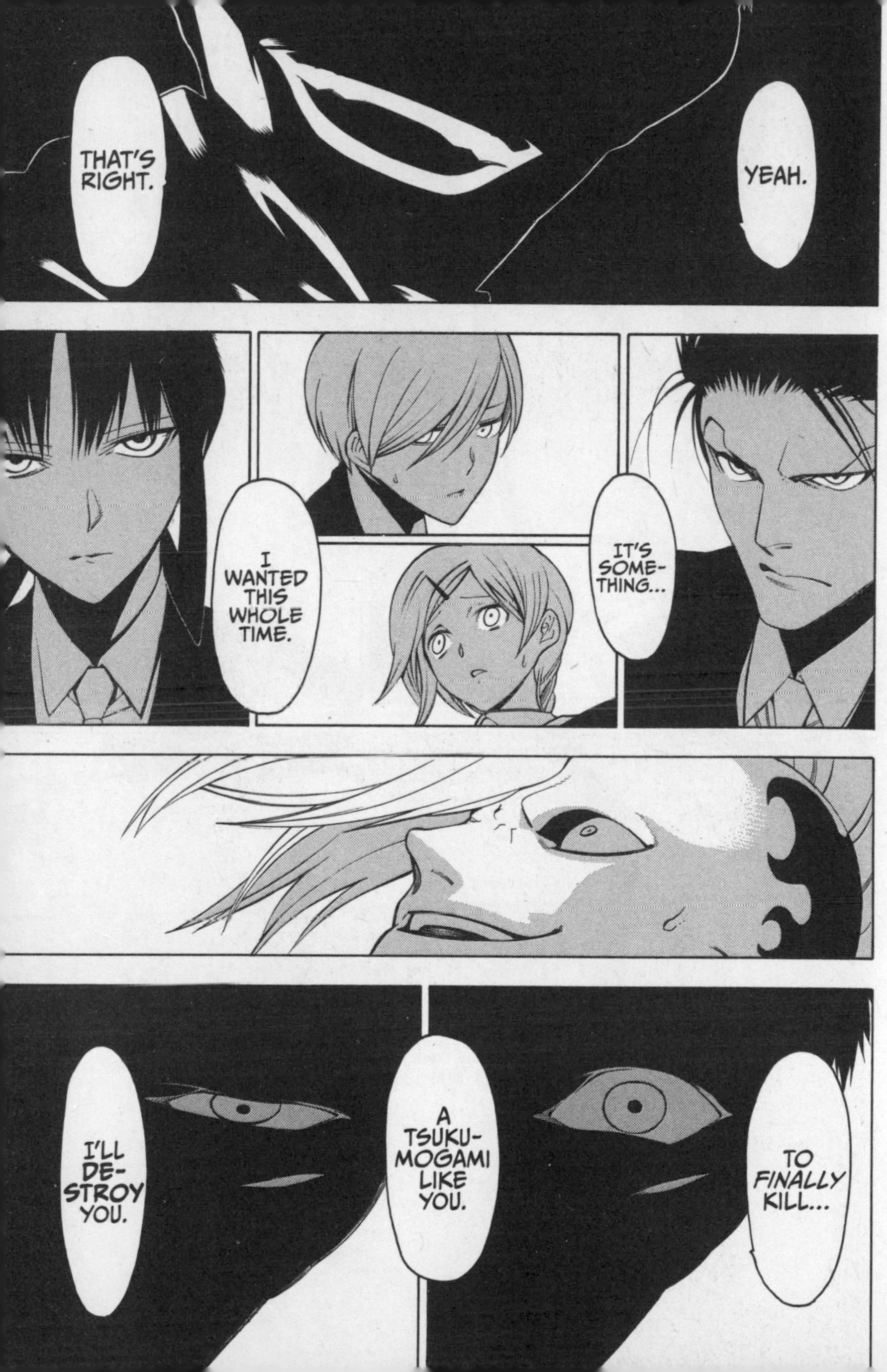
YEAH.
THAT'S RIGHT.
IT'S SOME-THING...
I WANTED THIS WHOLE TIME.
TO FINALLY KILL...
A TSUKU-MOGAMI LIKE YOU.
I'LL DE-STROY YOU.

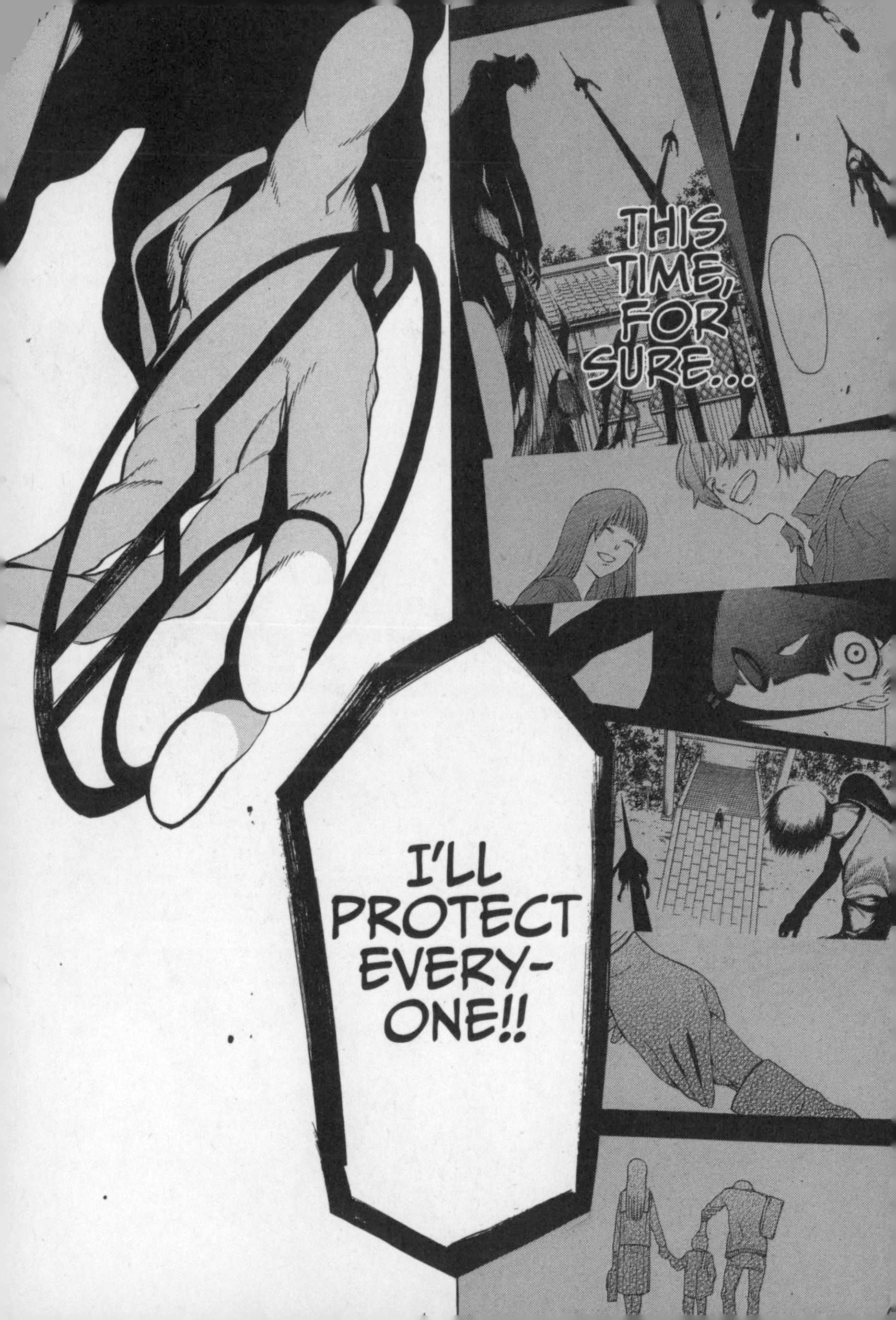
THIS TIME, FOR SURE...
I'LL PROTECT EVERY-ONE!!

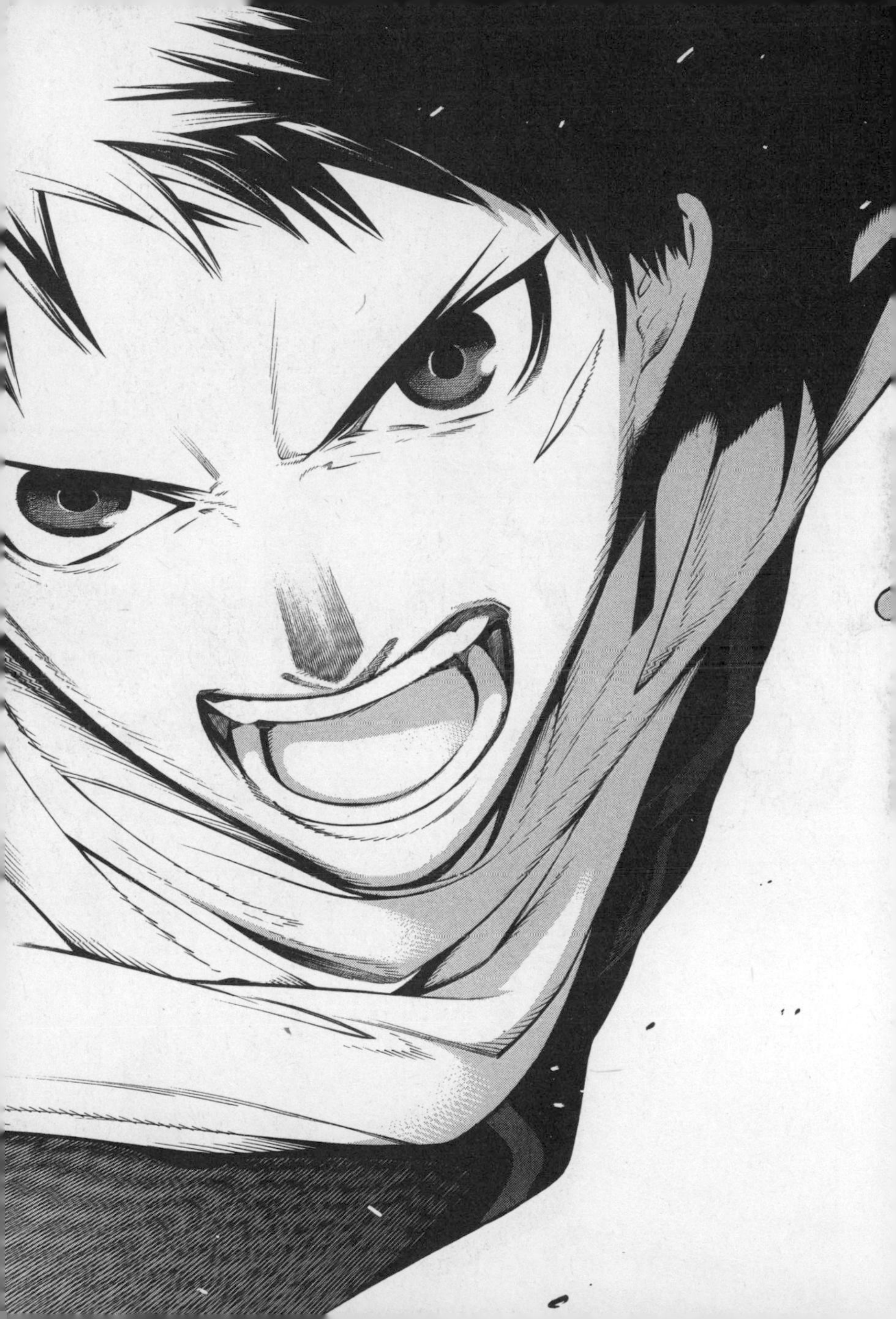

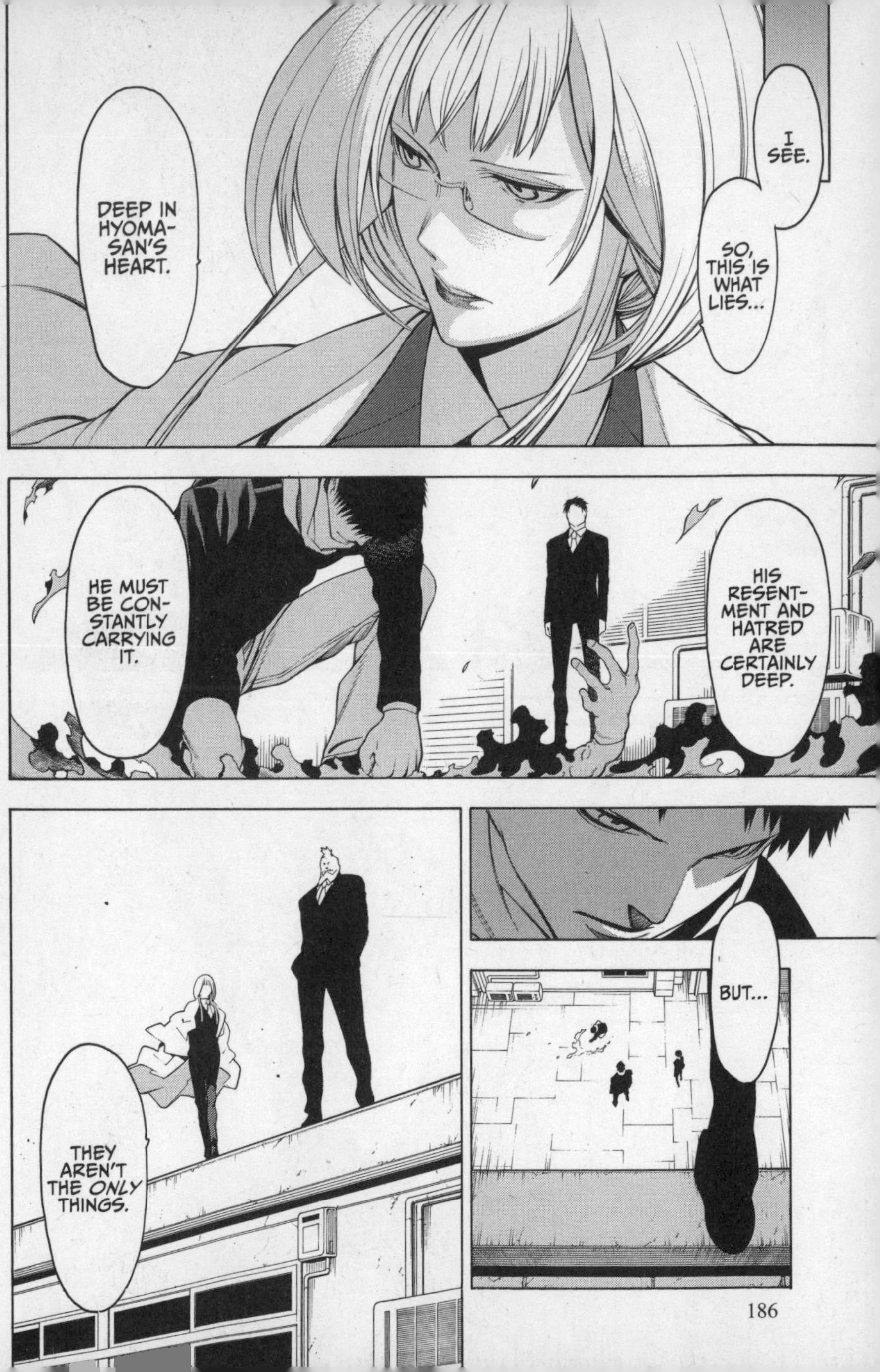
I SEE.
SO, THIS IS WHAT LIES...
DEEP IN HYOMA-SAN'S HEART.
HIS RESENT-MENT AND HATRED ARE CERTAINLY DEEP.
HE MUST BE CON-STANTLY CARRYING IT.
BUT...
THEY AREN'T THE *ONLY* THINGS.

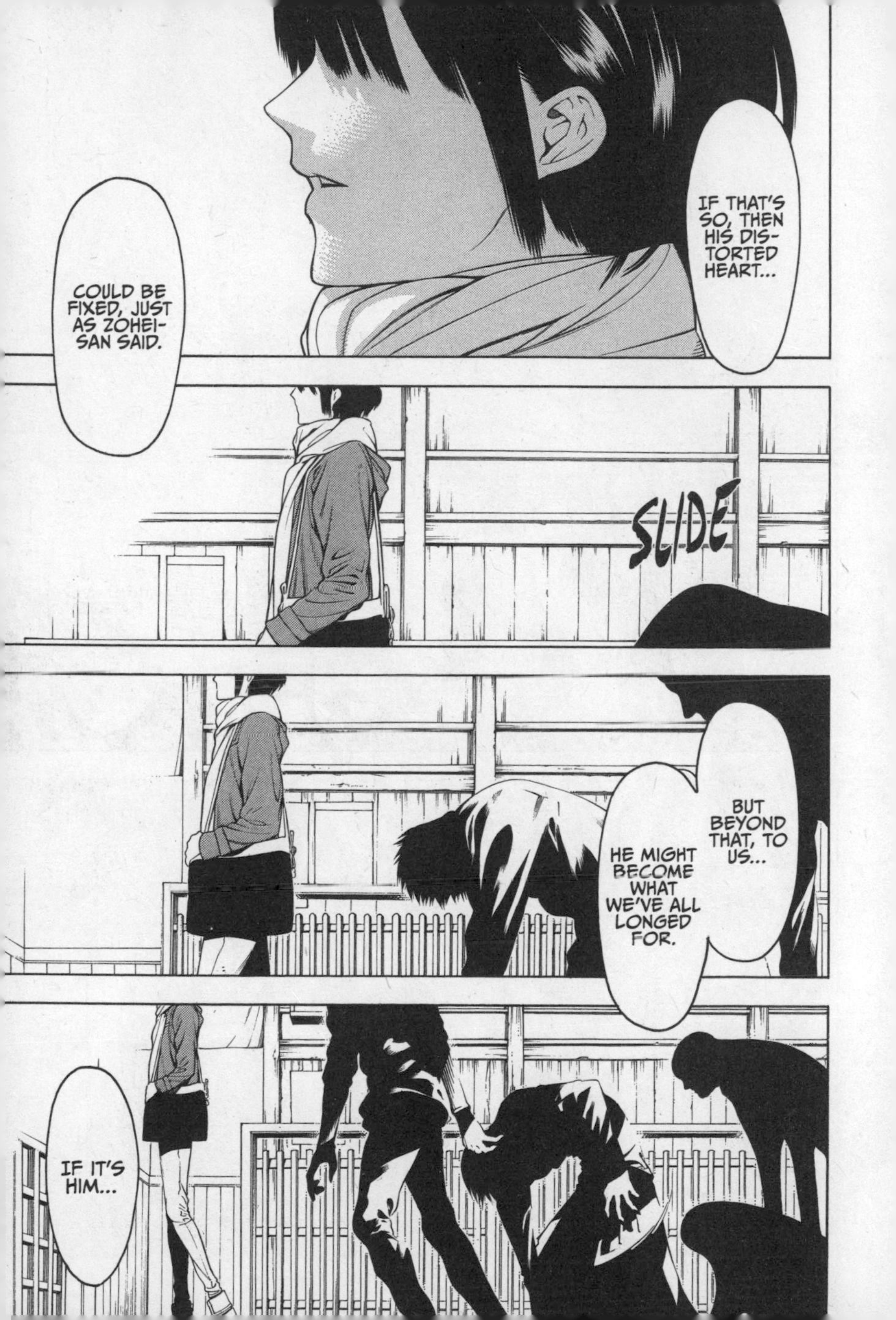
IF THAT'S SO, THEN HIS DIS-TORTED HEART...
COULD BE FIXED, JUST AS ZOHEI-SAN SAID.
SLIDE
BUT BEYOND THAT, TO US...
HE MIGHT BECOME WHAT WE'VE ALL LONGED FOR.
IF IT'S HIM...

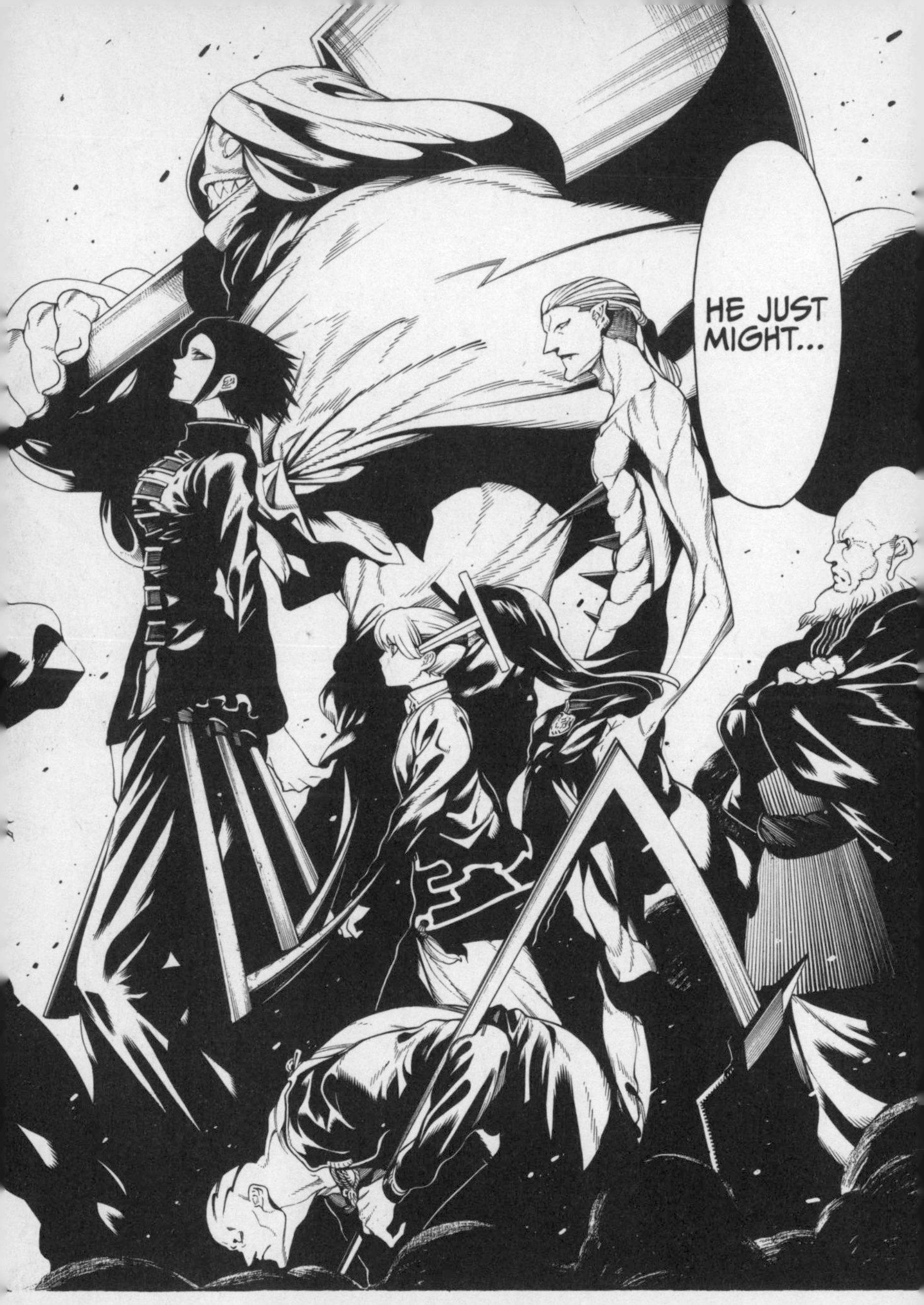
HE JUST MIGHT...

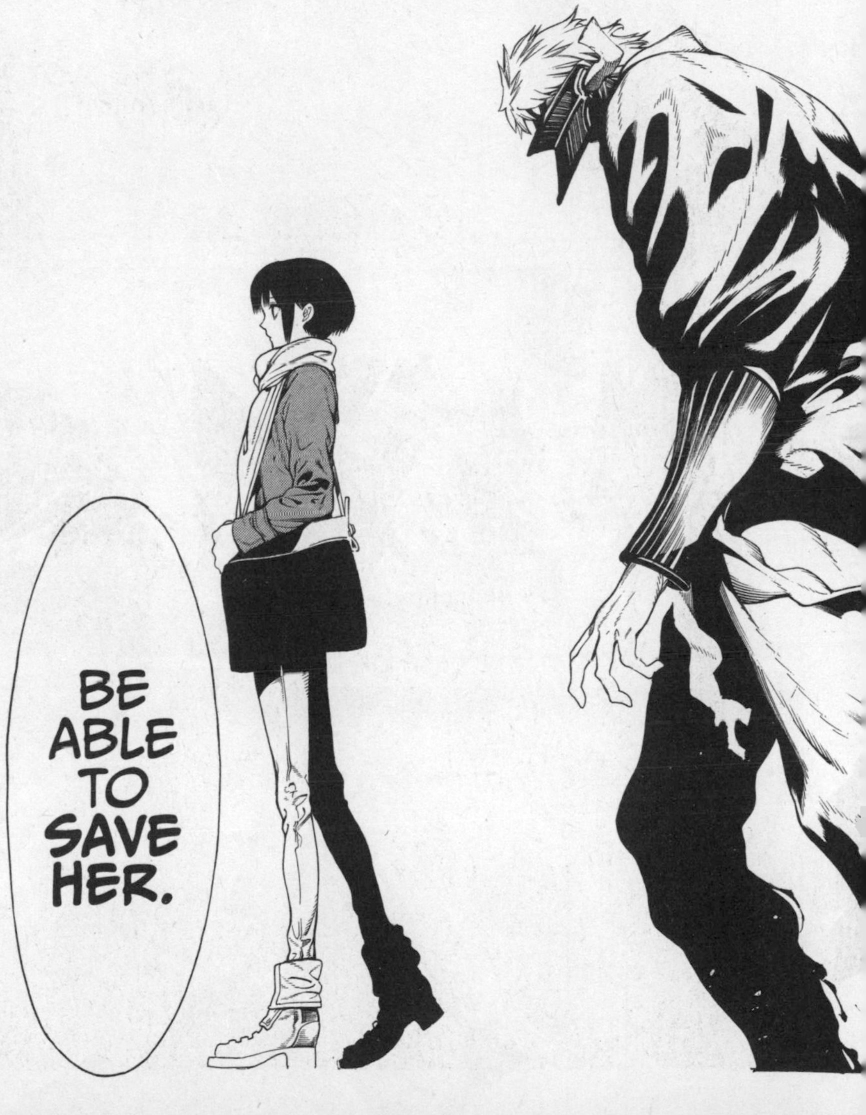
BE ABLE TO SAVE HER.

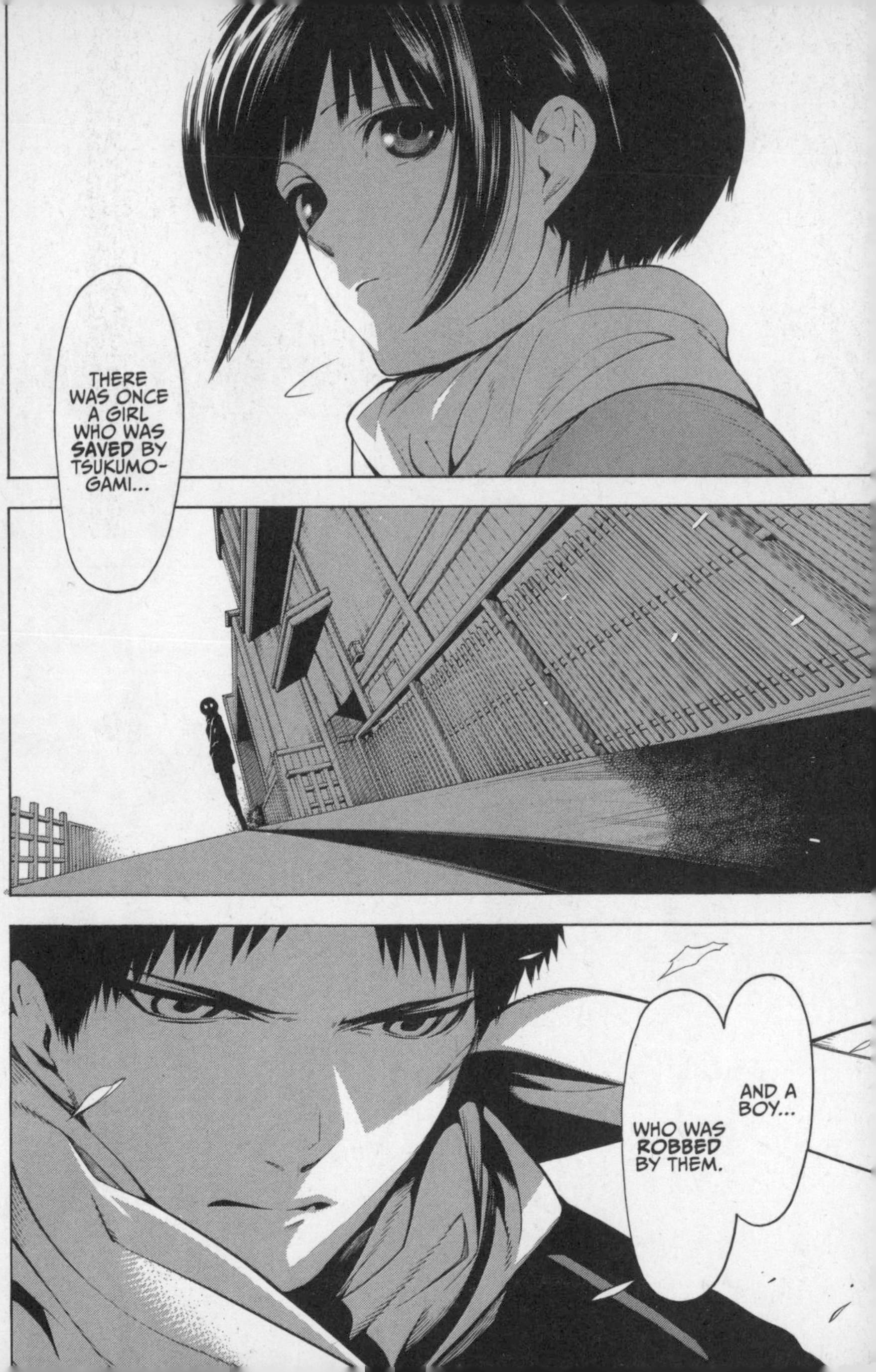
THERE WAS ONCE A GIRL WHO WAS SAVED BY TSUKUMO-GAMI...
AND A BOY...
WHO WAS ROBBED BY THEM.

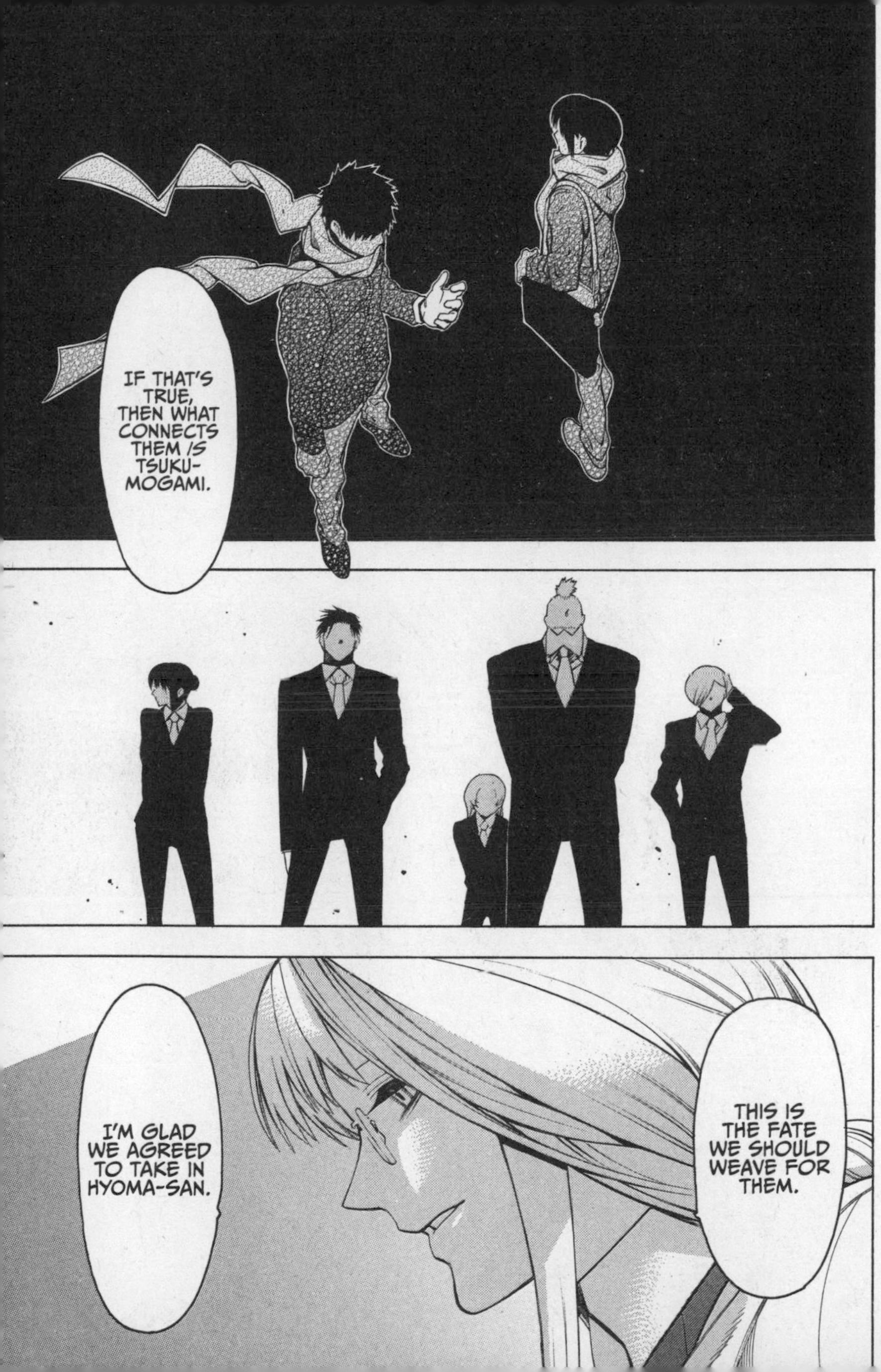
IF THAT'S TRUE, THEN WHAT CONNECTS THEM IS TSUKU-MOGAMI.
THIS IS THE FATE WE SHOULD WEAVE FOR THEM.
I'M GLAD WE AGREED TO TAKE IN HYOMA-SAN.

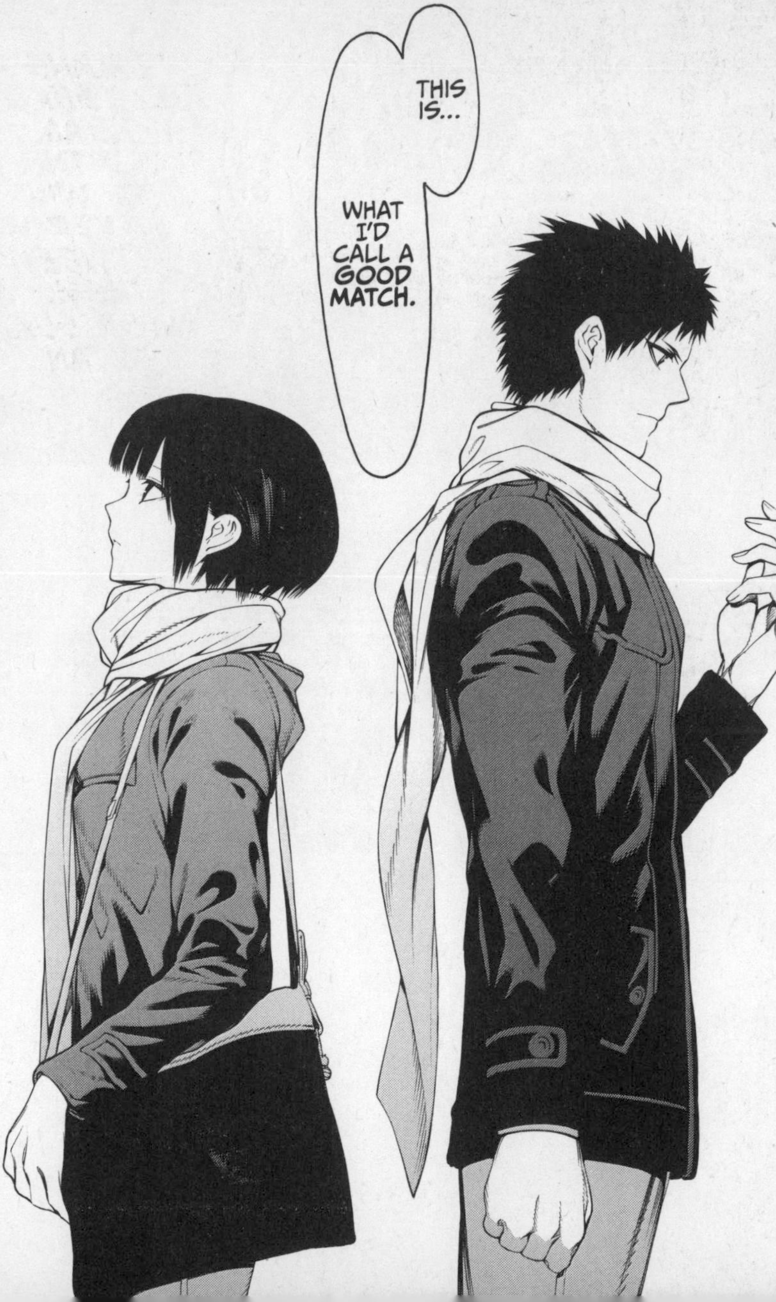
THIS IS...
WHAT I'D CALL A GOOD MATCH.

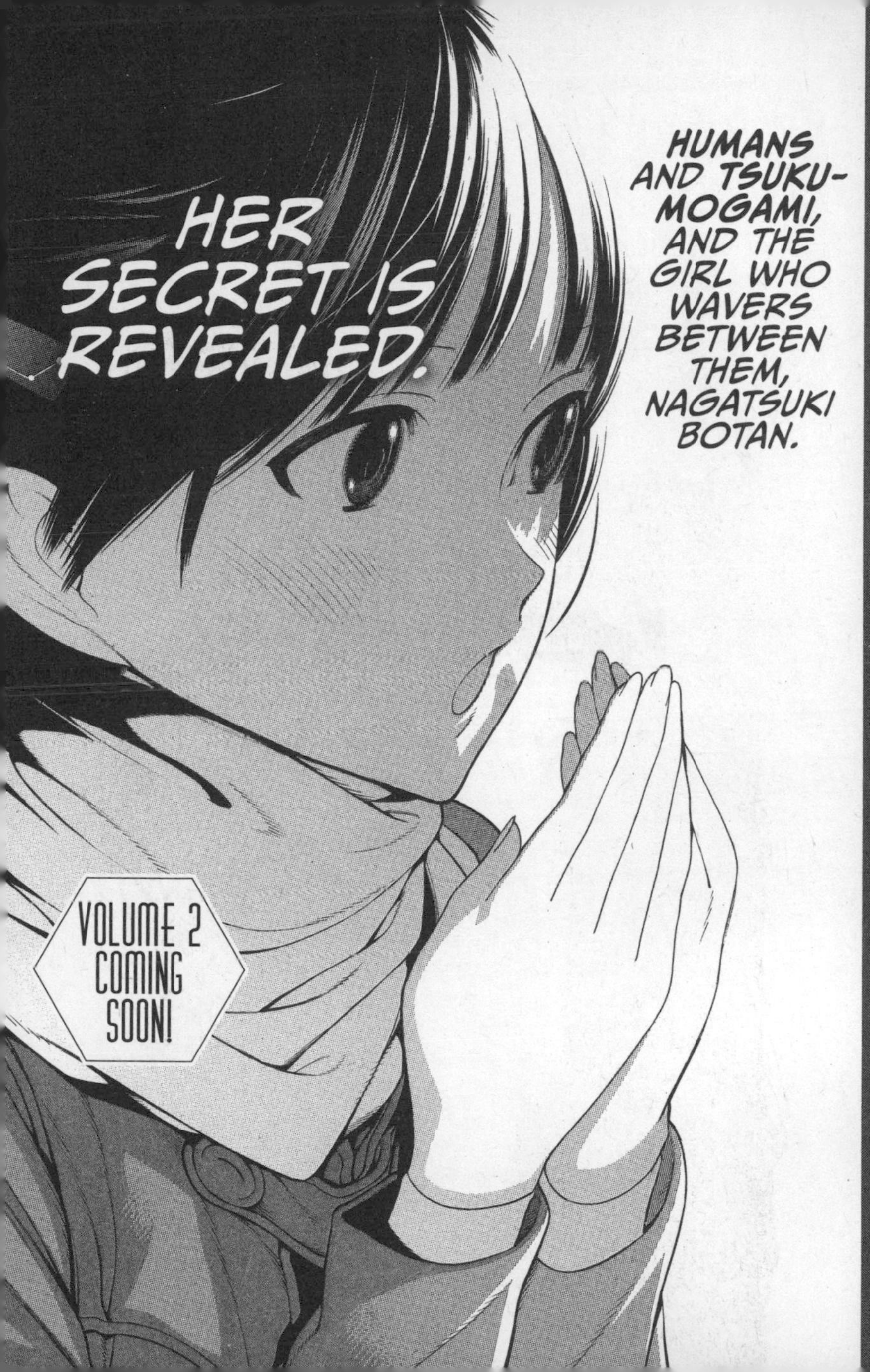
HUMANS AND TSUKU-MOGAMI, AND THE GIRL WHO WAVERS BETWEEN THEM, NAGATSUKI BOTAN.
HER SECRET IS REVEALED.
VOLUME 2 COMING SOON!

SEVEN SEAS ENTERTAINMENT PRESENTS

MALEVOLENT SPIRITS: monanogatari ①

story and art by ONIGUNSOU

TRANSLATION
Jessica Latherow

ADAPTATION
Asha Bardon

LETTERING
Chris Burgener

COVER DESIGN
Hannah Carey

PROOFREADER
Dave Murray

COPY EDITOR
Leighanna DeRouen

EDITOR
Robin Herrera

PRODUCTION DESIGNER
Christa Miesner

PRODUCTION MANAGER
Lissa Pattillo

PREPRESS TECHNICIAN
Melanie Ujimori
Jules Valera

EDITOR-IN-CHIEF
Julie Davis

ASSOCIATE PUBLISHER
Adam Arnold

PUBLISHER
Jason DeAngelis

MONONOGATARI
© 2014 by Onigunsou
All rights reserved.
First published in Japan in 2014 by SHUEISHA Inc., Tokyo.
English translation rights arranged by SHUEISHA Inc.
through TOHAN CORPORATION, Tokyo.

Seven Seas press and purchase enquiries can be sent to Marketing Manager Lianne Sentar at press@gomanga.com. Information regarding the distribution and purchase of digital editions is available from Digital Manager CK Russell at digital@gomanga.com.

Seven Seas and the Seven Seas logo are trademarks of Seven Seas Entertainment, Inc. All rights reserved.

ISBN: 978-1-68579-670-9
Printed in Canada
First Printing: January 2023
10 9 8 7 6 5 4 3 2 1

Withdrawn

////// READING DIRECTIONS //////

This book reads from *right to left*, Japanese style. If this is your first time reading manga, you start reading from the top right panel on each page and take it from there. If you get lost, just follow the numbered diagram here. It may seem backwards at first, but you'll get the hang of it! Have fun!!

Follow us online: www.SevenSeasEntertainment.com